Hoover Institution Publications

Eleven Against War

Eleven Against War

Studies in American Internationalist Thought, 1898–1921

Sondra R. Herman

HOOVER INSTITUTION PRESS

Stanford University · Stanford, California · 1969

Hoover Institution Publications 82
Library of Congress Catalog Card Number: 69–17295
Printed in the United States of America

*For my mother and father
and Frank*

Preface

In recent years Americans have become more self-examining than ever. The search for national definition, so persistent even during the first American Revolution, has naturally intensified in our own revolutionary times. Often this scrutiny takes place amid an angry cacophony that drowns out quieter observations. Yet at every level of society is felt the need for a few thoughtful moments, the young calling out for a renewed commitment to justice and their elders constantly reminding them of the value of loyalty and reconciliation. All feel the need for time to wonder and to question. All sense, even while denying it, that an understanding of our past is relevant to the shaping of our future.

In many areas historians as well as the public seek a usable past; and one area that has been most closely studied for our present enlightenment is early twentieth-century foreign policy. The traditional boundaries of diplomatic history are frequently ignored. Historians today are concerned with the relationships between domestic policies and foreign relations. Ideology as well as Utopia is often taken as a background for interpreting diplomatic relations. Historians are now just as likely to ask: What values did this policy embody? as they once were to ask: What specific situation called forth this response? But increasingly, particularly among students, another question is heard: What kind of people are we, anyway? It seems to me that both the detached professionals and the passionate novices deserve some answers. Such answers, however tentative, might focus either upon policies and achievements or upon ideals. In the search for a usable past, I have felt that the defeated causes and minority viewpoints have become as important to us as the programs that resulted in policies.

The present examination of one small segment of the American past considers just such a minority viewpoint—American internationalism. To the extent that this concept influenced policy at all, it did so by a severe adaptation to national interests. Otherwise, American internationalism was more a matter of hope than of action. From the ranks of the internationalists I have chosen only eleven: President Woodrow Wilson, Elihu Root, and Nicholas Murray Butler; Hamilton Holt, Theodore Marburg, A. Lawrence Lowell, John Bates Clark, and Franklin Henry Giddings, leaders of the League to Enforce Peace; and three representatives of a different kind of internationalism—community internationalism—Josiah Royce, Jane Addams, and Thorstein Veblen.

Other students of the subject will doubtless define the internationalist alignment differently and will choose other figures. I have made no attempt to produce an encyclopedic survey of internationalist thought. However, the bases of my selection do deserve mention. A number of years ago, when this study began, I had become curious about the extension of the American reform impulse into the arena of foreign affairs. I wanted to study specific peace proposals, even those later condemned as Utopian, proposals which the reformers had offered either in the heyday of the peace movement or in response to the crisis of 1914. I did not seek particularly influential reformers, nor concentrate upon men who influenced the formulation of policy. Rather, I wished to study individuals whose internationalism was related to their deeper values—men and women who understood the meaning of the world crisis within the framework of some life philosophy. My choice of internationalists reflects my basic assumption that our evaluations of foreign policy are not merely reactions to events, and not products of different degrees of expertise. They are mirrors of our most basic interpretations of the social nature of man. Clearly, some of the internationalists did consider subjects and problems ranging far afield from areas usually regarded as matters of national policy. None would today be considered an expert in foreign affairs. In this way, they were representative of an age better known for its criticism and its faith in progress than for its expertise.

Fundamentally the work has remained a study of ideas. And yet the question of why, in the end, the internationalists failed, lurks in the background begging to be answered. Upon that question I touch only briefly in the hope that other researchers will consider the problem.

One major theme, however, has emerged. Internationalism in early twentieth-century America represented neither a pure nor a unified set of beliefs. There seemed to be at the very least two different ideals of international society with very little agreement between them. Men who led the movements for a world court or a league of nations envisioned an international polity united by formal contracts and by a common allegiance to the rule of law. This was not very different from their ideal of the American polity as an organization of competing individuals and business corporations with differing degrees of merit and power. In international society the more or less powerful components of the system were the separate sovereign states. Wilson and Butler, Root and the leaders of the League to Enforce Peace, espoused this viewpoint. They tended to believe that the competition of individuals or of businesses or of nations, and the emergence of the strongest in that competition, while sometimes dangerous, served the interests of the whole society. They placed a high value on stabilizing this competition and on pacifying it. Often they considered wars the work of greedy national leaders or of jingoistic populations.

The community internationalists, Royce, Addams, and Veblen, considered international life potentially organic, and focused their attention upon social and economic changes which they believed would increase the sense of human unity. They combined a dynamic interpretation of human nature with a rejection of conservative Darwinism and competitive individualism. The community internationalists often regarded wars as the products of profoundly faulty social organization and of the limited mentality that accompanied it. Their criticisms of traditional patriotism were both broader and harsher than those of the political internationalists. Indeed, questions of loyalty, of relationships across national boundaries, and of rootlessness were extremely important to community internationalists.

The social position of the two groups was also somewhat different. The men of the polity led large organizations, including peace societies and universities. The communalists identified themselves with small but cosmopolitan groups of scholars and reformers, or with the disinherited. The world of the polity was much more the world of decision making, as we term it today, than was that of the community.

During the war years these views clashed, and the viewpoint of the polity won public attention, only to be undermined by its own compromises with nationalism and by the revolutionary age. Neither the community internationalists nor the political internationalists attracted to their respective causes any lasting loyalty from the American people. To most of his contemporaries, as to a later generation, Wilson represented the core of American internationalism. This was doubly tragic, for Wilson's limitations were taken to be the failings of a whole body of thought, and much that was wise and practical never received a fair test.

Anyone who undertakes a work of this nature incurs intellectual and personal debts far greater than can ever be repaid. I could not have completed this study without the help of many generous people.

Several years ago Professor John Higham of the University of Michigan encouraged me to study intellectual history. His treatment of the patterns of nativism in the late nineteenth and early twentieth centuries not only enlightened me, but aroused my curiosity about internationalism as a contrasting mode of thought. His scholarship has been an inspiration ever since, and I am deeply grateful for his continued interest and encouragement.

The work of Dean Henry R. Winkler of Rutgers University in British movements for a League of Nations greatly stimulated my parallel interest in American internationalism. Correspondence with the late John C. Farrell of Johns Hopkins and with Professor Daniel Levine of Bowdoin College furthered my research on Jane Addams. Professor Warren F. Kuehl of the University of Akron offered challenging comparisons with another approach to the study of internationalism and provided useful bibliographical information. Professor Lloyd C. Gardiner of Rutgers and Professor Richard M. Brown of the College of William and Mary helpfully criticized an earlier version of the work.

My greatest intellectual debt is to Professor Warren I. Susman of Rutgers, who has been an unfailing patient advisor, a cogent critic, and an illuminating guide. His pointed questions opened up many new areas of research. His ideas were a continual stimulus to my own, and I can never thank him enough for his insistence upon my exploring those ideas in depth.

Like all students of our past I am deeply obliged to those trail blazers whom I have never met except in their invaluable works. Foremost among them are Arthur S. Link, Merle Curti, Arno J. Mayer, and William Appleman Williams.

Nor could I have proceeded at all without the knowledgeable librarians who guided me to manuscript sources. Mrs. Arline Paul, head of the Reference Department of the Hoover Institution at Stanford University, and Mrs. Majorie Edwards of the Swarthmore College Peace Collection were particularly helpful. For the courtesy and kindness of many people I am grateful, especially to my patient and astute editor, Mrs. Edna Halperin and to Mr. Alan H. Belmont, Executive Assistant to the Director of Hoover Institution.

But to those to whom I owe everything personal, I can say far too little. My parents, Dorothy and Irving Kleinman, and my husband, Frank Herman, not only read and helpfully criticized the work but even supplied their own faith and courage whenever my own showed signs of fading.

Menlo Park, California
September, 1968

Acknowledgments

For giving me permission to quote from copyrighted material I should like to thank the following: Harper and Row, Publishers, Inc. for *The Public Papers of Woodrow Wilson,* edited by Ray Stannard Baker and William E. Dodd; The Macmillan Company, Inc. for *Newer Ideals of Peace* and *Twenty Years at Hull House* by Jane Addams, for "In Distrust of Merits" from the collection *Nevertheless* by Marianne Moore, and for *The Philosophy of Loyalty* by Josiah Royce; Viking Press, Inc., for Thorstein Veblen's *Essays in Our Changing Order,* edited by Leon Ardzrooni, and for Veblen's *An Inquiry into the Nature of Peace and the Terms of Its Perpetuation.*

Contents

CHAPTER I

Polity and Community:
Two Ideals of International Society

There is always a market for lesser-evil thinking which poses immediate alternatives; the need for thinking which confronts us with great hopes and great plans is not so evident. Yet without great plans, it is hard and often self-defeating to make little ones.

David Riesman, "Some Observations on Community
Plans and Utopia," 1947

Internationalism is an elusive concept for historians of early twentieth-century America. At the turn of the century the term suggested advocacy of an active role for the United States in world politics, support for peaceful settlement of international disputes through arbitration or mediation, and even for American membership in a world confederation of nations. Historians have generally agreed that the majority of the American people were not internationalists either before or during World War I. But a search through the literature dealing with this period has failed to turn up any consistent definition of the beliefs of those few Americans who did have internationalist leanings.

The present study treats internationalism as a spectrum of social and ethical philosophies culminating in the ideal of a peaceful world society of national societies. American internationalists were reformers dedicated to changing the relationships of national states with the avowed aim of preventing future wars. They wished to arouse Americans to the necessity of continuous cooperation with other nations. Unlike diplomats concerned with the negotiation of individual bilateral agreements, internationalists hoped to achieve an orderly world by the creation of some formal organization to settle international conflicts, or by encouraging broad programs of economic and social cooperation to promote a sense of international community.

International reform programs and the assumptions underlying them varied greatly. Nevertheless, there were a few fundamental propositions, I believe, which defined the twentieth-century internationalist frame of mind. Some of these beliefs distinguished internationalism from an earlier cosmopolitanism as well as from the nationalism of the reformers' contemporaries. The most characteristic internationalist assumptions were the following:

1. International society was both many and one. It was unrealistic to attempt to reduce national cultures to some cosmopolitan unanimity.

The Stoic and medieval universalists had cherished the wholeness of world society rather than its diversity. Idealizing the eschatological unity of mankind, they tended to regard ethnic contrasts as temporal and therefore as essentially unreal.[1] Even with the rise of the modern state-system, the ideal of one Christendom pervaded the federative peace plans of the sixteenth and seventeenth centuries and the natural law concepts upon which international law was based. The eighteenth-century universalists found validity, as Robert R. Palmer has observed, in the abstract notion of humanity. They regarded variety as "a sign of error."[2] In early nineteenth-century Europe, the ideal of a single political organization declined as liberal reformers devoted themselves to the freedom and unity of nationalities. By the beginning of the twentieth century, it was no longer possible to ignore the strength of national loyalties.

2. Nations shared a life transcending their plurality. The society of societies shared a multitude of legal, social, and commercial bonds that made members interdependent. More important, ethical obligations in the interdependent world were universal.

Internationalists emphasized that the human condition itself obliged men to seek peace. Some stressed also the obligation of states to honor the equal rights of other states. The first assertion stemmed from the ancient Judeo-Christian ethic, the brotherhood of man, the latter from the Enlightenment natural rights philosophy. By the early twentieth century this ethical uni-

[1] Hans Kohn, *The Idea of Nationalism: A Study in Its Origin and Background* (New York, Macmillan, 1944), pp. 65-66; Ernst H. Kantorowicz, "The Problem of World Unity," *The Quest for Political Unity in World History*, ed. Stanley Pargellis (Washington, U.S. Government Printing Office, 1944), pp. 33-35.
[2] "Humanity and Nationality," *Quest for Political Unity*, p. 141.

versalism was no longer treated as an abstraction. Internationalists often emphasized the harmony between the pursuit of national interests and the search for peace. A few, however, believed that peoples would have to submerge their national ambitions altogether in order to achieve international cooperation. All considered a narrow conception of national interests immoral. It was this sense of obligation beyond national boundaries that distinguished internationalists from their contemporaries.

3. All wars resembled one another not in their circumstances but in their deeper origins. The roots of modern wars lay beneath the immediate situations that prompted outbreaks of violence. Among the real causes were the selfishness and irrationality of group action, the national state-system itself, the absence of international controls over armaments, economic rivalries, the dichotomy between common human needs and the actions of governments. The pervasiveness of these causes made possible a general peace program. If one could not predict the circumstances leading to wars, one still could offer suggestions for substantial changes in international behavior.

4. Progress toward peace was a real possibility. There was nothing inevitable about either war or peace. Both were man-made; both were chosen.

Before World War I some internationalists firmly believed that evolution toward a peaceful world was inevitable. Faith in such progress was strong within the American peace movement. Frederick Lynch of the Church Peace Union predicted in 1912 that the twentieth century would be "an age of treaties rather than an age of wars. . . ." In 1910 Andrew Carnegie commissioned the trustees of the Carnegie Endowment for International Peace to use the proceeds of his investment for the next most palpable evil afflicting men after the scourge of war had been eradicated.[3] Many internationalists, however, did not expect such complete moral regeneration. They believed in the possibility, not the inevitability, of good will and rationality in international affairs. They sought a peace that would be more than an armistice, insisting, as Immanuel Kant had a century earlier, that "we must act as if . . . perpetual peace existed—though it may not exist; we must endeavor to make it real. . . ."[4]

5. Even if the United States or other nations failed to accept a proposal

[3] Clarke A. Chambers, "The Belief in Progress in the Twentieth Century," *Journal of the History of Ideas*, XIX (April 1958), 210, quotes Lynch's prediction. Andrew Carnegie to Board of Trustees of the Carnegie Endowment for International Peace, Dec. 10, 1910, Carnegie Endowment for International Peace Archives: Secretarial and Administrative Division, I, 20, Special Collections, Columbia University.

[4] Addendum to *Perpetual Peace*, 1785, trans. and ed. Lewis White Beck (Indianapolis, Bobbs-Merrill, 1957), p. 58.

for international cooperation, there was an obligation to offer it. Such plans might educate the public to the requirements of peace. Change was the law of life not only in international affairs but in men's attitudes and beliefs as well.

Beyond these few precepts there was little agreement among American internationalists. Not only did they hold most diverse conceptions of international cooperation, but the fundamental ideas upon which they based their proposals varied greatly. Contrasting world views were implied in their attitudes toward human nature, patriotism, the causes of war, the nature of international society. Not all the internationalists directly answered such questions as: Was man naturally peaceful and gregarious or militant and selfish? What was the relationship between internal social structure and a nation's propensity toward war? How was patriotism related to war? Was there such a thing as national character? Why and when did nations obey international law? What was the essential meaning of peace, progress, society, international organization? Many reformers were more concerned with the detailed structure and functions of a proposed international organization than with these questions. Nevertheless, their writings implied answers and indicated a close relationship between ideas about the future of American society and their hopes for international society.

Except in a few histories of Wilsonian progressivism,[5] this relationship between domestic and international reform attitudes has remained unexplored. The ideational derivation of various American peace plans of the early twentieth century has not been the concern of students of internationalism. Modern American internationalism has been treated either as a direct outgrowth of an essentially West European body of thought, or as a branch of American missionary nationalism itself.

Both the linear studies of internationalism and the critical realistic ones, emphasizing the tragic influence of American idealism on twentieth century foreign policy, have made valuable contributions to our knowledge of international ideals. The surveys of Sylvester Hemleben, Sir John A. R. Marriot, Christian L. Lange, and August Schou indicate the rich variety of European and Anglo-American internationalism over many centuries.[6]

---

[5] William Diamond, *The Economic Thought of Woodrow Wilson* (Baltimore, Johns Hopkins Press, 1943), *passim;* Eric Goldman, *Rendezvous with Destiny: A History of Modern American Reform* (New York, Vintage Books, 1959), pp. 209–13; Richard Hofstadter, *The American Political Tradition and the Men Who Made It* (New York, Vintage Books, 1954), pp. 254–57, 276–79.

[6] Sylvester John Hemleben, *Plans for World Peace Through Six Centuries* (Chicago, Univ. of Chicago Press, 1943); Sir John A. R. Marriot, *Commonwealth or Anarchy: A Survey of Projects of Peace from the Sixteenth to the Twentieth Century* (London, Allan, 1937); Christian L. Lange and August Schou, *Histoire de*

Implying that a humane, reforming spirit arose in the West after every major war, these scholars have used internationalist theories as arguments for the necessity of a strong peace-keeping organization. The critical realists, examining the same peace plans, have recently demonstrated the ineffectiveness of theory divorced from the realities of power. F. H. Hinsley, for example, has insisted that in spite of the gradual departure from Dante's medieval ideal of a Christian empire toward European federation and then toward a confederation of nations, internationalism repeated an unimaginative revolt against the national state system. Twentieth-century internationalists revived seventeenth-century federalism as if nations had not already rejected the federal policy, as if Kant, Rousseau, and others had not criticized federalist plans in the interval. Professor Hinsley contrasts the justly neglected plans of the theorists with the realistic wisdom of statesmen who sought an equilibrium of power.[7]

In the 1950s this appreciation for the realities of international politics and for the persistence of contrasting national interests led tough-minded critics of American foreign policy to attack the American Utopian tradition. Nothing so discredited utopianism as the swift descent from some supposed Allied unity into the Cold War. Reinhold Niebuhr, Hans J. Morgenthau, George F. Kennan, and others could discredit a whole way of thinking about foreign affairs, with the sure confidence that students and the public held vividly in their minds also the contrast between the expectations of 1919 and the realities of the 1930s; between the principles of the Atlantic Charter and the actuality of Hiroshima. In brief, utopianism was for fools, and internationalism was believed to be the major tenet of utopianism. The realists usually characterized internationalism as too abstract a belief to guide decision-makers. They mentioned it largely in the process of teaching Americans to avoid such self-deceptive naïveté.[8]

While these critics conceded that a well-tempered idealism provided a needed brake upon Machtpolitik, they implied that the realistic pursuit of

---

l'Internationalisme, 3 vols. (Oslo, Publications of the Nobel Institute, H. Aschehoug, 1919–63).

[7] *Power and the Pursuit of Peace: Theory and Practice in the History of the Relations Between States* (Cambridge, Cambridge Univ. Press, 1963), pp. 3–4, 7–8, 14–15, 37, 40, 51–52, 60 ff., 266.

[8] R. C. Good, "National Interest and Political Realism: Niebuhr's 'Debate' with Morgenthau and Kennan," *Journal of Politics*, XXII (Nov. 1960), 579–619, indicates more diversity within political realism than I have suggested. George Kennan, *American Diplomacy 1900–1950* (New York, Mentor Books, 1964), pp. 82–84, condemns international idealism as the "legalistic-moralistic approach to international problems." Hans Morgenthau, *Scientific Man vs Power Politics* (Chicago, Univ. of Chicago Press, 1946), pp. 95–99, 101, 103; Reinhold Niebuhr, *The Structure of Nations and Empires* (New York, Scribner, 1959), 183, 190 ff.; Roland N. Stromberg, *Collective Security and American Foreign Policy from the League of Nations to NATO* (New York, Praeger, 1963), Chapter I and p. 238.

national interests could be moral in itself. Only national states gave men security in an imperfect world. American idealists, especially the internationalists, so lacked an appreciation for the roots and persistence of international conflicts that they failed to prepare the country for her twentieth-century responsibilities. Robert E. Osgood, for example, in a masterful study of the contests between moralists and national Egoists emphasized how the extremes of hope and selfishness both reinforced Americans' "isolationist predispositions" and contributed to a dangerous instability in American foreign policy after 1898.[9] The success of American policy in contributing to the growth of American power and influence in the world was far too little credited. And it was not until the 1960s that the danger of a decline of idealism was fully appreciated.

Far from implying that the realists did not consider the search for international peace and stability important, their criticism of early twentieth-century idealism suggested that they thought peace too vital a matter for idealist rhetoric. George F. Kennan brought to a climax the realists' attack upon moralism by picturing its dire influence upon US policy in World War I. Wilson's pursuit of ideal ends, Kennan argued, "provided both rationale and objective" for the holy crusade that destroyed old Europe. It prevented Americans from considering the practical difficulties of postwar conditions. It resulted in a bitter peace, leaving a terrible resentment. It was just such a peace as Wilson, ironically, had hoped to avoid.[10]

Kennan's condemnation of Wilsonianism was as much moral as practical. American self-righteousness, not ineffectiveness, brought the sharpest reproach. In the works of Reinhold Niebuhr such idealism represented in a peculiarly well-intentioned form man's sin of pride—a sin courting tragedy as inevitably as had the protagonists of ancient Greek drama. While in the past decade Wilson scholars have tempered Kennan's harsh judgment of the president by demonstrating the extent to which he considered national interests as well as ideals in foreign policy,[11] the belief remains that Wilson represented a consensus of internationalist thought.

I question this assumption, and hypothesize in the present study a sharp division in American internationalist thought between political internationalism and community thinking. My examination and analysis of five peace programs, in addition to Wilson's, suggest not only this division but a considerable diversity within each group. The social philosophies underly-

[9] *Ideals and Self-Interest in America's Foreign Relations: The Great Transformation of the Twentieth Century* (Chicago, Phoenix Books of Univ. of Chicago, 1964), pp. 12, 27.

[10] Kennan, *American Diplomacy*, pp. 60–62.

[11] Daniel M. Smith, "National Interest and American Intervention, 1917, An Historiographical Appraisal," *Journal of American History*, LII (June 1965), 5–24.

ing internationalist programs emerged from studies of the thought of each individual or group who advanced them. Elihu Root and Nicholas Murray Butler were prominent conservative spokesmen for the creation of a permanent world court of justice before and during World War I. Abbott Lawrence Lowell, Hamilton Holt, Theodore Marburg, John Bates Clark, and Franklin Henry Giddings, founders of the League to Enforce Peace, demonstrated the tensions within the movement for collective security. These two groups, as well as President Wilson, provide clues to the predominance of political conceptions in internationalist thought.

Community internationalism, a very different mode of thinking, less popular, less frequently studied, is represented by Josiah Royce, Jane Addams, and Thorstein Veblen. Royce propounded an essentially religious interpretation of the community of man and proposed a plan for international insurance. Jane Addams, representing the mixture of pacifism and internationalism in the woman's peace movement, advocated an international welfare community. Thorstein Veblen symbolized the alienated intellectual's disillusionment with Wilsonianism. His program for "peace by neglect" was truly a revolt against the national state system.

Only two of these internationalists, Woodrow Wilson and Elihu Root, were ever in a position to formulate foreign policy. Although the others hoped to influence policy, they were theorists as well as propagandists, and it is as theorists that they will be treated here. Their plans were Utopias—models of a peaceful international society. Nevertheless, the internationalists did not engage in fantasy. They were interpreting contemporary reality and offering what they regarded as practical proposals for change. For a Utopia can be, as David Riesman remarked, a rational belief in a potential reality, violating neither the holder's long-range interests, nor his knowledge of human nature.[12] The internationalists' proposals were Utopian chiefly in this sense.

TÖNNIES' SOCIAL ANALYSIS

In 1887 the German sociologist Ferdinand Tönnies published his *Gemeinschaft und Gesellschaft,* a major analysis of two different social relationships and two different modes of thought and behavior. *Gemeinschaft* was a natural community of family, friends, and fellow villagers. Intimate and warm, it was valued for its own sake. *Gesellschaft* was the impersonal type of association that was rapidly overtaking the community in the Western world. It was represented by businesses, by organizations, by government itself—in fact by all forms of public life which individuals

[12] "Some Observations on Community Plans and Utopia," *Yale Law Journal,* LVII (1947), 175.

created for the sake of some object external to their relationship. "In a most general way," Tönnies observed, "one could speak of a *Gemeinschaft* comprising the whole of mankind," a concept in accord with the Church's view of itself. "But *Gesellschaft* is conceived as mere coexistence of people independent of each other."[13]

Although there is no evidence that the American internationalists were directly influenced by Tönnies, there is evidence that they were conscious of a way of life (simpler, more intimate than urban living) that was passing. Their internationalist ideals fell into two patterns suggested by Tönnies' analysis. The political internationalists, Root, Butler, Lowell and his associates, and Wilson, in spite of occasional references to community, conceived of international society as a polity. Its functions were juridical or governmental. National states themselves created it by treaty agreements. The members of this society remained independent of one another. The polity was truly an international organization—formal, atomistic, and described in constitutions and other contracts. Complete at any moment in time, it could acquire more functions by custom, contractual arrangements, and legal precedents.

The community, by contrast, was envisioned as an organic, natural unity embracing all the peoples of the world and pervaded by the spirit of fellowship. It was never actually complete, nor identifiable with one organization, but always changing and growing. Josiah Royce caught its essentially unfinished nature by linking communities to interpretation, an endless social process.[14] It could be primarily spiritual (yet practical) as Royce conceived it, or secular as Miss Addams implied when she spoke of the "solidarity of the human race."[15]

In spite of the vague character of the international community, Royce, Addams, and Veblen described precisely those activities that would make it grow in human consciousness. International insurance, education, and the regulation of trade, would affect the lives of individuals directly. The administrative experts, scientists, insurance men, performing them, acted for the community at large. Their personal nationality was irrelevant to the performance of their duties. By contrast, the members of the proposed League Assembly and Council represented various national states. The judges of the permanent world court, while not representing governments, so strongly retained their national identification that a specific method of choosing them became the chief stumbling block to the creation of the

[13] *Community and Society (Gemeinschaft und Gesellschaft)*, trans. and ed. Charles P. Loomis (New York, Harper Torchbooks, 1965), pp. 33–34, 42–43, 71, 103.
[14] *The Problem of Christianity* (2 vols., New York, Macmillan, 1913), II, 159–60.
[15] *Twenty Years at Hull House, with Autobiographical Notes* (New York, Macmillan, 1910), p. 126.

court. In the polity, one had to balance representation among great and small states. In the community, informal and non-organizational, the states as such were not represented.

These two conceptions, polity and community, may be considered as representing useful analytical tools rather than as the internationalists' own rigid ideologies. Public figures such as Root and Butler, Jane Addams, and Lowell and his associates considered the practical achievements of international bodies more important than ideological consistency. The polity meant judicial settlement of international disputes, or enforcement of the consideration of such disputes—both suggesting the atomistic character of international life. Community activities, largely economic, social, and cultural, cut at the roots of this atomism and even at the psychological sources of national antagonism. Yet two such contrasting approaches to world peace, even if they lacked ideological consistency, inevitably reflected more fundamental ideational contrasts.

Each conception of international society derived from a particular *Weltanschauung*. The political internationalists were, for the most part, Spencerians. Insisting upon the natural inequality of men and often (but not always) upon man's natural selfishness and aggressiveness, they believed in an evolution from military barbarism toward a peaceful, industrial civilization. This peaceful new order would retain competitive features, but in the non-violent form of trade rivalries and individual striving. Beneath the conflict of interests existed a natural harmony.

In spite of these precepts of classical *laissez faire,* the institutionalists came to accept and even to advocate large-scale organization. In part, their very restricted conception of the functions of international organization supported this acceptance. But their own roles in the *Gesellschaft* also led them to the belief that formal organization was the one method for the solution of complex problems. Courts and councils, leagues or federations both expressed man's increasing rationality and became the means of civilizing him. The men of the polity paradoxically depended upon this increasing rationality for the growth of peace, and then debated the question of using force to support international decisions.

The community thinkers, if similar to one another in few ways, were all anti-Spencerian. Royce considered evolution only a partial view of the ever-hidden truth about the universe. Addams and Veblen accepted Darwinism, but strenuously rejected the social Darwinian viewpoint, which the institutionalists took for granted. The communalists refused to view man as an isolated being, measuring pains and pleasures. Nor were they concerned with rating the virtues of various nations, classes, or income groups. They viewed man much as did John Dewey, James M. Baldwin, Henry Demarest Lloyd, and other contemporary psychologists and intellectual progressives, as a creature of dynamic social instincts. Man's very consciousness emerged in relationships. Assertive individualism, such a virtue to most of the institutionalists, appeared to the communalists as social amorality. Such individualism, enlarged upon the world scene in the form of national rivalries, made formal restraints futile. The communal internationalists rejected the morality of the pursuit of national interests, and concerned themselves with the question of how man acquired the will to war. They sought not a restraint of this will, but its moral sublimation. They were looking for some practical realization of the Enlightenment ideal of a single humanity, but rejected the *Philosophes'* abstract conception of man.

RESPONSES TO THE COMMUNICATIONS REVOLUTION

The contrast between institutional and communal internationalism emerged in diverse responses to the communications revolution. The traditional internationalist search for an orderly world grew more intense in the 1890s as the cumulative effects of the rapid technological development of the preceding decades registered both in America and in Western Europe. Internationalists who reached maturity in the last two decades of the nineteenth century were convinced that they were living in a world quite different from that of their parents. They perceived a marked increase in what Jane Addams called "group loyalty." They were disturbed by tensions between the newly arrived immigrants and old Americans, between workers attempting to organize and employers resisting such attempts, between farmers, now dependent upon a world market, and an assertive urban plutocracy.[16] Not only did the reformers find the fragmentation of American society bewildering, but they were concerned about the potentials of international disintegration. Many, though by no means all, internationalists observed the potential dangers of the arms race, the imperial contests for power, prestige, and profits, the strident military activism of the age. Yet at the same time the dynamic technology of the early twentieth century had given Americans an excessive faith in human reason and in man's ability to control destructive forces.[17]

One of the strongest advocates of social planning, John Dewey, testified that his generation had witnessed the most rapid and extensive revolution in world history as communications created a world-wide market, hastened

[16] Rowland Berthoff, "The American Social Order: A Conservative Hypothesis," *American Historical Review*, LXV (April 1960), 507; George Mowry, *The Era of Theodore Roosevelt 1900–1912* (New York, Harper, 1958), p. 15.

[17] Chambers, "Belief in Progress," p. 198; Charles A. Beard, "Introduction" in J. B. Bury's *The Idea of Progress: An Inquiry into its Origin and Growth* (New York, Macmillan, 1932), pp. xxii–xxiv.

urbanization, redistributed the world's goods, and even profoundly affected the most cherished religious and moral beliefs.[18]

Both Dewey's contemporaries and recent economic historians have confirmed his observations. The new order, emerging in the 1870s was the first world-wide international economy. Formerly isolated trading areas were knit together both by the great international migrations and by the tremendous flow of international capital through a small number of major financial centers, the most important of which were London and New York. Geographical specialization in agriculture and industry increased. The coincidence of periods of prosperity and depression in widely separated parts of the globe marked a new interdependence.[19]

During this same period there existed a cultural and social interdependence too. The 1890s and 1900s were preëminently the decades of the penny press and mass communications. News was no longer local nor even national, but in some senses international. Paul Reinsch, political scientist and legal scholar, observed in 1911:

The psychological unity of the world is being prepared by the service of news and printed discussions by which in the space of one day or one week the same events are reported to all the readers from Buenos Aires to Tokyo, from Cape Town to San Francisco.[20]

But he failed to note that British, French, and German press associations, carrying the news world-wide, were by and large influenced by the business, governmental, and social interests of their own national states and served to consolidate national loyalties and imperialist sentiments. For their readers they placed a wide variety of interpretations on the "same political dramas," the "same catastrophes," the "same scientific achievements."[21]

There was a marked contrast between the technological unity of the world—its economic interdependence—and its political diversity. What did this situation imply? To political internationalists, to readers of John Fiske and Norman Angell, it suggested first that war would be commercially and socially disastrous to all nations. Angell emphasized that the belief that one

---

[18] "The School and Social Progress," *American Social Thought,* ed. Ray Ginger (New York, Hill and Wang, 1961), p. 19.

[19] David A. Wells, *Recent Economic Changes and Their Effect on the Production and Distribution of Wealth and the Well-Being of Society* (New York, Appleton, 1893), pp. v–vi, 1, 6, 29–34; William Ashworth, *A Short History of the International Economy since 1850,* 2nd ed. (London, Longmans, 1960), pp. 182–87, 194–95; A. B. Usher, "The Steel and Steam Complex and International Relations," *Technology and International Relations,* ed. William Fielding Ogburn (Chicago, Univ. of Chicago Press, 1949) pp. 60–62.

[20] *Public International Unions, Their Work and Organization: A Study in International Administrative Law* (Boston, Ginn, 1911), p. 3.

[21] *Ibid.;* Robert Leigh, "Mass Communications and International Relations," *Technology and International Relations,* pp. 133–35.

power or a group of powers could benefit from war was a "great illusion." Fiske believed that commercial self-interest would compel nations to concentrate upon industrial rather than on military production. Diversion of resources to the arms race would only feed social discontent and revolutionary fires.[22] Such beliefs could issue either in cheerful optimism or in cautious preparations. By the turn of the century Elihu Root, Secretary of War, was arguing that the tensions of a smaller world did not allow disarmament. Other institutionalists tended to think that the creation of an international organization would have to precede mutual disarmament. The United States had to be strong enough to rule its new empire. But war among the civilized (imperial) powers must be prevented.[23] There no longer was any frontier at home or abroad to absorb the expansionist impulse.

With the closing of the international frontier, the question of whose influence would prevail became paramount to the institutionalists. Some of them, Franklin Henry Giddings, for example, anticipated a rivalry between the autocratic empires of the East and the democratic ones of Great Britain and the United States. Hamilton Holt, the most optimistic political internationalist, perceived an irresistible world-wide trend toward liberal democracy. The imperialism supported by the institutional thinkers, after 1900, was most benign. America's conquest of the world was to be moral, not political or military. Holt believed that the Pan-American conferences, the Hague conventions, the growth of the Anglo-American peace and arbitration societies signalized a world-wide readiness to accept an American-type federation. His friend Hayne Davis actually produced a timetable of traveling distances between the world's major cities to convince members of the Interparliamentary Union that the train for the "parliament of man, the federation of the world" had arrived.[24]

Nicholas Murray Butler and Elihu Root were not ready to board that train, but they too conceived of the polity as a mirror of American institutions. The expansion of American interests in the international econ-

---

[22] Norman Angell, *The Great Illusion: A Study of the Relation of Military Power in Nations to their Economic and Social Advantage* (New York, Putnam, 1910) ; John Fiske, "The Arbitration Treaty," 1897, *A Century of Science and Other Essays* (Boston, Houghton Mifflin, 1899), p. 187.

[23] Elihu Root, "The Monroe Doctrine," Dec. 20, 1904, in *Miscellaneous Addresses,* eds. Robert Bacon and James Brown Scott (Cambridge, Harvard Univ. Press, 1917), p. 269; Theodore Marburg, "A Modified Monroe Doctrine," *South Atlantic Quarterly,* X (July 1, 1911), 229; Arthur N. Holcolme, "Edwin Ginn's Vision of World Peace," *International Organization,* XIX (1965), 2.

[24] Franklin Henry Giddings, *Democracy and Empire* (New York, Macmillan, 1900), p. 357; Hamilton Holt, "The United States Peace Commission," *North American Review,* CXCII (Sept. 1910), 304; Hayne Davis, *Among the World's Peacemakers: The Epitome of the Interparliamentary Union* (New York, Progressive Publishing Co., 1907), p. 395.

omy probably increased their confidence, for they had personal and business associations with Andrew Carnegie, J. P. Morgan, and other financial titans with international connections. Between 1897 and 1914 American foreign investments increased five-fold. For the first time American bankers were floating large loans abroad, although the United States remained a debtor nation until World War I. Not only were American companies investing in mining, agricultural production, and oil rights outside the United States, but many of them had established manufacturing and sales subsidiaries abroad.[25] Under these circumstances the political internationalists regarded direct American political control over the so-called backward areas as superfluous. They felt that the advantages of imitating American free institutions would be patent to all. Eventually, other nations would accept the American image of international organization.

Their confidence grew also with the assumption that powerful Great Britain would agree with the United States as to the necessity of creating permanent international institutions. After the Spanish-American War the British and Americans had demonstrated the methods of peaceful settlement in a number of touchy matters, such as the Panama Canal treaties, the Alaska boundary settlement, the Newfoundland fisheries arbitration. Instead of attributing these agreements to British eagerness for American friendship,[26] the institutionalists interpreted them as examples of the practical political wisdom of the Anglo-Saxon. Although they felt close ties with the British, and although their respect for British and American political traditions was not markedly different from that of the racial Darwinists of the same day, the political internationalists appeared to lack the deep-rooted racist fears, the anti-Catholicism, the extreme insecurities of place and position that made Darwinism so strong a support of nativism for many Americans. They reacted, for example, to Japan's surprising victory of 1905 by assuming thereafter that Japan was, of course, a progressive nation. If they felt any apprehensions about the "yellow peril," they remained surprisingly silent, although some of their friends did not.[27]

---

[25] Cleona Lewis, *America's Stake in International Investments* (Washington, D.C., Brookings Institution, 1938), pp. 1–2, 176 ff., 605–606.

[26] Charles S. Campbell, Jr., *Anglo-American Understanding 1898–1903* (Baltimore, Johns Hopkins Press, 1957), pp. 13–19, 21–23.

[27] Nicholas Murray Butler, *Across the Busy Years* (2 vols., New York, Scribner, 1939–40), I, 101–102; II, 22–32; Butler, "A Voyage of Discovery," Jan. 21, 1916, *The Faith of a Liberal* (New York, Scribner, 1924), pp. 329, 335 ff.; Theodore Marburg, *Expansionism* (Baltimore, J. Murphy Co., 1900), pp. 40–58; Abbott Lawrence Lowell, "The Colonial Expansion of the United States," *Atlantic Monthly*, LXXXIII (Feb. 1899), 145–54; Hamilton Holt, "Japan and America," *Independent*, LXV (Oct. 29, 1908), 1007; John Bates Clark, "Powerful Agencies Working for Peace in the World," *Lake Mohonk Peace and Arbitration Conference* (cited hereafter as *Mohonk*), XI (1905), 54–56.

This attitude demonstrated one of the institutionalists' most fundamental beliefs, namely, that worldly success, military or economic, signified the inherent virtues in a nation. The institutionalists combined a social Darwinian emphasis upon struggle and inequality with the expectation that civilized nations would support an international tribunal. The great powers and smaller industrialized states would automatically insure the success of international institutions, for support of international organization was the only rational future course. Did not great success indicate great rationality?

The community internationalists believed just as firmly that it did not. They rejected the assumption equating success with virtue, often finding a higher morality among primitive peoples and conquered nations.[28] This bias signalized much more than sympathy for the weak. At the heart of community internationalism lay a profound distrust of political power. Moreover, except for Royce's and Veblen's revulsion against Prussian statecraft during World War I, the communalists seemed completely unconcerned with the emergence of a *Pax Britannica* or *Americana*. International activities were to be more than reflections of the Anglo-American accord.

Thus the communal response to the communications revolution differed from that of the institutionalists. The communalists tended to view the new technology as a neutral force. It might educate men to a new scientific objectivity (Veblen often thought so), but it offered no guarantees of peace and cooperation. Jane Addams knew, for example, that without freedom of travel the immigrants would not have had their opportunity to mingle in American cities and to learn new ways of living. But she also considered how machine technology had become an instrument for exploiting the labor of these same people. Royce appreciated the new unity of scientific knowledge, but contended that mass communications made men easier prey to demagogic control. Both Veblen and Miss Addams were sensitive to the manipulation of war sentiment by the press.[29]

There is no evidence that facility of communication paved the way toward international understanding. More often it quickened nationalist antagonisms. The public international unions, created largely to prevent

[28] Jane Addams, *Newer Ideals of Peace* (New York, Macmillan, 1907), pp. 8, 11–14, 17–18; Addams, *Peace and Bread in Time of War,* reprinted with a 1945 introduction by John Dewey (Boston, G. K. Hall & Co., 1960), pp. 75–76, 92–96; Josiah Royce, *The Hope of the Great Community* (New York, Macmillan, 1916), pp. 3, 56–57; Royce, *Race Questions, Provincialism, and Other American Problems* (New York, Macmillan, 1908), pp. 43–45; Thorstein Veblen, *Imperial Germany and the Industrial Revolution* (Ann Arbor, Univ. of Michigan Press, 1966), pp. 312–14.

[29] Royce, *Race Questions,* 74–75; Veblen, *Imperial Germany,* 78–79, 133; Veblen, *An Inquiry into the Nature of Peace and the Terms of Its Perpetuation* (New York, Huebsch, 1917), pp. 21–22; Addams, "The Food of War," *Independent,* LXXXIV (Oct. 11, 1915), 55–56.

national interference with communications, had not escaped political hindrances, although they were concerned with such apolitical matters as continuity of cable services; the exchange of information about agriculture blights, criminal syndicates, and epidemic diseases; and the standardization of weights and measures. They lacked the power to take substantive action without the unanimous consent of the member governments. The nations were too jealous of their sovereignty to accord the unions independent powers. International lawyers and the hopeful institutionalists argued that the very existence of the unions paved the way toward political accords. They would make future wars less likely or less total, and nationalism itself more humane.[30] But the communal internationalists maintained that modern nationalism, in the age of the technological revolution, was more destructive and antagonistic than ever.

On the other hand, there appeared to the communal internationalists much cause for optimism in the rich and varied international life that flourished in the very period of imperial tensions. Jane Addams, as much as the institutionalists, rejoiced in the formation of international unions, especially in those humanitarian, scientific, and social reform private unions that sprang up as if in resistance to nationalist divisions. For all the internationalists the shock of the First World War was tremendous because, as George Mead observed in 1915, it seemed to them that an international society had in fact existed before 1914. Men were engaged in a life of international trade, industry, science, and education, "beyond comparison more vivid and intimate than the national life in any country of Europe one hundred years ago."[31] Josiah Royce frequently observed the community relations of scientists all over the world, united in one enterprise—the search for truth. Veblen contrasted the political dissension of the age with its technological knowledge, which was cosmopolitan.

Thus, while the institutionalists regarded the smaller world of the twentieth century as an arena for American (peaceful) influence, the communalists looked upon it with mingled apprehension and hope. There were international bonds, but no international community; a cosmopolitan inheritance, but national loyalties; a mingling of peoples, but an increase in armaments. For all these reasons the communalists came to distrust the exclusively political man. The institutionalists, however, tended to place more and more faith in him.

[30] Reinsch, *Public International Unions,* pp. 3–13, 164, 170–85; Simeon E. Baldwin, "The International Congresses and Conferences of the Last Century as Forces Working Toward the Solidarity of the World," *American Journal of International Law,* I (1907), 564–78.

[31] "The Psychological Bases of Internationalism," *Survey,* XXXIII (March 6, 1915), 604.

COMMUNITY AND POLITY—SOCIAL MILIEUS

The community and the polity were more than contrasting life-philosophies. They represented life-styles as well. There can be no explanation for the differences between the formal governmental approach to international peace and the community approach without some sense of the contrast between the social milieu of a Thorstein Veblen and that of a Nicholas Murray Butler. Veblen worked in the great university institutions, but Butler, President of Columbia University, was *of* them. In general, the political internationalists were very much at home in large-scale organizations, in businesses, in peace societies, in governments, in newspaper enterprises, in institutions of learning. This was not the world of the communalists. In particular, the political internationalists were frequently leaders or organizers of nation-wide peace and international legal organizations. Although in 1915 Jane Addams had helped to establish a peace organization —the Woman's Peace Party—and although she was endowed with executive talent of no mean degree, she never appeared to think in quite the same terms as the business associates of the polity, the men of the *Gesellschaft*. She referred, in letters to Lillian Wald, to the settlement "household" and called a fellow-worker "sister"[32]—a suggestion of her very personal orientation to the world about her.

What were these peace and arbitration organizations with which the institutionalists were involved? They constituted, as Theodore Marburg observed, the "peace movement practical." By the 1870s the British and American peace societies were beginning to lose (but had not entirely lost) their mid-century Quaker character and anti-government orientation. The Civil War wrecked the old American Peace Society because many of its members were abolitionists and almost all unionists. As it re-emerged in the Gilded Age, the peace movement became the province of practical men who were unreceptive to radical proposals of any kind. The absolute pacifists, for example, were losing control of the movement to men who wished to accommodate peace programs to the national interest. The old-liners of the American Peace Society suffered abuse and humiliation for opposing the Spanish-American War, but a surprising number of newcomers approved the "splendid little war," or appreciated its results.[33]

After 1900 peace organizations flourished and multiplied. More associations of international lawyers formed an influential part of the movement.

[32] Addams to Wald, April 8, 1899, Sept. 22, 1899, Papers of Lillian Wald, New York Public Library.
[33] Merle Curti, *Peace or War: The American Struggle 1636–1936* (Boston, Norton, 1936), pp. 74, 76, 97, 128, 134–35, 141, 154–55, 170–71, 182; Hinsley, *Power and the Pursuit of Peace*, pp. 124–26.

Some of these law associations originated in the 1870s as both the Franco-Prussian War and the success of the *Alabama* claims arbitration stimulated an Anglo-American movement for an international code of law. Although Elihu Burritt and James B. Miles of the American Peace Society initiated the codification drive, the law associations were led by continental and British legal scholars rather than by American pacifists. These experts explored customary international practices, treaties, and arbitration agreements, and actually initiated the codification of copyright and maritime law and financial regulations.[34] In so far as they considered international organization at all, they proposed a juridical structure that the governments would accept.

In 1873 the Swiss legal scholar, Johann Bluntschli, told the Universal Peace Union that pacifists should restrain their desire for the unconditional arbitration of every dispute not settled by negotiation. The states could not be expected to sacrifice their vital interests. The pacifists were initially shocked by this cold splash of caution.[35] But within two decades many of the leaders of the American peace societies were agreeing with Bluntschli. Their task, they then felt, was not to declare absolute principles of international morality (although they still did), but rather to win the governments' consent to particular methods of peaceful settlement. As plans for international organization emerged, the political internationalists defended them largely on the grounds that they were both necessary and politically acceptable. The idea of an irreversible progress toward peace[36] meshed completely with the growth and operation of the peace societies.

The gradualism of the peace societies and the lawyers' influence within them increased after the First Hague Peace Conference. In 1899 Czar Nicholas II, looking for proposals for halting the arms race, called a conference to consider "the great idea of universal peace." (The Russians, as is now well known, could not then afford to replace their artillery with equipment that would match the rapid-fire field guns their Austrian rivals were about to adopt.) British and American peace societies, stunned and delighted by such a proposal from such a source, rallied to the Czar's cause without quite appreciating the reasons for his noble gesture. In spite of American refusal to arbitrate the issues with Spain, and in the face of governmental disinterest in disarmament, the peace organizations mounted a campaign to induce the United States to accept the Czar's offer and to use the conference for the adoption of a permanent world court that should be the nucleus of a world organization.

---

[34] Irwin Abrams, "The Emergence of the International Law Societies," *Review of Politics*, XIX (July 1957), 361–80.

[35] Hinsley, *Power and the Pursuit of Peace*, p. 128.

[36] Stromberg, *Collective Security*, pp. 5–6.

Instead of establishing such a court, the conferees adopted a Draft Convention for the Pacific Settlement of Disputes, which created a shadow institution (a panel of arbitrators) called the Hague Court of Arbitration. Two decades of work at step-by-step codification bore fruit as the conference accepted codes relating to maritime warfare and to the humane treatment of prisoners. The pacifists were indignant at this approval of the rules of war. Nevertheless, they considered the conference an important first step toward world organization. This appreciation of a mere gesture toward their sentiments by policy-makers revealed the change overtaking the peace movement, for it is undoubtedly true, as Calvin DeArmond Davis has written, that the results of the conference were "paper achievements" masking failure.[37]

The new relation between the peace movements and the governments of Western Europe and the United States was epitomized in the Interparliamentary Union. This association of members of parliaments and supporters of international organization was founded in 1889 by British M. P. Randal Cremer. After its 1904 St. Louis meeting, it enrolled over two hundred American congressmen and senators, some of whom were leading proponents of world federation. The federalists viewed the Union itself as an embryonic world legislature. Yet the resolutions of the Union, often tempered by the suggestions of government ministers, did not seem very radical. The Union, which optimists called the most practical organization in a practical peace movement,[38] in fact offered no assurances that nations would sacrifice their sovereignty to a truly federal world organization. Very few federalists would have dared make such a suggestion.

In general, then, the turn-of-the-century American peace movement was eminently respectable. Its leaders cherished their communication with policy-makers and often imagined they were influencing them when in fact they were not. The tendency to seek approval from on high so enforced the elitist tone of the peace societies that Jane Addams, Hamilton Holt and John Bates Clark appealed for greater support from organized labor[39] to prevent the societies from assuming an exclusively middle-class character. In spite of such labor support (largely from the American Federation of Labor), it was men like Andrew Carnegie, Nicholas Murray Butler, and

[37] *The United States and the First Hague Peace Conference* (Ithaca, Cornell Univ. Press, 1962), pp. 37, 44–46, 61–63, 213.
[38] Hayne Davis, *The World's Peacemakers*, pp. 113–14, 118; Holt, "U.S. Peace Commission," p. 304; Curti, *Peace or War*, pp. 192, 218–19.
[39] Addams, "The Interests of Labor in International Peace," Universal Peace Congress, *Official Report of the Thirteenth Congress* (Boston, Oct. 3–8, 1904), pp. 145–47; Holt to Frederick Lynch, March 16, 1912, New York Peace Society Archives, Swarthmore College Peace Collection; Clark, "The Part of Organized Labor in the Arbitration Movement," *Mohonk*, XIV (1908), 61.

Edwin Ginn who gave the movement its tone. It is hardly surprising that such men thought of international society as a creation of the rational leaders of the various nations. Their internationalism challenged educated patriotism not at all.

The very structure of the peace movement contributed to the institutional ideal of a formal large-scale organization. At the turn of the century the societies themselves experienced an organizational revolution. Their membership and financial resources increased enormously. As Merle Curti observed, perhaps the growth of the societies was a response both to the ease and prestige of supporting the peace cause and to the tensions of the arms race.[40] It was also a reflection of faith in progress and in man's ability to direct his future. In either case, the societies acquired a new complexity after 1900. The new organizations—the New York Peace Society, the Church Peace Union, the Carnegie Endowment for International Peace, the World Peace Foundation—now required for their intricate operations of fund-raising, research, and publication, a permanent reservoir of administrative talent.[41] The peace organizations, like business corporations, universities, and labor unions, were entering upon a new phase of large-scale development. Many of the new men of the societies and law associations either managed or organized businesses, institutions of learning, or similar enterprises. Their assured status in such organizations enabled them to reconcile a commitment to *laissez faire* with appreciation for concentrated power. Even those institutionalists who used the vocabulary of classical Manchesterian economics did not feel threatened by government activism *per se*. They identified themselves with those who governed.[42]

From their very engagement in the *Gesellschaft,* as well as from their beliefs about war, human nature, change, and tradition, the institutionalists derived the ideal of an atomistic polity. The national states seemed to them more real than any spiritual unity. And their approach to problems of all dimensions was, in the words of Hamilton Holt, to organize "men about ideas."[43]

The communalists, by contrast, emphasized the threat to individuality and freedom in the bureaucratic development of their time. They were not involved in large political and business enterprises. (Jane Addams' commitment to the Progressive Party in 1912 was an unusual display of partisan-

---

[40] *Peace or War*, pp. 197–98.

[41] *Ibid.,* pp. 199–201. The correspondence of Samuel P. Dutton, New York Peace Society Archives, and of James Brown Scott, Carnegie Endowment Archives, as well as a general survey of the Secretarial and Administrative Division of the Carnegie Endowment Archives, reveals the businesslike character of these new societies.

[42] Elihu Root, *The Citizen's Part in Government* (New Haven, Scribner, 1907), pp. 6–10, discusses the citizen's choice to "govern or be governed."

[43] "Results," *Independent,* XCI (July 14, 1917), 45.

ship, undertaken for the sake of a cause she considered greater than political parties.) If anything, the communalists' life-style indicated a lack of identification with any organized social group. "I have been," Josiah Royce observed in 1915, "socially ineffective as regards genuine 'team play,' ignorant of politics, an ineffective member of committees, and a poor helper of concrete social enterprises . . . always . . . a good deal of a non-conformist."[44] Royce was too modest, but his self-identification as an apolitical intellectual was accurate; and his description fit Thorstein Veblen as well.

Although Jane Addams was the chairman of many committees and small organizations, her associations were, as I have observed, communal rather than institutional. Significantly she told the story of Hull House in a series of vignettes about herself and her friends, about the immigrant families and their living conditions. It became clear that she and the other communalists lived in a world of personal contacts, cherishing ideas and what sociologist Charles Cooley called "primary groups," with continuous, undifferentiated, face-to-face relations.[45] The political world, where great decisions influenced large numbers of people the decision-maker never saw, was not their milieu. The world all about them was organizing, but they responded with considerable resistance to organizations. Veblen refused to accommodate himself to the regulations and mores of the university. Royce was convinced that great enterprises destroyed individual effectiveness and even self-awareness. Addams could never identify with any one class or distinct status group but only with individuals, who constituted for her the whole of humanity.

Some of the paradoxes of communal thinking seem to reflect the peculiar social position of the American intellectual. As intellectuals were unorganized, so the communalists could not accept international organization uncritically. In spite of this they actually were internationalists, believing both in the reality of ethnic groups and in the potential reality of ethical and cultural bonds between them. As intellectuals they considered their own communities of knowledge universal, but rejected the abstract universalism of the past. Almost nostalgically they idealized small primitive social groups, long dead or dying—Royce's early Christian church, Miss Addams' immigrant peasant families, Veblen's savage tribes with their ethic of "live and let live." Yet they realized that the kinship spirit of such groups could not be projected in a world community. Thus they proposed substantial and imaginative changes. They neither accepted the world of international

[44] "Words of Professor Royce at the Walton Hotel in Philadelphia, December 29, 1915," *Papers in Honor of Josiah Royce on His Sixtieth Birthday* (New York, Longmans, 1916), p. 282.

[45] Charles P. Loomis and John C. McKinney, "Introduction," *Community and Society*, pp. 14–15, discuss Cooley's theory of "primary groups" in relation to Tönnies' sociology.

politics as it was, nor rejected it as hopeless. Instead they criticized it, pointing out that community was precisely the ingredient international relations lacked.

These complexities of communal thought balanced the very different complexities of political internationalism. The institutionalists offered much more detailed programs and were caught up in the compromises of practical politics. Without both modes of thinking American internationalism would have lacked depth and concreteness. It was precisely this intellectual exchange that made American internationalism more than an outmoded Victorian faith in progress.

CHAPTER II

Elihu Root and Nicholas Murray Butler: The Polity as International Judiciary

A nation that is either intellectually, morally, or politically turbulent is not in any position to assume leadership in the development of international affairs on a peace-loving and orderly basis.

Nicholas Murray Butler, "The International Mind," 1912

In the summer of 1905 President Theodore Roosevelt, after extended private negotiations, brought together representatives of nearly defeated Russia and of exhausted but triumphant Japan to sign the Portsmouth Treaty ending the Russo-Japanese War. Roosevelt's immediate concern was the prevention of either Japanese or Russian predominance in East Asia and a restoration of the balance of power that would keep the continent open to expanding American influence. He wished also to educate Americans for a new active role in world affairs appropriate to their great power.

Not far from Portsmouth, New Hampshire, at the Lake Mohonk resort hotel of Quaker Albert Smiley, another group of Americans considered the question of the nation's readiness for such participation. Among the members of the 1905 Lake Mohonk Conference on International Arbitration were State Department lawyers, international legal scholars, and supporters of the Roosevelt administration who believed that continued peace society pressure for arbitration of all international disputes was not an adequate answer to the complex problems of world peace. Americans were still faced with the necessity of acquiring a sense of their international obligations as well as of their rights. International laws must be made both more definite and broader in coverage. Above all, American respect for international law as an "essential element of good citizenship" had to be encouraged. Oscar S. Straus, Roosevelt's Secretary of Commerce, recalled in his memoirs that these objectives had long concerned prominent men at the Lake Mohonk conferences. He called upon James Brown Scott, Professor of International Law at Columbia University, to help him form a new society devoted to the extension and public understanding of international law. Scott, soon to become secretary of the society and its hardest-working administrator, was joined by George W. Kirchway, Dean of Columbia Law School; John Bassett Moore, author of a famous digest of international law based largely upon American arbitrations; Andrew D. White, American delegate to the First Hague Conference; Chandler P. Anderson of the State Department; John W. Foster, former Secretary of State; Robert Lansing, and others. During that winter Scott and Straus presented the plan to the New York Bar Association, which thereupon formed the American Society for International Law, with Secretary of State Elihu Root as its first president.[1]

The Society symbolized the lawyers' deep concern over the course of American thinking about international relations. Elihu Root's presidential addresses (from 1907 to 1924) frequently focused upon popular influences in diplomacy. Some members of the law society undoubtedly considered wars the outcome of clashes of vital interests between nations. But more often they agreed with Root that mass emotions, insulting behavior, and jingoism made it difficult to avoid armed conflict. Root emphasized the situations in which governments tried to settle their differences by constructive compromise while their peoples remained "uncompromising and belligerent," insisting upon the "uttermost view of their own rights."[2]

The elitist interpretation of the origins of wars was not peculiar to international lawyers. It reflected a more pervasive conservative distrust of the rule of the majority in decision-making. Nicholas Murray Butler, a frequent chairman of the Lake Mohonk conferences, for example, shared this view. He preached the doctrine of the international mind, by which he meant a reasonable self-control over nationalist emotions, a tendency to regard other nations as cooperating equals in foreign affairs. In Butler's

---

[1] Oscar S. Straus, *Under Four Administrations from Cleveland to Taft* (Boston, Houghton Mifflin, 1922), pp. 333–34; George A. Finch, "The American Society of International Law, 1906–1956," *American Journal of International Law*, L (April 1956), 295–97; "Editorial Comment," AJIL, I (Jan. 1907), 129–30.

[2] In *Addresses on International Subjects*, eds. Robert Bacon and James Brown Scott (Cambridge, Harvard Univ. Press, 1916), see: "The Need of Popular Understanding of International Law," 1907, p. 3, and "The Japanese Treaty," April 19, 1907, pp. 8, 11, 12.

estimation, relatively few men possessed this international mind, and it devolved upon the remainder to follow their example.[3]

This attitude thoroughly merged with the belief that almost all controversies among nations were ultimately reducible to conflicts over legal rights. Such conflicts could be adjudicated by a court, providing the laws were precise and broad enough. Translating national interests into national rights, the international legalists considered the prospect of a permanent world court as mankind's best hope for peace. In general, these legalists interpreted international organization as a juridical structure and valued its slow steady growth by treaty agreements, codification, and court precedents. Many believed that once a custom or practice had become almost universally recognized in international relations, it became part of the municipal law of every national state. Legalism was defined, in brief, as the attempt to convert international conflicts into cases and to supplement diplomatic negotiations by judicial decisions.

Although the international law societies worked for structural reforms in foreign relations, their orientation toward national policy, as toward society generally, was conservative. The legalists cherished stability over change; they exhibited a Hamiltonian distrust of human nature; and they wished to preserve the contemporary distribution of power not only among national states but within American society. The *leitmotiv* of the American conservative, as Robert G. McCloskey has observed, was the exaltation of "economic privilege to the status of an absolute." Those who had acquired property were, by social Darwinian standards, deemed fit in the struggle for survival. Liberty became a natural right both as to expression and as to property. It was distinguishable from license because liberty implied self-restraint,[4] obedience to law, and acceptance of the *status quo*. The conservatives lauded constitutional restraints upon popular will. They believed, contrary to Justice Oliver Wendell Holmes's dictum, that the fourteenth amendment to the Constitution did indeed enact Herbert Spencer's *Social Statics*. Cherishing the Supreme Court as the institution best devised for protecting the American polity against disorder and egalitarian legislation, they projected its image upon the international polity. In international society they wished to reform in order to preserve an established order.

[3] "The International Mind," May 15, 1912, *The International Mind: An Argument for the Judicial Settlement of International Disputes* (New York, Scribner, 1912), pp. 101–102.

[4] *American Conservatism in the Age of Enterprise, 1865–1910* (New York, Harper, 1964), pp. 22, 27–28; Nicholas Murray Butler, "Liberty," June 3, 1914, *Scholarship and Service: The Policies and Ideals of a National University in a Modern Democracy* (New York, Scribner, 1921), pp. 332–33; Butler, "Greetings to the New Russia," April 23, 1917, *Greetings to the New Russia,* Carnegie Endowment for International Peace, Division of Intercourse and Education, no. 13 (Washington, D.C., 1917), p. 12.

One can readily discern how Root and Butler acquired their taste for a conservative tradition. In the 1880s, an age of "conservative crisis" in the legal profession when many young lawyers were aligning themselves with reform movements in the cities, Elihu Root was already a well-established member of the New York Bar and a close ally of the great financial interests of the city. He had come to New York City from Hamilton, New York, determined to make his way in the market place, and he had succeeded. Shortly after completing his legal training at New York University (1865–67) he joined the Union League Club where "he was definitely marked as a staunch and respectable Republican." Not even his defense of Boss Tweed in a corruption case had hurt his reputation. Rather, it had given him the opportunity to work with some of the best attorneys in the city, including David Dudley Field, the famous codifier of international law. By 1885 he was engaged almost full time in the lucrative practice of organizing corporations and consolidating businesses.[5] He was not only a learned lawyer with a keen, logical mind, but an expert conciliator and administrator—talents that would serve him well in public life. Witty and warm in private, he displayed a rather austere public personality and so became more the party tactician than the dramatic platform orator. He acquired completely that outlook which Alexis de Tocqueville had described in 1835 as belonging to the bench and the bar. The lawyers had, Tocqueville observed,

. . . certain habits of order, a taste for formalities and instinctive regard for the regular connection of ideas which naturally render them very hostile to the revolutionary spirit and the unreflecting passions of the multitude.[6]

Like most American conservatives, Root rarely displayed any public hostility toward the multitude, but spoke in the accents of the democratic tradition. His social attitudes, however, emerged in his ardent appreciation of the wealthy corporation organizers. He pictured Carnegie and Morgan, for example, as kindly, noble men who had grown rich "not by injuring any living being but by conferring great benefits upon society."[7] He offered the Horatio Alger myth as an explanation for their success and considered

---

[5] Philip Jessup, *Elihu Root* (2 vols., New York, Dodd Mead, 1938), I, 71, 81–82, 93; Richard W. Leopold, *Elihu Root and the Conservative Tradition* (Boston, Little Brown, 1954), pp. 13–14, 16–17.

[6] *Democracy in America*, Henry Reeve text, ed. Phillips Bradley (2 vols., New York, Vintage Books, 1954), I, 283.

[7] Root to Theodore Roosevelt, Dec. 13, 1899, quoted in Jessup, *Elihu Root*, I, 208; Root, "Andrew Carnegie," April 25, 1920, *Men and Policies*, eds. Robert Bacon and James Brown Scott (Cambridge, Harvard Univ. Press, 1924), pp. 51–52; Charles W. Toth, "Elihu Root, 1905–1909," *An Uncertain Tradition: American Secretaries of State in the Twentieth Century*, ed. Norman A. Graebner (New York, McGraw Hill, 1961), p. 57.

puritanical values and community service characteristic of business leaders
and political leaders of his time, despite all the contrary evidence of the
Gilded Age. Such commendations made Root anathema to progressives but
a very useful link between Roosevelt and the conservative Republicans.

Nicholas Murray Butler also joined the conservative wing of the Eastern Republican Party. His father had been a party organizer and president
of the School Board in Paterson, New Jersey; and Butler always combined
the same two interests. Even as an undergraduate at Columbia University,
he was ambitious to know the top men and quickly cultivated President
Frederick Barnard, who influenced him to study educational theory and
philosophy instead of law. A year of postdoctoral study at the University
of Berlin (1884–85) was the most critical one in Butler's formal education,
for he acquired, as he later recalled, an "ineffable impression of . . . what a
university was,"[8] and determined to help fashion Columbia University after
the continental image. From the first, his ambitions toward university
administration outweighed his scholarly interests. Although determined
that Columbia should uphold the traditions of *Lehrfreiheit, Lernfreiheit,*
and the pursuit of science for its own sake, he wished to make the
university a training-ground for public life. The university's most vital
function, he stated in 1902, was to supply the nation's leadership in
diplomacy, in domestic politics, and in business as well as in intellectual life.
Its theorists should always instruct "men of practical affairs."[9] More than
that, the university must preserve a "reverence for that which lasts . . . for
that which bears the mark of excellence," and must uphold the American
institutions of the common law, free speech, representative government,
private property, and the separation of church and state.[10] In spite of his
devotion to academic freedom, Butler could tolerate the rebel only within
clearly defined limits.

As president of Columbia (1901–44), Butler assumed an almost condescending attitude toward the faculty. Pontifical and eloquent, he proved an
outstanding administrator and fund-raiser, forming close associations with
the business leaders of New York. He loved pomp. (Carleton J. H. Hayes
recalls that he even criticized King Haakon of Norway for not acting regal
enough.) It was symptomatic of his early and continued veneration of the
successful that he made it a point, even while a student in Europe, to win

---

[8] "A Voyage of Discovery," Jan. 29, 1916, *The Faith of a Liberal* (New York,
Scribner, 1924), pp. 327–28, 345; *Across the Busy Years, 2* vols., (New York, Scribner, 1939–40), I, 73–75.

[9] "Scholarship and Service," 1902, *Scholarship and Service,* pp. 12–13; "The American College and University," 1895, *The Meaning of Education: Contributions to a
Philosophy of Education* (New York, Scribner, 1917), p. 271.

[10] "The Service of the University," October 10, 1912, *Scholarship and Service,* p. 65;
"The University as a Conservative Force," New York *Tribune,* June 19, 1902, p. 3.

introductions to Gladstone, Bismarck, and other political leaders. Over the years he developed an enormous correspondence with American presidents, European prime ministers, party leaders, and educational administrators, particularly in France, Great Britain, and Germany. Living thus in this restricted world of the rich and strong, he came to conceive of internationalism as the unique possession of the educated few. He perceived a contest between these rational men, the upper classes of "broad intellectual outlook," and the vulgar demagogues who too often excited the uninformed public.[11]

He responded quite naturally, by organizing the educated leadership. In 1900 Frederick Holls, Secretary of the American delegation to the First Hague Conference, introduced Butler to Baron d'Estournelles de Constant, a member the French delegation. Constant, Leon Bourgeois, and other members of the French Senate and Academy had formed the Association for International Conciliation to encourage "men of good will" (the educated elite) to exchange visits. The international visitors would lecture in the host country and return home to encourage among their fellow countrymen more understanding and presumably friendlier attitudes toward foreigners. Butler quickly formed an American branch of the Association and edited its journal, *International Conciliation*. Many of the same men who had worked for the American Society for International Law helped him. In addition, there were old-line peace leaders such as Andrew Carnegie and Benjamin Trueblood, Interparliamentary Union men like Hayne Davis and Representative Richard Bartholdt.The organization retained its elevated tone when Butler carried its functions into the Division of Intercourse and Education of the Carnegie Endowment for International Peace. Root, Butler, Henry Prichett, and Joseph Choate, a leader of the New York bar, advised Carnegie on the creation of the Endowment. Carnegie himself had decided that the Anglo-American entente and President Taft's campaign for an arbitration treaty with Britain offered sufficient promise of the growth of peace to warrant a major investment in the cause.[12]

Under Butler's guidance, the Carnegie publications stressed scholarly interpretations of international conflicts rather than peace propaganda. With Root as president of the Endowment, and James Brown Scott as head

[11] *Across the Busy Years*, II, 83; Carleton J. H. Hayes, "Impressions of Nicholas Murray Butler," Oral History Collection, Columbia University (New York, 1960), pp. 1, 22; and in the same collection, James T. Shotwell, "The Reminiscences of James T. Shotwell," (New York, 1949), pp. 10–13.

[12] Butler to James Brown Scott, April 18, 1911, and July 12, 1913, Carnegie Endowment for International Peace Archives, Secretarial and Administrative Division I, IV, Special Collections, Columbia University; and, in the same collection, Elihu Root, "The Purposes of the Carnegie Endowment for International Peace," Dec. 29, 1910, I, 44–45; also, Baron d'Estournelles de Constant, "Program of the Association for International Conciliation," *International Conciliation*, no. 1 (1907), 1–4.

of the International Law division, the early legalistic emphasis of *International Conciliation* was fixed. Altogether the Carnegie Endowment, the American Society for International Law, and the American Society for the Judicial Settlement of International Disputes, which was formed in 1910 by Taft supporters and legalists, were in the forefront of the movement for a permanent world court. Butler used the Division of Intercourse and Education not only for international visits but for the encouragement of college international relations clubs, for the restoration of libraries destroyed in World War I, and for the creation of "international mind alcoves" in British, Commonwealth, and American university libraries. In February 1914 he boasted that the Division had as accurate a picture of European affairs as any foreign ministry. The guns of August swiftly refuted his claim, but in one respect Butler's pretensions were borne out. He often said that he went abroad as a private ambassador, and truly he was received in just that manner.[13]

LAW, SOCIETY, AND HUMAN NATURE

It is hardly surprising that men of such associations and interests as Root and Butler should feel a threat to their profoundest beliefs in the rising social reform movements of the early twentieth century. They believed that the success of self-government depended upon popular adherence to fixed moral and political principles such as were embodied in the American Constitution. The mass of the population, ignorant of the complexities of the governing process, had no choice but to rely upon expert leadership. Since men were unequal in talent and ambition, and since material rewards came always to the fit, a truly free society would necessarily be one in which property and power were unequally distributed. The conservatives found each of these ideas challenged by new intellectual and political currents, and uneasily suspected that their own social status was at stake in the contest.

Butler, for example, delivered many an emotional address against the relativism he felt inherent in the pragmatic revolt. As intellectual progressives emphasized the application of philosophy to social reconstruction, and the uses of history for "explaining the present and controlling the future of man,"[14] Butler responded by asserting that the pragmatists were playing to

---

[13] Butler, "The Carnegie Endowment for International Peace," *International Conciliation*, no. 75 (Feb. 1914), 6; *Across the Busy Years*, II, 93–94, 101–104, 111–13, 121–23; Shotwell, "Reminiscences," Oral History Collection, p. 13.

[14] Morton G. White, *Social Thought in America: The Revolt Against Formalism*, 2nd ed. (Boston, Beacon Press, 1959), pp. 6–8.

the mob and encouraging lawlessness.[15] His own Kantian and Hegelian training had left him with a firm, but not closely examined, static idealism. He pictured the cosmos as a "self-active totality"—a grand abstraction confirmed by every scientific insight.[16] His was truly the "bloc universe" that William James rejected. But Butler had neither the time nor the philosophical depth to vindicate his assertions. Instead, he accused the progressives of undermining the nation's moral fiber, of contributing to the decline of time-honored creeds and of weakening both religious faith and popular attachment to "principles of American government."[17] He imagined a public lacking reverence for an intellectual elite, amenable to demagogic control, and striving to attain an equal distribution of property.

Whenever any major reform issue arose, Root and Butler eventually led the argument around to the question of minority rights and the state of the law. They were sure that movements for initiative, referendum, and recall reflected an unjustifiable loss of faith in the agents of governments. In fact, progressivism as a whole was nothing more than the jealousy of the unfit. It implied, Butler asserted, the "crude and dangerous notion" that one man was as capable of governing as any other.[18] Since the Constitution was the great guardian of individual rights and of the fundamental principles of the American political order, any attempt to change it would eventually lead to anarchy. Both Butler and Root assumed that procedural reforms would infect constitutional law and make it as amenable to the will of a fickle, powerful majority as statutory law. A terrible democratic absolutism would result and private ownership would be destroyed. This black picture of a disorderly and socialist society gave to the conservative appreciation of the law a strident, defensive character.

Such men, although ardent advocates of *laissez faire,* were often willing to accept traditional Hamiltonian notions of a strong government in alliance with business. State welfare legislation, however, posed an immediate threat to their interests. As *laissez faire* receded in economic theory and was refuted by state and municipal practice, it found its last refuge in the courts and in constitutional law. The Supreme Court and judicial review thus became, for most conservatives, the zenith of American political

---

[15] In *Scholarship and Service,* see: "The Age of Irrationalism," June 7, 1911, pp. 313–15; and "Making Liberal Men and Women," June 30, 1920, pp. 184–85.

[16] *Philosophy* (New York, Columbia Univ. Press, 1911), pp. 16–18, 21–23.

[17] "The Call to Citizenship," July 6, 1909, *Why Should We Change Our Form of Government* (New York, Scribner, 1912), pp. 98–99. Cf. "True and False Democracy," March 23, 1907, *True and False Democracy* (New York, Scribner, 1907), pp. 38–39.

[18] "The Education of Public Opinion," June 22, 1899, *True and False Democracy,* p. 59. Cf. Root, *Experiments in Government and Essentials of the Constitution* (Princeton, Princeton Univ. Press, 1913), pp. 33, 37, for distinctions between reforms promoting efficiency and those hindering the legislative process.

achievement. These men were living in an age when, as Arnold Paul has noted, due process of law, once primarily procedural, became "solidly substantive as well."[19] The Court's interpretation of the fourteenth amendment and freedom of contract allowed corporations to contest the state police power in the regulation of wages, hours, and working conditions. Conservative legal thought guided the Court majority, combining Spencer's antipaternalistic support of restrictions upon legislative interference with business, with the traditional legal concern for an orderly society.[20]

These very values—individual and corporate liberty and an orderly, inegalitarian society—were Root's and Butler's highest. These men reacted sharply to charges of judicial legislation, and even more stridently to any suggestion of popular control over the judiciary. Butler cited Eugene V. Debs's appeal to recall "capitalist judges" to prove that judicial recall was a socialist plot. He largely ignored the fact that recall was not directed against the Supreme Court. Earnest Taft supporters, they tried to turn the 1912 election into a contest over fundamental constitutional principles by asserting that the principle of limited government was threatened. If judicial recall succeeded, it would mean a "socialistic democracy," Butler asserted. A majority would take "direct and responsible control of your life, your liberty, your property."[21]

Both Root and Butler feared an imminent attack of class legislation by the poor. Confident that the majority of American workingmen would not accept socialism as a dogma, they foresaw an inadvertent growth of socialist legislation. To this threat they responded with a double appeal that was to assume prime significance in their conception of the international polity. First, they emphasized the importance of ignoring class lines and of uniting all Americans by patriotic devotion.[22] It was first and foremost the nation, not the class nor any brotherhood of man, that was to be the unit of any true internationalism. Second, they came to regard law (not only substan-

[19] Arnold M. Paul, *Conservative Crisis and the Rule of Law. Attitudes of the Bench and Bar, 1887–1895* (Ithaca, Cornell Univ. Press, 1960), p. 235; Butler to Root, June 15, 1909; Root to Butler, June 18, 1909, Papers of Nicholas Murray Butler, Columbiana Collection, Columbia University; Root, Debate on Income and Corporation Taxes, *Congressional Record,* Senate, 61st Cong., special sess., June 23, 1909, pp. 4002–4004, strongly suggests that the conservatives combined Hamiltonian views of the national government with more typical *laissez-faire* principles.

[20] Paul, *Conservative Crisis,* pp. 4–5, 235–36; Butler, *The American As He Is* (New York, Macmillan, 1908), pp. 28–29, presents a typical expression of the idea of the judiciary as protector of constitutional liberties against willful majorities.

[21] "Why Should We Change Our Form of Government?" Nov. 27, 1911, *Why Change Our Form of Government,* pp. 31, 42–43. Cf. Root, *Experiments in Government,* p. 72.

[22] Root, "The Spirit of Self-Government," *International Conciliation,* no. 62 (Jan. 1913), 6–10; Butler, "To New Made Americans," Jan. 3, 1924, *Faith of a Liberal,* p. 166.

tive legislation but the eternal rules of "right reason") as the essential element in any political organization. A veneration of law itself was so basic in their thinking that they conceived of international reform as purely legal. The ground was thus laid for their pervasive distrust of any international system that was not primarily juridical.

Although they regarded the law with an almost pious reverence, as indeed many middle-class Americans did in the late nineteenth and early twentieth century, neither Root nor Butler precisely defined what they meant by the law.[23] At a time when Oliver Wendell Holmes Jr. was exploring the process by which judges made law, and Louis D. Brandeis was calling for a positive legal recognition of actual social conditions and needs, Root and Butler still spoke of law as the embodiment of abstract principles of justice. They clung to natural law concepts and insisted that judges discover them. The natural law, the rules of justice, and the principles of the American Constitution coalesced. Constitutional limitations were made "impersonally, abstractly, dispassionately, impartially, as the people's expression of what they believed to be right."[24] Thus the "ought" and "is" became indistinguishable, and constitutional law came to be identified with morality itself.

Both Root and Butler made this quite clear in their discussions of human nature and law. The law symbolized order, stability, individual liberty. It was the essential ingredient of any society. Their discussion raised the image of the founding fathers, not only because they centered it upon the constitution, but because they so thoroughly shared Alexander Hamilton's distrust of popular majorities and related it to the need for legal restraints. "The reason for restraining rules," Root declared in 1912, "arises from a tendency to do the things prohibited . . . to press the exercise of power to the utmost under the influence of ambition . . . of selfish interest and arrogance of office."[25] The law was a constraint upon a deep and fundamentally evil human desire for power, which Root termed the "worst element in our nature." If men had been even rationally selfish (as Root and Butler occasionally implied they were in defending *laissez faire*), the path of government would have been considerably easier. But the mass of men were both self-interested and impulsive. "When a man thinks he thinks,"

[23] Henry Steele Commager, *The American Mind: An Interpretation of American Thought and Character Since the 1880's* (New Haven, Yale Univ. Press, 1959), pp. 360–61, discusses the persistence of natural law concepts in America. Lawrence Stapleton, *Justice and World Society* (Chapel Hill, Univ. of North Carolina Press, 1944), pp. 9–10, 21–23, considers natural law a liberal and liberating rather than a conservative influence on thought.

[24] Root, *Experiments in Government*, p. 51.

[25] *Ibid.*, pp. 59–60. Cf. Root, *The Citizen's Part in Government* (New York, Scribner, 1907), pp. 17–20, for a discussion of the function of law in inculcating habits of self-restraint and in making democratic government possible.

Butler contended, "he usually merely feels, and his instincts and feelings are powerful precisely as they are irrational."[26]

Thus, without any clearly defined psychological theory, the legalists expressed traditional and static conceptions of a divided human nature. The lower impulses of man were passionate, imitative, animalistic, and evil. Man's higher nature reflected the standards of his surrounding culture, from which he acquired reason and rational free will. It was this reason, embodied in the standards of civilization, that the law expressed. Inevitably then, man's highest duty and most enlightened self-interest lay in obedience to the law.

This concentration upon the reasonableness and justice of the law led Root and Butler to argue the traditional ideas of *stare decisis*. They cherished the very steadiness of the law and rejected any idea that it could be an instrument for reforming an inegalitarian social order. As Felix S. Cohen has observed, the argument that law cannot save a man from his own mistakes is frequently a defense against the embodiment of social reform in statutes.[27] So it was for the conservatives in the first decade of the twentieth century. Root often advocated the adoption of a single code of domestic, federal law and the codification of international law. He worked for legal precision and efficiency and was in that sense a reformer.

But he frequently would caution audiences that the law could not bring a Utopia, because the errors and evils of human nature would remain. He did not wish Americans turning toward the federal government for their economic salvation. No law could "give to depravity the rewards of virtue, to indolence the rewards of industry."[28] Below substantive laws there existed a law of human nature—the unequal endowment of men. In any social order, Butler emphasized, there would be energetic, rising men and unambitious poor. The statement left unanswered the question of whether the existing social order offered equal opportunity to both. Butler presumed it did. The poor were poor, he argued, because, like George Bernard Shaw's Mr. Doolittle, they were "undeserving." This was Butler's major argument against both welfare legislation and socialism. The "deepest law of our nature," he maintained, was "that all progress is the result of inequality or difference. . . . Set a thousand men free at this moment and make them absolutely equal, and tomorrow at sundown, no two of them would be alike. Nature forbids."[29] It was this stress upon inequality among both individuals

---

[26] "The Revolt of the Unfit," Dec. 8, 1910, *Why Change Our Form of Government*, p. 149; cf. "What Knowledge is of Most Worth?" July 9, 1895, *Meaning of Education*, p. 68, where Butler indicates how man's acquired rationality sets him free from his animal passions.

[27] *The Legal Conscience: Selected Papers of Felix S. Cohen* (New Haven, Yale Univ. Press, 1960), p. 29.

[28] *Experiments in Government*, p. 19.

[29] "Public Opinion in the United States," 1921, *Faith of a Liberal*, p. 53.

and groups that distinguished the political internationalists' concept of human nature from that of the community thinkers. The men of the polity were intent upon proving the justice of the distribution of power within American society; the communalists either contested this elitism or disregarded it.

THE COURSE OF EMPIRE

When President McKinley appointed Root Secretary of War in 1899 because he needed not a soldier but a lawyer "to direct the government of these Spanish islands," the Filipino revolt under Emilio Aguinaldo was for the first time being directed against the Americans. Up to that time neither Root nor Butler had said very much about racial differences. Root's experience in directing the suppression of the revolt and defending the military action against democratic and anti-imperialist attacks gave to his notions of human inequality a racial connotation. The institutionalists generally believed that the British and American experience in self-government was unique. This experience established a tradition of liberty under law which no other people had nor were likely to acquire except under long Anglo-American tutelage. For the sake of civilization, therefore, it was the duty of Americans to retain the Spanish possessions won in 1898, and to mold the Filipinos, the Puerto Ricans, even the independent Cubans and other Latin Americans, in the American image.

In spite of the harshness of the guerilla warfare in the Philippines, in spite of Root's characterization of the followers of Aguinaldo as primitives "but little advanced from savagery,"[30] there was a genuine paternalistic idealism inherent in his imperialism. Believing that the illiteracy of former Spanish subjects made representative government unworkable in the new US possessions, Root acceded only reluctantly to the demand by Congress for popularly elected legislatures. He did, however, hasten the transition from military to civilian rule and instruct his governors to respect local customs as far as possible. Material progress, security, and, above all, social order were the Rootian ideals for American protectorates and possessions. For example, he defended American military occupation of Cuba as absolutely necessary for the promotion of conditions essential to self-government and for the prevention of "continuous revolution and disorder."[31]

[30] Root to Senator John Morgan, July 8, 1902, Papers of Elihu Root, Manuscript Division, Library of Congress. Cf., from the same collection, Root to William Howard Taft, Oct. 25, 1902; and "The United States and the Philippines," Oct. 24, 1900, *The Military and Colonial Policy of the United States,* eds. Robert Bacon and James Brown Scott (Cambridge, Harvard Univ. Press, 1916), pp. 39–42.
[31] Root to Charles Eliot, May 4, 1900, quoted in Jessup, *Elihu Root,* I, 288; cf. Henry L. Stimson and McGeorge Bundy, *On Active Service in Peace and War* (New York, Harper, 1947), p. 118.

The conservatives asserted that because the Filipinos and Puerto Ricans and Cubans were "ignorant of the art of self-government," and because their material progress depended upon the flow of American capital, which needed a secure political environment, they could not be released completely from American guidance. Thus, Root and Butler never believed in the capacity for nationhood among the Filipinos or Puerto Ricans. Possibly if either people had attained nationhood while Root and Butler still lived, neither man would have denied the islanders' rights, for the conservatives' respect for an international legal position was great. However, Root, like Roosevelt, believed that American expansion was the expansion of civilization. The possessions should remain possessions. Butler, on the other hand, imagined a distant future when the peoples of Puerto Rico and the Philippines would have acquired a greater political talent and could be members of some American commonwealth.[32]

In spite of this overriding zeal to educate the Spanish-speaking peoples to American ways, strategic considerations played a determining role in the conservatives' desire for empire. Root insisted that Americans had gone to war in defense of the just quarrel of the Cuban people. But eleven years after the close of that war he defended the Platt Amendment, which had made Cuba a protectorate, on the grounds that Cuba guarded the approaches to the Isthmus of Panama and must therefore be kept under American influence.[33] Similarly, Butler had warned President McKinley in 1898 that German ambitions in the Far East threatened world peace. The United States should prevent their fulfillment by retaining control of the Philippines.[34] Finally, Root justified the Roosevelt Corollary to the Monroe Doctrine, which stipulated United States unilateral exercise of an "international police power," by claiming that self-protection involved an estimate of the effects of actions beyond national borders. The stability and independence of Latin American governments was a condition of United States independence.[35]

In brief, Root and Butler had deep-felt convictions both of Anglo-Saxon

[32] Root to Mrs. H. Fairfield Osborn, Dec. 24, 1917, Root Papers; Butler to McKinley, Sept. 14, 1898, *Across the Busy Years*, II, 348; Howard K. Beale, *Theodore Roosevelt and the Rise of America to World Power* (Baltimore, Johns Hopkins Press, 1956), p. 70; Leopold, *Root and the Conservative Tradition*, pp. 27, 37.

[33] Debate on the Payne-Aldrich tariff, *Congressional Record*, Senate, 61st Cong., special sess., June 23, 1909, p. 3704. Root himself was author of the Platt amendment he defended. In the tariff debate, he argued against raising the tariff on Cuban sugar and pineapples. The general welfare of American protectorates concerned him more than a protective tariff serving individual capital interests.

[34] Butler to McKinley, Sept. 14, 1898, *Across the Busy Years*, II, 347–48.

[35] "The Real Monroe Doctrine," April 22, 1914, *Addresses on International Subjects*, pp. 111, 113.

superiority and of the necessity of expanding American interests in Latin America and Asia. Their attitudes toward the Latins were never as openly condescending as Roosevelt's, nor as self-righteous and missionary as Wilson's. On a 1906 tour through Latin America, for instance, Root emphasized the common interests of the Americas, his respect for Latin culture, and his faith in Latin ability to create strong governments. He projected a future in which the Americas would be economically independent of Europe because they were interdependent among themselves. The United States would encourage political stability in the area. American capital would flow in as a natural concomitant. Latin America would then be brought "out of the stage of militarism and into the stage of industrialism." Friendly feelings would develop from this commercial bond just as Anglo-American friendship had developed out of close commercial links between the two countries.[36] It is unlikely that Root ever pictured the Latin American nations equal in power to the United States, but neither did he think the flow of American capital would impair Latin independence. Quite the contrary, he wished the Latins to achieve a higher status in world politics.

For such an improved status the first requirement was the creation of Pan-American institutions for the peaceful settlement of disputes. In November 1907, when fighting again broke out on the Mexican-Nicaraguan border, Root invited all the Central American representatives to Washington to help settle the dispute. Under his guidance, and with the example of the Second Hague Conference still fresh in all minds, the Central Americans created a Central American Court of Justice with compulsory jurisdiction over all intergovernmental and private international disputes. The Court was a miniature of the one Root envisioned as the world court. In this smaller version, however, every nation had its judge.[37]

The second condition was European acceptance of Latin American nations in the councils of nations. This Root achieved at the Second Hague Conference. If he imagined that the South Americans would strengthen the US position, he was sadly disappointed. Following the lead of Argentinian foreign minister Luis Drago, the Latins insisted upon complete prohibition of debt collection by force and on multilateral inter-American implementation of this interpretation of the Monroe Doctrine. Caught between Euro-

[36] In *Latin America and the United States*, eds. Robert Bacon and James Brown Scott (Cambridge, Harvard Univ. Press, 1917), see: Presidential Address at the Third Conference of American Republics at Rio de Janeiro, July 31, 1906, pp. 7 ff; Address to English and American Residents of Buenos Aires, Aug. 16, 1906, p. 91; and "How to Develop South American Commerce," Nov. 20, 1906, pp. 263–64.

[37] James Brown Scott, "Elihu Root, Secretary of State, July 7, 1905–Jan. 27, 1909," *American Secretaries of State and Their Diplomacy*, ed. Samuel Flagg Bemis (New York, Knopf, 1929), IX, 266–67.

pean creditors and Latin American debtors, the United States offered a compromise which forbade the use of force, except in a case where the debtor either refused to arbitrate or rejected a verdict of arbitrators. The Monroe Doctrine was thus to remain unilateral.[38]

Brazil and the South Americans then insisted upon a vote for each nation on the court, a scheme Root believed would turn the court into an assembly. When it proved impossible to reach a compromise between the great and small nations, the delegates adjourned, pledging to create a world court as soon as the question should be resolved.

Root did not permit this setback to diminish his patience nor his gentlemanly forbearance. The "Root Doctrine" of "honorable obligation" and "kindly consideration"[39] continued to guide his approach to weaker nations. As long as Root remained Secretary of State, the velvet of good manners always clothed the fist of American power.

The Root Doctrine was symptomatic of the patrician character of conservative internationalism generally. It presupposed a dominant Anglo-American influence in the world combined with a gentle respect for the contrary beliefs of other nations. On the one hand, the conservatives assumed that races and nations differed in their political skills (an argument that justified Anglo-American tutelage of backward peoples). On the other hand, they insisted that internationalism did not mean compelling other nations to act like Americans or even expecting them to do so. Butler's thinking appeared to involve a conflict between the necessity of converting others to the American political culture and an insistence that Americans learn to respect national differences. When he asked, "Shall we keep to ourselves the great fundamental American accomplishments, or shall we use our influence to teach others . . . and spread them abroad,"[40] it sounded a bit selfish not to spread them abroad. Yet he was equally convinced that "real internationalism" meant an appreciation that such traits as the "Puritan conscience in America," the "French spirit," and "German idealism," were not abstractions but realities which any international organization should respect. Patently, the only resolution of this contradiction would be a voluntary acceptance of those American ways that were deemed essential for world peace. Other nations should work for a

[38] Arthur P. Whitaker, *The Western Hemisphere Idea: Its Rise and Decline* (Ithaca, Cornell Univ. Press, 1954), pp. 98, 102–103, discusses Roosevelt's and Hay's first postponement of Drago's proposal and Root's skillful denaturing of the doctrine in the American "Porter resolution."

[39] James Brown Scott and Robert Bacon, "Introductory Note," in Root, *Addresses on International Subjects,* p. viii, considered Root's practices distinctive enough to constitute a "doctrine."

[40] "Nationality and Beyond," Aug. 8, 1916, *International Conciliation,* no. 107 (Oct. 1916), 6.

great tribunal settling conflicts in "formal and stated fashion."[41] The only question that remained was: Were the nations ready to take so bold a step?

This was a question the legalists could not answer. The spread of constitutional government seemed to them a hopeful sign. But their fears of popular intervention in diplomatic matters ran very deep. Experiences such as the San Francisco school board's segregation of Oriental children served to confirm the thesis that ignorant defiance of international law could bring nations to a crisis.[42] Yet something more than jingoism threatened the imperial rivalry of the great powers. Neither Root nor Butler ever openly discussed this, but it colored their judgments of the future during the whole decade before 1914. Both had an uneasy feeling that the balance of power was unstable. Only by repeated compromises could it be maintained. This belief led Root and Roosevelt to seek an understanding with Japan. Nevertheless, one could never take for granted such understandings as the Root-Takahira agreement.[43]

From his first days with the McKinley administration, Root had been, and remained, an advocate of a strong military establishment. He initiated the moves that were to place the American army on a modern footing. He instituted the general staff system, tightened civilian control over the military, and founded the Army War College to train officers to advise the general staff on strategic matters.[44] Root justified this course of action by claiming that the very progress of medical science had ended the "Malthusian checks to population." Nations were "jostling against each other," preparing to defend their rights in the "closer contact and conflict of modern life."[45]

Like the strategic view of American predominance in the Western Hemisphere, Root's defense of military preparedness was distinctly antithetical to the traditional views of the peace movement. Butler and Root both felt they were caught between the assertive nationalists and the soft-hearted, but naive, pacifists. They wished to be constructive but realis-

---

[41] "The Progress of Real Internationalism," May 22, 1907, *International Mind*, p. 5.

[42] Root, in *Addresses on International Subjects*, see: "The Japanese Treaty," pp. 11–12, 21; and "Nobel Prize Address," 1914, p. 171; and in *Latin America*, Address at the Mexican Academy of Legislation and Jurisprudence, Oct. 4, 1907, p. 190.

[43] Toth, "Root," p. 51; Leopold, *Root and the Conservative Tradition*, pp. 61–62. The Root-Takahira agreement, as Leopold points out, has been subject to intricate and often conflicting interpretations. In it Japan and the United States recognized each other's interests and possessions in the Pacific and agreed to consult one another in case of a threat to the *status quo*. Whether or not this contradicted American Open Door pledges or granted Japan any rights in Manchuria is at least questionable.

[44] Leopold, *Root and the Conservative Tradition*, pp. 38–42.

[45] "The Monroe Doctrine," Dec. 22, 1904, *Miscellaneous Addresses*, eds. Robert Bacon and James Brown Scott (Cambridge, Harvard Univ. Press, 1917), p. 269.

tic. Without much enthusiasm, therefore, Root and Roosevelt probed the
great powers' reactions toward arms limitation. (Arms reduction and certainly disarmament were out of the question.) An agreement on the size of
ships and armaments budgets seemed most practical, particularly if it
allowed, as Roosevelt and Alfred T. Mahan insisted, the replacement of
worn-out ships with efficient ones. When the new Liberal British government gave the proposal only lip service, and Germany, France, and Russia
rejected it, Root decided against a public proposal at the Second Hague
Conference.[46] In defending his position before the National Peace and
Arbitration Congress of 1907, he analyzed in almost classical terms the
idealist-realist confrontation. Every civilized nation displayed the practical
motives of self-preservation on the one hand and the humane, Christian
impulse of brotherhood on the other. Men of public responsibility naturally
had an obligation to advance national interests, which included "the material interest of their countrymen. . . ." Such practical administrators were
understandably impatient in the presence of men taking the "humanitarian
view," for the theorists were "not burdened by the necessity of putting
theories into practice." But the idealists often were repelled by the hardness
of the practical man.[47] Thus Root urged the Arbitration Congress not to
expect miracles from the Second Hague Conference.

Accepting Root's decision that the powers could not afford to disarm,
Butler nevertheless assumed that good will was sufficiently strong among
the civilized nations for them to halt the arms race where it stood. Significantly omitting references to Roosevelt's naval program, Butler urged the
British to forego their ambitions for a two-power fleet. Germany surely
intended no evil; Britain, at any rate, could be defended only by the growth
of international justice, not by her fleet![48] In ignoring the practical motive,
Butler revealed the depth of his elitist bias. Surely the men he trusted (the
British Liberals) would not ignore his suggestions unless they too were
trapped by their irrational populace. This was not so much an analysis of
war as an assignment of blame.

There were indications that Root, even while he adhered to this view, felt
uneasy with it. It implied a hopefulness he could not sustain, for he
believed that war was deeply rooted in human nature. The evil passions

[46] Beale, *Theodore Roosevelt*, pp. 340, 342, 346–48; cf. Root, "Instructions to the
American Delegates to the Hague Conference," May 31, 1907, in James Brown Scott,
The Hague Peace Conferences of 1899 and 1907 (2 vols., Baltimore, Johns Hopkins
Press, 1909), II, 183. Root encouraged the American delegation to support any other
proposals for arms limitation which seemed reasonable within the framework of their
instructions.

[47] "The Hague Peace Conferences," April 15, 1907, *Addresses on International
Subjects*, pp. 131–33.

[48] "The World's Armaments and Public Opinion," May 19, 1909, *International Mind*,
p. 30.

would not down. Man's warlike tendencies were part of the survival mechanism that Darwinian biology suggested. "In attempting to bring mankind to a condition of permanent peace," Root declared in his Nobel Prize Address of 1914, . . . "we have to deal with innate ideas, impulses and habits, which became part of the cave man's nature of necessity . . . and still survive dormant under the veneer of civilization."[49]

The conservatives' estimate of the source of wars then came down to this: All men are belligerent, but some are more belligerent than others. The old Calvinist sense of human sinfulness brought no humility, but rather reinforced the social Darwinian emphasis upon natural inequality. To reconcile the elitist view of war causation with the contention that war was rooted in all men's natures, the conservatives insisted that the masses of people could be saved if they followed instructed and competent leaders in all questions of foreign policy, particularly those involving national rights. International conflicts were even more complex than domestic conflicts and should therefore be even less amenable to direct popular control. Yet all signs pointed to an even stronger popular influence upon diplomacy in the future. This prospect created proportionately greater need for the enlightenment of the public. Progress away from war would come gradually and only by the cultivation of new habits of national behavior.[50]

In particular, the international lawyers and educated legalists would have increasing responsibilities in the future. They would be obliged to train all the nation's youth to respect the law and to understand and accept profound national differences of views with regard to international relations. Since most men failed to realize that preconceptions of rights varied from nation to nation, training in the diversity of man's cultures was essential. Eventually the public would learn that not all the right was always on the side of one's own country nor all the duties on the side of others.[51]

Still, above this cultural diversity hovered those universal moral standards of international right behavior—standards embodied in international law and thus obligatory for all nations. These universals the conservatives could not relinquish even in the midst of a discussion emphasizing their

[49] *Addresses on International Subjects,* pp. 156–57. In Dec. 1913 the Nobel Foundation conferred the peace prize for 1912 upon Senator Elihu Root for his services both to the Hague Conference of 1907 and to the Central American court. He was to deliver his address in Stockholm in Sept. 1914, but the war prevented his trip. For the process of his nomination see: James Brown Scott to Representative Richard Bartholdt, enc. in Bartholdt to Carnegie, Jan. 11, 1909; Root to Carnegie, Jan. 12, 1909, Papers of Andrew Carnegie, Manuscript Division, Library of Congress.

[50] Root, Address to a Conference of Teachers of International Law, April 23, 1914, *Addresses on International Subjects,* pp. 127–28; "A Requisite for the Success of Popular Diplomacy," Sept. 15, 1922, *Men and Policies,* pp. 478–80, 484–85.

[51] Root, "Opening Address," American Society of International Law: *Proceedings of Fifteenth Annual Meeting* (Washington, D.C., April 27, 1921), p. 4.

appreciation of diversity. The easy relativism essential to practical politics and diplomacy lodged together in the conservative mind with a sturdy moral absolutism.

PUBLIC OPINION AS A SANCTION

Whenever Root or Butler spoke of the standards of national behavior or of the equality of national rights, they implied that the same natural law conceptions found in domestic law pervaded international relations. International law consisted of those rules governing relations between states which were "founded upon justice, equity, convenience, the reason of the thing, and confirmed by long usage."[52] Yet the definition did not wholly exclude the legal positivism of the late nineteenth and early twentieth century which was eroding natural law conceptions. Neither Root nor Butler was a legal scholar, and neither troubled to distinguish between the varying positions in the controversy over the nature of international law. Root suggested that it was the consent of sovereign states that gave international law its force; the specific rules, treaties, customs, and generally accepted codes formed its content. The recognition of law as binding upon national states made it, in fact, the law. This was a strongly positivist view. What he could not accept (and what most American international lawyers strenuously rejected) was the positivism of John Austin. Austin had declared that law required visible means of enforcement before it actually could become law.[53] This view suggested to Root the necessity for more international organization than he was willing to accept.

The atomism implicit in international law made as profound an appeal to the conservatives as the individualism they believed implicit in constitutional law. The only equality recognized in international law was the equality of sovereign rights. Each state, Root declared with satisfaction, had the right to "redress an injury or not to redress it," to determine its own actions within the limitations imposed by recognition of the equal rights of others. The nations' liberty under law corresponded to the economic and civil liberty of individuals in a constitutional polity. This meant

[52] "Nobel Prize," pp. 161–62; "The Basis of Protection to Citizens Residing Abroad," April 28, 1910, *Addresses on International Subjects*, pp. 48–49.

[53] "The Function of Private Codification in International Law," April 27, 1911, *Addresses on International Subjects*, pp. 59–60, 65; "The Conditions and Possibilities Remaining for International Law After the War," April 27, 1921, *Men and Policies*, pp. 425–26; Charles G. Fenwick, *International Law*, 3rd ed. (New York, Appleton, 1948), pp. 27, 30–31, expounds the consent theory. Georg Schwarzenberger, *The Frontiers of International Law* (London, Stevens & Sons, 1962), pp. 25–27, indicates how the consent theory reveals the "overriding consideration" of power in international relations. Irwin Abrams, "The Emergence of the International Law Societies," *Review of Politics*, XIX (July 1957), 361, discusses Austin's influence and its decline.

that there was no legal remedy for inequalities of power, territory, or national wealth. The law neither brought states into existence nor equalized their resources; it simply recognized their rights. All else was left to the free play of international politics. Even if political competition erupted into violence, the law allowed this. Defensive and just wars were legal, although wars of aggression were not.[54]

It was thus the very incompleteness of international law (its implied acknowledgment of the *status quo*) that constituted its attraction to conservatives. They were satisfied that the United States was strong enough to make its influence felt in international councils. American interests were safe. The real question was: Would other nations accept and abide by the rules of international law? In answering this question Root was defending the legalistic position against both the Austinians, who questioned the existence of a law without positive sanctions, and the world organization men in the Anglo-American peace movement who began a drive for a true international organization with an international executive. The executive, Root contended, already existed. International law was truly law because it was in fact obeyed. No one ordered the powers to obey it. They did so voluntarily, and frequently against their own short-range interests. There existed a tendency among states, as among men, to conform to the standards of their society, because they feared ostracism, if not violent punishment. "The force of law is the public opinion that prescribes it."[55]

The communications revolution, the conservatives argued, made possible a genuine world public opinion which criticized and judged every nation's behavior. It is difficult to decide just what Root and Butler meant by public opinion, for they sometimes implied, as Abbott Lawrence Lowell did, that there could be no true opinion unless there was rational consideration of all sides of a question. Yet, they often insisted that the mass of men never decided questions in this manner, so that opinion seemed not to exist at all. Once again the idea of an elite resolved the issue. In the final analysis, the action of public opinion was in fact the reaction of the great civilized powers to violations of international law. Root defended the extra-territorial rights of the powers in China by charging that that isolated country had ignored public opinion in her treatment of foreigners. The powers then

[54] Root, Remarks, June 18, 1920, quoted in James Brown Scott, *The Project of the Permanent Court of International Justice, and Resolutions of the Advisory Committee of Jurists,* Carnegie Endowment for International Peace, Division of International Law, no. 35 (Washington, D.C., 1920), p. 33. Root, "The Relations Between International Tribunal of Arbitration and the Jurisdiction of National Courts," April 23, 1909, *Addresses on International Subjects,* pp. 33–34. Schwarzenberger, *Frontiers,* pp. 238–40.

[55] "The Sanction of International Law," April 24, 1908, *Addresses on International Subjects,* pp. 26, 28.

intervened to protect their interests, and China's very "disorder, oppression, poverty, and wretchedness," marked the "penalties which warn mankind that laws established for the guidance of national conduct cannot be ignored with impunity."[56]

Public opinion then emerged out of the reciprocal interests of great powers. The principle of reciprocity in international law seemed its foundation. However, Root did not state so explicitly. He called public opinion frequently uninformed, misinformed, or chaotic. Only if it could be made precise would it act as an enforcer of international law. This in turn meant that the rules of law had to be defined specifically. "The advantage of having a moral sense about a particular rule crystallized into a rule of law is that it takes the subject out of the field of controversy and leaves opinion free from uncertainty," Root told the American Society of International Law. Sovereign nations could not be compelled to obey the law, but if the law was certain, they would obey it voluntarily. To the argument that world public opinion did not exist because there were different national interpretations of international law, Root replied: However complex the issues of any particular international controversy, they could still be brought under the "aegis of public opinion" by demands that they be "submitted to an impartial tribunal," and that the decision of that tribunal be accepted.[57]

The path by which Root and Butler arrived at their conclusion that a permanent world court of justice had to be created was the following: (1) Nations generally obeyed international law because they found it neither beneficial nor easy to disregard world public opinion. (2) The advantage of a legal polity was that it allowed the actual disparity of power among states and still recognized the equal rights of small and large nations. (3) The major difficulty in the enforcement of the law lay in its uncertainty. (4) Therefore, controversies over the interpretation of the law had to be settled both decisively and justly by impartial judges who would discover the one meaning of international codes.

The conservatives recognized that the Hague Court, created in 1899, could not serve this function. It was, in truth, not a court at all, but a panel of arbitrators from which disputing nations could, if they wished, select four members (the four would elect a fifth as umpire) to settle a dispute. The trouble with this system was that the nations had no faith in it. They

[56] *Ibid.*, p. 30; "International Law at the Washington Conference on the Limitation of Armaments," April 27, 1922, *Men and Policies*, p. 454.

[57] "Sanction of International Law," pp. 31–32; "Washington Conference on Limitation of Armaments," p. 463.

used it only to settle minor disputes that did not concern their vital interests. Moreover, they could ignore its decisions if they had not agreed to abide by them. Root believed the difficulty lay not in the good intentions of the national states but in the method of arbitration itself. The system had no real advantages over diplomatic negotiation, which the powers naturally preferred.[58]

While respecting the manners and mores of the old diplomacy, Root had a profound distrust of diplomacy itself. The negotiators would be, he felt, increasingly the captives of nationalistic sentiment. The bargaining process would inevitably reflect the relative power of the two parties, and the ultimate threat of war itself remained in the background, with the result that the method could not be as certain nor as peaceful as a judicial proceeding. If the crises of his time were, as he and Butler tended to think, conflicts over "rights which are based on facts and therefore justiciable," then only judges who would be immune to popular pressures should decide them. The conclusion was clearly drawn from the example of a conservative Supreme Court, as Root himself pointed out:

If there could be a tribunal which would pass upon questions between nations with the same impartial and impersonal judgment that the Supreme Court of the United States gives to questions arising between citizens of the different States, or between foreign citizens and the citizens of the United States, there can be no doubt that nations would be much more ready to submit their controversies to its decision than they now are to take the chances of arbitration.[59]

There were other advantages to judicial decision. The difficulty of arbitration lay in the expectation that the arbitrators' decision might clash with national rights. This could hardly happen in a court where those rights were defined. The court's decisions would act as precedents guiding the legal actions of national states, thus building up a code of law.[60] More important, by this participation in the process of judicial review, the nations would have an opportunity to realize the significance of judicial limitations upon popular passions. Root and Butler believed that given time the world court could actually provide the nucleus of a world-wide movement for imitation of the American judicial system. Judicial review meant, Root told Latin audiences, that government was secure "against the tyranny of the mob," that civil liberties and property rights were protected. It seemed only natural to Americans that a court without any power to enforce its decisions (except the confidence of public opinion) should judge the acts of

[58] "Instructions to American Delegates, 1907," p. 191.
[59] "Instructions to American Delegates, 1907," p. 191.
[60] Butler, "The United States of Europe," Oct. 18, 1914, *A World in Ferment: Interpretations of the War for a New World* (New York, Scribner, 1917), pp. 36–37.

men who did hold power. The judicial process exercised such a stabilizing influence upon American political life that Americans hoped to win other supporters for the world court.[61] Yet, no matter how far the legalists went in comparing the Supreme Court and the prospective world court, they could not escape the fundamental contrast between the anarchistic world polity and the American federal government. The nations were neither culturally nor legally united. Nor were the conservatives eager to promote world federation. They considered such wild schemes potentially dangerous and actually ridiculous.[62] The United States Constitution, however, prescribed a method of choosing federal judges, and in any judicial international polity this was the crucial question.

As Brazilian action at the Second Hague Conference demonstrated, and as Root's frequent, and at first fruitless, attempts to reconcile the large and small powers showed, no one actually did consider the judges impartial. In some sense, whatever their qualifications, they remained national judges. Root himself admitted as much when he declared that in any arbitration the choice of arbitrators virtually decided the issue. It was on this rock that the Second Hague Conference foundered.

Root considered that substantial progress had been made because the members agreed to constitute a permanent world court and to choose jurists "of recognized competence in matters of international law."[63] But as the conference adjourned, the actual establishment of the court by the powers seemed nebulous. The attempt to define with greater precision the international law of prize and to constitute a Prize Court as an experiment in international adjudication also failed. As of August 1914 the powers' acceptance of the rules of the Declaration of London was still equivocal.

POSTWAR PATRICIANS

The legalists' battle for codification of the rules of maritime warfare was swiftly dwarfed between 1914 and 1918 by actual battles on land and sea. The belligerents shattered the very notion of civilized warfare. The world of the gentlemen-lawyers was turned upside down. Few now expected public opinion to prevent violations of international law. Still fewer saw any evidence of the international mind among the leaders of the great powers. Butler, who had so derided the warlike masses, completely reversed his interpretation of the causes of war, or at least the causes of this war.

[61] Address at University of San Marco, Lima, Peru, Sept. 14, 1906, *Latin America*, pp. 141–42.

[62] Warren Kuehl, *Hamilton Holt, Journalist, Internationalist, Educator* (Gainesville, Univ. of Florida Press, 1960), p. 72; Root, "Nobel Prize," p. 57.

[63] "The Real Significance of the Declaration of London," April 25, 1912, *Addresses on International Subjects*, pp. 84–85.

We can all testify that the statement that kings and cabinets were forced into the war by public sentiment is absolutely untrue. . . . A tiny minority in each of the several countries whose conduct was hostile . . . may have desired war, but the militarist spirit was singularly lacking among the masses of the population in Germany, in Austria-Hungary and [in] Russia. . . .[64]

Root, who often considered wars the products of conflicts over legal rights, now admitted that the issues were considerably more complex. The nature of modern warfare, he believed, had completely overtaken the slow growth of international law. Having denied the need for any sanction for international law, he nevertheless rejoiced in August 1914 that the Allies "resolved themselves into an international police force for the purpose of disciplining a big, destructive, intolerable bully." Recalling his old suspicions of German designs in the Caribbean and the Far East, and German recalcitrance at the Algeciras conference, Root concluded, the "Kaiser has no doubt intended all his life to wage a great European war."[65]

As the war in the trenches dragged on and as the submarine issue was pulling America ever closer to the conflict, the conservatives' interpretations of the war were becoming more pro-British. In 1914, for instance, Butler had blamed the militarists of both sides. He had even contended that government ownership of munitions factories would be a justifiable invasion of the "sphere of liberty." But by 1916 he was arguing that the American public had made up its mind about the real aggressor in this war.[66] Root's devotion to Britain's "revered principles of Constitutional liberty," his high personal regard for former Ambassador to the United States Lord Bryce (who had worked with him to bring the Newfoundland Fisheries dispute to the Hague), and his reconciliation with Roosevelt in 1916, led him to join the strongly pro-Allied branch of the party. Britain was fighting America's fight for democracy. The Central Powers were fighting for autocracy.[67] The complex issues of the war had finally resolved themselves into that simple pattern. Thus while Butler for a time agreed with Wilson's mediation policies and was even willing to accept Wilson's idea of a peace without victory,[68] Root from the first advocated an unconditional Allied triumph. He joined his friends in the movement for national preparedness and became a leader of the National Security League.[69]

[64] "The Onrush of War," Sept. 1914, *World in Ferment*, p. 17.
[65] Interview with William H. Short, Aug. 7, 1914, quoted in Jessup, *Elihu Root*, II, 313.
[66] "Cosmos" (pseud.), *The Basis of an Enduring Peace* (New York, Scribner, 1917), pp. 10–15; "Onrush of War," p. 16.
[67] Leopold, *Root and the Conservative Tradition*, pp. 99–100, 105.
[68] *Enduring Peace*, pp. 4–6.
[69] Jessup, *Elihu Root*, II, 32–26; Leopold, *Root and the Conservative Tradition*, p. 114.

The 1916 campaign naturally intensified the pro-Allied Republican dispute with Wilson. Butler and Root shared Roosevelt's contempt for the President's diplomacy.[70] And both underestimated the effect of the slogan, "He kept us out of war." Years later, Butler, still oblivious to the progressives and pacifists who supported Wilson in a close race against a Republican reformer, Charles Evans Hughes, claimed that if the Republicans had nominated conservative Root and had campaigned on a pro-Allied platform, they would have won![71] Root had a more modest and realistic evaluation of his public appeal. Moreover, before February 1917 he carefully avoided interventionist statements. But he did take a different line from Wilson. Like Butler he maintained that neutrality allowed a clear and open judgment of the issues of the war, including assessment of blame.

Although he had not mentioned it in 1914, he decided in 1916 that the United States should have protested German violation of Belgian neutrality. Like Butler he declared that the violation itself made the United States an interested party, for it was a German breach of contract with the American government. Therefore, the United States should be heard "in the assertion of our own national right."[72] Root's concern in this argument reached far beyond mere partisan advantage; he considered the very future of the legal polity in danger. The war did not make international law irrelevant. It was the very situation to which the rules were supposed to apply. If the powers disregarded the rules, how could law be said to exist at all? By Root's own former arguments it could not.

But the President of the American Society for International Law could hardly accept this conclusion. He insisted that the world needed a whole new code to match the swift changes in the nature of warfare. And more importantly, this code should include a declaration that violation of international law concerned all nations and not just the immediately interested parties.[73]

Root's plea for swift codification and ratification of new rules of international law really evaded the major issue of the polity, and he knew it. The question was not what the rules should be, but how the powers should prevent the rules from being violated. Demands for an international organization much stronger than a court, with the power to enforce, if not the law, at least the process of arbitrating disputes, became overwhelming. The

[70] Root, "Foreign Affairs, 1913–1916," *Addresses on International Subjects,* p. 440.
[71] Butler to George Wickersham, Feb. 13, 1925, in *Across the Busy Years,* I, 347–48.
[72] "Foreign Affairs," 443–44; Butler, "The Present Crisis," Feb. 2, 1917, *World in Ferment,* p. 148.
[73] In *Addresses on International Subjects,* see: "The Outlook for International Law," Dec. 28, 1915, pp. 399–401; and "Should International Law Be Codified?" Dec. 30, 1915, pp. 406–407.

resultant pressures triggered a movement for collective security in both Britain and the United States. By 1915 both Butler and Root were acknowledging that a whole new approach had to be taken. In August 1915 Butler wrote Theodore Marburg of the League to Enforce Peace: "It did not require the events of the past year to bring me to the point of favoring the introduction of the element of force in international institutions."[74] Nevertheless, neither Root nor Butler accepted membership in the League to Enforce Peace. Each raised strong objections to the program for collective sanctions long before the issues had crystallized in the Senate debate over the Covenant of the League of Nations.

Root and Butler defended national freedom of action without opposing international cooperation. They feared that a League commitment would obligate the United States to engage in military or economic reprisals when its national interests were opposed to such action. They were willing, therefore, to approve automatic consultation of the great powers (the concert system) in times of international emergency, but not a pledge to use force against an aggressor. Butler perceived one key objection to the plan for automatic sanctions. It "is not always so easy to determine . . . which of several parties to an agreement is the first aggressor," he wrote in 1916, "so as to warrant the terrible consequences that would follow from treating as an act of aggression [that which a nation] . . . considered an act of self-defense."[75] The system of collective security would mean that minor wars, if considered the result of violations of the League agreement, would automatically become great wars.

Root added another, more immediately practical, objection. The system, demanding so much of the great powers, would itself encourage violations of the agreement. The American people were not ready to support the application of sanctions in every case the League might deem necessary. When Colonel Edward M. House asked Root for his opinion of the Wilson and House early drafts of the League Covenant, Root replied:

No agreement in the way of a league of peace should be contemplated which *will probably not be kept* when the time comes for acting under it. Nothing can be worse in international affairs than to make agreements and to break them. It would be folly therefore for the United States, in order to preserve or enforce the peace after this war is over, to enter into an agreement which the people of the United States would not regard as binding on them. I think that the observation applies to making a hard and fast agreement to go to war upon the happening of some future event *beyond the control of the United States.*[76]

[74] Butler to Marburg, August 10, 1915, Papers of Theodore Marburg, Manuscript Division, Library of Congress.
[75] *Enduring Peace,* pp. 98–99.
[76] August 16, 1918, quoted in Jessup, *Elihu Root,* II, 378 (italics added).

Here was the key conservative objection to the League system. In spite of the US vote on the Council of the League of Nations, the League itself would be too broad a body to make it an instrument of American foreign policy. The United States would be sacrificing too much of its freedom of decision. The traditional distrust of concentrated power in the hands of others now assumed an international form. Root interpreted the League program as a demand for an international police force. Few members of the League to Enforce Peace demanded an international force. Certainly neither House nor Wilson contemplated such a strong League. They even objected to French plans for such a force on the grounds that it would turn the League into a military alliance. However, Root anticipated the evils of such a force, "perverted by ambition, desire for power, or gain, and by all those motives which have been the cause of wars."[77] While admitting that a new international authority was essential, Root and Butler thought of it primarily as a loose organization centering around an international court of justice, with the assembly operating as a general meeting house for the exchange of views and the council for consultation among the great powers. After the court had become established, and the nations had assimilated the practice of automatic consultation, they might be ready to accept a stronger authority if it grew step by step.

The conservatives then presented the following program: (1) The powers should call a conference immediately after the war to draw up an international code of laws, completing the work of the first two Hague conferences. (2) They should come to an agreement about the membership of the world court and set it in operation. (3) They should agree to mutual reduction of tariffs and armaments and accept the "open door policy in the broad sense." (4) The present Hague Court should decide all non-justiciable international disputes not settled by negotiations. (5) There should be three areas for the enforcement of the world court's decisions and the decisions of the Hague Court of Arbitration—Asia, Europe, and the Americas. The United States would remain the international policeman for the Americas and would decide under what circumstances it would support the action of the great powers in the other two areas.[78] Significantly, this program protected exclusive American predominance in the Western Hem-

---

[77] "Remarks of Mr. Root on Further Progress in Establishing an International Court," Executive Committee of the Board of Trustees, March 27, 1915, Carnegie Endowment for International Peace Archives, Secretarial and Administrative Division, V (separate pamphlet), p. 6.

[78] Butler, *Enduring Peace*, pp. 16–18, 87, 91, 93–95; "A League of Nations," *International Conciliation*, no. 131 (Oct. 1918), 527; Stimson and Bundy, *Active Service*, p. 103; also, in *Men and Policies*, Root, "Amendments to the Constitution of the League of Nations," enc. Polk to Lansing, March 27, 1919, p. 245; and Root to Will H. Hays, March 29, 1919, pp. 259–61.

isphere, the policy of economic expansion through the open door principle, and the idea of spheres of influence under the shield of juridical institutions.

Root's reservations to the Covenant of the League made it quite clear that he had this program in mind. First, he wanted the same reservations he had proposed for the Taft arbitration treaties of 1911. Nothing in the Covenant should be construed "to imply relinquishment by the United States of America of its traditional attitude toward American questions." Root suggested that this meant both an incorporation of the Monroe Doctrine into the Covenant and protection for American immigration policy. He then added reservations for compulsory jurisdiction of the world court over justiciable disputes, for obligatory arbitration of non-justiciable disputes, for conferences for revision of the Covenant after five years, and a provision for voluntary withdrawal of members after five years. In only one area outside of the judiciary did Root contemplate a strengthening of the League. He would have granted a Permanent Commission on arms control the power of inspection and verification over all the processes of disarmament the members accepted.[79]

The crux of the League debate was Article Ten of the Covenant, by which members agreed to "respect and preserve as against external aggression the territorial integrity and existing political independence of all the members of the League." Root thought that this commitment of American forces to preserve the settlement of 1919, which was but an "accommodation of conflicting interests . . . the shading of justice by expediency," was so unnecessarily strong that he contemplated its entire removal from the treaty. "Change and growth are the law of life and no generation can impose its will . . . upon succeeding generations."[80] But he shortly reconsidered and conceded that in spite of its deficiencies the article should run for five years before the Covenant revision. This was not a concession to Wilson, however. Root and Butler by 1919 considered the President's views on the League structure hopelessly wrong and his treatment of the Senate despicable. Moreover, they considered repudiation of the article essential both for America's interests and "in the interest of the peace of the world."

Why then did they change their minds? After the Bolshevik revolution, Butler and Root developed an entirely different conception of the League. They began to think of it as a powerful, if temporary, Western alliance against Soviet Russia. In June 1917 President Wilson had sent Root to

[79] Root, "Amendments to Constitution of League of Nations," *Men and Policies,* pp. 246–47.

[80] Root to Hays, March 29, 1919, *Men and Policies,* p. 262; and in the same volume, see Speech at National Republican Club, New York City, Oct. 19, 1920, 286.

head an American delegation to the Provisional Russian government. Root's primary mission was to convince the Russians to continue fighting the Central Powers. Speaking with Prince Lvov and other members of the first revolutionary government, Root gained the impression that the Bolsheviks had no substantial support among the population and no understanding of the true desires of the Russian people. If the Bolsheviks should attempt to seize power, Lvov told Root, the army and the people would revolt against them. Root agreed. Bolshevism could be counteracted by American aid to the Russian liberals, and by a propaganda campaign among the Russian soldiers.[81]

After the Bolshevik revolution, the conservatives took a more fearful view of what Butler called the "collectivism" of this "fanatical," "Oriental" faith. In the long run its appeal would be strongest in the East,[82] but in the chaotic postwar situation it posed an immediate threat to Central Europe. Thus, although Root and Butler continued to hope and expect that the Soviet government would fall by its own inefficiency and material exhaustion, they wished to use the League as an instrument for preventing world revolution. Root summarized the situation in a letter to Will Hays, Chairman of the Republican National Committee, explaining why he was willing to accept Article Ten temporarily.

The vast territories of the Hohenzollerns, the Hapsburgs, and the Romanoffs have lost the rulers who formerly kept the population in order, and are filled with turbulent masses without stable government, unaccustomed to self-control, and fighting among themselves like children of the dragon's teeth. . . . Since the Bolsheviki have been allowed to consolidate the control which they established with German aid in Russia, the situation is that Great Britain, France, Italy and Belgium, with a population of less than 130,000,000 are confronted with the disorganized, but vigorous and warlike population of Germany, German Austria, Hungary, Bulgaria, Turkey, and Russia, amounting approximately to 280,000,000, fast returned to barbarism and the lawless violence of barbarous races. Order must be restored. The allied . . . determinations must be enforced. . . . Under these circumstances, the United States . . . must [perform] its duty, and the immediate aspect of Article X is an agreement to do that.[83]

[81] Interview with Prince Lvov, n.d., Root Papers (Letter Box 136); Root to Secretary of State, June 17, 1918, Department of State: *Papers Relating to the Foreign Relations of the United States, 1918: Russia*, I (Washington, D.C., 1931), pp. 121–22; and in same volume, Lansing to Wilson, Aug. 27, 1917, pp. 147–53. George F. Kennan, *Russia Leaves the War: Soviet American Relations* (Princeton, Princeton Univ. Press, 1956), pp. 21–22, notes the futility of the Root mission. Its only effect was to further complicate the lives of the busy members of the Provisional Government and to emphasize the connection between American support and the Russian war effort.

[82] Butler, *Problems Confronting the Carnegie Endowment for International Peace*, speeches by Butler and Root contained in a pamphlet reprint of minutes of semi-annual meeting of the Board of Trustees, Dec. 7, 1920 (Washington, D.C., 1920), p. 11.

[83] Root to Hays, March 29, 1919, *Men and Policies*, p. 263.

In the eyes of the conservative internationalists, the League of Nations could make two major contributions to world peace. In the first place, as Root's letter to Hays suggested, it could provide the means for preventing the spread of revolutionary disorder in the immediate postwar period. By 1921 the conservatives were more confident that the prospects for world revolution had declined. They still awaited the fall of the Soviet regime under the impact of its own economic and political failures. Root felt that the League members had already abandoned the collective security function of the League and that it was unnecessary in any case.[84] In the second place, the League provided an opportunity for continuous, obligatory conferences of the members so that they could use it to settle their political (not legal) disputes in the usual diplomatic manner, that is, by using the "motives of expediency."[85] On this basis, Butler and Root supported American membership in the League with the Lodge reservations. They were not, however, disturbed very deeply when the United States did not join; and they blamed Wilson for the Senate's rejection of the Covenant.[86]

Neither man considered the economic and social aspects of the League's specialized agencies of any particular importance. In fact, they considered schemes for international economic reconstruction essentially frivolous. Each nation should solve its own economic difficulties in its own way and should reach trade and other agreements with the others without the League's assistance.[87] For example, Butler proposed that Americans meet the threat of socialism by voluntary, private economic reform, the adoption of profit-sharing schemes and other means of cooperation between laborers, investors, and managers.[88] Both men considered the atomistic internationalism of the legal polity (the law's protection of national independence) and the cutting off of trade with Soviet Russia sufficient answers to the tyrannous internationalism of communism.[89]

[84] Root, "International Law after the War," April 27, 1921, *Men and Policies,* pp. 432–434. Root's statement indicates to what extent he regarded the League as a continuation of the war-time alliance, directed in the immediate postwar period against Germany and Russia. Cf. Butler, "Columbia and the War," November 11, 1918, *Scholarship and Service,* p. 239.

[85] Root, "Law After War," p. 436; "The Codification of International Law," *American Journal of International Law,* XIX (Oct. 1925), 678.

[86] Butler, *Across the Busy Years,* II, 201; Root to Marburg, Jan. 6, 1920 in *The Development of the League of Nations Idea: Documents and Correspondence of Theodore Marburg,* ed. John Latane, 2 vols., (New York, Macmillan, 1932), II, 665.

[87] Butler and Root, *Problems Confronting Carnegie Endowment,* p. 10; Root, "Law After War," p. 435.

[88] In *World in Ferment,* see: "Is America Drifting?" Feb. 1917, pp. 162–63; and "Looking Forward," April 1917, pp. 200–201.

[89] Butler, "Introduction," *World in Ferment,* pp. 6–8; Root, "Law After War," pp. 427–28; "How to Interest Democracy in Foreign Affairs," March 1, 1923, *Men and Policies,* 497–98.

After the war they concentrated, therefore, upon the creation of a legal polity, a world court, and upon a campaign for American membership. In this area their contributions to international institutions, particularly Root's, were significant. It was in large measure Root's talent for ingenious legal compromises that finally solved the problem of the selection of judges for the world court. The Covenant directed the League Council to prepare a statute for an international court and to submit it to the membership for approval. In March 1920 Root accepted the invitation of Secretary-General Eric Drummond to serve on the ten-man Advisory Committee of Jurists. After winning the Committee's approval for the 1899 and 1907 Hague Conventions as the basis of their own work (thereby assuring that judges would be selected according to their legal qualifications), Root turned to the problem of large and small nation representation. He noted that the League Assembly provided equal representation for all members, while the Council represented only the great powers. The situation recalled quite naturally to an American the great compromise of the Constitutional Convention of 1787.[90]

Root and Lord Phillimore of Great Britain then presented their plan. Each member of the Hague Court should nominate four members to the world court. (This significantly allowed the United States, although not a member of the League, to become a member of the Court. In the first few years of the Court's operation American jurists declined to make nominations, although American judges were selected.) The Assembly and Council, voting separately, would choose from among the nominees eleven judges and four supplementary judges. A conference committee of the Assembly and Council would iron out any differences that developed between the two bodies, just as did the conference committees of the United States Congress. This plan the League adopted, and it worked well even after the Court had been enlarged.[91]

A second, equally important, consideration was the Court's jurisdiction. Root believed in a strong, active court with compulsory jurisdiction over all juridical questions. The first problem was a definition of juridical disputes. Here Root accepted the Five Power Plan (of Norway, Sweden, Holland, Denmark, and Switzerland), which held that the Court could hear questions involving international law (whether governmental or private), interpretations of treaties, former court decisions, facts "which if established would constitute a breach of international obligations," and questions of reparations for such a breach. He strongly felt that the nations were ready for general obligatory jurisdiction on all such questions. It should be

[90] Scott, *Permanent Court of International Justice,* p. 32.
[91] *Ibid.,* pp. 40–41; Jessup, *Elihu Root,* II, 420–21.

possible for one nation to hail the other into court, even against its will.[92] Once the nations agreed to the plan, they would automatically accept the Court's decision in any such case. Moreover, Root was sure that legal questions would not involve sacrifices of vital national interest. No such reservation on the court statute was necessary. International law had as its foundation the equal independence of every nation, and no nation made treaties against its own vital interests![93] Here again was evidence that the conception of a legal polity was a most limited one allowing the free play of political forces which neither Root nor Butler wished to see hindered by international institutions under any circumstances.

It is ironic that with such high regard for national sovereignty, and with such deep concern for the cultivation of the international mind, the legalists should again have encountered nationalistic resistance to the court plan. The members of the League, led by Great Britain, would not accept any general provision for obligatory jurisdiction. Instead they compromised and allowed each signatory to decide for itself the question of obligatory or case-by-case jurisdiction when it ratified the court treaty. Root was satisfied with this, the logical conclusion of his own respect for national freedom of action. He liked to quote a homely English proverb to illustrate his conception of the progress of international institutions: "Leg over leg the dog went to Dover." But he was deeply disappointed by the US Senate's rejection of the court statute, for Root had always been deeply solicitous of senatorial privilege in foreign affairs, and thought he understood the reasons for such reservations as the Senate frequently applied to arbitration treaties. Yet the efforts of Butler and the Carnegie Endowment for International Peace could not counter the belief that American membership in the Court would be the back door into the League.[94]

While the dream of the legalists was fulfilled in the creation of the Permanent Court of International Justice, the immediate hope for American membership was not. At the end of his long career Root was still trying to achieve a compromise with the Senate.[95] In spite of considerable presidential and public support, he failed; and it was not until after World War II that the United States did join. By that time the vision that had inspired the legal polity had faded. It had been a vision of nations voluntarily

---

[92] Extracts from Debate in the Advisory Committee of Jurists, June 26, 1920, *Men and Policies*, pp. 351–52.

[93] *Men and Policies*, p. 347; and "Law After War," p. 429.

[94] In *Men and Policies*, see Root, "Address before American Society of International Law," April 26, 1923, pp. 407, 413–15; and "Address before New York City Bar Association," Oct. 21, 1920, pp. 399–400; also *Problems Confronting Carnegie Endowment*, p. 34.

[95] Leopold, *Root and the Conservative Tradition*, pp. 163–66.

accepting the rule of law in all their relations, and of skilled and intelligent diplomacy smoothing out the political conflicts of nations whose basic interests were in harmony. The vision simply did not fit the realities of the thirties and forties. The gentlemen's world of social privilege, judicial supremacy, and international good manners had been consumed by war and revolution even before the emergence of the world court itself.

CHAPTER III

The League to Enforce Peace: The Polity as *Posse Comitatus*

*Men who are alike, who have common interests, can live to-
gether on a basis of mutual agreements, without any coercive
power above them to keep them in order. Men of differing nationalities and faiths, if also of discordant minds, can live and
work together for a common purpose only when a coercive power
maintains order among them. . . .*

Franklin Henry Giddings, *Democracy and Empire,* 1900

The concept of an international organization maintaining peace by the
collective force of its members is one of the oldest in Western history.
Before there were nations in the true sense of the word, there were
defensive alliances among city-states. In the centuries of nation-building,
plans for European or world federation captured the imagination of scholars and princely advisors. William Penn, in the seventeenth century, and
the Abbé Saint Pierre, in the eighteenth, envisioned international organizations based upon the principle of collective security. The Concert of Europe
in the early nineteenth century operated imperfectly, but maintained the
idea of great-power enforcement of compulsory mediation. In large measure the Concert also discredited the idea, for it was an instrument for
suppressing threats to the *status quo*.[1] Each attempt at alliance or international organization was confronted by similar problems. Could the organi-

---

[1] Roland N. Stromberg, *Collective Security and American Foreign Policy from the
League of Nations to NATO* (New York, Praeger, 1963), p. 5.

zation accommodate to peaceful change? Would it disintegrate when the circumstances of its creation no longer existed? Would members actually use force in the future as they pledged? Would one state control the others through the use of collective force? Agreements that appeared simple and self-enforcing in principle were by no means certain of application when a crisis arose.

This was true also of the idea of a league* to enforce peace which emerged out of debates and discussions within the British and American peace movements in the fall of 1914. The idea was simplicity itself. The civilized nations of the world would establish a court to settle all justiciable disputes not resolved by negotiation. A council of conciliation would similarly make recommendations to members concerning their political disputes. To prevent any member from going to war before a hearing, the nations would pledge to use jointly their economic and military forces against any one of their number committing acts of hostility. The signatories would not enforce acceptance of the court's decisions, but they would enforce consideration of the dispute and a cooling-off period.[2] The practices of the Concert of Europe combined with the pledges contained in Secretary of State William Jennings Bryan's conciliation treaties were expected to prevent most conflicts that were neither just nor inevitable.

In June 1915 the American League to Enforce Peace adopted such a platform. The American debate began in September 1914, when Hamilton Holt, editor of the New York weekly, the *Independent,* published an editorial called, "The Way to Disarm: A Practical Proposal." Holt took the position that a league, whose members should arbitrate disputes and mutually guarantee one another's territory and independence, would be able to reduce their armed forces until their collective strength was a certain percentage higher than that of the most heavily armed outsider.[3] When the New York Peace Society's Plan of Action Committee adopted Holt's suggestion, Theodore Marburg, a leader of the American Society for Judicial Settlement of International Disputes, proposed that a group of

---

* In this section and hereafter, in order to avoid ambiguity, the American organization known as the League to Enforce Peace will be referred to by its full name or will be called the League. The League of Nations will be cited by its full name wherever the context requires it for the sake of clarity. But league in lower case will refer to plans or ideas about an international organization, or to general proposals or discussions about international organizations.

[2] In *Development of the League of Nations Idea: Documents and Correspondence of Theodore Marburg,* ed. John H. Latané, 2 vols. (New York, Macmillan, 1932); see: Theodore Marburg, "Leading American and European Plans for International Organization (Other than League to Enforce Peace Proposals) Given Out from 1914 to 1919," II, 776, and "League of Peace (later League to Enforce Peace) Platform Adopted at Meeting at Century Club, April 9, 1915," II, 790.

[3] "The Way to Disarm: A Practical Proposal," *Independent,* LXXIX (Sept. 28, 1914), 428.

"scientific men" criticize it. They should present their conclusion to "practical men," who would then help launch a new society to win American and foreign support for a league of peace. The "scientific men" soon dropped Holt's provision for territorial guarantee and adopted instead the proposals of Viscount James Bryce, who was launching a similar society in Great Britain.[4] On 9 April 1915 the "practical men" led by Abbott Lawrence Lowell, President of Harvard, and ex-President William Howard Taft approved the plan. Lowell added a provision for pledging immediate and automatic military sanctions upon a breach of the peace. Taft, at Lowell's urging, consented to help organize the society.[5] The "League of Peace" became "The League to Enforce Peace."

Since neither Taft nor Lowell, nor most of the members of the American peace societies for that matter, had approved the idea of collective security before the war, the plan has been called part of a shocked reaction to the events of 1914. The testimony of Marburg, Oscar Straus, and Franklin Henry Giddings supports this interpretation.[6] In Marburg's words, "the crimes committed in this war, the very assault itself, were, before the event, simply unthinkable . . ." to men of the humanitarian spirit of the early twentieth century. Those who had been reluctant to advocate the use of force in any international relations, even by an international organization, suddenly decided that peace could not be achieved without it.[7]

Yet shock does not provide the entire explanation. Deeply committed pacifists, such as Jane Addams and William Jennings Bryan, were also horrified by the outbreak of war, but would not accept the collective security idea. Ardent nationalists, such as Theodore Roosevelt and Henry Cabot Lodge, saw deep flaws in it. Legalists, like James Brown Scott, Nicholas Murray Butler, and Elihu Root, feared that Americans were

---

[4] Marburg, "Condensed Summary of Discussions at Original Four Dinners at Which the League of Nations Project was Discussed," March 30, 1915, *Development of League Idea,* II, 711; Ruhl Bartlett, *The League to Enforce Peace* (Chapel Hill, Univ. of North Carolina Press, 1944), p. 32. The League to Enforce Peace program fairly consistently paralleled that of the Bryce Group in Great Britain. For a discussion of "limited league" plans in Britain, see: Henry R. Winkler, *The League of Nations Movement in Great Britain 1914–19* (New Brunswick, Rutgers Univ. Press, 1952), pp. 7–23.

[5] Marburg, "Condensed Summary," April 9, 1915, *Development of League Idea,* II, 715, 717.

[6] Stromberg, "The Idea of Collective Security," *Journal of the History of Ideas,* XVII (1956), 250; Oscar S. Straus, "Address," League to Enforce Peace, *Independence Hall Conference, held in the City of Philadelphia, June 17, 1915* (New York, League to Enforce Peace, 1915), pp. 26–28; Giddings, "Introduction," *Towards an Enduring Peace: A Symposium of Peace Proposals and Programs 1914–1916,* ed. Randolph S. Bourne (New York, American Association for International Conciliation, 1916), pp. viii–ix.

[7] *The League of Nations,* 2 vols. (New York, Macmillan, 1917), I, 37.

unprepared to accept the obligations of membership in any organization that pledged automatic sanctions. In spite of its broadly based membership, then, the League to Enforce Peace, did have a distinctive *Weltanschauung*. It combined decayed ideals of world federation with the traditional peace program of unlimited arbitration. It was pervaded with the old dream of a British and American empire of democratic institutions spreading its influence throughout the world. The prewar thinking of five of its leaders—Holt, Marburg, Lowell, Giddings, and John Bates Clark—illustrates this strange admixture. Let us consider the background of each of these public figures.

Hamilton Holt was an ardent social reformer. He had transformed the *Independent* (in which his family had long owned a share) from a Congregationalist journal propagating the opinions of Henry Ward Beecher, into an organ of the new progressivism. By 1900 the *Independent* was a strong defender of American expansion in the Pacific and Caribbean, and also supported direct election of senators, referendum and recall, woman suffrage, compulsory labor arbitration, and municipal ownership of public utilities. By far Holt's most prized reform was a plan for international federation, which Hayne Davis and Richard Bartholdt of the Interparliamentary Union discussed at length in the columns of the *Independent*. In 1903 Davis had brought Holt a plan for a world legislature. The more Holt considered it, the more convinced he became that an international organization had to have an executive as well. A union of the armed forces of member nations was essential to peace. With this plan in mind he became a founder of the New York Peace Society.[8]

Theodore Marburg, an amateur economist, President of the Baltimore Peace Society, and the scion of a wealthy German immigrant family, was convinced that Holt was moving too fast for the sentiments of most members of the American peace movements. Like Holt, he admired the work of the members of the two Hague conventions and felt that international institutions, rather than the stimulation of pacifist sentiment, provided the answer to the problem of wars. Almost as passionate an internationalist as Holt, Marburg was a considerably more ardent expansionist and Anglophile. A supporter of William Howard Taft, he had for most of his adult life devoted himself to the cause of arbitration of all international disputes. Lord Bryce, however, was his *beau ideal*. Very early in the war he turned to Bryce for suggestions on the construction of a league of peace,

---

[8] Warren F. Kuehl, *Hamilton Holt, Journalist, Internationalist, Educator,* (Gainesville, Univ. of Florida Press, 1960), pp. 3–8, 11–12, 34–36. Holt summarized the *Independent's* editorial policy in "A Backward Glance and a Look Ahead," *Independent,* LXXVI (Oct. 2, 1913), 5–6.

just as he had sought his support for various prewar reform organizations.[9] It was only natural that Marburg, who had been Taft's minister to Belgium in 1912 and 1913, and who had stayed on in the first year of the Wilson administration, should become a passionate interventionist early in the war. His familiarity with the British league movements and his many contacts in Western Europe soon led to his selection as chairman of the Committee on Foreign Organization.[10] Like Holt, Marburg considered the program of the League to Enforce Peace part of a broader movement for a strong international organization. He too was unwilling to compromise that conception of a league of peace.

Abbott Lawrence Lowell displayed a very different temperament. A Brahmin gentleman, as conservative in his fundamental philosophy as Root and Butler, he shared none of Holt's optimism. His works displayed the same distrust of emotional reformers as did those of Root and Butler. Lowell was a member of the Board of Trustees of Edwin Ginn's World Peace Foundation, a trained lawyer and a political scientist by profession. His works on European and British government and comparative colonial administrations had established his reputation, even before he assumed the presidency of Harvard University, as a shrewd, practical observer of political behavior. His most famous work, *Public Opinion and Popular Government* (1913), was more than an analysis, however. It was a mugwump's appeal for efficient government with strong political leadership. Lowell made the perfect Executive Chairman of the League to Enforce Peace, for he applied what he considered the art of government—the discovery of practical compromises between absolute political principles.[11] He came to prize the League's program itself as a compromise between narrow nationalism and vague cosmopolitanism.

John Bates Clark and Franklin Henry Giddings represented that group of "scientific men" to whom Marburg first appealed. Clark, America's foremost neo-classical economist, an expert logician of marginal utility

[9] Henry A. Atkinson, *Theodore Marburg: The Man and His Work* (New York, Morton Littman Printing, 1951), pp. 11–12, 45; Marburg to Bryce, Nov. 22, 1912, and other Marburg-Bryce correspondence, 1910–12, demonstrating their prewar relationship may be found in the Papers of Theodore Marburg, Manuscript Division, Library of Congress. For exchanges concerning the structure of international organization, see: Marburg to Bryce, Feb. 1, 1915, March 15, 1915, April 21, 1915, *Development of League Idea*, I, 19–20, 25–26, 34–35.

[10] John H. Latané, "Introduction," *Development of League Idea*, I, vi.

[11] Henry Aaron Yoeman's *Abbott Lawrence Lowell 1865–1943* (Cambridge, Harvard Univ. Press, 1953), Chapter I, pp. 82–91, 501–502; Lowell, *Public Opinion and Popular Government* (New York, Longman's 1913), pp. 62–68, 147–151, 160–161, 235; Lowell, *Conflicts of Principle* (Cambridge, Harvard Univ. Press, 1932), pp. 3–4, 10–12, 20, 94, 100–101.

economics, had long worked with Holt in the New York Peace Society and on the *Independent*. Like Marburg, he was deeply interested both in labor arbitration and in anti-trust legislation as means of preventing class conflict.[12] When he joined the faculty of Columbia University, his skillful exposition of *laissez-faire* ideals so endeared him to Butler that he was appointed director of the Carnegie Endowment's Division of Economics and History. James T. Shotwell, his successor, captured the essence of Clark's thought when he stated that it reflected a pre-revolutionary world "that had not lost the contours of its historic mold."[13] The forces of economic life were, to Clark, predictable, or at least susceptible to logical analysis and economic laws. In his optimistic early work, the *Philosophy of Wealth* (1886), Clark had emphasized the inevitable moral and material progress of man which the churches had to further by encouraging mutual respect, fraternal feeling, and fairness in all economic relations. Later he concentrated upon the ideal "equilibrium" which real economic forces approached if government action or monopoly did not hinder them.[14] In either case, the goal of progress was perfect justice.

In later works, Clark equated this with perfect competition, by which each man got his due. The free capitalist economy most nearly approached this dynamic equilibrium, and it was this world of competition and eventual justice which needed the League of Nations as its protector. So thoroughly did Clark link the League to preservation of the capitalist economy ("peace abroad" and "peace at home") that as the war closed, he viewed the League as an instrument against socialist revolution.

Clark's colleague and early collaborator, Franklin Henry Giddings, supplemented Clark's work by describing the evolving social structure that underlay the play of economic forces. He considered himself a positivist, developing a science of social relationships that would take account of their complexity and yet be based upon fundamental conceptions as easily

---

[12] *The Philosophy of Wealth: Economic Principles Newly Formulated* (Boston Ginn, 1886), pp. 64–68 illustrates Clark's early Christian Socialist view of class conflict and arbitration. *Essentials of Economic Theory as Applied to Modern Problems of Industry and Public Policy* (New York, Macmillan, 1907), pp. 384–386, shows his later neo-classical contrast. For a complete statement of Clark's anti-trust arguments, see: Clark, *The Control of Trusts: An Argument in Favor of Curbing the Power of Monopoly by a Natural Method* (New York, Macmillan, 1901).

[13] James T. Shotwell, "John Bates Clark, 1847–1938, A Tribute," *Carnegie Endowment for International Peace Yearbook* (Washington, D.C., 1938), p. 157. On Clark's early work for the Carnegie Endowment, see: Nicholas Murray Butler, "Speech at a Dinner in Honor of John Bates Clark," *Economic Essays Contributed in Honor of John Bates Clark*, ed. Jacob H. Hollander (New York, Macmillan 1927), pp. 356–57.

[14] Clark, *Philosophy of Wealth*, pp. 175–87, 196–97; John Rutherford Everett, *Religion in Economics: A Study of John Bates Clark, Richard T. Ely, Simon N. Patten* (New York, King's Crowns Press, 1946), pp. 41–42.

quantified as conceptions in the natural sciences. He hoped to go beyond his great mentor, Herbert Spencer, by establishing the psychological foundations of any society in the stimulus-response mechanism.[15] Thus, he arrived at the idea that cooperative or conflicting social relationships derived basically from mental perceptions of likeness or difference in human beings. It was "consciousness of kind" that led to family coherence, to the formation of racial, ethnic, and political groups. To Giddings the atomistic polity was a natural product of social evolution, national states were the "natural aggregations of people which have developed social organization" out of "like-mindedness,"[16] and the League to Enforce Peace a necessary answer to the conflicts between these groups.

THE DEMOCRATIC EMPIRE

The League leaders did not propound a unified interpretation of human nature to account for their conclusion that collective force was needed in support of international institutions. Giddings' theories of conflict and cooperation, however, came closest to such an interpretation. The world of nations was without a doubt what he termed a "heterogeneous society," lacking the institutions necessary for peaceful progress. But that did not mean that he believed aggression inherent in human nature. Instead Lowell and Giddings suggested that man was a creature of impulses (sometimes generous, sometimes not). Men imitated others, particularly the leaders of social groups, and reasoned only when some environmental situation compelled reasoning. For example, in *Public Opinion* Lowell argued that most men had neither the time nor the inclination to reason about affairs of state. Political leaders did the reasoning for them, and then presented issues to the public for a simple yes or no answer. It was at this point that public argument began, opinion formed, and eventually a democratic decision evolved.[17] To Giddings, the men who took the lead were distinguished from their fellows by ability, effort, and training. They were the "rational

---

[15] Giddings, "The Concepts and Methods of Sociology," *Congress of Arts and Science: Universal Exposition, St. Louis, 1904,* ed. Howard J. Rogers (Boston, 1906), V, 788–90, 798; John L. Gillin, "Franklin Henry Giddings," *American Masters of Social Science,* ed. Howard W. Odum (New York, Holt, 1927), pp. 196–97; F. H. Hankins, "Franklin Henry Giddings, 1855–1931: Some Aspects of His Sociological Theory," *American Journal of Sociology,* XXVII (Nov. 1931), 350–52.

[16] "The Mind of the Many," 1898, *Democracy and Empire* (New York, Macmillan, 1900), p. 52; *Principles of Sociology: An Analysis of the Phenomena of Association and Social Organization* (New York, Macmillan, 1896), pp. 17, 322–23.

[17] *Public Opinion,* pp. 16, 18, 22–24, 53, 69, 88–91; cf. Giddings, *Principles of Sociology,* pp. 100–114, 123, for man's "survival instincts and their social conditioning."

conscientious" types who led advanced societies.[18] Giddings, Marburg, and
Lowell also considered certain nations to be the natural leaders of an
international polity, in part because their governmental experience had
developed more rational leaders than had other nations.

Clearly, the interpretations of human nature propounded by the League
leaders were designed to fit specific arguments rather than to explain
human behavior in general terms. During the period when Clark was a
Christian Socialist, he believed man's fundamental instincts altruistic.
When he became a neo-classicist, he emphasized man's ability to make a
rational calculation of his self-interest. In pleading for international cooperation, Marburg emphasized man's altruistic nature. In defending sanctions,
he spoke as a Utilitarian, describing the League's function as instituting
pains and penalties.[19]

An important part of league thinking on the subject of human nature
revolved around the conception of public opinion. Lowell insisted the term
meant group agreement on an issue, leading to the selection of one choice
among two or more that might be rationally held.[20] The very structure of
the collective security plan was based upon the assumption that once
conflict had been avoided (by the threat of force and the court and council
action), the decisions of the league bodies would prevail because public
opinion would accept them. "The great weapon we rely upon is public
opinion," Lord Robert Cecil, a British league leader, told the House of
Commons in July 1919, "and if we are wrong about it, then the whole thing
is wrong."[21] This concept was indeed paradoxical, for the advocates of a
league parted from the legalists by asserting that world public opinion was
not yet perfect enough to support compulsory arbitration of disputes. Yet
they assumed it did exist to enforce acceptance of the arbitral decision. It
somehow emerged during the cooling-off period.

Before the war, Marburg and Clark had strenuously held that a major
cure for immoral economic practices was exposure of the issues. Holt based
his faith in the future "parliament of man" on a similar assumption. In any
conflict there was a morally right side and an evil side. If the people knew all

[18] See *Readings in Descriptive and Historical Sociology* (New York, Macmillan,
1906), pp. 214–18, for Giddings' complete classification of human "types."
[19] Clark, *Philosophy of Wealth*, pp. 39–44, gives his earlier view of human nature. In
Essentials of Economic Theory, p. 39, he briefly discusses rational selfishness in
classical terms. Marburg, *League of Nations*, I, 66; Marburg, "The League to Enforce
Peace: A Reply to Critics," *Enforced Peace: Proceedings of the First Annual
National Assemblage of the League to Enforce Peace, Washington, May 26, 27, 1916*
(New York, League to Enforce Peace, 1916), p. 129.
[20] *Public Opinion in War and Peace* (Cambridge, Harvard Univ. Press, 1923), pp.
13–14, 78–79.
[21] Quoted by Hans J. Morgenthau, *Politics Among Nations: The Struggle for
Power and Peace*, 3rd ed. (New York, Knopf, 1962), p. 260.

the facts they would choose the good. Therefore, one of the most important roads to international peace was "first hand acquaintance with the views of . . . other classes and parties," responsible journalism, international contacts, and, above all, open airing of national conflicts of policy.[22] The same assumptions that underlay Wilson's plea for "open covenants openly arrived at"—a basic faith in the eventual rationality and enlightenment of man—formed the underpinning for this aspect of league thought.

There was another side to it, however. For if men were so enlightened, why was force needed at all? There was the darker interpretation of human contacts and social relations put forth by Giddings. Acquaintance with the views of others did not always bring peace (as Holt supposed). Instead, it increased group consciousness, by contrasting the likenesses within societies with the differences between them. Thus "consciousness of kind" arose after "painful" impressions of consciousness of difference.[23] Moreover, the differences to which peoples of various races and nationalities reacted accounted for different degrees of civilization. In America the red and black races were backward. Only the white had the inherent capacity to make "independent advances." Among the white people of America those of British descent were inclined to be most "progressive."[24]

Several conclusions followed this assumption. First, Marburg asserted (out of a racism simpler but essentially similar to that of Giddings) that the spread of "justice loving peoples," the British and Americans particularly, was of great moment to the peace of the world. Therefore, expansion of their influence in direct colonization or indirect predominance would further the cause of peace.[25] Second, it was vital to keep the American population as homogeneous as possible both by immigration restriction and by every reasonable social reform that would eradicate class conflict.[26] Third, in any heterogeneous society, domestic or international, men would not form "spontaneous" communities. They could, as Giddings remarked, "live and work together for a common purpose only when a coercive power maintains order among them."[27]

[22] Holt to Carnegie, April 11, 1912, Papers of Andrew Carnegie, Manuscript Division, Library of Congress.

[23] Giddings, *Principles of Sociology*, pp. 104–105.

[24] *Ibid.*, pp. 328–29.

[25] Marburg, *League of Nations*, II, 73.

[26] Marburg, "Admissions and Restrictions upon Admissions of Aliens," *American Society of International Law: Proceedings of Fifth Annual Meeting* (Washington, D.C., 1911), pp. 90–94; Giddings, "The Survival of Civil Liberty," 1899, *Democracy and Empire*, pp. 296–97; Lowell, *Governments and Parties in Continental Europe*, 2 vols. (Boston, Houghton Mifflin, 1896), I, 102–103; II, 46, 57, 334–36, discusses the relationship of class and ethnic composition to political stability in various countries, indicating how multi-lingual Switzerland proves the case for homogeneity by overcoming linguistic differences with economic uniformity.

[27] "Mind of the Many," *Democracy and Empire*, p. 63.

In such discussions of American society at the turn of the century, the future leaders of the League to Enforce Peace anticipated their wartime proposals concerning the character and composition of an international organization. Marburg and Giddings maintained that Anglo-American predominance of the league would make for peace. Marburg even wanted membership restricted to "progressive" peoples. Lowell, believing that genuine public opinion could emerge only when there were unspoken agreements on fundamental political principles,[28] assumed that such agreements existed among rational leaders of the Western nations. Their contacts around the green baize tables would be friendly.[29] Holt, on the other hand, was by far the most optimistic observer of human nature, and the least inclined toward a racial interpretation of society.[30] Far from considering the heterogeneity of American society a threat to democratic institutions, he argued that it was precisely this aspect of America (as well as the US successful experiment with federalism) that prepared the nation for leadership in a world organization.[31] One way or another these leaders of the collective security movement accepted the idea of American predominance in a league. But it was significant that some ideas about force had racial overtones, while Holt's stress upon an executive for a league derived from his federalism.

As we shall see, the divergence between Holt, the optimist and progressive, and Lowell, the practical conservative, was to crystallize in the League debate of 1919. The nature of this difference had been revealed much earlier in contrasting beliefs about American democracy and political and economic reform. As early as the 1880s Lowell's deepest fears were of an "unbridled democracy," destroying the stability and freedom of constitutional government. If socialism were to come, it would be better controlled by an intelligent autocrat than by a popular assembly that could defy the minority with impunity. "Far better a Bismarck than a Jacobin convention," was Lowell's motto.[32] It was such dangerous popular tyranny that

[28] *Public Opinion*, pp. 36, 42, 44.
[29] Lowell and Henry Cabot Lodge, "Joint Debate on the Covenant of Paris," March 19, 1919, *A League of Nations* (World Peace Foundation Bound Pamphlets, Boston, 1919), II, 66–67. Lowell was replying to Lodge's argument that points of contact are "points of friction."
[30] Kuehl, *Holt*, pp. 46–48; Holt, "International Amity," *Independent*, LIV (Nov. 12, 1908), 1137; Holt, "How Shall We Keep Peace with Japan?" *Free Synagogue Pulpit*, III (June 1915), 98–99, 102.
[31] "Way to Disarm," p. 429.
[32] *Essays on Government* (Boston, Houghton-Mifflin, 1889), pp. 19, 66.

direct democratic reforms would encourage. The cures for boss-rule, therefore, should be civil service reform, an extension of *droit administratif* (to
remove complex economic issues from the political arena), not the creation
of more democratic machinery. No political internationalist had more respect than Lowell for the expert administrator as the savior of stable
government in a complex society. Few emphasized the importance of the
League secretariat as much as he.[33]

Holt took a different approach to reform, largely because he considered
corrupt politics a consequence not of industrial complexity, but of "plutocratic domination." Public education and greater popular control of the
party machinery through primaries, initiative, and referendum would cure
boss-rule. There had to be "experimentation with government machinery,"
and new organizations for the majority.[34] In international affairs, too, Holt
relied upon organizational resolutions to social and economic disorders,
while Lowell relied upon intelligent political leadership and compromise.

The most revealing attitudes toward conflict resolution emerged in the
League leaders' discussions of economic competition, progress, and labor
arbitration. To Lowell and Giddings, orthodox Social Darwinists, life was
a race in which the runners should have equal opportunity but would
inevitably display different abilities. The race was to the swift. The competitive system, so essential to progress and freedom, necessarily caused the
incompetent to suffer. What then should be done? To avoid revolutionary
discontent, the strong should offer some protection to the utterly helpless.
Lowell considered freedom of contract too "essential to the progress of
society" to accept a welfare state. But like Giddings and Clark he was
occasionally willing to compromise *laissez faire* in order to correct intolerable abuses and to prevent the growth of extreme opinions. Thus, he
considered the extent of government regulation a question of expediency,
but resistance to corporate (business or union) selfishness a matter of
principle.[35]

Like Clark and Marburg, Holt emphasized labor arbitration as a road
away from class conflict. Unlike either, he was a strong advocate of
compulsory government arbitration and did not regard the arbitral process
as a suppressed conflict. On the contrary, it was an instrument of peace, as
he had learned from his own experience as arbitrator in garment-industry

---

[33] *Public Opinion*, pp. 104–109, 161, 276–77; "Oscillations in Politics," *Annals of the
American Academy of Political and Social Science*, XII (July 1898), 95, 98; Lowell,
et al., "The Covenanter: Letters on the Covenant of the League of Nations," A League
of Nations (World Peace Foundation Bound Pamphlets, Boston, 1919), II, 122.

[34] In the *Independent*, see: "Democracy in America," LIV (Sept. 18, 1902), 2260–62,
and "The Referendum," LIV (Nov. 20, 1902), 2789–90.

[35] Yoemans, *Lowell*, p. 412; Lowell, *Essays on Government*, pp. 9–14; Giddings,
"The Costs of Progress," 1893, *Democracy and Empire*, pp. 77–78, 93–95.

negotiations in New York.[36] But arbitration was not enough. For many years, Holt, unlike any of the other leaders of the League, supported Socialist candidates in New York and advocated municipal ownership of public utilities. The economic sphere, he maintained, was the proper place for socialism. The private sphere of personal conduct and opinion was the proper place for individualism. While Giddings and Clark and Marburg stressed the repressive nature of socialism, while Lowell emphasized the connection between private ownership and progress, Holt identified social justice with moderate socialism.[37] Thus, Holt's general economic orientation was much closer to the British Labor Party than that of Lowell, Marburg, Clark, or Giddings. Like some of the Fabians, he regarded the collective security league as a compromise with an ideal solution to international conflict—world government.

The fundamental purpose of social reform measures, as Giddings saw it, was to strengthen the nation's social cohesion so that America would be a stronger rival of other nations. Lowell turned the matter the other way: the fundamental purpose of American expansionism was to preserve frontier opportunity so that the United States could escape the ills of static societies. In either case the acquisitions of 1898 were valuable. Lowell was unwilling to see America's inheritance frittered away by misconceptions of democracy. The civil liberties of America's wards should be protected, but in no case did this imply the granting of citizenship or the vote. Like the conservative legalists, Lowell refuted the "widespread belief that all men are fitted to govern themselves." The "Anglo-Saxon race" had been prepared for self-government "by centuries of discipline under the supremacy of law." Other peoples could achieve self-government only by a similar process.[38]

[36] In the *Independent*, see: Holt, "Labor Disputes," LII (Feb. 28, 1901), 517; "The Solution of Industrial Peace," LXXIV (Feb. 6, 1913), 273–75; Clark, "Do We Want Compulsory Arbitration?" LIV (Nov. 13, 1902), 2682; Kuehl, *Holt*, pp. 49–50.

[37] In the *Independent*, see: Holt, "The Bugaboo of Individualism" LVI (March 31, 1904), 743; "The Representative With a Million Constituents," LXXX (Nov. 23, 1914), 281; "Socialism and Socialism," LVIII (Dec. 8, 1904), 1337–38. The anti-socialist arguments of the other League leaders were largely based upon inegalitarian interpretations of human nature. See, Clark, *Social Justice Without Socialism* (Boston, Houghton Mifflin, 1914), pp. 6–7, 48; "Education and the Socialistic Movement," *Atlantic Monthly*, CIII (June 1909), 436–37; Giddings, "The Ethics of Socialism," *International Journal of Ethics*, I (Jan. 1891), 242; Marburg, "Amendment of the Sherman Anti-Trust Law," *Annals of the American Academy of Political and Social Science*, XXXII (July 1908), 35, 39–40; Lowell, *Essays on Government*, pp. 14, 16–17.

[38] Lowell, "The Colonial Expansion of the United States," *Atlantic Monthly*, LXXXIII (Feb. 1899), 145, 150–51, 154. "The Status of Our New Possessions," *Harvard Law Review*, XIII (Nov. 1899), 155; Giddings, "A Political Program," *Independent*, LIII (Sept. 27, 1900), 2305–2306; "Industrial Democracy," 1891, *Democracy and Empire*, p. 115.

Lowell's and Giddings' defenses of expansionism, designed to prove that democracy and empire were not antagonistic phenomena, converged with traditional imperialist themes. The spread of American rule meant the spread of justice and liberty. The responsibilities of governing colonies would preserve America's adventurous spirit and manliness. Empire would even create the international mind. As Giddings observed, Americans would become involved "in complications from which we can hope to emerge unscathed only by the exercise of tact and knowledge."[39] What was crucial in these arguments was not the assumption that American rule was as beneficial to the colonizers as to the wards, but the identification of forcible expansion with progress—moral, political, and economic. By giving progress a lateral as well as temporal dimension, Marburg, Giddings, and Lowell prepared the way for the belief that international organization, backed by force, would also be an instrument of civilizing backward or evil peoples.

John Bates Clark laid the foundations for this belief in his economic theory. Contrasting a civilized economic sphere of freely exchanged labor and capital with a backward one of industrial stagnation, Clark asserted that the more civilized nations (the Western nations, Australia, and Japan), annexed the uncivilized areas, the greater would be the chances for world peace and economic progress. True, there were "unhappy attendant incidents," such as imperialist clashes, to this annexation, but the end result would be a world-wide dynamic economy and the spread of competition. In the future, wars would cease and there would be only the peaceful "contentions of the market through which progress is assured."[40]

Giddings agreed that progress was likely if the empires allowed local liberty and "struggle and competition enough to assure the continuation of natural selection." The difficulty was that democratic empires confronted an "autocratic" empire ruling a "superstitious and ignorant multitude." Thus, the real fate of civilization depended "upon the predominant influence of either the English-speaking people of the world or of the Russian Empire."

---

[39] Giddings, "Imperialism?" *Political Science Quarterly,* XIII (Dec. 1898), 602; Marburg, *Expansionism* (Baltimore, J. Murphy, 1900), pp. 40–58, presents the usual arguments associating "Aryan" rule with liberty, justice, and progress. In the *Independent,* see: Holt, "Hawaii American Territory," L (July 7, 1898), 127; "Our Conditions to Spain," L (July 21, 1898), 196–97; "Can We Let Them Go?" L (July 21, 1898), 266; "Mr. Van Dyke and the Philippines," L (Aug. 15, 1898), 920. These editorials generally emphasize the duty of protecting colonies from less just people. Albert K. Weinberg, *Manifest Destiny: A Study of Nationalist Expansionism in American History* (Baltimore, Johns Hopkins Press, 1938), pp. 254–82, 288–304, describes the moralism and determinism that provided a setting for these beliefs.

[40] *Essentials of Economic Theory,* pp. 212–14, 231, 235–36; In *Lake Mohonk Peace and Arbitration Conference* (cited hereafter as *Mohonk*) see: Clark, "Address" VII (1901), 48, and "Address," III (1897), 77.

The autocratic one would suppress local liberty and individual initiative and establish socialism, and the end would be "degeneration."[41] In 1917, when Giddings' nightmare of an autocratic socialist empire materialized in Russia, he began to view the League of Nations less as an instrument of international cooperation and more as a means for advancing the Anglo-American political culture. His anticipation of the Russian-Western confrontation had prepared him for this outlook.

It was Theodore Marburg who forged the strongest link between international organization and empire in the prewar period. In 1911 he persuaded Holt to discard plans for an international federal executive as too strong a dish for the American peace movements.[42] But Marburg was deeply concerned over the imperial contests for backward territory. Uncivilized peoples were constantly committing outrages against Western traders, whereupon European governments would step in to rescue their nationals. The Europeans would remain and set about monopolizing the trade of the backward areas. Economic and political conflicts resulted. Horrified that war might break out between the progressive powers, Marburg recommended that a world court be empowered to settle colonial questions, and to order "certain things to be done" in backward areas "by the united action of the chancelleries of the great powers."[43] Marburg failed to appreciate that he was in effect restoring Holt's executive function, but he did later realize that he had proposed an embryonic mandates system whose chief goals would be order and preservation of the open door.[44] Thus Marburg's own collective security thinking, contrary to his testimony, had begun not with his shock over the German invasion of Belgium, but three years earlier in anticipation of a general war.

FROM FEDERALISM TO COLLECTIVE SECURITY

The prewar movement for international organization, unlike the post-1914 collective security movements, was highly optimistic and confident. The first decade of the twentieth century witnessed very little activity for the prevention of aggression, and much planning for disarmament by advocating adoption of an international police force. Thus it is difficult to equate

[41] In *Democracy and Empire*, see: "Preface," p. v, and "The Gospel of Non-Resistance," 1900, p. 357.

[42] Kuehl, *Holt*, pp. 68–69.

[43] "A Modified Monroe Doctrine," *South Atlantic Quarterly*, X (July 1911), 229.

[44] Marburg to Sir Gilbert Parker, April 5, 1919, *Development of League Idea*, I, 626–27; Holt, "For a Holy War," *Independent*, XCII (Dec. 15, 1917), 497–98, expanded Marburg's idea into the only League to Enforce Peace declaration on mandates. He acknowledged the origin of the idea. See Holt to Marburg, Dec. 20, 1917, Marburg Papers.

the two movements, even though the ideas proposed by each were similar.

Neither the numbers nor the influence of the prewar federalists should be exaggerated. An overwhelming majority of the members in the British and American peace movements equated international organization with a world court and a permanent arbitration system. Few contended that the decisions of the court should be backed by force.[45] But these few are worthy of attention if only to remind us that the notion of collective security did not spring full-grown out of the trenches of France. The movement started with peace society agitation in support of the Anglo-American arbitration treaty of 1897, grew more vocal during the Hague conferences, and reached a climax before it declined in 1911 with the Senate's defeat of the Taft arbitration treaties.

At first the federalists were hardly distinguishable from other advocates of unlimited arbitration on all international questions. Benjamin Trueblood of the American Peace Society, for example, wrote a work titled *The Federation of the World* (1899), in which he proposed a permanent system of arbitration, systems of regional cooperation involving arms reduction by members of each regional federation, and eventual consolidation of the regions into a world federation. Trueblood was still thinking in traditional terms, as evidenced by his contention that the spread of true Christian influence would reduce national animosities and undermine the "war-system."[46]

But in 1909 a few leaders of the New York Peace Society and some contributors to the *Independent* (W. H. Short, Henry G. Granger, W. J. Barnett, Oscar T. Crosby) joined Richard Bartholdt, Hayne Davis, and Hamilton Holt in forming the World Federation League. These men were departing from the traditional pacifist emphasis of Trueblood's work and they knew it. Crosby, for example, drew up "Articles of Federation for the Federated States of the World," with provisions for universal citizenship, weighted voting in a federal court, and an international navy under the court's direction. The federalists' major objective was to hasten "the day of the establishment of some form of central government empowered to keep the peace."[47] Hamilton Holt's interpretation of the "Constitution of the

[45] Stromberg, *Collective Security and American Foreign Policy*, pp. 5–7.

[46] *The Federation of the World*, 3rd ed. (Boston, Houghton Mifflin, 1899), pp. 66–67, 91–92, 122–23, 128–32.

[47] In the World Federation League, *The Peace Movement: The Federation of the World* (New York, World Federation League, 1910), see: Oscar T. Crosby, "Articles of Federation for the Federated States of the World," pp. 52–58, for a discussion of the use of the Federation's forces within national states as well as for keeping peace between them; and "Platform of the World Federation League," p. 1. Holt, "An American Peace Commission," *Independent*, LVIII (June 20, 1910) 1455–56, describes the formation of the organization.

World" preserved some national control over the major portion of the
world's armed forces. Holt simply required national pledges of contributions to an international force. The Hague conferences were to become
continuous, evolving into the federation's legislature. The Hague Court,
with obligatory jurisdiction, would become the world judiciary. A council
of the Interparliamentary Union would constitute the executive. So little
did the federalists consider the legal and substantive obstacles to their plans
that some cheerfully acknowledged the federation as sovereign, while Holt,
Davis, and Bartholdt insisted that no sacrifice of sovereignty or national
interest would be required.[48]

In 1910 Holt sent Andrew Carnegie the Holt-Davis plan for a world
constitution and urged Carnegie to try to persuade Theodore Roosevelt to
support the idea in his Nobel Peace Prize speech. At Christiania, Norway,
Roosevelt did propose a modified version of the international police force
idea, quoting enough of Holt's editorial to convince the optimistic journalist
that he was a convert. A rather naive World Federation League campaign
was started to persuade Roosevelt to pressure the powers into pooling their
navies—a campaign of flattery which pictured the former President as
founder of the United Nations and even "world president."[49] Holt was sure
Roosevelt would follow along. After all, federation was an American idea.
("The Constitution of the United States furnishes the key to universal
peace among nations."[50])

Neither Holt nor the other federalists understood the fundamental disparity between Roosevelt's balance of power concept and their own cheerful certainty that world organization was a real solution to the problem of
war. The group continued to push for its cause. Representative Bartholdt
proposed a joint Congressional resolution urging an American Peace Commission to promote disarmament and federation. Even when Congress
adopted a much weaker resolution, without the federative feature, Bartholdt was encouraged. But the plan died aborning. President Taft, cautioned by Root and Butler, refused to appoint the commission.[51]

Holt did not lose heart, however, until Roosevelt joined Henry Cabot

[48] Holt, "A Constitution of the World," *Independent*, LXII (April 11, 1907), 826;
cf. Crosby, "Articles of Federation," p. 53.
[49] In World Federation League, *Peace Movement*, see: Walter John Barnett,
"Theodore Roosevelt and the Peace Movement," p. 41; Henry G. Granger, "Mr.
Roosevelt, a Suggestion," pp. 64–65. Holt, "Work for a Nobel Prize Winner,"
Independent, LXVIII (Feb. 24, 1910), 429–30, offers more modest suggestions for
Roosevelt in preparation for the third Hague Peace Conference.
[50] "Mr. Roosevelt at Christiania," *Independent*, LXVIII (Feb. 17, 1910), 377.
[51] Kuehl, *Holt*, pp. 85–87; Holt, "The United States Peace Commission," *North
Atlantic Review*, CXCII (Sept. 1910), 301–16 discusses the hopes of the federation
movement, its justification, and the prospective work of the peace commission. This
article is an important summation of the whole movement.

Lodge in a campaign against the Taft arbitration treaties. This was too much for the optimistic editor, who felt that "public opinion" had passed "the stages of conciliation and even arbitration," and was "ready for world federation."[52] The crippling of the Taft treaties, more than any other event before the war itself, contributed to both Holt's and Marburg's disillusionment. Marburg became permanently distrustful of parliamentary participation in foreign affairs. Not only did Holt turn to pacifism after 1911, but he increasingly suspected "the interests" (the arms manufacturers, the idle rich, the statesmen with personal stakes in the *status quo*) of undermining the cause of international organization.[53]

Nor was Holt the only one to espouse the devil theory of war. Even the calm Clark was beginning to turn in that direction. His Lake Mohonk addresses on international arbitration had always been optimistic. Clark believed, in fact, that international peace would be easier to achieve than peace between the classes. Like Fiske, he considered that the most important aspect of promoting international arbitration was that the money saved on armaments would increase the health of the domestic economy, thereby preventing social revolution.[54] But after the Balkan wars, Clark began to suspect that the matter was not so easy. The very economic ties that bound nations exacerbated their jealousies. The growth of armaments warned of "the awful danger of a possible war that has never been equaled for its destructiveness." This fear of a war promoted by chauvinists and the arms interests led Clark to propose in May 1914 a "standing committee of the powers," to settle political disputes and prevent any nation from going to war before arbitrating.[55]

In 1912, Giddings, who had not previously advanced any particular peace

---

[52] "The Federation of the World," *Independent*, LXVIII (May 12, 1910), 1044.

[53] Holt to James Brown Scott, n.d., Carnegie Endowment for International Peace Archives: Secretarial and Administrative Division, IV, Special Collections, Columbia University. Holt suggested topics for research including: "armies and navies as berths for the idle rich"; "armies and navies as foes of progressive democracy"; and "war debts in relation to public debts and high finance." Cf. Holt, "Call the Third Hague Conference Without Delay," *Independent*, LXXXVI (Dec. 4, 1913), 429–31, for the theory that the statesmen opposed international organization because they feared losing their position. Andrew D. White gave this explanation, and was quoted by W. H. Short to George Kirchway, Nov. 19, 1913, enc. to Holt, New York Peace Society Archives, Swarthmore College Peace Collection. Cf. in the *Independent*, Holt, "Armaments Scandals," LXXIV (May 1, 1913), 946; "The Armament Octopus," LXXVIII (April 13, 1914), 80. For Marburg's opinions on parliamentary control of foreign affairs, see: Marburg to Christian L. Lange, Aug. 9, 1915, *Development of the League Idea*, I, 60; and *League of Nations*, I, 111.

[54] In *Mohonk*, see: "Address," II (1896), 38; "The Part of Organized Labor in the Peace Movement," XIV (1908), 62; cf. "An Economic View of War and Arbitration," *International Conciliation*, no. 32 (July 1910), 7.

[55] John Bates Clark and Sir George Paish, "A Proposed Standing Committee of the Powers," *Mohonk*, XX (1914), 121–23.

plan, addressed the American Sociological Society on the relationship between social theory and public policy. Giddings began by declaring that a balance of power would provide the substantive foundation for international institutions. In mid-course, however, he made a significant shift. The choice between maintaining peace and going to war was determined not by the distribution of power, but by individual national leaders. Since their action not only determined policy but guided the thinking of multitudes, these exceptional men were in "the final throwing of the dice of fate . . . the causes of peace and war. . . ."[56]

This intellectual shift from social determinism to moral judgment was the most significant in collective security thinking. Nothing was more fundamental in the plans for enforcing the peace than the notion that wars resulted from the calculated actions of an identifiable aggressor. As Roland Stromberg remarked, the advocates of collective security believed that "the will to war was everything."[57]

When the storm erupted, the last shred of faith in inevitable progress disintegrated. As Giddings correctly observed, that faith had been a reflection of tremendous pride in material achievement and in scientific knowledge, and of an assumed relationship "between reason and reasonableness."[58] It was only natural that the devil theory should flourish when such self-satisfaction was dissolved. Men looked for someone to blame; it did not take long to settle on the Kaiser. As the German government defended the invasion of Belgium on grounds of *Kriegraison,* the future leaders of the League to Enforce Peace were sure they had discovered the evil destroyers of their peaceful world. They were not alone in their beliefs, of course, but their passions were rather extreme for citizens of a neutral nation. As early as September 1914 Marburg made an impassioned plea for open American support of the Allied cause, calling the German militarists heartless and war mad.[59] Since the Germans were not amenable to reason, he argued, only force would educate them. Nor was Marburg surprised at the war's extent, for it was part of the faith in an interdependent world that war anywhere eventually meant war everywhere.[60] The support for a world-wide peace-keeping organization indeed depended upon such an assumption, for if all members were not threatened by the breach of peace,

[56] "The Relation of Social Theory to Public Policy," *International Conciliation,* no. 58 (Sept. 1912), 9, 11–12.

[57] Stromberg, "Idea of Collective Security," 255.

[58] "How Social Progress Depends on the Success of the League Platform," *Enforced Peace,* p. 171.

[59] New York *Tribune,* Sept. 18, 1914, quoted in *League of Nations,* II, 130–31.

[60] *League of Nations,* I, 37; cf. Lowell, "Safeguarding the Future," *Win the War for Permanent Peace: Addresses Made at the National Convention of the League to Enforce Peace in Philadelphia, May 16, 17, 1918* (New York, League to Enforce Peace, 1918), p. 39.

why would they supply forces to prevent war? In the *Independent* of 10 August 1914, Giddings testified that he had abandoned all hope for the balance of power. The system itself was the instrument of militarists. His attack upon the mad European contenders faced a full-page picture of Kaiser Wilhelm II labeled simply "The Aggressor."[61] The identification of righteous force with a world-saving mission, which had been implied in expansionist arguments at the turn of the century, was growing stronger.

Holt was then faced with a difficult choice. On the one hand, the whole tone of his journal implied agreement with Marburg and Giddings. But his alliance with the pacifists meant an entirely different interpretation and response to the war. He could not make up his mind. When the Woman's Peace Party proposed continuous mediation by a conference of neutrals, he applauded them. When Wilson adopted a program of moderate preparedness, he supported him (although the pacifists did not). For the war itself, he offered no explanation. Holt's biographer correctly assesses the first two years of the war as the most confused in Holt's thinking.[62]

For Holt, the idea of collective security was not only logical: it was an emotional necessity, providing the way out of his own ideological dilemma. Sprucing up the last of his federalist plans (one dating from 1911), he called it significantly "The Way to Disarm." There were three kinds of force, he insisted. Force for aggression was "wholly evil"; national defense was a "necessary evil." But international force was "almost wholly good."[63] This kind of moral measurement was typical of collective-security thinking. The same self-righteous judgments had been made in the past about backward nations and justice-loving peoples. Holt had never before confronted the contradictions between his advocacy of collective force and his pacifism, because prewar plans were formulated in a hopeful spirit.

The essence of prewar federalism had been the demand for an international organization whose bodies would have the power to enforce their decisions. Charles Eliot, former President of Harvard, revived this suggestion. The league should have an international police force. Holt did not press for this feature of his old plans. Marburg told Eliot that the "practical men" of the League opposed it. There was a "danger of oppression

[61] "Whom the Gods Would Destroy," *Independent,* LXXIX (Aug. 10, 1914), 195–96.

[62] Kuehl, *Holt,* p. 106. In the *Independent,* see, Holt, "The High Duty of the United States," LXXIX (Aug. 10, 1914), 195; "A Task for the Thirty-five Neutrals," LXXXII (May 24, 1915), 308–309; "A Conference of Neutral Nations," LXXXII (May 29, 1915), 443–44; "Woman's Peace Congress," LXXXII (May 10, 1915), 228; "Three Roads and One," LXXXIV (Nov. 22, 1915), 292–93; "The President's Program of Preparedness," LXXXIV (Dec. 20, 1915), 455–56, for Holt's conflicting attitudes on neutral mediation and preparedness and his accommodation to Wilson's program.

[63] "Way to Disarm," p. 428.

connected with such a purpose."[64] Lowell carried the argument further. The United States would not keep several hundred thousand men in the field awaiting "the order of an international council composed mainly of foreign nations." The plan was visionary and unworkable.[65] The first, and perhaps most critical, decision of the League to Enforce Peace was against having the international police force and in favor of using force to compel a cooling-off period.

The second decision derived from Lowell's argument that the league treaty should contain a pledge for instant, automatic military sanctions— force against violence. The *posse comitatus* reflected the frontier nature of international society: each nation armed to the teeth, just as had been each man in pioneer settlements where no government existed to maintain order. On the frontier "people did not wait for a gradual improvement by the preaching of higher ethics and a better civilization. They felt that violence must be met by force, and when the show of force was strong enough, violence ceased."[66] Suppose the powers agreed only to confer in a crisis as Root suggested? Then, Lowell replied, the outlaw would have a chance to argue with the policeman while his own armies moved. No. The only security for the members of the league would be in their pledge of joint force.[67]

This frontier interpretation of international security rested on three unproven assumptions: (1) easy identification of the outlaw; (2) the certain effects of a threat of force; (3) the unity of the *posse comitatus*. The men of the League believed that an aggressor could be identified in any critical situation because the nation that refused to arbitrate a dispute or to expose its views to public opinion obviously had a poor case. Moreover, the league itself at some future time would define aggression. Such a definition, Lowell believed, might include a first declaration of war, armed invasion of another's territory, or the use of force on the seas if not disowned within forty-eight hours.[68] It is noteworthy that this assumption of easy identification of the aggressor ignored the month of confusion and countermobilizations that followed Sarajevo. The advocates of collective security believed that Germany's invasion of Belgium was the first real act of the war. Their moral absolutism made a significant contribution to the theory that wars are caused by deliberate criminal actions. It followed then that an incipient aggressor had to be stopped in time, as Germany might have been stopped by a standing committee of the powers in August 1914.

[64] *League of Nations,* I, 63–64, 69–71; "Reply to Critics," p. 132.
[65] "A League to Enforce Peace," *Towards an Enduring Peace,* p. 152.
[66] "A League to Enforce Peace," League to Enforce Peace Pamphlet (Boston, 1915), Society Publications, Hoover Institution, p. 10.
[67] "League to Enforce Peace" *Towards an Enduring Peace,* pp. 153–54.
[68] "League to Enforce Peace" (1915, Society pamphlets, Hoover Institution), pp. 13–14.

As Lowell emphasized repeatedly, if the intentions of such a committee or *posse comitatus* were sincere and clear, aggression could be prevented. The mere threat of concerted force would be enough to assure a cooling off period. For if any member of the league contemplated aggression, it would have to consider going "to war with the whole world. . . . There is no more danger" of that, "than there is of a rough attacking a dozen policemen. It does not happen; it cannot happen; it will not happen."[69] The real purpose of the threat of force, then, was to prevent the actual use of force.

If that were so, then the threat had to be convincing. This in turn assumed that the members of the league would unite against a potential attacker. But if they already had the will to cooperate they clearly needed no coercion to induce cooperation. If, on the other hand, they entered the organization with mental reservations, then how dependable would their cooperation be in a crisis? Either the members of a league trusted one another or they did not; either their national interests were common interests or they were not. Lowell, Marburg, and most leaders of the League were never certain on this point.

Early in 1915 John Bates Clark began to probe this contradiction. The assumption that national interests coincided at all times ill-fitted his own ideas of competition and self-interest. He concluded that some threat from outside the league would have to exist to reinforce solidarity within. If the league had universal membership, there would be no outsiders. The conflict of interests among the member nations would cause disintegration. The solution was to constitute a league immediately out of one of the warring alliances and the neutral nations. Clark, of course, assumed that the Allies would form a league and the United States would lead the neutrals into it. The league would then become a defensive alliance.[70] (The fact that it would already be at war did not seem to trouble Clark.) Most important of all, such an arrangement would assure the preservation of national sovereignty, for in joining alliances voluntarily nations did not sacrifice their freedom of action. Clark felt so strongly about his concept of the league as an alliance that he strenuously protested the tendency of Holt and Marburg to refer to league bodies as a "legislature," a "ministry" or as the "executive."[71]

Although Lowell did not agree with Clark on the immediate necessity of

---

[69] "Debate Covenant," *A League of Nations,* II, 72–73. See also "The International Policeman," *Independent,* LXXXII (June 14, 1915), 460–61.

[70] "Existing Alliances and a League of Peace," *Towards an Enduring Peace,* pp. 138, 140–41. Clark's concern over the potentials of league disintegration, and other problems relating to the motivations of league members, is recorded in his diary from May to September 1915 in the Papers of John Bates Clark, Special Collections, Columbia University.

[71] Clark to Marburg, Jan. 28, 1918, Marburg Papers; Clark to Marburg, Oct. 30, 1917, *Development of League Idea,* I, 335.

creating a league out of the Entente, he did share Clark's awareness of the national resistance to any scheme that resembled a world government. Moreover, he opposed Holt's idea that economic sanctions should be tried before military sanctions were imposed. Holt based his position upon the assumption that all nations would join the league. The smaller nations would find military sanctions difficult to apply and perhaps would fear to attempt such a measure. Lowell replied that if non-intercourse were tried first, every nation would experience constant domestic opposition from interests hurt by the boycott, "a fact that would be perfectly well known to the intending belligerent" and that would "reduce its fear of a boycott."[72] A well-prepared aggressor could resist such pressure. The great powers would find in any case that blockade required military enforcement. Finally, if the blockade failed, then the "fire is ablaze and can be put out only by blood. The object of the league is not to chastise a country . . . breaking the peace, but to prevent the outbreak of war . . . by the immediate prospect of such appalling consequences to the offender that he will not venture to run the risk."[73]

By adopting all sanctions, diplomatic, economic, and military, without suggesting the order of use, the League to Enforce Peace in effect decided for Lowell. The only compromise with Holt's views was a provision that small neutral powers might stand aside or use only commercial measures, while the great powers and those immediately involved in the conflict would use force.[74] The responsibility of the "standing committee of the powers," the league council, was fixed. As Lowell told Lord Bryce in September 1918, agreement among the great powers was "the vital point of the whole league."[75] It has since proved to be the vital flaw in international organization, for there is nothing automatic about the harmony of interests in international relations. The leaders of the League to Enforce Peace (with the exception of Clark, as we have seen) assumed that harmony was automatic. Lowell, for example, refused to adopt Bryce's suggestion that some punishment for breach of treaty obligations (outside of the basic obligation to submit disputes) be instituted. That would suggest bad faith among the Allies.[76]

This concept of an underlying harmony of interests among nations

---

[72] Holt, "A Declaration of Interdependence," *Independent*, LXXXII (June 14, 1915), 447; Lowell, "League to Enforce Peace," pp. 155–56.

[73] "League to Enforce Peace," p. 156.

[74] "Tentative Draft of a Treaty for a League of Nations" (Executive Committee of the League to Enforce Peace, New York, April 11, 1918), Appendix IV in Bartlett, *League to Enforce Peace*, p. 223.

[75] Lowell to Bryce, Sept. 6, 1918, Marburg Papers.

[76] *Ibid.* Giddings' faith in the unity of the future league was based upon Britain's honoring of the Belgium neutrality treaty, as well as upon a general theory that war

united the men of the polity whether they were legalists or collective security advocates. Both groups asserted that patriotism, as well as a realistic conception of national interests, could be reconciled with true internationalism. When speaking of this reconciliation, however, they invoked a specialized conception of internationalism. Assuming that Anglo-American friendship was, as Giddings termed it, the "nucleus of a perfected internationalism," they tended to rate other nations on a descending scale of enlightenment after the British and Americans.[77]

Their idea of a potential international concord did not actually derive from the assumption that all nations shared similar viewpoints. Instead the political internationalists presented a double argument for harmony of interests. First, they insisted that when international laws were clarified and international disputes exposed to public opinion, right thinking men would agree upon the interpretation of any conflict. Secondly, they believed that Great Britain and the United States, and the smaller nations of the world influenced by them, would exert a predominant influence in any international organization. In the last analysis, it was upon Anglo-American leadership and power that they depended.

Why then did the League men go farther than the legalists? In part, the differences between Lowell and Taft on the one hand, Root and Butler on the other, stemmed from the legalists' long attachment to the court as the only institution needed to assure peace. The founders of the League to Enforce Peace insisted that the deepest conflicts between nations were conflicts of policy, not conflicts of legal right. Root did not think that nations would accept the decision of any international body that dealt with questions of vital interest. Taft had long been committed to referring just such questions to an international court.[78] Lowell rested his case for collective security on the presumed effect of the threat of force as a deterrent. Both Root and Butler seemed to concentrate their attention on the possibility that the United States would actually have to use its forces in fulfillment of the treaty obligations. The willingness or unwillingness of the population to act constituted a practical objection to the plan. These were differences

---

was the strongest force in "reconditioning" men's minds. See "Intellectual Consequences of the War," 1918 Typescript, Papers of Franklin Henry Giddings, Columbiana Collection, Columbia University, pp. 7–8, 14–15.

[77] Giddings, "Introduction," *Towards an Enduring Peace,* p. xi; *The Responsible State: A Reexamination of Fundamental Political Doctrines in the Light of the War and the Menace of Anarchism* (Boston, Houghton Mifflin 1918), pp. 14–15, 46 ff.; Marburg, "The World Court and the League of Peace," *Annals of the American Academy of Political and Social Science,* LXI (Sept. 1915), 280–81.

[78] Bartlett, *League to Enforce Peace,* pp. 19–20. On March 22, 1910, Taft specifically referred to questions of "national honor," and later that year thought "every issue" not negotiated could be arbitrated.

of degree of commitment to international organization *per se*. They did not
constitute differences of substance. The essential features of the atomistic
polity were its preservation of national independence, and its limited legal-
political nature when contrasted to the organic, non-mechanical community.
These it preserved whether the polity had a police force or not; whether it
centered around the court or had many institutions. We can see the
fundamental resemblance between Lowell's arguments and those of the
legalists not in their debate over sanctions, but in their attitudes toward
national sovereignty. Lowell insisted that in

. . . trying any novel social experiment, it is wise to disturb the existing
traditions and habits as little as possible in order to raise the fewest possible
objections to its acceptance and to reduce the friction with customary practice to a minimum. In a League of Nations this means interfering with
national autonomy as little as may be.[79]

The statement was one with which the legalists could agree, however
much they differed with Lowell and Holt upon the kind of structure that
constituted an interference.

WILSONIANS AND CONSERVATIVES

While the dialogue between collective security advocates and legalists
revealed the institutional consensus, the one between President Wilson and
the League to Enforce Peace exposed the difficulty of finding practical
solutions. Holt had long considered territorial guarantees the heart of an
international organizational agreement. His plan for a league of peace,
making such guarantees, predated the war crisis. "The Way to Disarm,"
repeated it. President Wilson, quite independently of Holt or of any other
world organization man, reached the same conclusion shortly after the
beginning of the war.[80] In 1916, at the Pan-American Scientific Congress,
he openly proposed mutual guarantees of territory and political independence. In the context of Latin American-US relations, the proposal had
distinctly anti-revolutionary connotations that Holt quickly detected. At the
time, Holt did not regard the league as anti-revolutionary. He thus asked
the President to consider seriously how a provision for territorial guarantee
could be reconciled with the need for change in Latin America. American
power should not "guarantee the permanence of existing regimes," nor
prevent revolutions.[81]

Colonel House provided the answer. An international organization would

[79] "The Covenanter," *A League of Nations*, II, 99.
[80] Quincy Wright, "Woodrow Wilson and the League of Nations," *Social Research*,
XXXIV (Spring 1957), 70; Charles Seymour, *The Intimate Papers of Colonel House*
(4 vols., Boston, 1926–28), I, 209, 224, indicates the connection of the idea with
Wilson's original league conception and with Pan-Americanism.
[81] "Monroe and Wilson," *Independent*, LXXV (Jan. 17, 1916), 73.

make provision for peaceful change through its council and court. The guarantee would simply provide for protection against external aggression. This feature of the League Covenant, Article Ten, satisfied Holt. Unlike the other leaders of the League to Enforce Peace, he had long sympathized with Wilson's neutrality policies and was not a militant interventionist after the *Lusitania* sinking. Therefore, although a Republican, he became an all-out Wilson supporter.[82] His loyalty to the President was to have a significant bearing upon the future of the League to Enforce Peace.

Marburg, being a friend of Taft and an early interventionist, did not share Holt's sympathies until the critical period of the treaty debate in the Senate. Then he too decided that the pledge of mutual respect for territory and political independence was the heart of the Covenant. At first his position did not differ from Taft's (or did not seem to). But Taft and Lowell had accepted Article Ten only reluctantly and without considering it essential, while Marburg had gone over completely to Holt's point of view. This difference was to prove crucial.

Lowell was in the most equivocal position of all. His temperamental and philosophical inclinations were very like Taft's and much closer to Root's than to Holt's. He considered himself, above all, a realist. The passionate pacifists with whom Holt first allied, regarded Lowell as a deep-dyed conservative.[83] Still, he was not as partisan an opponent of Wilson's as were Taft, Root, and Butler, and he had very little sympathy with Lodge. If partisanship alone had molded the League of Nations debate, Lowell might very well have come out for Wilson. He had supported him in 1916. And even before that, he had been a most sympathetic supporter of Wilson when Wilson was President of Princeton. But that was not enough, for after the war ended, Lowell began to harbor increasing doubts about the quality of Wilson's leadership. Unaware that House and Wilson had created the American Inquiry to prepare American peace proposals and positions for the Peace Conference, Lowell appealed to the President to appoint a commission to work with the British and French in advance of the conference. When Wilson turned him down, Lowell began to doubt the President's practicality. Wilson's call for a Democratic Congress in 1918 confirmed Lowell's evaluation. The President did not know how to compromise.[84]

[82] Kuehl, *Holt*, p. 62; Holt, "Which is the Party of Progress?" *Independent*, LXXVIII (Oct. 9, 1916), 52, indicates Holt's dilemma in 1916. The *Independent* supported Hughes. Holt did not vote. "Woodrow Wilson," *Independent*, XCVIII (Jan. 19, 1918), 89, indicates Holt's worshipful attitudes toward the President. "No Divided Counsels at Washington," *Independent*, XCV (Aug. 17, 1918), 210–11, presents the argument for a Democratic Congress very much in Wilson's terms.

[83] Lucia Ames Mead to Jane Addams, n.d., 1915 Jane Addams folder, Woman's Peace Party Correspondence, Swarthmore College Peace Collection.

[84] Yoemans, *Lowell*, pp. 154, 184, 296, 356, 462; cf. Bartlett, *League to Enforce Peace*, p. 100, for Taft's denunciations of Wilson in the 1918 campaign. Lowell took no

Even as Wilson was engaged in writing the Covenant, battle lines were forming within the League to Enforce Peace. They were lines between conflicting ideals of international organization, reflecting old divergencies. Lowell's erstwhile skepticism about purely procedural reforms contrasted with Holt's faith in them. Lowell's ideas about a limited league contradicted Holt's expectation that the League of Nations would and should evolve into a world government. Lowell's tendency to distinguish between political expediency and moral principles was in sharp contrast to Holt's tendency (very much like Wilson's) to see political and moral issues as essentially the same. While Wilson was in Paris, Holt was urging him to make sure the conferees created a "league of peoples," not a "league of governments." The Assembly should have the power to initiate international legislation that the Court and Council would consider binding upon the signatories.[85] At the same time, Lowell and Taft were urging the President to modify the Covenant in the opposite direction. There should be specific provisions protecting the Monroe Doctrine and the right of every nation to form its own immigration policy. The acceptance of mandates should be voluntary. After a five-year period any member-nation should have the right of withdrawal upon giving the League of Nations a year's notice.[86]

Because Holt and Marburg were such passionate supporters of Wilson's work, while Lowell and Taft were mildly critical, the League to Enforce Peace shrewdly decided that Lowell and Taft were in the best position to meet Lodge's opposition. In March 1919 Lowell and Lodge debated the provisional draft of the Covenant. The debate not only revealed the schisms within institutional internationalism, but some of the reasoning and prejudice behind them. Lodge emphasized the conflict between those who supported a league, but felt that sanctions should be regional (Root and Butler's position and also that of Theodore Roosevelt), and those who, like Wilson, favored a universalized Monroe Doctrine. Lowell replied that the only conception of the Doctrine which the Covenant vitiated was the idea that the Western Hemisphere should be America's "game preserve." If the United States was not a hunter, then it could consider no other nation a poacher.[87] He refuted Lodge's contentions that the Covenant would violate

---

part in the campaign. Lowell's early relations with Wilson are treated in: Henry W. Bragdon, "Woodrow Wilson and Lawrence Lowell—An Original Study of Two Different Men," *Harvard Alumni Bulletin*, XLV (May 22, 1943), 595–97.

[85] "The Birth of the League of Nations," *Independent*, XCVII (Feb. 15, 1919), 217; Kuehl, *Holt*, p. 140.

[86] "Covenant Debate," *A League of Nations*, II, 76, 82–84; Bartlett, *League to Enforce Peace*, p. 124. Taft added an amendment protecting US tariff policy, largely to disarm Wilson's critics. Otherwise his amendments resembled Lowell's. In communicating with Wilson, however, the L.E.P. confined its suggestions to one change protecting the Monroe Doctrine.

[87] "Covenant Debate," *A League of Nations*, II, 51–52, 85.

the constitutional prerogative of Congress to declare war (any more than did any other treaty of mutual guarantee), and that the Council would order American troops into foreign wars. The Council made recommendations. It did not give orders.[88] Clearly the same sensitivity to the issue of sovereignty operated in both debaters, but their interpretations of the relationship between League of Nations bodies and sovereign nations differed. Lowell did not express any hesitancy about Article Ten at this point. Neither did Taft. But Lodge was beginning to muster his forces against that provision to "respect and preserve as against external aggression the territorial and existing political independence of the members of the League."

The more Lodge concentrated his attack on Article Ten, the more Wilson defended it as the heart of the Covenant. Lowell's middle position was becoming untenable. In July 1919 Taft forced the issue. To prevent a split in Republican ranks, Taft himself would offer an amendment on the article. If the members of the League to Enforce Peace did not agree, Taft would resign his presidency of the organization. Lowell saw that Taft's resignation would undermine the position of the mild reservationists. He supported Taft's reservations.

In the course of the struggle, however, Will Hays, Chairman of the Republican Party, without authorization from Taft, made public Taft's reservations. At this point Taft decided to hold that reservations were necessary for the Senate's acceptance of the treaty. He thus inadvertently allied himself with the Lodge group. Holt then challenged Taft's position by asking the executive committee specifically to reject the Lodge reservations. It was too late. Lowell and the majority of the committee supported Taft. The League to Enforce Peace would accept whatever reservations the Senate as a whole approved. The Holt-Lowell schism now spread down through the ranks.[89]

Did the split result from a series of tactical blunders and from mere partisanship? Not entirely. Holt believed that concessions to Lodge would only induce him to add stronger and stronger reservations in order to defeat the treaty. Lowell had depended upon Wilson's acceptance of mild reservations to win enough votes away from Lodge.

When Wilson and his Senate floor-leader, Gilbert Hitchcock, refused to accept reservations, Lowell found himself in the position of having to bargain with the Republican leadership. Deciding that the Republicans

[88] *Ibid.*, pp. 74–76, 85–88.

[89] Bartlett, *League to Enforce Peace*, pp. 144–48, 151–53, 172–74. Raymond B. Fosdick, who attended the crucial Nov. 13, 1919 meeting of the League to Enforce Peace executive committee, believed the organization split "right straight in two on partisan lines." R.B.F. to Arthur Sweetser, Nov. 14, 1919; Fosdick, *Letters on the League of Nations* (Princeton, Princeton Univ. Press, 1966), p. 61.

would in all likelihood win the election of 1920, he appealed to Root and to other limited internationalists to prevent the election from becoming a referendum, as Wilson wished. In an effort to win some commitment from the Republican candidate that would prevent his falling into the arms of the irreconcilables, they should declare their support for the League and for Warren G. Harding. Root drafted the carefully worded "Statement of Thirty-one Republicans." Holt and Marburg, however, concluded that the 1920 election was the Covenant's last remaining hope. They joined Irving Fisher's Pro-League Independents and supported James G. Cox.[90]

Much more than partisanship was revealed in this schism. The contrast between the Wilsonians and the conservatives reflected two widely disparate conceptions of the League of Nations. For Holt and Marburg, Article Ten became the very pledge envisioned by the League to Enforce Peace—a pledge against aggression. Marburg reasoned that if the United States abjured this pledge, and applied sanctions at its own discretion, other nations would follow suit. The League would then lose its collective force and become a "voluntary institution, a change which will be fatal if we hope for the discouragement of war under it."[91] Lowell contended that the sanctions articles would still apply. The League to Enforce Peace program was fulfilled, for the organization had not based its plan on territorial guarantees. The purpose of the League of Nations was to deter sudden attack, not to deny the aggressor the fruits of victory. Moreover, Article Ten would neither prevent aggression nor delay war. Any great power knew that if "defeated she would have no chance to seize territory, and if victorious she would not be prevented from doing so."[92]

What was implied here? The Wilsonians associated collective security with the protection of the independence of small nations. They stressed the atomism of the doctrine. The conservatives regarded collective security as a means of maintaining order. To them, this was both the beginning and the end of the League's functions. It was Wilson's veneration of self-determination that was splitting the league movement. Holt's federalism strangely embraced both world government and territorial guarantees. But Lowell had never held as high a regard for nationalist movements, which he

---

[90] Kuehl, *Holt,* pp. 143–44; Marburg to Wilson, March 20, 1920, *Development of the League Idea,* II, 671. The last Holt-Marburg plan was one for Presidential resubmission of the Covenant with any reservations Wilson accepted. The controverted clauses should then go to the people in a national referendum.

[91] Marburg, "Address to the faculty of New York University," Oct. 31, 1920, *Development of the League Idea,* II, 759; Holt, "Article X—The Soul of the Covenant," *Independent,* C (July 5, 1919), 15–16, indicated how Wilson modified Article Ten to accommodate peaceful change and how a similar, but separate, article was still in the Covenant.

[92] Lowell to Hitchcock, Dec. 30, 1919, quoted in Yoemans, *Lowell,* pp. 456–57.

considered essentially disintegrating forces.[93] It is significant that he, like Root and Butler, associated the drive for self-determination with revolutionary disorder, while the Wilsonians focused upon the anti-autocratic aspects of such movements.

"THE LEAGUE OR BOLSHEVISM"

On one important issue, however, both sides agreed. Socialist revolution constituted a threat to the liberty and order of the atomistic polity. It was the specter of Bolshevism that aroused the passions of the Covenant debaters. For, as Holt had written, all supporters of either *the* League of Nations or of *a* league realized the implications of Europe's postwar chaos. It was "the League or Bolshevism."[94]

This nightmare caused the normally cool-headed Clark to thrash about with one contradictory suggestion after another. He was convinced that the League of Nations must be a defensive alliance. But the question was: What was to be done about Germany? First, assuming that the Germans were unrepentant militarists, he insisted that they be tied hand and foot by reparations, harsh demands, security treaties in the West. On the other hand, one could not allow them to link up with Soviet Russia, thereby spreading Bolshevism and military control over Central Europe. Clark visualized the horrible prospect of German efficiency and Russian socialism conquering the world. The primary tasks, therefore, were to free a reformed Germany from socialist control, to reduce tariffs, to lessen reparations, and to admit Germany to the League of Nations. Otherwise a "sinister political agitation" would sweep through Europe "seizing what wealth there is."[95]

As if this contradiction between a League of Nations with German support against Soviet Russia, and a League primarily the West's defense against Germany were not enough, Clark began to consider alternatives to the League of Nations. Because the United States rejected the Covenant, it was imperative that an alternate means of controlling revolution be found. The Western nations should devise formal methods of economic association and cooperation. The United States should support the League's social agencies. The peace societies should begin a fresh campaign to win American membership in the world court.[96]

[93] Lowell, *Governments and Parties in Continental Europe,* II, 96–97, 122–23.
[94] "The League or Bolshevism," *Independent,* XCVIII (April 5, 1919), 4.
[95] "A Workable League," New York *Times,* Nov. 11, 1918, p. 14; "If This League Fails," *Ibid.,* June 1, 1919, p. 2; "Annual Report to the Board of Trustees of the Carnegie Endowment for International Peace," 1919, quoted in Shotwell, "John Bates Clark," *Carnegie Endowment Yearbook,* p. 162.
[96] Clark to Charles Levermore, May 11, 1922, Clark Papers.

Giddings experienced a similar red scare and similarly adjusted his conception of a league to it. Defiantly facing audiences of radical sympathizers at the Rand School in New York, Giddings asserted that Bolshevism was "not socialism . . . not cooperative communism," but the "massing and turmoil of the criminal elements of society let out of jail and on the loose."[97] True to his social Darwinian principles of the natural inequality of man, Giddings railed against all proposals for economic leveling. Bolshevism, he insisted, defied all the known truths of social science. It was instituting rule by incompetents, and this could only be sustained by brute force.[98]

His program for warding off socialist discontent at home and abroad combined immigration restriction (presumably to give American labor a favorable market and to keep out revolutionary infections), bold police action against strikers, and fairness to the workers in the face of rising profits and prices. There should be profit sharing, collective bargaining, and voluntary social insurance.[99] These domestic measures depended for their success upon a vigorous international program. The key to this program was Anglo-American cooperation and predominance through the League of Nations. The most hopeful result of the war, according to Giddings, was the triumph of the two English-speaking peoples. If they remained strong, the forces of militarism and revolution could be contained.[100]

Apparently then, the specter of revolution had revived Giddings' hopes for a democratic empire. But league thinking on this point did not revert to its imperialist origins. The mandates system had made direct expansionism out of date. The war had broken down the notion that primitive peoples involved the powers in conflicts. Now the Germans were the ones who had left the civilized sphere, and evidently the Russians too. The idea of enforced peace carried a different connotation after 1914. Instead of becoming an instrument of cooperation among "civilized" peoples, it became an instrument of control of any one of their number at any given time. Nor could the optimistic spirit of the prewar federalism persist in the face of war and revolution. In 1920 the old talk of world constitutions, unlimited arbitrations, and international executives seemed dated. With the League of Nations a reality, the issue of whether the constitution of the world would mirror the American constitution was irrelevant.

[97] Hankins, "Franklin Henry Giddings," *American Journal of Sociology*, XXVII (Nov. 1931), 353; Giddings, "The Bolsheviki Must Go," *Independent*, XCVII (Jan. 18, 1919), 88.

[98] "Absolutist Communism," *Independent*, CIII (July 3, 1920), 14–15.

[99] In the *Independent*, see: "The Immigration Tangle," CVI (Sept. 24, 1921), 144; "The Supreme Law," XCIX (Sept. 27, 1919), 442–43; "What is Fair," XCVIII (June 21, 1919), 437.

[100] "What the War Was Worth," *Independent*, XCIX (July 5, 1919), 16–17.

Yet just such hopes, fears, and proud assertions had given birth to the collective security idea. To a few of its adherents collective security was the first step toward world government. To others it was a practical necessity in the face of militarism and revolution. Most of the leaders of the League to Enforce Peace considered the League of Nations an instrument for assuring peace through the Anglo-American rule of law. Obviously, the idea was shot through with contradictory assumptions. When men hope for miracles —even practical miracles—logic is almost sure to go by the boards.

CHAPTER IV

Josiah Royce: The Community of the Loyal

Whoever seeks any truth is loyal, for he is determining his life by reference to a life which transcends his own. And he is loyal to loyalty; for whatever truth you try to discover is, if true, valid for everybody, and is therefore worthy of everybody's loyal recognition. The loyal then are the truth seekers; and the truth seekers are loyal. And all of them live for the sake of the unity of all life. And this unity includes us all, but is superhuman.

Josiah Royce, *The Philosophy of Loyalty*, 1908

The concept of an international community was not one that institutionalists ever attempted either to define or to understand. For those who assumed a universal applicability of clear legal standards, wars appeared to be criminal actions punishable by all states together. The men of the polity made no distinction between an aggregation of states and groups of men of various nationalities who had acquired a sense of community. In the case of those who insisted that the international mind combined an acquired rationality with genteel good manners, the importance of a more endogenous sense of belonging was overlooked. For the most part, political internationalists tended to believe that the antiquated methods of old world diplomacy or the organizational mechanism of international relations was faulty.

On the other hand, those who took the position that an organization for settlement of international disputes, however necessary, could not touch the deeper destructive tendencies of national groups, were likely to consider the question of what actually did constitute a community. For the term "community" suggests a relationship of cooperation and the absence of genuine antagonism, as well as a specific locality and a shared tradition.[1] To the communal internationalists it suggested, as well, a sense of belonging to one organic society. Harmony was of course implicit in this conception, but not a harmony that magically descended upon those only apparently in conflict. The harmony would have to be created by a real change in social relationships from those of conflict, which was actually present and built into one way of life, to those of solidarity.

Such a conception was difficult and unusual for twentieth-century American internationalists. It implied an up-in-the-air utopianism that did not appeal to the "peace movement practical." The conception was not prevalent in the American peace societies. More important, it seemed to contradict notions of a pluralistic society. What was this unity? Could individuals and nations be free if they accepted it? Federal structures so closely approximated the American experience that they were at least understandable. But the *Gemeinschaft* appeared foreign and strange. The paradox of communal internationalism lay in the fact that, for all its European connotations (and these, as we shall see in this chapter, were strong), it did accord with American ideals and experience. The Puritan ideal of the "city on the hill" was a *Gemeinschaft* of shared religious values and prophetic vision; frontier families and immigrant families were communities that left deep impressions upon internationalists such as Josiah Royce, Jane Addams, and Thorstein Veblen. More pervasive than all these was the American faith in a community of free individuals united by shared hopes in a democratic future.

Still, it was the exceptional internationalist who projected a communal ideal into the dialogue about war, peace, and international organization that took place in America from 1898 to 1921. Communalism raised complex problems of the relationships of individual nations to the whole. Jane Addams solved these by viewing the community as one of activity and sentiment in which the issue of sovereignty became irrelevant. Thorstein Veblen rejected the notion of sovereignty and made the community a cosmopolitan technological and scientific unit as well as a potential psychological one for the common man. Josiah Royce viewed the community as a spiritual, but practical, kinship of all loyal men. He faced the unity-plurality problem often. Each consideration of the problem left an imprint upon his international thought. His metaphysics gave the community its structure and described the process of interpretation that united individuals. Royce's

[1] E. C. Lindeman, "Community," *Encyclopedia of Social Science* (New York, Macmillan, 1937), III, 102–103; Baker Brownell, *The Human Community: Its Philosophy and Practice for a Time of Crisis* (New York, Harper, 1950), pp. 198–99, 204–205, 207–208, emphasizes small size, cooperative relationships, diversity of functions, and "face-to-face" encounters, or the possibility of them, as features of a community.

psychology and ethics established the foundation of man's need for community. His Pauline Christianity led to the rejection of facile optimism and enhanced Royce's appreciation of the contrast between political unity and true community.

By embracing tragedy as a necessary and significant element in the emergence of human morality, Royce indicated the difference between his *Weltanschauung* and that of the typical political progressive. He could not accept easy and quick cures for deeply imbedded social wrongs.

[What] you and I really most need and desire is not the new, nor yet the old. It is the eternal. The genuine lover of truth is neither a conservative nor a radical. He is beyond that essentially trivial opposition.[2]

This expressed Royce's whole attitude toward political and social reform. He desired neither change for its own sake, nor tradition for its venerableness, but whatever moral teaching would make men aware of the truth that was always within them. Nevertheless, he felt impelled to connect this teaching with practical concerns and to offer an ethic that should really make a difference in the way men lived together. This was one of the major purposes of his *Philosophy of Loyalty* (1908). To cite one example, highly relevant to internationalist thinking: Royce asserted that there was no necessary connection between war and loyalty. Loyalty was not a militant virtue. There was, however, a necessary connection between an individual's loyalty and his spiritual peace, and between this peace and man's cooperation with his fellows. Eventually Royce would make individual self-possession and devotion to a cause which others shared, one.[3] His connection between internationalist ethics and social psychology was typical of communal thought.

Although before World War I Royce had not discussed international relations, he was profoundly concerned all his professional life with war and peace, atomism and unity. His faith in a community of mankind did not come suddenly, as a result of the shock of 1914. It grew bit by bit out of a long quest for community—a quest both intellectual and deeply personal.

FRONTIER INDIVIDUALISM AND ROYCE'S QUEST

Royce, the mature philosopher, felt that the experiences of his very early years had exerted a profound influence upon his thinking. He believed that

[2] "On Certain Limitations of the Thoughtful Public in America," n.d., *Race Questions, Provincialism, and Other American Problems* (New York, Macmillan, 1908), p. 163.

[3] Josiah Royce, *The Philosophy of Loyalty* (New York, Macmillan, 1908), pp. 12–13, 37, 46–47, 80, 95–98.

his interest in community (although it would remain undefined for a long time) really began in his childhood on the California frontier.[4] There, from the sight of new communities emerging out of disorder and violence, he readily acquired a sense of their importance. Psychologically, Royce never completely abandoned the frontier. He cherished the free individual and sorrowed at free-wheeling, assertive individualism. He was a lonely man who glorified society, a highly self-reliant thinker who sought to prove that man could attain truth only in a community of thinkers.

In the summer of 1849, six years before Josiah was born, the Royce family had made the dangerous and lonely trek across prairies and deserts from eastern Iowa to the California gold country. Sarah Royce, a highly educated, devout woman, later recalled for her son her mystic sense of God's protecting presence in the desert.[5] Although Royce was fascinated with his mother's religious experience, he was much later to reject such mysticism and depend upon the "social religious experience" as the essence of Christianity and the necessary condition of salvation.[6] Perhaps this preference began with a child's sense of where security lay. Family loyalty and deep moral and religious ties enveloped the small boy, while the world outside, the world of fortune-hunters and of pleasure-seeking men and women, abounded with uncertainty. Even to a boy who met his mother's strict Sabbath observance and endless Bible-reading with "passive resistance," as he recalled, the lesson was impressive and lasting.[7]

In 1866 the family moved from Grass Valley to San Francisco where Royce's formal education began. (He had up to this time been tutored by his mother.) Royce's introduction to the "majesty of the community" was "impressive" and "disciplinary." He looked odd—a large-headed, red-haired, "countrified and quaint" little boy whose schoolmates rejected him. At the age of fifteen he had only one friend, a harmless lunatic who imagined himself emperor of California. At the same age, William James, sociable and at ease among his fellows as Royce would never be, was

[4] "Words of Professor Royce at the Walton Hotel in Philadelphia, December 29, 1915," *Papers in Honor of Josiah Royce on His Sixtieth Birthday* (New York, Longmans, 1916), pp. 279, 282.

[5] Sarah Royce, *A Frontier Lady: Recollections of the Gold Rush and Early California,* ed. Ralph Henry Gabriel (New Haven, Yale Univ. Press, 1933), p. 44. Royce drew upon his mother's experience in describing the effects of the westward journey, in his history, *California from the Conquest in 1846 to the Second Vigilance Committee in San Francisco: A Study of American Character* (Boston, Houghton Mifflin, 1886), p. 246.

[6] *The Problem of Christianity,* 2 vols. (New York, Macmillan, 1913), I, xv–xvi. Royce was contrasting his own communal religion with James's interest in individual religious experience in *Varieties of Religious Experience.*

[7] "Words of Professor Royce," p. 280; cf. Sarah Royce, *Frontier Lady,* pp. 104, 109–10, 115.

touring the continent with his brother.[8] Royce's early social experiences were thus far from cosmopolitan.

At the newly formed University of California at Berkeley, Royce developed a strong and persistent interest in romantic literature, evolutionary science, and mathematics. An impressive senior thesis brought him a scholarship and a chance to study the post-Kantian idealists with Herman Lötze at Göttingen. Lötze was helping to undermine Hegelian absolutism with an empiricism that William James, but not Royce, appreciated. Nevertheless, Royce learned Lötze's method and, like his mentor, wanted to remain empirical without rejecting idealism. He dismissed Lötze's system but retained the desire to erect a grand synthesis of knowledge.[9] Although Royce strenuously, and by and large correctly, insisted that he was not a Hegelian (he was much more indebted to Kant, to the German romantic poets, to Schopenhauer, and above all to the American logician Charles Spenser Pierce),[10] his admiration of Hegel's ideas of consciousness and of Hegelian ethics was evident particularly in his early works.

George Santayana called Royce's ethical philosophy divided on the deepest question. "What calm could there be," Santayana asked, "in the double assurance that it was really right that things should be wrong, but that it was really wrong not to strive to right them?"[11] Royce often did express this belief in a variety of ways, for his first task as a religious philosopher was to explain and justify the existence of evil in God's world. The Hegelian belief that one attains virtue only in struggling against evil and in overcoming tragedy seemed to Royce a revelation of the "very life of this passionate deeper Self."[12] Not the least paradoxical aspect of Roycean idealism was his glorification of moral courage in the midst of works designed to assure readers (and perhaps himself) that in God's good world the suffering of innocents was in the final analysis, meaningful.

After returning from Germany and receiving his doctorate in philosophy at Johns Hopkins, Royce became a teacher of literature and composition at the University of California. But he had earlier decided that his career would be that of a metaphysician, and William James had encouraged him. He thus wrote to James early in 1880, "There is no philosophy in California, from Siskiyou to Fort Yuma, and from the Golden Gate to the summit of the Sierra. . . . Hence the atmosphere for the study of metaphysics is

[8] "Words of Professor Royce," p. 281; Ralph Barton Perry, *In the Spirit of William James* (New Haven, Yale Univ. Press, 1938), pp. 6–7.

[9] Vincent Buranelli, *Josiah Royce* (New York, Twayne, 1964), pp. 60–61.

[10] *Problem of Christianity*, I, xi–xii; "Words of Professor Royce," p. 282.

[11] *Character and Opinion in the United States* (New York, Scribners, 1920), p. 78.

[12] *The Spirit of Modern Philosophy* (Boston, Houghton Mifflin, 1899), p. 305. See also pp. 207–11 for a discussion of Hegelian social consciousness and interpretations of evil, both strongly influential in Roycean idealism.

bad."[13] James persuaded the president of Harvard to offer Royce a post. At first Royce only filled in while James took a leave of absence, but upon James's return he was given a permanent appointment. As Royce remarked, the Harvard seminars became his own personal community.[14]

James's relationship with Royce played a significant role in the philosophical development of both men. While James admired the skillful argument and deep feeling of Royce's earliest exposition of absolute idealism (*The Religious Aspect of Philosophy*, 1885), he could no more accept Royce's ideas than he could (at first) refute them. To Royce the fragmentariness of actual individual experiences, the recognition that much of reality was not verified by individuals, and the belief that the real must be experienced led inexorably to one conclusion: there must be an Absolute Being who verifies and experiences reality. Royce even used the logical possibility of error (which he believed was a mental fragment of a higher thought which corrected it) to establish the existence of an Absolute as all-knower.[15] By 1893 James had become convinced he could refute this argument by proving that ideas and objects might be linked entirely within the finite individual's mind. Royce's Absolute was "the idle witness of an achievement which does not require its services."[16] To Royce, the Absolute was logically necessary. To James, Royce's Absolute was simply one individual's way of confirming faith and gaining assurance. Between these divergent points of view there could be no compromise.

Even Royce's incorporation of James's voluntarism served the cause of absolute idealism. Truth was not external and passively accepted by men. Any definition of truth had to include the purpose of the believer. The process of searching for truth was intensely active and personal. Both James and Royce agreed that the intentions of individual wills entered into this pursuit. But then Royce added, "The only question is whether the will really aims at doing something that has a final and eternal meaning."[17] Here James demurred. In satisfying a demand or confirming a hypothesis, a specific idea possessed truth, he thought. But to Royce the truth had to be single and universal. As he indicated in 1908 in an extended discussion of

[13] Royce to James, Jan. 1880, quoted in Ralph Barton Perry *The Thought and Character of William James*, 2 vols. (Boston, Little, Brown, 1935), I, 784. Royce acknowledged James's early encouragement (see p. 799).

[14] *Ibid.*, 794–97; "Words of Professor Royce," p. 283.

[15] *The Religious Aspect of Philosophy* (Boston, Houghton Mifflin, 1913), pp. 385, 391–405, 425, 431; J. Harry Cotton, "Royce's Case for Idealism," *Journal of Philosophy*, LIII (1956), 116–18.

[16] Perry, *Thought and Character of James*, I, 799.

[17] "The Problem of Truth in the Light of Recent Discussion," 1908, in *William James and Other Essays in the Philosophy of Life* (New York, Macmillan, 1911), p. 233. Royce thought the will sought a truth that possessed completeness. "We will the eternal" (see p. 235).

loyalty and truth, his ethical as well as his metaphysical scruples were involved. How would we regard a witness, Royce asked, who swore to "tell whatever is expedient and nothing but what is expedient, so help me future experience"?[18]

This characterization of the pragmatic witness revealed the spirit of the debate between the two men. Each honed his logic upon the other's resistance. Each was completely in earnest and gave no quarter. Yet both were full of comradeship, humor, and loyalty. The debate had much to do with Royce's conception of the community of loyal men, for both were devoted to the truth. James's pluralism and other challenges eventually led to Royce's substitution of the Community of Interpretation for the Absolute.

Well before this culmination of his career as a metaphysician, Royce was deriving his ideas of community from another source—California history. How the contrast between Germany's long-settled communities and conditions in California specifically affected Royce we can never know with certainty, for he did not record any social impressions of Germany. But he did write history very much under the influence of German organicism. For Royce, what the frontier lacked was a sense of social relatedness, tradition, loyalty to one place and to the people in that place. He depicted the Bear Flag War as a shabby episode in which the greed, skill, and opportunism of the Americans overcame the indolence and the innocence of the Mexican Californians. After the conquest there was law (of a sort) in the mining camps and even a passion for righteousness. But the miners turned against both strangers and foreigners when their luck and good humor ran out.[19] Royce's 1886 conclusion seemed completely the judgment of a Hegelian. It was "the State, the Social Order" that was divine, and a reformer's first duty was "patient loyalty to the actual social order."[20] Still, Royce was not writing a political tract, but something more, a "study of American character," and it was therefore significant that he found the political talents of the Americans (talents which he admired as strongly as the men of the polity did) not an aid to community development but rather a hindrance, giving men more confidence in paper solutions than they should have had.[21] The true lesson of California history was a "lesson in reverence for the relations of life."[22]

[18] *Philosophy of Loyalty*, p. 331.
[19] *California*, pp. 134, 139, 149–53, 277–83, 313–25, 328.
[20] *Ibid.*, p. 501; "An Episode in Early California Life: The Squatter Riot of 1850 in Sacramento," 1885, in *Studies of Good and Evil* (New York, Appleton, 1898), p. 325.
[21] *California*, p. 275.
[22] *Ibid.*, p. 500.

A similar moral imperative concluded Royce's *The Religious Aspect of Philosophy* (1885). Insisting that the true goal of a good life was not personal happiness but increased human unity, Royce regarded those who dedicated their lives to public service, art, science, and scholarship as more truly free than the violent individualists of the California frontier. By the 1880s, then, Royce had discovered that men were free not when they pitted themselves against a community or escaped from one, but when they found their own meaningfulness within community.[23]

REALITY, KNOWLEDGE, AND FAITH

The late nineteenth century witnessed one of those great confrontations of ideology and creed that usually foreshadow revolutionary times. As an idealist Royce felt that a philosopher's task in such times was to direct men's attention to the meaning of their own beliefs in order to demonstrate the deeper truth that lay in the synthesis of these ideas. This synoptic possibility was especially marked in the so-called conflict between faith and evolutionary science. Royce began by criticizing romantic optimism of superficial faiths. Such optimism, he pointed out, ignored the graver and indeed the tragic truths of traditional Christianity.[24] He concurred with Schopenhauer's darkest picture of man's fate and morality. But he refused to let either pessimists or naturalists have the last word. For example, he considered Spencer's evolutionism uncritical, dogmatic, and naive in its assertion of some unknowable that hovered over the evolutionary process. Evolution, a partial truth, displayed what men considered a natural tendency toward complexity and heterogeneity. Royce accepted evolutionary science as adequate only for the "world of description," which was a world of fragmentary truths hinting at a far deeper cosmic truth.[25] The reality which men learned bit by bit and incompletely was known all at once, as one truth, by the Absolute Self. Royce thus used evolution as he had used his acknowledgment of the reality of evil and sin to glorify God.

Very early in his discussion of the way in which men acquired truth, Royce hinted at the emergence of the community idea. He thought that men had a social consciousness that appreciated nature before they described it. Nature (reality) for men was essentially social and ethical. The scientific world itself was social, as Charles S. Pierce pointed out. Scientists ac-

[23] *Religious Aspect of Philosophy*, pp. 212–15; Ralph Henry Gabriel, *The Course of American Democratic Thought* (New York, Ronald Press, 1956), p. 306.

[24] *Spirit of Modern Philosophy*, pp. 8, 81, 293, 441.

[25] *Ibid.*, pp. 297–99, 392, 405, 410–11; "The Nature of Voluntary Progress," 1879, *Fugitive Essays*, ed. Jacob Loewenberg (Cambridge, Harvard Univ. Press, 1920), p. 130.

cepted as fact only that "which others are conceived to be capable of veri-
fying. . . ."[26]

Royce's Community of Interpretation eventually replaced the Absolute
Self largely because James and other philosophers challenged Royce's "bloc
universe." Accepting James's notion of the real plurality of individuals and
of the centrality of purpose and will within them, Royce set out to prove
the relationship of both to a cosmic will and purpose. They were real only
as parts of an Infinite. On the other hand, the British idealist, F. H.
Bradley, argued that the existence of an actual Infinite was self-contradic-
tory. It was an abstraction of experience only.[27] Royce contended that since
scientific truth was more than an isolated discovery (each hypothesis and
finding was criticized, retested, corrected, and synthesized with previous
knowledge), reality itself was both many and one.

On Pierce's recommendation, Royce used the new mathematical studies
of infinite series to answer Bradley. A series was infinite when the relationships between finite numbers reflected the structure of the whole. Between
any two members it was possible to insert an infinite series of fractions.
Therefore members interpreted one another and the whole through their
fractions. Actual examples of mathematically well-ordered series would
include a map, picturing the map itself, consciousness of self-consciousness,
knowledge of knowledge.[28]

Further challenge by James and the pluralistic idealists (for example,
George H. Howison) led to exploration of the relationship between meaning (as intention) and meaning (as interpretation), until in 1913 Royce
used Pierce's doctrine of "signs" to establish that reality itself was neither
static nor abstract but full of purpose and relationship. Available evidence
was a "sign"; a scientific hypothesis was an interpretation, and the person
to whom this was addressed, the interpretee. Since real events in time were
also "signs," reality became an historical, triadic, relational process, a
Community of Interpretation. *"By the 'real world,' "* Royce concluded, *"we
mean simply the 'true interpretation' of this our problematic situation."*[29]

Royce was performing much more than a dialectic feat. His purpose had

[26] "Natural Law, Ethics, and Evolution," 1895, *Studies of Good and Evil*, pp. 129,
137.
[27] John Herman Randall, Jr., "Josiah Royce and American Idealism," *Journal of
Philosophy*, LXIII (1966), 61, 63.
[28] *Ibid.*, p. 61; Herbert Schneider, *A History of American Philosophy* (New York,
Columbia Univ. Press, 1947), pp. 487–88; Richard Hocking, "The Influence of
Mathematics on Royce's Metaphysics," *Journal of Philosophy*, LIII (1956), 81, 91.
Royce's answer to Bradley was contained in a Supplementary Essay to the first volume
of his *magnum opus, The World and the Individual*, 2 vols. (New York, Macmillan,
1900–1902).
[29] Royce, *Problem of Christianity*, II, 228, 230, 251, 264–65, 270–71, 284 (Royce's
italics).

been to prove that the very life of the scientific world and the reality of the universe were communal. Therefore, the significance of Christianity for the modern man was the reflection of this reality in the heart of the religion. Christianity was above all the religion of a Beloved Community that was united by faith in the Spirit dwelling within the body of the faithful. Acting then as a sympathetic interpreter of Christianity to a scientific world, Royce indicated that love for the community, salvation of the sinful individual by the community, and loyalty inspired by belief in Christ, were the essentials of Christianity. He then demonstrated that the community was a triadic Community of Interpretation, suggesting a correspondence between this Beloved Community and reality.[30] This argument made individuals significant and real only in their relationships with others, and the world itself social. Loyalty pervaded the whole conception of the community, even to its metaphysical essence.[31]

The ultimate significance, for this inquiry, of the metaphysical structure and religious loyalty of the community was Royce's incorporation of both into his view of international relations. He considered the triadic process of interpretation as the essence of any peaceful relationship. He looked for practical communities of interpretation to answer the deeply rooted problems of war.

THE ALIENATED AMERICAN

One cannot, however, depend entirely upon Royce's metaphysical structure for an understanding of the significance of the international community. His beliefs about war and peace emerged from his social psychology, which in turn illuminated his interpretation of American problems. Royce was indeed a synoptic philosopher, perceiving relationships among apparently distinct phenomena. Every reflection about human nature confirmed the central truth of his Pauline Christianity, "The detached individual is an essentially lost being."[32]

Deeply indebted to James Mark Baldwin as well as to William James for his psychological insights, Royce combined a primary emphasis upon will as the essence of the individual with an almost equal emphasis upon man's social nature. Man's very instincts, judgments, reasoning, and self-con-

---

[30] *Ibid.*, I, 14, 39, 105, 410; II, 324–25. Royce believed that a denial of the community was self-refuting. "For if there is no interpreter, there is no interpretation. And if there is no interpretation, there is no world whatever" (see II, p. 325).

[31] *Ibid.*, II, 218–19.

[32] *The Hope of the Great Community* (New York, Macmillan 1916), p. 46; cf. Jacob Loewenberg, *Royce's Synoptic Vision* (Baltimore, Johns Hopkins Press, 1955), pp. 14–16. By calling Royce's philosophical method synoptic, Loewenberg meant that it was concerned primarily with the inner relationships of individuals and ideas.

sciousness were social. For example, man's ideas were, as James suggested, plans of action that included a fringe of feeling about possible consequences. Royce asked how men became conscious of such plans of action. Their acknowledgment of their own ideas was possible only within a social environment that made them conscious both of objects and of rational behavior in their presence. The acquisition of ideas illustrated the higher development of man's instinct of imitation.[33] The instinct had for Royce a neutral and plastic character. It did not imply, as for some of the political internationalists, an inevitable herd-like passivity among the masses, in contrast to the rationality of the few.

Nor did man's innate sociability mean for Royce, as it did for Addams and Veblen, an innate or instinctive peacefulness. Royce was too much a Pauline Christian not to give some hint of man's sinful nature even in his discussion of naturalistic psychology. He saw both the human tendency to resist others and to set up a contrast between the self and others as fundamental. Social opposition stemmed from the biological tropism Jacques Loeb described. Human restlessness not only produced mental initiative but also lay "at the root of a social tendency called Individualism."[34] It could be creative or antagonistic, depending upon the individual's setting. By and large, individualism meant, as Royce would later indicate in discussing war and peace, that man's sociability was strangely asocial. Individuals could neither live peaceably with others nor live at all without them. Not inherently aggressive, man was above all sensitive—reacting to others both by imitating and by opposing them.

In brief, Roycean psychology predicated the society as primary in the formation of the individual. Society was for Royce more than the sum of individual lives. It had a life of its own. And social life made the individual what he was. He even took the position that self-consciousness was primarily social. "I am dependent upon my fellows, not only physically, but to the very core of my conscious self-hood."[35] The ethical side of the individual was his conscience. But the conscience itself, Royce declared in a statement almost anticipating Freud's concept of the superego, was but "an imitation, a brief abstract, and an epitome of our literal social life."[36]

Believing so thoroughly in the interdependence of individual and society, Royce even went so far as to make free will social. The will was an active process of judging one's own actions and choosing one above the other. One

[33] Royce, *Outlines of Psychology* (New York, Macmillan, 1903), pp. 275, 290–91, 295. See also pp. 276–80, and "Preface," p. xiii, for Royce's debts to James and Baldwin.

[34] *Ibid.*, pp. 277, 307–308, 326–27.

[35] "Self-Consciousness, Social Consciousness and Nature," 1895, in *Studies of Good and Evil*, p. 201.

[36] "Anomalies of Self-Consciousness," 1895, *Studies of Good and Evil*, p. 193.

learned to choose freely in a social environment. Choosing meant that social duties were evaluated, not imposed. "For my duty is only my own will brought to a reasonable self-consciousness and is not an external restraint."[37] Hardly any statement could make as clear the distinction between legal-political attitudes and communal philosophy. In institutional thought, individuals sacrificed an anarchistic freedom in order to live within society. The sphere of liberty was one area in which there was no governmental action. In Royce's social ethics the isolated individual was the one most enslaved by his own irrational desires and drives. Men became truly free only within small communities where they cooperated with others. The contrast between government and liberty was to his mind a sign of social decay, not a self-evident truth. As men of the polity accommodated their *laissez-faire* philosophy to the world of large-scale organization, Royce regarded great organizations and true communities as opposing forces.

Thus to Royce the core of the American problems of his time was alienation. As society grew more complex and vast, individuals lost a sense of their own significance within it. The power of great economic organizations and the power of government appeared external and oppressive to them. No one identified himself with his society.

The government in such vast social orders represents the law, a dictation that the individual finds relatively strange to himself. Or, again, the power of the state, even when it is attractive to the individual, still seems to him like a great nature force, rather than like his own loyal self, writ large.[38]

Alienation was the source of all social illnesses because the freedom of the individual and the healthy progress of society were in truth completely interdependent.

In 1902 Royce proposed that the individual, so crushed by bigness, could save himself in the "province." The province was Royce's earliest version of the community. He defined it as any part of the national domain sufficiently unified by ideals, customs, and local pride to "possess a sense of its distinction from other parts of the country."[39] In a province, individuals cherished local customs and traditions as their own. They felt at home and socially effective.

Anticipating much later defenders of regionalism, Royce described the evils of alienation that might be overcome by provincialism.[40] The first evil of American society, and also of world society was excessive mobility. The

[37] "Immortality," 1907, *William James and Other Essays,* pp. 289–90; "The Problem of Job," n.d., *Studies of Good and Evil,* p. 21.
[38] *Philosophy of Loyalty,* p. 239; cf. "Provincialism," pp. 77–78.
[39] "Provincialism," p. 61.
[40] *Ibid.,* pp. 63–64; Morton and Lucia White, *The Intellectual versus the City: From Thomas Jefferson to Frank Lloyd Wright* (New York, Mentor Books, 1964), p. 185.

uprooted man, frequently changing his dwelling-place, felt at home nowhere, as Royce's own California experience had told him. Although it was the duty of communities to welcome strangers, it was not healthy for the influence of mobile men to predominate in any one local area.[41] Clearly Royce was considering the disorderly social and political life that prevailed in communities of transients. So long as strangers remained strangers, no real sense of community existed among them. Jane Addams would describe how a sense of community emerged among the outcasts themselves, but it was more significant to Royce that so long as they viewed their new surroundings only as a source of material opportunity, only as a region to be exploited, they could attain neither a sense of belonging nor an opportunity for loyalty.

Secondly, Royce asserted, the growth of the mob-spirit and the increase in passive conformity was subverting man's real freedom. Although he wished the newcomers to learn to love their adopted country, Royce never confused assimilation with conformity. Like Alexis de Tocqueville and many other observers of American customs, Royce noted that Americans already were far too ready to let the majority dictate their views. Unlike Tocqueville, however, Royce attributed this excessive conformity both to a lack of a sense of belonging, and to the effects of mass communication, not to the absence of a traditional aristocratic leaven. Individuals on the receiving end of the same news and opinions were bound to be similarly molded by events, so long as they refused to take the trouble to think. Like an unseen mob they simply reacted to stimuli and echoed slogans. In contrast to the political internationalists who believed liberty was threatened by the increasing number of governmental restrictions upon private economic initiative, Royce insisted that the greatest threat to liberty was the individual who no longer regarded himself as an individual, but who willingly became part of a mob. The effects of modern social pressures upon the discriminating mind concerned him most. He studied the mob-spirit and contrasted it with the community spirit which cherished and encouraged individual critical faculties.[42]

Finally, Royce appreciated the hidden alliance between aggressive individualism and modern collectivism. Each intensified the other, for without the willing conformity of the many, the few could not become giants. Both

---

[41] "Provincialism," p. 69; "Provincialism Based upon a Study of Early Conditions in California," *Putnam's Magazine,* VII (1909), 239.

[42] *Race Questions,* pp. 76–78, 86–89, 95. Royce used Gustav Le Bon's *The Crowd* as his source for mob psychology, but, unlike Le Bon or some of the more conservative internationalists, he did not regard the mob-spirit as inherent in the modern, democratic social order.

depended upon the obliteration of individuality. The paradox could be explained in terms of Saint Paul's observation about man's sinful nature: the greater the external authority over men, the more assertive and danger-ous man's self-will. The real goal of individualists was not freedom but power. "The more the social will expresses itself in vast organizations of collective power, the more are individuals trained to be aware of their own personal wants . . . and of the vast opportunities that would be theirs if they could but gain control of these social forces."[43]

The observation had religious roots, but political implications. It was, in fact, the same fearful prediction that Giddings and Lowell were making when they associated mob-rule with tyranny. But there was one important difference. Royce did not associate mob-rule with socialism, nor socialism with totalitarianism. On the contrary, he connected the very ideas of self-interest that the men of the polity opposed to socialism, with the totalitarian mentality. The demagogue, the child of the twentieth century, was not a socialist but an individualist *par excellence*. This did not mean that Royce supported socialism or revolution. His opposition to collectivism was strong whether the collectivism was governmental or private. The communalists, however, had no vested interest in anti-socialism.

There was one other important contrast between Royce's ideas of mob-tyranny and those of the political internationalists. Unlike Marburg and Giddings, Royce did not interpret civilization as the product of advanced or progressive races. His attitudes toward racial interpretations of history and toward race theory generally were profoundly skeptical. To Royce, irra-tionalism and the mob-spirit belonged not to certain races but to the racists. Once again his approach to the problem of conflicts was psychological and ethical rather than political and self-righteous. He analyzed not the charac-ter of races, but the character of race-prejudice. His first approach was to question the use of the term "race" as implying a "distinct hereditary variety of mental constitution." This had not been proven, and thus he considered race "sciences" false. "I begin to wonder," Royce remarked dryly, "whether a science which mainly devotes itself to proving that we ourselves are the salt of the earth, is after all so exact as it aims to be."[44]

Perhaps the differences between teachable peoples, like the Germans, and backward races reflected the method of education. The Germans had long been in contact with civilization before they entered history; they had come down to Rome as conquerors. If Caesar had taught them quickly by modern means, "unlimited supplies of rum, of rifles, and of machine guns," they, like the colored peoples of the nineteenth century, might have furnished

[43] *Problem of Christianity*, I, 152–53.
[44] "Race Questions and Prejudices," 1904, *Race Questions*, pp. 9, 39.

models of debasement for race theorists. "Dead men not only tell no tales; they also, strange to say, attend no schools, and learn no lessons. And hereby they prove themselves in the eyes of certain students of race-question to have been always of a much lower mental type than the cultivated men who killed them."[45]

Having indicated the uncertain nature of race "science" and its deep confusion over inherited and environmental influences upon character, Royce then analyzed racial antipathies as developing from a natural but neutral social sensitivity. When fear or anger heightened sensitivity, men focused upon any physical feature of an opponent as significant. The "scientists" then named and insisted upon the prejudice until it became "a sort of sacred revelation of truth, sacred because it is felt, a revelation merely because it has won a name and a social standing."[46] This analysis of race prejudice reflected Royce's more pervasive distrust of purely emotional reactions and sympathies.

Although Royce did not apply the same analysis to nationalism, his association of pride with fear (as the roots of prejudice) bears a striking resemblance to Veblen's interpretation of patriotism as a longing for collective prestige, and to Addams' idea that patriotism derived in part from fear of the outsider. In each case, the communalists rejected not only plans for controlling backward peoples by force, but the entire expansionist *Weltanschauung* upon which such plans were based. By focusing upon the inner character of group relations instead of upon the external appearance of conflict alone, they criticized solutions that depended simply upon restraints (either by law or by force), emphasizing instead the cooperative maintenance of order. Royce's appreciation of the black constabulary in Jamaica and his references to his "negro countrymen" who might help solve the South's social problems made this abundantly clear.

Still living in an age of racial Darwinism, Royce could not entirely free himself from the American racial bias. He addressed the fearful white Southerner rather than the constrained blacks, a not too surprising course, given the circumstances of segregation. Nor did he attack the institution of segregation as such. What was remarkable in the context of his times was his focus upon white prejudice, including his own, as a psychological phenomenon, and as the source of racial conflict. "I am a member of the human race," he concluded, "and this is a race which is, as a whole, considerably lower than the angels, so that the whole of it very badly needs race-elevation."[47] Such a conclusion demonstrated very well the spirit of loyalty, even before he formulated the heart of his ethical beliefs.

[45] *Ibid.*, pp. 41–44.
[46] *Ibid.*, pp. 48, 51–52.
[47] *Ibid.*, p. 53.

"LOYALTY TO LOYALTY"

Royce's major ethical work, *The Philosophy of Loyalty*, has been viewed in various contexts. Modern critics of his philosophical idealism often infer that he preferred a romantic virtue to wisdom and self-restraint.[48] There is some justification for this judgment. Roycean ethics were profoundly heroic in tone. Royce viewed the contemplative life as only one example, and not always the best example, of the good life. However, Royce himself defended his choice of the highest good in terms that constitute a reply to such critics. If wisdom and self-restraint were good, then the individual should acquire them. But individuals by themselves could not become wise or self-restrained. They needed a cause to teach them these virtues. They learned by uniting the self with others.[49]

Because Royce was deeply concerned with specific problems of individual conscience in the self-estranged society of late nineteenth-century America, a historical interpretation of his philosophy assumes a different dimension from the ethical analyses. Ralph Henry Gabriel, for example, views *The Philosophy of Loyalty* as an attempt to answer naturalistic relativism and agnosticism, and more broadly as an effort to reconcile the free individual with the higher law without an appeal to political theory.[50] Gabriel emphasizes Royce's uniquely apolitical interpretation of freedom and community.

Still another historical interpretation of Roycean loyalty might describe his philosophy as an effort to glorify the active and practical virtues inherent in community by demonstrating that peaceable loyalties could provide the "moral equivalent of war." This interpretation is not as clear-cut, however, for it must be granted at the outset that Royce was no pacifist. He did not expect to do away with war, and he did not particularly value non-resistance. He was not engaged, like William James and Jane Addams, in an attempt to make pacifism itself virile. While proving, however, that the patient and practical devotion of the individual to a cause (loyalty) was "the whole moral law," he also indicated that misunderstanding of loyalty was in part responsible for the exclusive association of war and loyalty. He analyzed man's love of war not as a relic of his barbarism, nor proof of his need for war, but as proof of his need for loyalty. Thus, although the self-sacrificing soldiers were Royce's first ex-

---

[48] Howard B. White, "Royce's Philosophy of Loyalty," *Journal of Philosophy,* LIII (1956), 99–100; Stuart Gerry Brown (ed.), "Introduction," *The Social Philosophy of Josiah Royce* (Syracuse, Syracuse Univ. Press, 1950), p. 27.

[49] *Philosophy of Loyalty*, p. 31; cf. *Problem of Christianity,* I, 188, for an expression of the psychology of an individual's need for community.

[50] *Course of American Democratic Thought,* pp. 304, 307.

ample of loyalty, they were not his last.[51] Like James, who coined the phrase, he had found a "moral equivalent."

Clearly Royce was evolving his philosophy in two contexts. First, there was the challenge of rival philosophies and beliefs—moral relativism, pragmatism, ethical individualism, each of which Royce treated in turn. Then there was the social challenge of estrangement, militant nationalism, class warfare, and imperialism. Royce even referred to the "self-estranged social mind," as an "imperialistic sort of national consciousness."[52] He seemed as clearly alive to the conflict between Roosevelt's activism and the traditional doctrines of the peace societies as was James or Miss Addams. For with all his admiration of the soldierly virtues, Royce was too much a seeker of the community to be satisfied with the church militant, or with loyalty that resulted in conflict. Thus in 1907 when Professor Rudolph Steinmetz of the Netherlands wrote a *Philosophie des Krieges,* Royce decided that his own work in progress concerning truth, conscience, and loyalty would answer the prevalent view of militant activists—that if war disappeared moral decay would follow.[53] (James's "Moral Equivalent of War" [1910] and Addams' *Newer Ideals of Peace* [1908], were answers to the same assertion.)

In this context one may assess Royce's *Philosophy of Loyalty* as a logical disassociation of virtue from militancy. He analyzed the effects of war upon the individual conscience. In peacetime a man was torn between the value of altruism (self-sacrifice) and that of individualism (self-assertion against others, or cultivation of one's own life). Each had a claim upon his conscience but he could not hold the two together. In wartime the patriot or soldier experienced a strange resolution of this conflict. His individual life suddenly had a plan and purpose, acquired because the individual had fused his life with that of others in devotion to a cause. True, the cause was destructive and the fusion perhaps irrational and emotional. Royce exhibited no admiration for the war-spirit *per se,* but saw its significance in its (temporary) resolution of a conflict of conscience between self-will and social demand.[54] Thus, Royce indicated that what men loved and needed was not war but a cause to which they might be loyal. It was loyalty, and not the external circumstances alone, that gave their lives direction and unity.

Essentially then, the moral demand of the loyalty principle was simple: choose your cause and be faithful to it. Now Royce was confronted with

[51] *Philosophy of Loyalty,* pp. 43, 54. Royce thought his own discussion of soldiers and samurai placed too great an emphasis upon the connection of loyalty with martial virtues and vices (see also p. 102).

[52] *Ibid.,* p. 239.

[53] *Ibid.,* pp. 12–13.

[54] *Ibid.,* pp. 39–42.

critics similar to those moderns who have held loyalty too romantic and irrational. He had to prove that loyalty was not inherently as destructive as the soldierly example suggested. Therefore, he predicated a pacifying and unifying character to the loyalty ethic itself. In choosing a cause, a person had to reflect upon its relation to other men's causes, and on its effects upon the universal principle of loyalty. The choice made should further the cause of "loyalty to loyalty." Royce was not propounding an abstraction. He meant something very definite and practical. "If loyalty is the supreme good, the mutual destructive conflict of loyalties is, in general, a supreme evil." Thus, men had a standard for judging their choices; whatever cause required the destruction of another's life, property or the destruction of his means of loyalty, violated the principle of "loyalty to loyalty."[55]

Royce recognized that this was perfectionism. One could not know in advance all the demands that would be made upon an adherent to a cause. He was deeply conscious of the disparity between his ideal and actual human behavior. But that did not relieve him of the duty of explaining the ideal completely, any more than loyalty relieved the individual of the obligation to continue to judge his own cause and that of others. The significance of "loyalty to loyalty" as it applied to internationalist thought was twofold: First, it demonstrated the prevalent internationalist discrimination between enlightened patriotism, which was peaceloving, and destructive emotional nationalism (a distinction Veblen refused to accept). Second, it led logically to the pluralism of Royce's international community, or the Great Community, as he called it. In the Great Community men would still be loyal to their nations, but their loyalties would no longer be antagonistic. This community was a goal, and Royce recognized it as a perfectionist one. He assumed that enlightened loyalty strove to reconcile particular and specific causes. He did not admit that so long as the causes themselves remained limited, the individuals were not aiming at reconciliation.[56]

Finally, Royce saw the significance of loyalty to a lost cause. In the imperfect world of conflicting causes, the ideal of the harmony of all causes inevitably lost. Yet defeat could not destroy the goodness of loyalty itself. "This good of the causes is essentially superhuman in its type, even while it is human in its embodiment. For it belongs to a union of men, to a whole of human life which transcends the individuality of any man, and which is not

[55] *Ibid.*, pp. 115–17, 120–21; Loewenberg, *Synoptic Vision*, p. 28, observes that "loyalty to loyalty" indicated that Royce denied the exclusive goodness of any one cause. Causes were only worthy of loyalty in that service to them would foster universal loyalty.

[56] George H. Mead, "The Philosophies of Royce, James, and Dewey in their American Setting," *John Dewey: The Man and His Philosophy: Addresses Delivered in New York in Celebration of His Seventieth Birthday* (Cambridge, Harvard Univ. Press, 1930), pp. 91–92.

to be found as something belonging to any mere collection of men."[57] Thus Royce's philosophy reconciled morality and religion, a reconciliation which was ever his goal. Loyalty became "the Will to Believe in something eternal, and to express that belief in the practical life of a human being."[58]

In a similar way Royce's Great Community, essentially spiritual and never completely attainable, was, however, supposed to guide men in the practical conduct of their lives. The actual earthly defeat of the cause of universal loyalty was the fundamental reason for Royce's skepticism about the conquest of war. The true warfare of "enlightened loyalty" was spiritual only. The loyal spirit did not rejoice in great armies. It regarded militancy as unenlightened loyalty at best, "and at its worst one of the basest of disloyalties to universal loyalty."[59] Yet, as Royce's and the world's experience would soon confirm, enlightened loyalty was the rarest of virtues.

THE INSURANCE COMMUNITY

World War I put Royce's philosophy of loyalty to the practical test. The results, as might have been expected in any confrontation with complex reality, were contradictory and tragic. Royce in a sense was a war-casualty. The contrast between the Germany of his spiritual birth, the Germany of Kant, Goethe, and Schopenhauer, and the realm of Kaiser Wilhelm contributed toward hastening his death.[60] He could no longer accept the Hegelian dictum that the state was divine. He had long ago replaced that belief with "loyalty to loyalty." Yet here was Germany acting upon the premise that no higher loyalty than blind national obedience existed. Horace Kallen recalled hearing Royce's vigorous denunciation of Germany after the sinking of the *Lusitania,* and thinking what an ironic position this was for one so indebted to German philosophy and so sure of the harmony of all loyalties.[61] George Santayana, perceiving that Royce could not reconcile his old Hegelian concept of evil with the loss of innocent lives on the *Lusitania,* noted playfully:

Was not the Universal Spirit compelled to bifurcate . . . Germans and Americans, in order to attain self-consciousness by hating, fighting against and vanquishing itself? Certainly it was the American duty to be angry, as it was the German duty to be ruthless.[62]

[57] *Philosophy of Loyalty,* p. 354.
[58] *Ibid.,* p. 357.
[59] *Ibid.,* pp. 214–15.
[60] George Herbert Palmer, "In Dedication: Josiah Royce," *Contemporary Idealism in America,* ed. Clifford Barrett (New York, Macmillan, 1932), p. 8.
[61] Horace M. Kallen, "Remarks on Royce's Philosophy," *Journal of Philosophy,* LIII (1956), 133.
[62] *Character and Opinion,* pp. 77–78.

There is strong point in Santayana's criticism. Royce, the philosopher of loyalty, could not accept the consequences of wartime loyalty. His perfectionism was too demanding. He became not gently tolerant, as the loyalty ethic implied, but aflame with righteous sincerity as an Old Testament prophet. He could no longer be neutral, he told a British friend, about the appeal that Germany made to the world. It was a "perfectly deliberate and merciless" attack upon every form of loyalty.[63]

At first glance there seemed very little that was unusual in Royce's militant idealism. Anti-Prussianism was a common enough attitude among the internationalists (with some notable exceptions), especially after May 1915. But Royce's reaction to Germany was unique, for it was predicated not upon the premise of Anglo-American solidarity but upon the idea that Germany had betrayed the whole international community.

In a paradoxical sense Royce's Hebraic denunciations which so contradicted loyalty to loyalty, also grew out of that principle as he had extended it in *The Problem of Christianity* (1913). Here he discussed the whole problem of loyalty and treachery in relationship to the concept of community. Loyalty, he asserted, was the willing and *"practically devoted love of an individual for a community."*[64] (The metaphysical community was triadic in structure, interpretative in function, and both many and one. Its significance for Roycean internationalism is discussed later in this essay.)

At the moment it is important to realize that the community was something more than a metaphysical concept. For Royce it was natural, human, and explicable in social terms as well. It required social communication among members, their willing and knowing cooperation, and historical development. The members of any community shared a past which they remembered, the present in which they were joined in cooperative activity, and a future. Thus Royce spoke of a "community of memory" and a "community of hope."[65] His most important social contrast was between organizations and communities. In organizations men worked together without knowing why they cooperated. The work of a modern factory, for example, was mechanically cooperative, but not truly communal. In a community each member could say, " 'This activity which we perform together, this work of ours, its past, its future, its sequence, its order, its sense, all these enter into my life, and are the life of my own self writ large.' "[66] Identification between the individual and the whole through an interpretation which each member made of his own life was the essence of the human community.

[63] Royce to Professor L. P. Jacks, n.d., published in London *Morning Post*, July 5, 1915, and in *Great Community*, pp. 22–23.
[64] *Problem of Christianity*, I, xvii (Royce's italics).
[65] *Ibid.*, II, 37, 50–51, 67.
[66] *Ibid.*, pp. 87–89.

So long as Royce confined his attention to the religious community, the Pauline Church, his interpretation held. Although critics might argue that the historical reality of Jesus was essential for Royce's conception of the Beloved Community (an issue upon which he refused to commit himself), they did not dispute that belief in Jesus' life and death and resurrection bound the members of the community. Each Christian accepted these events as significant in his own past. Each one's hope for life after death was the same goal that united the community. Moreover, this body of believers had a very potent human interpreter in Paul, and identified the suffering God Jesus as the very spirit of the community. Love of God and of the community (Pauline charity) provided one spiritual bond.[67]

It was in this context that Royce first spoke of the sin of treachery. It was ever a tragic possibility in the Beloved Community, for loyalty had to be willing and free. The members remained faithful because they chose loyalty. "The beloved community demands for itself such freely and deliberately steadfast members. And for that very reason, in a world where there is such free and good faith—there can be treason."[68] Treachery shattered the community. The tragic sin both required, and gave the occasion for, community-creating deeds that would transform the loss into a gain. This was Royce's explanation for the significance of the Christian doctrine of atonement.

Almost unconsciously Royce translated this religious ideal to the political world, a world he knew was very far from the ideal. He had in 1913 spoken of natural communities as bound by ties of kinship, language, and culture,[69] suggesting an equation between nation and community. The philosophy of loyalty, however, predicated a universal community. Throughout the war, and particularly during the *Lusitania* crisis, Royce acted as if this universal "community of hope" actually existed. Its existence was, of course, in the future but Royce could not accept the possibility that this dream might not materialize. He thus turned against the traitor, Germany, considering its assault upon the community a very personal and deep one.

Before the sinking of the *Lusitania,* Royce had discussed the war in a calmer spirit. In a small volume, *War and Insurance* (1914), he had

---

[67] *Ibid.,* pp. 70, 72–76, 425.

[68] *Ibid.,* I, 299.

[69] *Ibid.,* pp. 64–65, 167–68. In the second of these two discussions of "natural" communities or nations, Royce recognized that their immorality was as great as the sins of individuals and more dangerous.

analyzed the causes of wars and the nature of modern warfare. Anticipating the ideas of modern Christian realists, Royce insisted that war was not simply a reversion to barbarism or a reflection of the evil side of man's nature. The very character of international relations and the strength of national consciousness contributed to man's warlike tendencies. Modern wars were waged for ideals. They were frequently planned and carried out by men who believed they were serving justice and the interests of humanity. The same humane sympathies that stirred men's hearts when they heard of tragedy and disaster, made their wars seem "morally indispensable," righteous, and "not only fascinating, but rational."[70] In brief, one could not hope for the elimination of war simply by the "progress of civilization."

Royce carried his rejection of the doctrines of sympathy and love (as cures for war) even further. One reason the Buddhist and Christian appeals to love were so futile was that they seemed both pallid and irrelevant in a war. Man's instinct for imitation was too strong, and men imitated "whatever was impressively vigorous about the will and power of interesting men and nations."[71] Giddings had used this argument to assert that it was leaders who were chiefly responsible for wars. Royce was using the same argument to prove the instability of emotions deriving from humane impulses. The question was: Why could the ethic of non-violence not affect the course of international relations?

Royce answered that the relationship between nations was one of natural conflict. At this point, modern realists have usually insisted that the causes of conflict were real clashes over vital interests—the inevitable struggle for power that has been endless in international society. Royce did not ignore the drive for power as a source of conflict. He had treated it in *The Philosophy of Loyalty* as an extension of individualism. But his treatment was purely an evaluation of the amorality and futility of the power drive.[72] He did not believe that conflicts of national self-interest alone explained international violence. Foreign relations were dangerous in their very structure. They were dyadic. Whether nations were in international organizations or out of them, in alliances or isolated, they faced each other in "dangerous pairs."[73] Their relations naturally became those of opponents, for that was the relationship of any pair that did not form part of a community.

---

[70] *War and Insurance* (New York, Macmillan, 1914), pp. 5–6.

[71] *Ibid.*, pp. 7–8.

[72] *Philosophy of Loyalty*, pp. 87–90; cf. *Great Community*, p. 57, for a contrast between powerful nations and those which had, at various periods, contributed to the community of mankind. Royce contrasted the spiritual and ethical contributions of ancient Greece with her political disunity. His discussion of Germany is even more revealing.

[73] *War and Insurance*, p. 39.

It is not good for man to be alone. Yet if you give man a companion, it is equally natural that the two should ere long quarrel!

Their quarrel need not be due to the fact that they are naturally malicious. But perhaps by mere accident, they soon get in each other's way."[74]

Here was Royce's interpretation of the essential reason for the futility of pacifist appeals. The dyadic relationship of love was inherently unstable. Whenever two social groups, two nations, confronted one another, they soon discovered how their interests conflicted. Love quickened into hate. Royce was not contrasting, as would Reinhold Niebuhr some twenty years later, "moral man and immoral society." He contended that the immorality of both was traceable to the absence of community. But his argument bore a strong resemblance to that of Niebuhr. The highest good that man achieved within national communities (loyalty) became, in the absence of international community, the worst evil. The very depth of man's attachment to his nation assured that he would nobly sacrifice his life and ignobly kill others for a national cause.[75]

Yet relationships within nations were very different from international relations. Families, churches, provinces, nations maintained their solidarity because they were communities. These communities did not form any higher community. National honor had no meaning because there existed no higher community to which nations owed honor and allegiance.[76]

At this critical point in his argument, Royce applied his metaphysical reasoning to international relations. What was essential for the creation of an international community, a community to which nations might give their loyalty, was a triadic relationship to replace the dangerous dyadic one. All stable communities, practical or metahpysical, familial or businesslike, were relationships of at least three. The strength of the community rested with one member who interpreted the other two to each other. The interpreter in large measure created a common will. In the business community he was the agent who brought together the principal, wishing to do business, and the client whose interest conflicted with his. Serving neither party exclusively, but both together, the agent created their community.[77]

If Royce had depended upon structure alone, he might at this point have invoked the international judiciary. But he was quite familiar with all the arguments for and against the court. The judicial community was structurally sound, he argued (judge, plaintiff, defendant), but totally inadequate in a world of passionate nationalism. It was necessary but insufficient,

[74] *Ibid.*, p. 29.

[75] *Ibid.*, pp. 21, 39. Cf. Reinhold Niebuhr, *Moral Man and Immoral Society: A Study in Ethics and Politics* (New York, Scribner, 1932), pp. xi–xii, 84, 85, 91 ff.

[76] *War and Insurance*, p. 88.

[77] *Ibid.*, pp. 51–53.

because nations owed it no loyalty and were not obliged to accept judicial decisions. "Exactly," replied the federalists, "the court needs the means of enforcement." But Royce did not consider the matter so simple. He perceived that the soldiers in any international force would still owe their loyalty to contending nations.

Will it be easy for the international army to arouse the enthusiasm which patriots now give to such demands as their country makes upon them for service? In other words, when the great stresses come, the international tribunal has to depend upon motives which seem, at best, drearily reasonable just at the moment when they most need to seem ideally inspiring.[78]

This observation was to be echoed by Jane Addams and other communalists who supported the court but found it insufficient. Moreover, like the advocates of collective security, Royce recognized that nations did not always quarrel over their rights even while they could accept an interpretation of these rights. Royce did not accept the theory of any international organization settling questions of policy. It was unrealistic to expect passionate nationalists to refrain from conflict at the command of a confederal body.[79]

Royce's criticism of international legal-political structures was simple. These coldly mechanical structures did not touch the deep emotions and loyal commitments that were infused into modern nationalism. They alone could not promote international loyalty, which was the essential ingredient of a true community of mankind. Yet Royce, wishing to be practical, would not abandon the problem as hopeless. He turned to the insurance community.

His choice was not only original but meaningful. Modern realists have insisted that a patriot's attachment to his nation in large measure reflects the uncertainty of modern industrial life. The national state protects its citizens, gives them a sense of security.[80] Patriotism itself may be a compensatory emotion combating insecurity and fear. While Royce did not interpret national loyalty in this way, he appreciated the security-providing function of insurance. Relationships of risk produced conflict. The insurance interpreter pacified the dangerous dualism between adventurer and beneficiary. Moreover, insurance provided security for larger and larger numbers of people and encouraged their assimilation with one another if only by bringing them together. Royce's mathematical studies convinced

[78] *Ibid.,* pp. 57–58, 88–89.

[79] *Ibid.,* p. 92.

[80] Hans J. Morgenthau, *Politics among Nations: The Struggle for Power and Peace,* 3rd ed. (New York, Knopf, 1962), pp. 106–109; Robert E. Osgood, *Ideals and Self-Interest in American's Foreign Relations: The Great Transformation of the Twentieth Century* (Chicago, Univ. of Chicago Press, 1964), pp. 10–11.

him that one "of the most widely applicable laws of nature," expressed in statistical, not mechanical terms, was that "aggregation tends to result in some further mutual assimilation of the members of the aggregate." Their cohesion in turn produced further growth.[81] Royce was suggesting, although he did not state it explicitly, that the enormous extension of insurance, both public and private, in the twentieth century might provide a means for easing class conflict. The union of the highly abstruse probability theory upon which insurance rested with the deeply social and practical effects of insurance attracted Royce quite naturally.[82] But it was above all the interpretive, triadic, and community-creating aspect of insurance that induced him to suggest a plan that might make wars in the future less terrible and total.

He offered the following proposals:

1. Because nations as well as individuals were subject to the risks of natural disasters, and moral and social upheavals as well—all entailing economic losses—they might unite to protect themselves in an international insurance community.

2. The interpreter of the community would be an International Insurance Board of Trustees with no political powers. The trustees would neither arbitrate disputes, nor command any force, but simply interpret insurance contracts.

3. The Board would first determine an actuarial basis for insurance by investigating the statistical regularity of such disasters as floods, famines, earthquakes, destructive storms, shipping losses, and epidemics. It would then investigate the loses of its clients, compensate them, and attempt through other agencies (for example, health agencies) to minimize risks and the effects of disasters.

4. The initial funds for the insurance coverage might come from the reparations claimed by the victors in the world war and/or from contributions by the members.[83]

5. The beginnings of the international insurance enterprise might be very small. Perhaps its first work would be to reinsure those interests that had been international in scope before the war—interests destroyed by the war itself. (German companies had largely been concerned with the rein-

[81] "The Mechanical, the Historical, and the Statistical," *Science*, N.S., XXIX (1914), 562, 564. Royce offered insurance as the practical example of assimilation and growth.

[82] Shepard Bancroft Clough and Charles Woolsey Cole, *The Economic History of Europe* (Boston, Heath, 1941), pp. 649–50, discuss the significance of the growth of life insurance at the end of the nineteenth century and the beginning of the twentieth. Royce, *War and Insurance*, pp. x, xlvii.

[83] Royce, *War and Insurance*, pp. xii–xiv, 74–77, 79–80.

surance business of protecting the insurers themselves; perhaps it was this form of insurance Royce had in mind when he offered reinsurance as an answer to his insurance company critics.) [84]

How would the plan lessen the possibilities of war? Because Royce's audience demanded direct solutions, Royce offered some that constituted the weakest part of his proposals. The Board could make wars less profitable by declaring that any conquered country no longer existed to receive insurance funds. The "dead state's" investment would revert to the general fund, where the conqueror could not touch it. (The fund would be widely invested and inaccessible.) Second, the Board might, without judging the merits of any conflict, simply cut off funds from whichever nation involved in a conflict committed the first overt act. [85] Even if Royce had interpreted wars as the results of rational economic planning, which he did not, these arguments seemed weak. Decisions concerning the first overt act would be uncertain. A victor, denied insurance funds, might still acquire much greater economic resources by conquest—territory, industries, a labor force and raw materials, for example. Royce's critics perceived that certain countries did not appear to be very good risks against such war-insurance. [86]

Royce admitted that the plan was imperfect and in need of revision. He placed no reliance at all upon these direct effects of insurance. The indirect effects "would from the very beginning far outrank in importance its direct accomplishment." [87] These indirect influences were to exemplify international loyalty in the performance of insurance duties, to bring men together in more thoroughly social and peaceful enterprises, to further the cause of universal loyalty by making practical and visible the community of mankind. In this Royce demonstrated once again that he was more interested in gradual and active (if difficult) social regeneration than in any specific mechanism for keeping the peace.

In formulating his plan, and in particular in evaluating the prospects for initiating it through reinsurance, Royce had consulted insurance men at the

[84] Sydney Preston and Alexander Ernest Sich, "Fire Insurance During the War," *War and Insurance: The Economic and Social History of the World War. British Series,* (London, Oxford University Press for the Carnegie Endowment for International Peace, 1927), pp. 95–96; Royce, *Great Community,* pp. 78–84.

[85] Royce, *War and Insurance,* pp. xxvi–xxvii, 71–72, 78.

[86] "Peace Through Insurance," *New Republic,* I (Nov. 14, 1914), 26; cf. New York *Times,* Nov. 29, 1914, Sec. VI, 535, for a more favorable review of the practical side of Royce's proposal.

[87] *Great Community,* p. 91; cf. *War and Insurance,* pp. xxxiv, 94–96 for a more extended discussion of the influence of insurance upon international loyalty. Royce recognized the practical interests promoting this loyalty. He had never thought of loyalty as selflessness in any case. See also, "Professor Royce on his Reviewer," *New Republic,* I (Dec. 26, 1914), 23, for a reply to critics along the same line.

Harvard Graduate School of Business Administration.[88] When he learned that a "World Congress of Insurance" was to meet in San Francisco in October 1915, he wrote to Chancellor David Starr Jordan of Stanford, who was consulting with the insurance men and with various peace groups that were to meet, calling Jordan's attention to the plan. Jordan thereupon invited Royce to the Congress and made him an honorary member of the Congress. But there is no evidence of Royce's attendance nor of the Congress' consideration of his plan.[89] The International Labor Organization, which was the international body most directly concerned with research into social insurance after the war, also ignored Royce's proposals. None of the statesmen or national representatives at Versailles considered them. Thus, ironically, Royce's most earnest attempt at practical proposals proved to be the least noticed aspect of his writings. It was almost as if he foresaw this result in 1908 in warning the "thoughtful public" in America against social panaceas. "We have to learn," he had insisted, "both to work and to wait. We have to learn to obey as well as to formulate. What saves the world can never be any one man's formulated scheme."[90]

In 1916, at the end of his philosophical career, Royce emerged as a most unusual internationalist. A moralist and an idealist, he was a Pauline realist as well. The paradox and the richness of his social thought lay in its union of sense of human imperfections with a persistent courage and assurance. Royce understood that the strength that came from a bland optimism was no strength at all. Yet he preached the doctrine of active loyalty in pursuit of an ideal. His words about the Great Community, which was surely an ideal, illustrate his own loyalty to truth. It was, he asserted,

. . . not ours to say, in the world in which we at present have to live . . . when and how the true revelation of the world's meaning is faced and found. We often do our best when we fix our mind on the thought which Kant expressed in the words: "If justice meets utter wreck, then there is no worth whatever in the continued existence of human life in this world." That word, at least, relieves us from the requirement of trying to prove that justice in mortal affairs will escape total wreck.[91]

Thus spoke the man who has become to modern interpreters more than a skillful dialectician imbibing wisdom at the fount of German idealism. His attempt to combine the ideal and the practical, unity and plurality, reflected

[88] *Great Community*, p. 92.

[89] Royce to Jordan, February 10, 1915; and Jordan to Royce, Feb. 16, 1915, David Starr Jordan Peace Correspondence, Hoover Institution. For accounts of the World Insurance Congress and the World Peace Congress and their concentration upon comparative insurance plans, neutral mediation, and league organization, see the San Francisco *Examiner*, Oct. 5, 1915, pp. 6, 20; Oct. 10, 1915, p. 1; Oct. 11, 1915, p. 6; Oct. 12, 1915, p. 20; Oct. 14, 1915, p. 6.

[90] "Limitations of a Thoughtful Public," p. 152.

[91] *Great Community*, p. 27.

his frontier American experience as much as his Germanic training. As a philosopher of loyalty, who was sensitive to the significance of alienation, he is better appreciated today than he was in his time.[92] As an "American thinker on the war" he imparted depth and challenge to the internationalist dialogue.

[92] Randall, "Royce and American Idealism," *Journal of Philosophy*, LXIII (1966), 73.

CHAPTER V

Jane Addams: The Community as a Neighborhood

Cease to be the shadow of man and of his passion of pride and destruction. Have a clear vision of the duty of pity! Be a living peace in the midst of war—the eternal Antigone refusing to give herself up to hatred and knowing no distinction between her suffering brothers who make war on each other.

Romain Rolland, quoted by Jane Addams, *The Long Road of Woman's Memory,* 1916

The pragmatism that Royce regarded as only a partial account of truth because it ignored the community of truth-seekers, had its own communal ethic. Grounded in evolutionary science, rather than in metaphysical logic, this pragmatism produced plans for social reconstruction and experiments in community living. John Dewey's attempt to make the school a miniature community—peaceful as well as active—was one such expression of this philosophy. Like Royce, Dewey was indebted to Hegel for the distinction between community and civil society. He too retained a certain nostalgia for small rural communities in the midst of his urban living. But while Royce's method was to elucidate the logical structure of the community of interpretation, and then to seek a practical application of it, Dewey encouraged intelligent scientific planning to further social welfare. Jane Addams and other settlement-house pioneers owed more to the insights of John

Dewey[1] than to the idealism of Josiah Royce. Dewey himself learned much from the settlement-house communities.

Absolute idealism was not then a necessary component of international communalism. It was not even essential for a religious view of the international community. Positivists, for example, rejected supernaturalism and made of humanity itself an object of worship. The ministers of the social gospel made human solidarity, cooperation, and brotherhood conditions for individual salvation. One could save one's soul only by redeeming the society. Even revolutionary nationalism could infuse political movements with mystical hopes for an international brotherhood. Mazzinian nationalism, paradoxically, was internationalist in just this way. In general, however, it was difficult to combine religious fervor with a pragmatic temperament. As Royce suspected, the two did not go well together. William James's appreciation of the "varieties of religious experience" was pragmatic, indeed, but not in itself religious. Still, this peculiar combination of an almost mystical reverence for humanity and a very pragmatic approach to social problems, leading to radical criticism of the *status quo,* was possible.

Jane Addams made this combination her own. As a pacifist she criticized the passive "dove-like" ideal of the peace movement. As a pragmatist she relied upon experience more heavily than upon theory. And then she would theorize. She had an almost mystical faith in the people, but never hesitated to point to their corrupt and often selfish behavior. She was an ardent feminist with Victorian standards of femininity, sentimental in the extreme, and yet an effective executive. Her contemporaries and more recent historians, as Christopher Lasch has pointed out, have been prone to sanctify her. "Praising her goodness, her saintliness, was a way to avoid answering her questions."[2]

The questions, however, had a disturbing way of re-emerging: Was industrial materialism crushing the spontaneous joy of youth? Could any group loyalty, even loyalty to the workers of the world, foster human unity? Could a war that intensified nationalistic hatreds "make the world safe for democracy"? Her questions turned most of all to her own beliefs, for she was never certain she was right. Thus when her friends deserted her in 1917, she asked whether her pacifism had degenerated into a dogma.

[1] Jane Addams, "John Dewey and Social Welfare," *John Dewey, the Man and His Philosophy: Addresses Delivered in New York in Celebration of His Seventieth Birthday* (Cambridge, Harvard Univ. Press, 1930), pp. 141–43; Morton White, *Social Thought in America: The Revolt Against Formalism,* 2nd ed. (Boston, Beacon Press, 1959), p. 96; Morton and Lucia White, *The Intellectual versus the City: From Thomas Jefferson to Frank Lloyd Wright* (New York, Mentor Books, 1964), p. 160.

[2] "Introduction," *The Social Thought of Jane Addams* (Indianapolis, Bobbs-Merrill, 1965), p. xiv.

It was not the loneliness, nor even her own mistakes, she feared, but the tendency toward self-righteousness in anyone who held himself apart from a mass emotion. Too much was at stake, however, for her to give up pacifism even for the sake of "mixing on the thronged and common road."[3] She would have had to sacrifice her faith that individual loyalty to one's "vision of the truth" was the beginning of social change; she would have had to deny her perception that a pervasive desire for peace and unity underlay even the hatreds of war. Above all, she was convinced that one could only teach by the deed.

For Jane Addams, loyalty to one's own vision was an overly individualistic, doctrinaire belief. Her pacifism did not stem primarily from doctrine. It was, in fact, fused with a belief in international community, and this came as much from experience as from theory. She identified herself with the interests and hopes of the immigrant community. This was truly a radical identification for so middle-class a lady although not really unusual among American intellectuals of the time.[4] Her experience on Chicago's West Side revealed that the crippling environment that drove apart immigrant and old American, young idealist and parent, rich and poor, also forced cooperation among the poor themselves. She appreciated that the immigrants were, in Oscar Handlin's words, "the uprooted," divorced from the familiar rural-village environment and longing for community. While Handlin has shown that the immigrant associations were community-creating instruments for the Germans, the Russians, and the Italians, separately, Jane Addams saw the birth of an international community in the tendency of the Polish neighbor to help the Austrian one, the Italian worker to join a union with the Jewish worker. The immigrant community was international not because many nationalities lived side by side, but because they were helping each other and "fusing."[5] Undoubtedly, observers with a lesser faith in natural gregariousness would have been more keenly aware of intergroup tensions; nor did Jane Addams completely ignore them. Like Prince Kropotkin, however, she argued that man would have to rely for his very existence upon mutual aid rather than upon competition. Like Tolstoy she saw salvation in the masses and the humble.

Tolstoyan Christianity and the settlement-house experience worked to-

[3] Democracy and Social Ethics, ed. Anne Firor Scott (Cambridge, Harvard Univ. Press, 1964), p. 6.

[4] Christopher Lasch, The New Radicalism in America, 1889–1963: The Intellectual as a Social Type (New York, Knopf, 1965), p. 147.

[5] Jane Addams, "Class Conflict in America," American Sociological Society: Papers and Proceedings, XI (Dec. 28–31, 1907), 153; "Toward Internationalism," Woman's Auxiliary Conference of the Second Pan-American Scientific Congress (Washington, D.C., Dec. 28, 1915–Jan. 7, 1916), p. 59; Oscar Handlin, The Uprooted: The Epic Story of the Great Migrations That Made the American People (New York, University Library, n.d.), pp. 173, 185–89.

gether in the creation of her pacifism, with the settlement and practical needs always taking the upper hand. She had very early been attracted to Tolstoyan beliefs, not particularly because they were pacifist, but because the great teacher of nonresistance embodied ethics in action. In 1896 she had gone to Yasnaya Polyana to visit the master, and had returned more a critic than a disciple, but with uneasy feelings of guilt. Tolstoy had examined the luxuriant sleeves on her dress and had commented upon the uses the peasant women would have applied to so much material. Learning that she derived part of her income from a farm in Illinois, he noted that she was an absentee landlord. Jane Addams was to observe many years later that she was disappointed in Tolstoy's position on nonresistance. "It seemed to me that he made too great a distinction between the use of physical force and that of moral energy which can override another's differences and scruples with equal ruthlessness."[6] But she did not mean to imply that Tolstoy had been wrong about her privileges in contrast with those around her. Upon returning from Yasnaya Polyana she determined to work in the Hull House bakery every day for two hours. Her father, a miller, had taught her to bake bread; and, as we shall see, the bread itself had as great a significance for her as for the advocates of "bread labor." But as always, realism prevailed over doctrine.

I held fast to the belief that I should do this, through the entire journey homeward . . . until I actually arrived in Chicago when suddenly the whole scheme seemed to me as utterly preposterous as it doubtless was. The half dozen people invariably waiting to see me after breakfast, the piles of letters to be opened and answered, the demand of actual and pressing human wants —were these all to be pushed aside and asked to wait while I saved my soul by two hours' work at baking bread?[7]

Here was a very early instance, but a crucial one, in her attempts to test theory by practice. Her experience with Tolstoy put an end once and for all to the irrelevant preaching of perfectionist dogmas. Yet she gained more than she lost through this experience, for she soon would apply to social problems what John Dewey called the "creative imagination," dealing with the materials at hand for the sake of what could be. William James caught the spirit of her work in a review of her *The Spirit of Youth and the City Streets* (1909). "She simply inhabits reality and everything she says necessarily expresses its nature."[8]

---

[6] *Twenty Years at Hull House, with Autobiographical Notes* (New York, Macmillan, 1910), pp. 268, 273.

[7] *Ibid.*, pp. 276–77.

[8] James quoted by Anne Firor Scott, "Introduction," *Democracy and Social Ethics*, p. lxii. For Dewey's definition of creative intelligence, see White, *Social Thought in America*, p. 145.

COMMUNITIES IN CEDARVILLE AND CHICAGO

Neither Jane Addams' pacifism nor her awareness of poverty stemmed from childhood experiences. She had grown up in the prosperous farming community of Cedarville, Illinois, under the guidance of her well-to-do father, a miller and grain merchant. Following her sisters to Rockford Seminary for girls, she had become a genteel, cultured young lady. Her determination to live among the poor in some great cosmopolitan city had come only in her late twenties, when she was seeking a fulfillment of the new woman's role in public affairs. If she had not struggled so painfully to discover herself, it is unlikely that she would have discovered "the depressed tenth." Her motives, as she herself implied, were subjective rather than charitable.[9]

Undoubtedly her father, whom she worshipped with a "doglike affection," was the strongest influence in her early years. Her mother had died in 1863 when Jane was only two, and the little girl turned to her father for love and for an interpretation of the life around her. John Addams, Cedarville's most respected citizen, a friend of Lincoln and a State Senator, had little use for religious doctrine. When his bewildered daughter had asked him what he was, he had replied without further elucidation that he was a Hicksite Quaker. Her questions about foreordination finally led to his revelation that such disputes meant nothing to him. He believed simply that "you must always be honest with yourself inside whatever happened." Throughout her childhood and her college years, Jane Addams searched for a secure religious haven. She entered settlement work partly out of religious motives. Eventually, however, Chicago taught her the limitations of traditional individual rectitude. She became a contented and a more democratic-minded agnostic.[10]

Her father's heroes, Lincoln and Mazzini, became her own. The Lincoln ideal taught her that democracy grew out of the fund of common experience between leader and people. The experiment in self-government could succeed only if the people themselves cooperated to foster it. The frontier community symbolized this ideal, and her father's experience in building a

[9] "The Subjective Necessity for Social Settlements," *Philanthropy and Social Progress: Seven Essays . . . Delivered Before the School of Applied Ethics at Plymouth, Mass., During the Session of 1892* (New York, Crowell, 1893), pp. 12–16; *Twenty Years at Hull House*, pp. 72–73, 77, 88.

[10] *Twenty Years at Hull House*, pp. 15–16; Margaret Tims, *Jane Addams of Hull House* (New York, Macmillan, 1961), pp. 17–19; John C. Farrell, *Beloved Lady: A History of Jane Addams' Ideas on Reform and Peace* (Baltimore, Johns Hopkins Press, 1967), pp. 61–63.

railroad with the financial aid of his Pennsylvania Dutch neighbors stood as a living example of it.[11]

The rural setting, the free and prosperous farmers who cooperated to bring the wheat of northern Illinois to Freeport and Chicago by rail, always spelled community to Jane Addams. The whole life of Cedarville seemed a natural setting for youth and age. It was perhaps here that Jane Addams' vision of an organic, classless society began.

Between her father's internationalism and her own there existed a tenuous connection, even though Jane Addams appreciated it only after she had discovered the meaning of her past. One day in 1872 the little girl found her father in mourning for the Italian patriot Joseph Mazzini. Why should he care about some foreigner he had never met? John Addams explained that just as he himself had formed the "Addams guard" to fight with the Union Army for freedom in America, Mazzini had fought for Italian liberty and for the freedom of all Europe's peoples. "I obtained a sense," she recalled in 1910, "of the genuine relationship which may exist between men who shared large hopes, and like desires, even though they may differ in nationality, language and creed."[12]

Rockford Seminary (later Rockford College) was one of the first institutions for higher learning for women in the Midwest. The environment of serious study and dedication, the girls' sense of unique opportunity, awakened Jane Addams' feminism. But Rockford was also a training ground for foreign missionaries, and the evangelism of the headmistress, Miss Sill, repelled the young doubter whose ideas of the divine were still in flux. Nevertheless, Jane Addams acquired a sense of Christian mission all her own and strong ideas of woman's role in society, which were just enough to make her restive with the life her vivacious, cultured stepmother had planned for her. Women's education, she told her fellow students in her junior class oration, neither confined them to the "arts of pleasing," nor sought to make them like men. Women claimed the right to "independent thought and action" while retaining the old ideal of the Saxon lady as "bread giver." Jane then planned a career combining scientific study with feminine service. She would become a doctor.[13]

[11] *Twenty Years at Hull House,* pp. 35–36; James Weber Linn, *Jane Addams: A Biography* (New York, Appelton, 1935), pp. 11–13, 16–17, indicates that John Addams' business ventures played a central role in the development of Cedarville.

[12] *Twenty Years at Hull House,* p. 21.

[13] "Bread Givers," Address at Rockford Seminary, April 21, 1880, Jane Addams MSS, Swarthmore College Peace Collection; Linn, *Addams Biography,* pp. 42–44, 54, 61; Lasch, *New Radicalism,* pp. 8–10, 16, 21–22.

The matter was not so quickly settled, however. In August 1881 John Addams died. His daughter lost all sense of purpose and plunged into an emotional and spiritual crisis from which she did not recover completely for eight years. She went on to the Woman's Medical College in Philadelphia only to decide, after six months, that she had mistaken her aptitude for science. A spinal disease temporarily immobilized her physically as well as emotionally. A trip to Europe with her stepmother failed to revive her spirits. When her stepmother moved the family to Baltimore, where Jane studied French and attended lectures at Johns Hopkins, she "reached the nadir of . . . [her] nervous depression and sense of maladjustment." She wrote her friend, Ellen Gates Starr, that she was "filled with shame that with all my apparent leisure I do nothing at all. . . . I have found my faculties, memory receptive faculties and all, perfectly inaccessible locked up away from me."[14] A second trip to Europe in 1887–88 turned the key, not because she had discovered "the other half" but because she decided to act at last upon a plan she had considered even before she embarked.

One evening in Madrid after she and her friends had enjoyed the bloody spectacle of a bullfight and she had stayed all day at the arena, the shock of her love for a beauty that was also cruel impelled her to stop cloaking her idleness in a "dreamer's scheme." She would tell Ellen of her plan and bring the dream to reality. She wanted to rent a large house in the cosmopolitan industrial district of a great city "where many primitive and actual needs are found," to give herself and others like her, too swamped with privileges and too steeped in intellectual pursuits alone, the "solace of activity."[15] The next day Jane Addams and her friend set out for Paris and London. They visited Toynbee Hall, the first settlement house, to learn how such an enterprise worked.

In 1889 as she and Ellen opened up Hull House in Chicago's immigrant district, Jane Addams saw that two needs were meeting and answering each other—the objective needs of a torn, divided, and impoverished area and the subjective needs of her own generation to create some harmony between their Christian ideals and their lives.[16] The settlement movement was a very class-conscious one. In England it was inspired by a sense of *noblesse oblige.* John Ruskin, whose writings first impelled Canon Barnett and the young men of Oxford and Cambridge to set up Toynbee Hall in the Whitechapel district, was concerned chiefly with the intellectual's obli-

---

[14] Jane Addams to Ellen Gates Starr, Feb. 7, 1886, quoted in Lasch, *Social Thought of Addams,* p. 5; cf. *Twenty Years at Hull House,* p. 77.

[15] *Twenty Years at Hull House,* pp. 85–86.

[16] In *Philanthropy and Social Progress,* see "Subjective Necessity for Social Settlements" pp. 1–2, 6, 17, 19; and "The Objective Value of a Social Settlement," pp. 29, 31.

gation to relieve the sins of his society.[17] In spite of all Jane Addams' efforts to understand rather than sympathize with the poor, she never quite lost this feeling of condescension.

Hull House was to bring high culture to the slums, if only to prove that the poor were not a lower order of men. The settlement workers learned neighborliness from their clients, but largely because these clients retained the "primitive" virtues of pity and mutual aid. Canon Barnett of Toynbee Hall had taught that whatever draws men together was deeper and more real than the environment that drove them apart. Jane Addams accepted this as her guiding philosophy. Yet the subjective and objective needs were, after all, different needs, and behind her goal of the classless society lay the haunting sense that such differences might not so quickly disappear.[18]

The salvation of privileged youth lay in answering the cries of the slums. For if they held aloof from the poor and from the "starvation struggle which makes up the life of at least half the race," not only would their sympathies deaden, but their guilt would bring a loss of vitality, which could only make them "pitifully miserable." Jane Addams regarded this longing for helpfulness and action as a "race memory" of the "starvation struggle" of ancestors. But when she spoke of girls trained to altruism and then bound by the "family claim," just as they would go out into the world to fulfill their obligations, it was clear that her own experience rather than any evolutionism molded her interpretation.[19]

In 1887, on her second trip to London, Miss Addams had heard the positivist Frederick Harrison speak of loyalty to humanity. Without yet understanding the practical implications of the idea, she was attracted to it. Her notebook recorded a visit to Ulm cathedral, where in the choir stalls were carved figures of Hebrew prophets, Greek philosophers, and Christian saints, symbols of the rich diversity of this "humanity" and of the "fellowship of common purpose" which transcended it.[20] Her vision of Hull House became this vision of human solidarity, and she quickly saw its fulfillment in her own activity. She plunged into work, minding the children of working mothers, preparing the dead for burial, acting as midwife for an unmarried pregnant girl whom all the good Irish matrons of the neighbor-

[17] Arthur Mann, "British Social Thought and American Reformers of the Progressive Era," *Mississippi Valley Historical Review,* XLII (March 1956), 683–84.
[18] Daniel Levine, *Varieties of Reform Thought* (Madison, State Historical Society of Wisconsin, 1964), p. 21; Addams, "Subjective Necessity for Social Settlements," p. 26.
[19] "Subjective Necessity for Social Settlements," pp. 10, 12–16.
[20] *Twenty Years at Hull House,* pp. 82–83.

hood had deserted. The Nineteenth Ward of Chicago, where Hull House stood, was the center of the tenement sweat-shop garment industry. Evening after evening, the Russian and Bohemian and Italian women staggered home under the weight of huge piles of garments to be finished in their crowded rooms. There the children waited for supper, and the ill lay on bedrolls on the floor. There the stink of the slaughterhouses and the noise of the streetcars and crowds drifted through the narrow windows. Typhoid, tuberculosis, smallpox, and diphtheria ran rampant through these tenements. And often the most pitiful savings went for funeral trappings much more magnificent than the clothing or shelter of the living.[21]

Jane Addams and Ellen Starr were learning what the "love of humanity" meant. It did not mean charity nor the handing out of a pittance of help.

Our very first Christmas at Hull House, when we as yet knew nothing of child labor, a number of little girls refused the candy which was offered them as part of the Christmas good cheer saying simply that they "worked in a candy factory and could not bear the sight of it." We discovered that for six weeks they had worked from seven in the morning until nine at night, and that they were exhausted as well as satiated. The sharp consciousness of stern economic conditions was thus thrust upon us in the midst of the season of good will.[22]

The clash between the dream of Christian fulfillment and the harsh reality of the slums brought the genteel Miss Addams and her friends up sharply. They were soon transformed from missionary philanthropists into radical critics of the ugly commercialism of the cities. Not only did they see youth and love and work degraded, but they learned at close hand that it was no simple matter to bridge the chasm of values between the rich and the poor. The traditional puritan virtues of hard work, abstinence, and thrift which the middle-class charity worker usually preached to her clients were meaningless to families who could find no work, or who could not possibly save when they needed every penny merely to live. The poor understood their naturally helpful and kindly neighbors. They understood the selfish rich who stayed uptown. What they could not understand was middle-class charity doled out as a reward for impossible "virtues."[23] Thus in the very first years of Hull House, the settlement workers discovered that the "overdifferentiation" of the lives of rich and poor could not be ended by even the most generous giving. Community had to start with mutuality. The women of Hull House, wanting to open the lines of com-

[21] *Ibid.,* pp. 109–10; "Objective Value of Social Settlements," pp. 29–31; Ray Ginger, *Altgeld's America: The Lincoln Ideal versus Changing Realities* (Chicago, Quadrangle Paperbacks, 1965), pp. 27–29.

[22] *Twenty Years at Hull House,* p. 198.

[23] *Democracy and Social Ethics,* pp. 29–31, 34–40, 51.

munication between the classes, had to transform charity into equality and comradeship. Only if they joined the real struggles—for labor legislation, for union rights, for accident insurance, for adequate medical care, for tenement legislation—would the community grow. Even the most immediate problems provided opportunities.

We quickly discovered that nothing brought us so absolutely into comradeship with our neighbors as *mutual and sustained efforts* such as the paving of a street, the closing of a gambling house, or the restoration of a veteran policeman.[24]

Thus the settlement workers became fighters. They campaigned against the ward boss (while quite appreciating why he held the neighbors' loyalty). They organized the Juvenile Protective Association, the Consumers' League, and women's trade unions. During these struggles Jane Addams began to appreciate two cardinal points that would later mold her pacifism. First of all, the struggle for social justice held forth as great a challenge and as much adventure as any war. Secondly, the very process of fostering the growth of human solidarity required the use of all the resources of government. A government so transformed by the demands of its own society might be compelled to adapt even its foreign policy to those demands.

All the while the settlement house was becoming a community—a community whose goal was to make city life more organic. And this meant, at the very least, hospitality to all visitors and to every viewpoint. The problems of industrial society were too complex to permit the social workers to apply any limited insight to the solutions. The neighbors must be heard, for it was their city. Evangelists and housewives, respectable reformers and eccentrics, conservatives, atheists, socialists—all used the Hull House platform. Chicagoans often misunderstood this hospitality and assumed that the residents agreed with those who spoke. Following the assassination of President McKinley, night after night the great house was surrounded by the Chicago police as they combed the district hunting for anarchists. After one particularly noisy meeting, a policeman turned to Dr. Alice Hamilton with a few pointed words: "Lady, you oughtn't to let bums like these come here. If I had my way, they'd all be lined up against a wall at sunrise and shot."[25] But the ladies found it all very stimulating. They understood that the real purpose of free speech was mutual enlightenment. One could not be "dogmatic concerning the final truth."[26]

The settlement house was more than a community of diverse viewpoints;

---

[24] *Twenty Years at Hull House*, p. 315 (italics added).
[25] Ginger, *Altgeld's America*, pp. 129, 138.
[26] *Twenty Years at Hull House*, pp. 447–48.

it was a community of nationalities and individuals as well. In the Nineteenth Ward, Russians and Poles, Jews and Hungarians, Italians and Irish, Czechs and Germans lived and worked together. And the Hull House little theater performed the Shakespearean histories and Greek tragedies for them all, while the immigrants themselves wrote and performed plays, gave dances, parties, and staged grand parades. "When men and women, boys and girls, work all day in sweatshops," Jane Addams observed realistically, "they want to have fun." Yet neither the residents nor the neighbors lost their identities in the mass. They were too strikingly individual to do so. Clarence Darrow often visited at Hull House and welcomed Governor John Peter Altgeld and Beatrice and Sydney Webb there. John Dewey served on the Board of Trustees and lectured at the Plato Club, both learning from and teaching the residents of Hull House. Julia Lathrop, a friend of Jane Addams from Rockford, combined law and social work and eventually directed the US Children's Bureau while furthering plans for psychiatric treatment of juvenile criminals. Dr. Alice Hamilton's studies of the "dangerous trades" helped to open the whole new field of industrial medicine. Florence Kelley, the most vociferous battler of them all, joined the movement for an eight-hour day and became chief factory-inspector in Illinois. Grace Abbott was superintendent of the League for the Protection of Immigrants, while her sister Edith joined Julia Lathrop and Sophonisba Breckinridge in founding the department of social research at the University of Chicago's School of Civics and Philanthropy.[27]

In brief, the residents of Hull House started out as amateur philanthropists; but within a decade they became scientific reformers, using the best available professional tools for the creation of an urban community. One of Jane Addams' first principles was her insistence upon expert knowledge and precise information as instruments of social progress. The settlement was not just a laboratory. Fellow feeling was more important to early social work than were analytical motives. Nevertheless, the acquisition of thorough information about urban society signalized the residents' break with the condescending and genteel charity work of the past. One of the most famous early collections of studies of urban population patterns, labor movements, and housing problems was *Hull House Maps and Papers, a presentation of nationalities and wages in a congested district in Chicago . . .* (1895). Not only did their investigations of urban problems greatly strengthen the settlement workers' arguments before city and state governing

---

[27] "Objective Value of Social Settlements," p. 28; Nicholas Kelley, "Early Days at Hull House," *Social Service Review,* XXVIII (Dec. 1954), 424–29; Ginger, *Altgeld's America,* pp. 129, 132–33, 135–36; Scott, "Introduction," *Democracy and Social Ethics,* pp. xxviii–xxx.

bodies, but they helped significantly to launch university studies in urban sociology.[28]

Thus the devoted expert played as crucial a role in Addams' Chicago programs as did the interpreter in Royce's insurance plans. And in many ways the social worker and expert served as interpreters between parties in conflict, even as in Royce's triadic scheme. It is not surprising, therefore, that during the international disintegration of 1914 Jane Addams, like Royce, would be mindful of the potentially helpful role of the neutral expert. She came to believe that the fundamental problems that gave rise to war could be understood better by scientists and doctors than by statesmen.

Within the settlement house itself many activities became bridges between groups isolated by class distinction, by generational experience, or by national background. Like Tolstoy, Jane Addams valued the arts for their inherent unifying qualities and for the emotional involvement they produced in the residents. She was delighted to discover that her neighbors cherished their native cultures and that they remembered the arts and crafts of their homelands.[29] Like Tolstoy, too, Miss Addams put to good use both in her writing and in her social reform work her own sensitivity to family misunderstandings. In a sense, perhaps because her own struggle for independence against the "family claim" had been so painful and so crucial to her development, she discovered the now familiar clash between immigrants and their Americanized children. Characteristically she discovered an activity reflecting the genuine cultural heritage of the European parents, to heal the alienation between them and their children. The women who used to spin and weave garments in the old country displayed their skills in the Hull House Labor Museum, teaching their children the origins of the garment industry in which those children worked. With a new pride in their parents, some of the children gained a sympathetic insight into all their parents had left behind in the peasant villages—acceptable social roles, useful work, respect.[30]

Class isolation presented more difficult problems. In Chicago, memories of strikes, police hunts, and the Haymarket bomb were bitter and enduring. The socialists did not entirely trust the Hull House ladies. Jane Addams, in fact, had indicated that although she fully sympathized with their goals and

---

[28] *Hull House Maps and Papers, a presentation of nationalities and wages in a congested district in Chicago. . . .* (New York, Crowell, 1895); Addams, "A Function of the Social Settlement," 1899, *Jane Addams: A Centennial Reader,* ed. Emily Cooper Johnson (New York, Macmillan, 1960), pp. 24–25; A. Elson, "First Principles of Jane Addams," *Social Service Review,* XXVIII (March 1954), 5–6.

[29] Addams, "Tolstoy's Theory of Life," *Chautauqua Assembly Herald,* XXVII (July 14, 1902), 2; Farrell, *Beloved Lady,* p. 65.

[30] *Twenty Years at Hull House,* pp. 235–37.

appreciated that they realized the true situation of the workers better than any, she found their interpretation of human nature too dogmatic and too rigid.[31] But these same middle-class ladies were useful interpreters to "respectable" Chicago of the immigrants' feelings and conditions. Both unionists and socialists recognized this fact. Often the residents arbitrated labor disputes when no one else could. They were profoundly sympathetic with the worker's drives for concrete gains and for the theme of solidarity, but they regarded the violence of the strikes as tragic. Still, Miss Addams rather idolized the labor movement. She criticized it only after its first struggling days, when it showed signs of adopting the business ethic which was so thoroughly corrupt in Chicago.[32]

Thus, long before Jane Addams knew she was a pacifist, her pacifism was growing, primarily out of her practice of reconciling conflicting interests without weak compromises. She would probe beneath appearances and look for some motive in her opponents that might be transformed into an instrument for reconciliation. This ceaseless activity of discovering bonds of unity in mutual needs formed the core of Addams' community.

THE PEACEFUL IMPULSES

In 1893 Chicago held a world's fair, the Columbian Exposition. A great white city, elaborate and overdecorated, arose in the midst of the filth and the smoke. A group of boys at Hull House joined the "Columbian Guards" and drilled in the gymnasium. One day Jane Addams visited them and told them that since the purpose of the Guards was to clean up the city, it would be more appropriate to parade with sewer spades than with rifles. The moment her back was turned they dropped the spades and took up the rifles once more. It was Miss Addams' first "Quixotic experiment" in pacifism,[33] inspired more by the needs of the city than by her readings in Tolstoy. She was reaching the conclusion that war and soldiering were futile, ineffective instruments for social change.

As she observed her neighbors in the Nineteenth Ward, especially during the Spanish-American War and the Philippines campaign that followed, she began to consider the sources of man's warlike tendencies. There was

[31] *Ibid.,* pp. 186–87.

[32] "The Significance of Organized Labor," *Machinists Monthly Journal,* X (Sept. 1898), 551–52; "The Present Crisis in Trade Union Morals," *North American Review,* CLXXIX (Aug. 1904), 179–93; "Trade Unions and Public Duty," *American Journal of Sociology,* IV (Jan. 1899), 448–62, offered her most extended discussion of the labor movement's faults and virtues. Most of the faults stemmed from the efforts of a "partial" movement to correct abuses that could only be cured by the whole public, represented by the government.

[33] *Twenty Years at Hull House,* pp. 444–45.

the basic human need to identify oneself with a group—a family, a class, or a nation. This primitive core of patriotism derived from the ancient tribe's need for self-protection against outsiders, and was infused with distrust and hatred. She felt that a civilized people could outgrow such aggressive patriotism, just as adolescents emerged from their gang loyalties into a fuller and more meaningful adult life.[34]

Men also showed a spirit of adventure, particularly when they were young. The same longing for excitement stirred the primitive hunter and warrior and the young men who revolted against factory labor by committing petty crimes and experimenting with drink and drugs.[35] The blandness of traditional peace dogma, not peace itself, repelled such adventurous spirits. Thus Jane Addams connected the activism of the 1890s with man's primitive needs. She concluded, however, that the martial spirit was not the only outlet for this desire for action and vitality.

In 1904, in two addresses to the thirteenth Universal Peace Congress in Boston, Miss Addams began to suggest two moral substitutes for war—the labor movement, with its ideal of human solidarity, and social reform, an experiment in trusting the people.[36] William James, at the same time, was developing his "moral equivalent of war." He commended Addams' suggestions, and called for the actual recruitment of youth in the tasks of building the industrial city. The heroism of physical labor, of socially useful work, might assume the same martial trappings as a soldier's life. James was convinced that warlike tendencies were deeply imbedded in human nature.[37] Addams believed that only the longing for adventure and group approval was. But the plans of both coalesced.

The concern for human nature, Jane Addams observed in 1907, had lately evinced an aggressive character; and yet it was international and might inspire an international loyalty. The campaign of German, British, French and American doctors against tuberculosis, for example, had

. . . its international congresses, its discoverers and veterans, also its decorations and rewards for bravery. Its discipline is severe; it requires self-control, endurance, self-sacrifice and constant watchfulness.[38]

[34] *Newer Ideals of Peace* (New York, Macmillan, 1907), pp. 12, 91, 210–11.

[35] *Ibid.*, p. 10; *The Spirit of Youth and the City Streets* (New York, Macmillan, 1912), pp. 51–52, 55, 59, 63, 70–71.

[36] In *Universal Peace Congress: Official Report of the Thirteenth Congress* (Boston, Oct. 3–8, 1904), see: "The Responsibilities and Duties of Women toward the Peace Movement," p. 121; and "The Interests of Labor in International Peace," pp. 145–46.

[37] William James, "The Moral Equivalent of War," 1910, *Essays on Faith and Morals,* ed. Ralph Barton Perry (Cleveland, Meridian Books, 1962), pp. 314, 323–26.

[38] *Newer Ideals of Peace,* p. 25.

This cause of service to the most primitive needs of humanity became Addams' equivalent of "loyalty to loyalty." It was universal, without restricting individual choice; peaceful, but far from passive. The choice also demonstrated why the Addams pacifism never assumed the isolationist character of Bryan's nor of some other anti-war progressives. She had conceived of social reform as international from the very beginning, and had found her own efforts for labor legislation supplemented by the efforts of reformers in other lands. For example, the Hull House residents quickly joined the International League for Labor Legislation because their own knowledge of the immigrants' past convinced them that the need was world-wide. Even campaigns in Illinois identified them with similar campaigns in Europe.[39]

The second substitute for war was a vital internationalism growing up among the immigrants themselves in the slums. In contrast to Butler's international mind with its cool rationality and patrician connotations, Addams' new internationalism was sentimental, empirical, and above all democratic. Both Root and Butler argued that the irrational masses drove the leaders to war. But Addams proclaimed the very opposite.

It is possible that we shall be saved from warfare by the "fighting rabble" itself . . . turned into kindly citizens of the world through the pressure of the cosmopolitan neighborhood. It is not that they are shouting for peace— on the contrary, if they shout at all, they will continue to shout for war— but they are really attaining cosmopolitan relations through daily experience.[40]

While there was nothing unusual in the belief in a natural progress toward internationalism—it was part of the motif of the turn-of-the century peace movement—the contention that the lowliest shall save was too thoroughly, Tolstoyan for most of the peace society leadership. The labor movement that did form a part of the American peace movement was an aristocracy among workers. But Jane Addams was speaking out for the unskilled, unassimilated masses whom neither the peace societies nor the American Federation of Labor embraced. What was it that caused her to adopt this course? Actually it was more than her own identification with the immigrants that impelled her in this direction. She had drawn for herself a blueprint of human nature that conformed in no way to the pattern of "fighting rabble."

Man, she believed, was a complex organism, changing psychologically throughout his life, molding his environment because he was a creature of dynamic instincts. Yet he was so "extraordinarily pliable" that the settlement workers could see no bounds to his moral capabilities "under ideal

[39] *Twenty Years at Hull House*, p. 230.
[40] *Newer Ideals of Peace*, p. 18.

civic and educational conditions."[41] The old concept of sinful human nature was refuted both by newer instinct theory and by the environmentalism which Jane Addams paradoxically combined.

It was not that she argued for the perfectibility of man. On the contrary, she often spoke of "our imperfect human nature" as being more real than eighteenth-century humanitarians thought. But in emphasizing man's pliability and vitality she was denying all rigid categorizations—the economic man of the classical economists, the political man of political scientists, even the proletariat and capitalist categories of socialist thought. Human beings were too complex and whole for these descriptions to be meaningful. To the Spencerians, she replied that man's economic success was no test of his fitness. There were virtues more important than the commercial ones. And if one individual or one family could barely endure the industrial environment, "larger social groupings," neighborhood organizations and unions, would find a greater fitness to cope with crushing burdens.[42] For man, above all, was an instinctively cooperative, gregarious, and creative creature. The few potent impulses (the "handful of incentives" Jane Addams called them) that really directed human conduct were life-giving and peaceful.

While recognizing the prevalent practice of immigrant families to send their children to work at an early age (as if the factories were no different from their old-country fields or the home workshop) and even importing young relatives to help support them, she insisted that such evidence of the corruption of poverty did not make child labor reforms, or any other reforms, in the phrase of William Graham Sumner "absurd efforts to make the world over."[43] On the contrary, conditions such as child labor only proved the need to free much deeper motives—the motives that inspired other poor people to sacrifice everything for family unity and the children's education, the motive that led old mothers to protect their criminal sons from further degradation. It was "family devotion," or as she frequently would term it, the "maternal anxieties," that kept the world sane and whole

---

[41] *Twenty Years at Hull House*, p. 452; Merle Curti, "Jane Addams on Human Nature," *Journal of the History of Ideas*, XXII (Oct. 1961), 252–53. Curti emphasizes Addams' extraordinary appreciation of unconscious motivations, as well as her knowledge of human growth.

[42] "In Memoriam, Henry Demarest Lloyd," Address, Chicago, Nov. 29, 1903, Jane Addams MSS typescript, p. 2; "Larger Social Groupings," *Charities*, XII (1904), 675; Donald Fleming, "Social Darwinism," *Paths of American Thought*, eds. Arthur M. Schlesinger, Jr. and Morton White (Boston, Houghton Mifflin, 1963), p. 140.

[43] Tims, *Jane Addams*, p. 11; Addams, "The Operation of the Illinois Child Labor Law," *Annals of the American Academy of Political and Social Science*, XXVII (March 1906), 328; Sumner, "The Absurd Effort to Make the World Over," 1894, in *The Conquest of the United States by Spain and Other Essays*, ed. Murray Polner (Chicago, Regnery, 1965), p. 55.

when every social force drove the family apart.[44] This instinct for nurturing the young, and the love of men and women which was so closely tied to it, became Miss Addams' basic explanation for the "revolt against war" in 1915.

Love and the nurturing instinct were not confined to the family. A sense of primitive pity served peasant peoples as much as a "thirst for righteousness" served young revolutionaries and as an impulse to justice served more sophisticated reformers.

In the depression winter of 1893, Jane Addams observed neighbors lending each other clothing and shoes, giving bread, advancing rent to families close to the breaking-point. The charity workers' concerns could hardly rival the kindnesses of the poor to one another.[45] True, other observers would have seen more terrible psychological effects of poverty. Jane Addams was hardly implying that poverty brought out the best in man. The fact remains that she observed that these primitive kindly instincts survived even in the worst environment, and faltered only when the young were overprotected, isolated from the "starvation struggle."

One reason for her insistence upon the basic nature of man's gregariousness was her observation that youth and primitive peoples exhibited more of it than the sophisticated. This Rousseauian romanticism she confirmed in describing the play instinct as the source of man's aesthetic and social drives. Children entered a world of imagination with their peers and could hardly be kept apart unless literally locked up. In adolescence the longing to assert individuality and vitality took the form of trying to prove oneself to others. The sexual instinct was, when not perverted by the glare of the dance halls, tender and romantic.[46]

All these longings for other beings and for love were fundamentally creative. Addams wrote of each of them not merely to prove man's sociability but also to attack the sordid ugliness of industrial life that thwarted man's normal nature. It was not the city she deplored (although she implied that rural life was more natural to man), but the crass materialism that corrupted the city and made it a place for profits instead of for civilization. For example, one of the social and creative instincts, man's "free labor quality" (similar to Veblen's "instinct of workmanship"), deteriorated in the tedium of mechanical and repetitious tasks in the factory. This quality found renewed expression in the immigrants' handicraft hobbies and artistic efforts. Having read John Ruskin and William Morris, Addams was

[44] *Twenty Years at Hull House,* p. 133; *Spirit of Youth,* pp. 31–33.

[45] *Twenty Years at Hull House,* p. 162; *Spirit of Youth,* pp. 142–43; *The Long Road of Woman's Memory* (New York, Macmillan, 1916), pp. 64–65; *Democracy and Social Ethics,* pp. 19–22.

[46] *Spirit of Youth,* pp. 15–16, 25–27, 29–30; "Work and Play as Factors in Education," *Chautauquan,* XLII (Nov. 1905), 253; *Newer Ideals of Peace,* pp. 171–72.

aware of the attack upon the factory system in the name of the artistic sense. She realized at the same time that the handicraft system would never come into its own again. But she called for a new socialized education that would put this instinct to use, bringing the workman a consciousness of the social usefulness of the product he shared in making. Like Veblen, she associated workmanship with peace, believing that even in the midst of war men longed to return to creative tasks.[47] Thus the "free labor quality" discussions were in reality a reformer's pleas. The same purpose pervaded her descriptions of the peasants who longed to cultivate the earth, a task which war thwarted. The instinct for labor was to become one of the bases of her association of peace and bread.

THE STATE—MILITARISTIC OR NURTURING

Jane Addams perceived the necessity of a radical transformation of the state into a community. She did not, however, call the change "community." Instead she spoke of *Democracy and Social Ethics* (1902), but what she had in mind was clearly a community transformation. Government would answer the primitive needs of the people. The population in turn would feel the government an extension of itself. In *Newer Ideals of Peace* (1907) Jane Addams insisted that peace itself was dependent upon such a transformation. Her 1902 collection of essays did not yet make the connection to international relations, but it did prepare the ground.

Democracy and Social Ethics was a rejection of the individualistic and commercial morality of the Gilded Age. Like the ministers of the social gospel, Jane Addams viewed the success ethic as a perversion of Christianity and a pervasive disorder throughout American society, infecting the relationship of parents to children, of teacher to students, of philanthropist to the recipient of aid. Her revolt against the gospel of wealth and economic individualism was not unique, but a part of the welfare-progressivism of the turn of the century. But it established certain themes for her later internationalism that were unique. First, there was the emphasis upon the importance of means for achieving any desirable goal. Failure in any reform effort, Miss Addams stressed, could come "quite as easily from ignoring the adequacy of one's method as from social or ignoble aims."[48] This

[47] "Child Labor Legislation—A Requisite for Industrial Efficiency," *Annals of the American Academy of Political and Social Science*, XXV (May 1905), 543–44; "Arts and Crafts and the Settlement," *Chautauqua Assembly Herald*, XXVII (July 9, 1902), 2–3; *Democracy and Social Ethics*, pp. 209–10, 219–20; "Labor as a Factor in the Newer Conception of International Relationships," Address, National Conference on Foreign Relations of the United States, Academy of Political Science at Long Beach, New York, May 31, 1917, Jane Addams MSS, pamphlet, p. 7.
[48] *Democracy and Social Ethics*, p. 6.

emphasis upon processes really defined her democratic faith. She could never look upon violent means as necessary for the achievement of any worth while goal, and rejected both the war to "make the world safe for democracy" and collective security on this ground. It was not the illogic of waging war for peace that troubled her, so much as a realistic appreciation that processes were always caught up in the results.

Second, her early ideas of leadership and individuality were to make themselves keenly felt during the war in her response to Wilson. She insisted, in 1902, that good could never be done to people, or even for them, but only with them. Certainly the Hull House experience confirmed this, but in *Democracy and Social Ethics* Jane Addams raised participatory democracy to a moral law. She recognized the importance and the effectiveness of organization, but questioned closely any organization that drew sharp lines between leaders and followers.

We have learned to say that the good must be extended to all of society before it can be held secure by one person or any one class; but we have not yet learned to add the statement that unless all men and classes contribute to the good, we cannot even be sure it is worth having.[49]

Thus, what Jane Addams perceived in the great strikes of her time was not simply class conflict, but a contest between an outdated individualistic ethic, which included even philanthropy, and a social ethic that was the essence of democracy. Her perceptive analysis of George Pullman as a well-meaning self-righteous Lear who would not let the labor movement, with its impulse toward brotherhood, grow up,[50] was the sharpest case in point. Her refutation of Spencer's contention that capitalistic individualism was peaceful began here—in her conception of capitalism's domineering character.

In *Newer Ideals of Peace* she developed the theme further, arguing that both the ideal and the reality of *laissez faire* were militaristic. The ideology of limited government, which so captured the American mind, had been a weapon against British royalism. *Laissez faire* still reflected martial origins. It was supported by static eighteenth-century ideas of human nature that had no relationship to real, imperfect human beings. The eighteenth-century idealists, Addams contended, had an aristocratic distaste for the

---

[49] *Ibid.*, p. 220.
[50] *Ibid.*, pp. 141–48; "A Modern Lear: Strike at Pullman," *Survey*, XXIX (Nov. 2, 1912), 131–37. In *Democracy and Social Ethics* Jane Addams did not mention Pullman directly, but her reference was clear. Instead she used the Lear image to portray generational conflict (see pp. 94–99). In "A Modern Lear," she gave not only a fuller account but her most sensitive portrayal of the ethical issues involved between Pullman and Debs's union. For another definition of democratic leadership, see "Exercises in Commemoration of the Birthday of Washington," Address, Chicago, Feb. 23, 1903, Union League Club of Chicago: *Memorial Bulletin* (1903), p. 6.

masses. The distinction they drew between government and freedom was but an extension of the English common-law distinction between ruler and ruled. No one who truly trusted the people to find their own solutions through government would have clung to the government-freedom dichotomy.[51]

Moreover, the eighteenth-century theories proved militaristic in their nineteenth-century applications. A government that took no account of the instincts for fellowship and mutual aid among the people naturally confined itself to military functions. Keeping order was, after all, a policeman's or a soldier's task. More than that, it encouraged a colonial relationship between employers and workers. The symbol of authority in the city was the privately-owned factory, just as the symbol of authority in medieval times was the fortified castle. From the factory, the employer looked down upon the workers as if they were a lower order of being. The workers responded with their group morality. Insofar as this morality bespoke the solidarity of all, it was an example of the social ethic. But it could become an exclusive and intolerant class-consciousness. The result of both attitudes was warfare. Terror was a proper instrument against class enemies, and violence characterized labor relations on both sides.[52] The negligent state became military, largely because it tolerated militaristic social relations.

Having thus denied Spencer's distinction between the peaceful capitalist order and the older militarism (Veblen was to do the same thing with very different methods), Jane Addams applied this interpretation to foreign affairs. Her life on Chicago's West Side had given her a unique insight into the connection between militarism at home and imperialism abroad. The ideal of enforcing order in the cities resembled the Anglo-Saxon idea of the rule of law over backward, colored peoples. Disparagement of the immigrant's culture enforced the racism of the expansionist mind.

Unrestricted commercialism is an excellent preparation for governmental aggression. The nation which is accustomed to condone the questionable business methods of a rich man because of his success will find no difficulty in obscuring the moral issues involved in any undertaking that is successful. It becomes easy to deny the moral basis of self-government and to substitute militarism.[53]

---

[51] *Newer Ideals of Peace,* pp. 33–36; see also p. 37: [We] "obstensibly threw off traditional governmental oppression only to encase ourselves in a theory of virtuous revolt against oppressive government, which in many instances has proved more binding than the actual oppression itself."

[52] *Ibid.,* pp. 149–50.

[53] *Ibid.,* p. 223. For a later interpretation of imperialism, emphasizing its relationships to dominant economic interests in the United States, see "Impressions of Mexico," *Women's International League for Peace and Freedom: U.S. Section,* pamphlet (April 1925), pp. 1–2, Society Publications, Hoover Institution.

Perhaps the barest explanation of imperialism that one could find among any of the American internationalists, this statement neglected Addams' own interpretation of primitive patriotism with its hatreds and fears. However, her tempering of economic interpretation with a socio-psychological one enabled her to make a unique analysis of the expansionist mind as one that equated morality with power, and thus denied the potential creativity both of the poor and of the inhabitants of the backward areas.

The real difficulty came when Miss Addams sought to prove that the welfare-state would be less inclined to imperialism and more toward peace. The evidence of Progressives who supported both welfare reforms and expansionism contradicted her contention. The Tory democracy of Disraeli was also the climax of Victorian imperialism; the Germany of Kaiser Wilhelm, with its elaborate provisions for social insurance had not abandoned militarism. Nevertheless, Jane Addams argued that a subtle psychological change was taking place in Germany and Britain that might eventually turn them away from the course of empire. In Britain the workers discovered that the cheap products of colonial labor debased their own standard of living. In Germany, the police who enforced health, insurance, and safety regulations were assuming the attitude of "helpers and protectors."[54] Orthodox Spencerians might doubt that either of these changes was taking place or that they would affect foreign policy. Addams' point was more pedagogical than logical. She was trying to make Americans feel guilty that more class-conscious, militaristic societies should have advanced social legislation while America with its egalitarian ideals had none.

She sought to indicate the connections between participatory democracy, welfare legislation, and peace. The welfare state, like the unions, would teach the immigrants the real rudiments of self-government in the only way these could be taught, by an appeal to the peoples' reliance on basic necessities.[55] The immigrants in turn would create a new patriotism, full of compassion for others, whether they were blood brothers or not. Therefore, if the government were to infuse this vital concern for human welfare into its activities, it would utilize this compassion. There was a kind of mystical "back to the people" fervor in all this, and perhaps Addams realized it; for she defended her conception of immigrant life. "We are often told that men under this pressure of life [poverty and the experience of being uprooted] become calloused and cynical, whereas anyone who lives with them knows that they are sentimental and compassionate."[56] It was a difficult argument

[54] *Newer Ideals of Peace*, pp. 89, 166.
[55] "Recent Immigration, A Field Neglected by the Scholar," Address, University of Chicago, Dec. 20, 1904, *University Record*, IX (Jan. 1905), 282.
[56] *Newer Ideals of Peace*, p. 18; "Recent Immigration," pp. 277–78, has specific suggestions for immigrant participation in the welfare government of the cities.

for those without settlement experience to counter; those with the experience tended to agree.

Even more determinative in the welfare state's peacefulness would be the women, who would connect their "maternal anxieties" with the new state's nurturing activities. Jane Addams did not claim that women were inherently more pacifist than men, but she did associate the maternal instinct with peacefulness. She was developing, along with Charlotte Gilmore Perkins and others, a new argument for female suffrage that had very little to do with the dogma of equal rights. The argument ran as follows: Woman's traditional functions had been the nurturing of the family, the protection of their health, the education of children. In an industrial city these tasks were literally stolen from her, for she no longer controlled the environment for raising children. The family health was undermined by industrial disease. She worked in a factory where she couldn't regulate her own hours as she could at home. She was being dehumanized. On the other hand, the government, as it began to concern itself with urban problems, was almost acting the mother role for its citizens. Clearly, the need of women for the vote, to regain their old functions, and the need of government for women, to gain their experience and motivation, were reciprocal.[57] In brief, women should have the vote not because they were like men, but because they were different.

By identifying women and the nurturing state in this manner, Jane Addams also connected exclusive male suffrage with an extinct militarism. Man's ability to bear arms was surely an irrelevant criterion for citizenship in an industrial democracy. She asserted finally that the military state and the nurturing state confronted each other as opposites in psychology, function, qualifications for citizenship, and the use of natural resources. The people could not have both butter and guns. They would have to choose. Thus she concluded her defense of the maternal state by interpreting Isaiah's prophecy of peace.

He contended that peace could be secured only as men abstained from the gains of oppression and responded to the cause of the poor; that swords would finally be beaten into plowshares and pruning hooks, not because men resolved to be peaceful, but because the metal of the earth would be turned to its proper use when the poor and their children should be abundantly fed. It was as if the ancient prophet foresaw that under an enlightened indus-

---

[57] *Newer Ideals of Peace*, pp. 184–88, 206–208; "Larger Aspects of the Woman's Movement," *Annals of the American Academy of Political and Social Science*, LVI (Nov. 1914), 4–6; "Votes for Women and Other Votes," *Survey Graphic*, XXVIII (June 1, 1912), 367–68. In 1912 Addams compared the need for women's votes by the welfare state to the need for middle-class votes by the commercial *laissez-faire* states of the early nineteenth century.

trialism peace would no longer be an absence of war, but the unfolding of world-wide processes making for the nurture of human life.[58]

It was not many years later that Jane Addams put the identification of peace and nurture to the test of action. The National Conference of Charities and Corrections (a national social workers' organization) elected her president in 1909, and in the same year began to draw up programs for "industrial minimums" that required immediate government action. In spite of their achievements in state welfare legislation, the social workers felt increasingly frustrated by serious discrepancies in state standards and by the attacks of the courts upon this legislation. They had reached the conclusion that some national party must take up their cause, but neither of the major parties was receptive. In the contest between the Taft Republicans and the insurgents, in the emerging Progressive Party the social workers saw a unique opportunity. Jane Addams, who had never held any public office higher than that of garbage inspector for the Nineteenth Ward, took the step of committing herself to Roosevelt's cause, because Roosevelt and his cohorts adopted the "minimums" into the platform.

She now began to realize the full difficulty and complexity of ethics in action even more than she had in the old campaign against ward boss Jimmy Powers. First, there was the lily-white complexion of the Progressives, which Jane Addams, a founder of the National Association for the Advancement of Colored People, found so repugnant that she almost bolted. Then she had to decide upon the platform that recommended the fortification of the Panama Canal and the building of two battleships a year.[59] Roosevelt and his fellow Progressives so identified the new nationalism with balance of power politics and expansionism that it was impossible to win a compromise on these points.

Addams defended the logic of her new pacifism. How could a government willing to expend hundreds of thousands of dollars to protect the Canal workers against malaria and yellow fever and the industrial workers against long hours, accidents, and the dangerous trades, threaten with destruction "the same sort of human stuff which it had so painstakingly" kept alive? A rift was evident between two streams within the Progressive

[58] *Newer Ideals of Peace*, pp. 237–38.
[59] *The Second Twenty Years at Hull House, September, 1909 to September, 1929, With a Record of Growing World Consciousness* (New York, Macmillan, 1930), pp. 20, 25–27, 31, 34–35, 37; "Charity and Social Justice," Address, National Conference of Charities and Corrections, St. Louis, May 19, 1910, *Survey*, XXIV (June 11, 1910), 441–43, indicates the change in the concept of philanthropy from aid to prevention, a change that required governmental action. Allen F. Davis, "The Social Workers and the Progressive Party, 1912–1916," *American Historical Review*, LXIX (April 1964), 673–74, 676–77, describes the development of the social workers' planks, and their difficulty with all-white Southern delegations.

Party—social welfare progressivism, which in part tended toward pacifism, and the new nationalism, which valued the state as a powerful
arbitrator between inevitably conflicting interests at home and abroad.

Jane Addams was never particularly inspired by Herbert Croly's
thought, although she advocated a strong state as a popular instrument. The
realism of Roosevelt with its emphasis upon the continual international
struggle for power was not her variety of realism with its focus upon the
human results of such struggles and the waste of human resources in
military preparations. Nevertheless, after considerable soul-searching Addams decided that the chance to enact significant welfare legislation should
not be ignored. Supporting the Progressives and campaigning in their
behalf, she reasoned that any group so committed to saving lives in industry
(where more were lost than on the battlefields) was "surely on the road to
peace."[60] Many years later she granted that perhaps this was a rationalization and she experienced a vague sense of guilt, even though she was still
passionately committed to the reforms the Progressives had advocated.
What she would not observe, perhaps because it was too self-complimen-
tary, was that this stand above all indicated the realistic nature of her
pacifism. The cause she cared about was the cause of the poor. Only in 1914
did this cause and the changing reality propel her into an extreme course.

"THE REVOLT AGAINST WAR"

All through the prewar years Jane Addams clung to her faith in the
progress of peace through the progress of the nurturing state. The 1912
defeat was not the end of progressivism, although after 1914 she parted
company with the Progressive Party. That summer, when the confrontation between nurture and militarism emerged into the open, she experienced
a sense of desolation that was almost as suicidal as the great war itself. The
whole world was changing, and her position would change with it, not
because she became less the pacifist, but because she began to feel the full
impact of an idea that formed the bedrock of her revolt against war:
namely, that the real evil of war was not the destruction of property or life
but the destruction of the human community. The nobility and sacrifice of
war-time patriotism were purchased at a frightful cost, the creation of a
dogmatic nationalism which consumed truth, fellowship, and the hope for

---

[60] *Second Twenty Years*, p. 37; William E. Leuchtenberg, "Progressivism and
Imperialism: The Progressive Movement and American Foreign Policy, 1898–1916,"
Mississippi Valley Historical Review, XXIX (Dec. 1952), 483–86, 492, 497–98, 500,
shows how compatible the ideas of the new nationalism were with imperialism. His
description of the majority of Progressives contrasts with Davis' description of the
social worker Progressives.

the future of the coming generation. No other communalist, not even Royce, saw the conflict between war and community in such stark terms. Veblen and Dewey, and most Wilsonian progressives, hoped to use the opportunity of the war to achieve long-sought goals of social control. But Jane Addams testified that the social reformer would have to combat the effects of the world war for years before the psychological foundation for social progress was re-established.

Most of her friends were to disagree with her and desert her in 1917, but in 1914 there was a glimmering of a social workers' revolt against war. In September, Lillian Wald of the Henry Street Settlement, Paul Kellogg, editor of the social worker's magazine, *Survey,* and veteran of the National Conference of Charities and Corrections, joined Miss Addams in calling upon other social workers to form a Union Against Militarism. Their anti-war protest reflected professional interests very directly. War eroded the generous impulses upon which the willingness to do justice depended. It shattered the immigrant community, turning neighbor against neighbor. It reduced the state to its primitive defensive functions, forcing an abandonment of those normal activities which governments had lately begun. War reversed democracy by unifying a population on the basis of coercion, instead of winning "inner consent." It "curbed the intelligence" by brutalizing men and demanding conformity.[61]

The social workers' revolt was a small and relatively weak one, but Jane Addams and Lillian Wald soon expanded it by making it a women's revolt. Never was American feminism more militant than in its pacifist crusade. The fighting spirit of the British suffragettes infused the American movement with an aggressive tone. Mrs. Emmeline Pethick-Lawrence, a veteran of the most violent phase of the British women's campaigns, came to Chicago. She was now, in 1914, an ardent pacifist. She pleaded with the women to follow their instincts and to demand an end to the war through American mediation. She brought with her the emerging program of the British Liberal-Labour organization, the Union of Democratic Control. In the fall of 1914 Mme. Rosika Schwimmer of Hungary, a journalist and founder of the International Suffrage Alliance, entered the fray. Both women were old comrades of Jane Addams, and their presence reminded her that she had considered suffrage an internationalist movement. Feminism was "spontaneous and universal," uniting the secluded Oriental

---

[61] Jane Addams, *Peace and Bread in Time of War,* reprinted with a 1945 introduction by John Dewey (Boston, G. K. Hall, 1960), pp. 3–4, 6; Jane Addams, Paul U. Kellogg, Lillian Wald, "Towards a Peace that Shall Last," *Towards An Enduring Peace: A Symposium of Peace Proposals and Programs 1914–1916* (New York, American Association for International Conciliation, 1916), pp. 233–37; Jane Addams, "Women and Internationalism," *Women at the Hague: The International Congress of Women and Its Results* (New York, Macmillan, 1915), p. 137.

women with the Western activists, the hard-working factory laborer and the privileged lady.[62]

As the women of Chicago and New York gathered to receive Mme. Schwimmer and Mrs. Pethick-Lawrence, Jane Addams conceived of a plan to unite the peace societies and the suffragettes. She asked Lillian Wald to contact New York pacifists and feminists to ask them to lend their support to an Emergency Peace Committee that would call for immediate American mediation. "It does seem a pity," she observed, "not to utilize all this enthusiasm."[63] The Chicago Emergency Peace Committee soon pondered the idea of a nation-wide organization. Carrie Chapman Catt, President of the International Suffrage Alliance, agreed to invite women's groups all over the country to attend a national peace meeting. The leading pacifists, such as Anna Garland Spencer and Lucia Ames Mead, quickly accepted and began to organize the conference. Every type of organization, from women's trade unions to associations of teachers to the Daughters of the American Revolution accepted the invitation, although some patriotic associations dropped out as soon as the platform emerged. This emergency meeting organized the Woman's Peace Party. Jane Addams became its president. During the war the party affiliated with British, German, Dutch, Belgian, Hungarian, and French peace groups, emerging in 1919 as the Woman's International League for Peace and Freedom. Their cause became Jane Addams' own as completely as Hull House had been in the early days.[64]

The ideas of feminine pacifism fused with the ideals of the nurturing state and of the internationalism of immigrants to form the whole *Weltanschauung* of Jane Addams' community. The association of maternal instinct with Tolstoyan "bread labor" gave Jane Addams' internationalism both its mystical and its empirical dimensions.

---

[62] Marie Louise Degen, *History of the Woman's Peace Party* (Baltimore, Johns Hopkins Press, 1939), pp. 28–29, 31–33; Jane Addams, "Larger Aspects of the Woman's Movement," *Annals of the American Academy of Political and Social Science*, LVI (Nov. 1914), 8. The Union of Democratic Control was formed in the fall of 1914 by C. P. Trevelyan, Ramsay McDonald, Norman Angell, and other leaders of the Liberal and Labour Parties. Its platform made parliamentary control of foreign policy, renunciation of secret alliances, nationalization of the arms industries preceding disarmament prerequisites for a democratic league of nations. See Henry R. Winkler, *The League of Nations Movement in Great Britain, 1914–1919* (New Brunswick, Rutgers Univ. Press, 1952), pp. 23–26.

[63] Jane Addams to Lillian Wald, Dec. 8, 1914, Papers of Lillian Wald, New York Public Library.

[64] The self-chosen epitaph on Jane Addams' tombstone reads, "Jane Addams of Hull House and the Woman's International League for Peace and Freedom"; Tims, *Jane Addams*, p. 15; Degan, *Woman's Peace Party*, pp. 35–38; Jane Addams and Carrie Chapman Catt's invitation to the women's organizations, Dec. 28, 1914, is in Jane Addams' Correspondence, Swarthmore College Peace Collection.

The Woman's Peace Party was a minority of a minority from the very beginning. In spite of their rejection of the Victorian sheltered life,[65] most American women related feminism to the rather barren ideals of career-women and to the sacrifice of family security. But the pacifists were even a minority of the feminist minority, and Jane Addams recognized this in declaring that most women allowed their political views to be molded by men.[66] Hers was a skillful and pointed argument, therefore, quite in keeping with her arguments for women's votes. It pictured the pacifist as not only a freer woman than her traditionally patriotic sister, but also as a more feminine one. Femininity did not mean frills and passivity and dependency, but a love-giving, life-giving assertion. In short, it was the maternal instinct that defined a woman, and this instinct created a unique obligation, for ". . . quite as an artist in an artillery corps commanded to fire on the *duomo* at Florence would be deterred by a compunction unknown to the man who had never given himself to creating beauty and did not know the intimate cost of it, so women, who have brought men into the world and nurtured them until they reach the age for fighting, must experience a peculiar revulsion when they see them destroyed, irrespective of the country in which these men may have been born."[67]

Jane Addams and the others traveled throughout the country asking the women to heed this instinct for life and utilize it. Instinct, she believed, could be a force for change. It was not religious conversion but true femininity in revolt that had, after thousands of years, brought to an end the ancient practice of human sacrifice to the gods, although the high priests were still declaring sacrifice essential to the survival of the tribe.[68] The ironic association of war patriotism and ancient superstition remained in the minds of her listeners, and Jane Addams, especially after 1917, spent an increasing proportion of her speeches in proving that the pacifists were not unpatriotic, but rather strongly insistent that patriotism retain its civilized meaning of nurturing all citizens and responding to economic changes through "rational and peaceful means."[69]

Nevertheless, it was quite clear from the beginning that the cause would mean considerable sacrifice for the women in belligerent countries who would be torn between their pacifism and the desire to be at one with their

[65] John Higham, "The Reorientation of American Culture in the 1890's," *Origins of Modern Consciousness,* ed. John Weiss (Detroit, Wayne State Univ. Press, 1965), p. 31.

[66] *Second Twenty Years,* pp. 109–10.

[67] "Women and Internationalism," p. 128.

[68] *Second Twenty Years,* p. 120.

[69] "Patriotism and Pacifism in Wartime," Address, Chicago, May 15, 1917, Evanston, Ill., June 10, 1917, Jane Addams MSS, separate pamphlet, p. 2; Linn, *Jane Addams,* 327–33, 349–56, 436, documents Jane Addams' isolation from former friends, and her defenses of her position.

countrymen.[70] The feminine revolt was useful, however, in two respects. It could expose other "revolts against war," and it might encourage practical changes in national policy. Jane Addams was sure there were other, more silent, rebellions against the war. In the summer of 1915, while she presented the Woman's Peace Party program for neutral mediation to the officials of belligerent and neutral nations, she discovered these revolts and used them as anti-war arguments.

During the war there were two currents in European thought flowing in opposite directions. The surface current was wartime nationalism, heroic, loyal, and full of passionate hatreds. Each additional day of war intensified this current, which was cutting disastrous channels into the foundations of democratic fellowship. Jane Addams, recalling her father's admiration of Mazzini, asserted that nationalism had once provided a unifying ideal. After the turn of the century, however, and especially after 1914, it became divisive and dogmatic. Like the religious fervor of the Spanish Inquisitors, the nationalism of modern Europe lived on its intolerance and persecutions. In 1919 she would interpret the red scare as but another manifestation of this religious nationalism, which feared heresy above all else.[71]

But beneath the obvious national hatreds flowed a deeper current seeking the channels of fellowship and a hopeful future. Civil leaders on both sides confided to Jane Adams their fears that the psychology of war would fix militarism and authoritarianism upon Europe for years to come. So prevalent was this apprehension that Miss Addams puzzled over the fact that neither the Allies nor the Central Powers understood the actual thinking of their supposed enemies. The waters of mutual interest were still and deep while violence frothed on the surface. She attributed this situation largely to a press which deliberately ignored such stirrings while adding color and emphasis to atrocities.[72]

The soldiers also revolted against war, although they fought well. Jane Addams learned that some refused to shoot, that many could be led into the brutal bayonet charges only after their scruples had been dulled by absinthe or brandy. It was not cowardice that gave rise to these scruples, she insisted, after Richard Harding Davis accused her of demeaning brave men —not cowardice but fellowship. The young soldiers had been outgrowing the rigid Victorian nationalism of their fathers when the old men's war

[70] Addams, *Long Road of Woman's Memory,* 116 ff.; "Women and Internationalism," pp. 124–25.

[71] "Americanization," *American Sociological Society: Papers and Proceedings,* XIV (Dec. 29–31, 1919), 206–209, 211–12; *Second Twenty Years,* pp. 153–55.

[72] In *Women at the Hague,* see: "The Revolt Against War," pp. 75–77; and "Factors in Continuing the War," pp. 88–89; in the *Independent,* see: "Peace and the Press," LXXXIV (Oct. 11, 1915), 55–56; and "The Food of War," LXXXIV (Dec. 13, 1915), 430–31.

thrust them back into it. (It is significant in view of her own experience that she interpreted the war itself as a conflict of generations more than as a conflict of nationalities.) The German lieutenant who told her that he realized there were good men on all sides, the French and British soldiers who confided they found it impossible to kill men who may have been fellow-students or business associates before the war, confirmed Jane Addams' idea that the new internationalism was as much a possession of youth as of the urban immigrants. The war was constricting it, just as the city constricted the family instincts. The wounded soldiers in the ambulances and field hospitals characteristically turned to women for support: "Cannot the women do something about this war? Are you kind to us only when we are wounded?"[73]

It was a sentimental view of women and war—the vision of Florence Nightingale and the mothers who did not raise their boys to be soldiers—but the pacifists drew enough inspiration from it to draw up a very concrete program. The January 1915 meeting of the Woman's Peace Party and the International Congress of Women at The Hague in April 1915 drew very heavily upon the British Union of Democratic Control platform. They advocated parliamentary control over the formulation of foreign policy, including, of course, feminine participation in parliaments and in executive positions. Self-determination meant the recognition of the rights of small nations and of primitive peoples at the peace conference, not great-power domination. They advocated an international organization with a legislature, a judiciary, and an international police force, viewing the latter as a replacement for national armies rather than as an instrument for enforcing peace.

The entire program, which emerged at the same time as the League to Enforce Peace, offered a sharp contrast to that organization. Where the League leaders troubled over questions of structure and sovereignty, the Woman's Peace Party neglected these issues entirely. The League to Enforce Peace was concerned with the nature of sanctions; the pacifists barely mentioned moral and economic sanctions to encourage arbitration. The women opposed the use of military force, and failed to examine the arbitral process. There was no fine distinction between juridical and non-juridical disputes in the Woman's Peace Party platform. The women did

---

[73] "Revolt Against War," pp. 59–69, 73–75. Jane Addams' address at Carnegie Hall, New York, July 9, 1915, on the "revolt" raised a storm of protest centering on her charge that stimulants were used before bayonet charges. See New York *Times*, July 13, 1915, p. 10; July 15, 1915, p. 3; July 16, 1915, p. 8; July 24, 1915, p. 4. She observed: "It brought me an enormous number of letters, most of them abusive, but a minimum number from soldiers who had actually been through bayonet charges, and these letters, I am happy to say, were always sympathetic and corroborative" (see *Second Twenty Years*, pp. 131–33; quotation from p. 133).

not consider the machinery of peaceful settlement as important as the prevention of the economic conflicts that led to war. Most of their program was substantive rather than methodological. The Hague Congress called for an end to all governmental protection of investors conducting business in foreign lands, for the opening of the Panama Canal and the Suez Canal and other international waterways to all traffic in peace and war, for nationalization of the arms industries preceding universal disarmament, and above all for neutral mediation.[74]

The idea of a continuous conference of neutrals mediating between the belligerents even before an armistice was the keystone of the Peace Party platform. Julia Grace Wales, a young English teacher at the University of Wisconsin, had formulated the plan. The Wisconsin legislature and Senator Robert M. La Follette endorsed it. The Wisconsin plan assumed that an open challenge to the belligerents, offered by men without diplomatic status or functions, would awaken latent peace sentiment in Europe. It would provide a means for mediation when the belligerents decided they wanted it. The continuous conference would draw up a peace settlement without consulting the two sides, would receive their replies and suggestions, would revise the proposals, and would continue this process until a settlement had been reached.[75]

Jane Addams, however, interpreted the Wisconsin plan somewhat differently. Emphasizing the apolitical character of the mediators, she declared that if the conference were composed of scientific experts, labor representatives, artists, and humanitarians all of whom shared an "international viewpoint" it would not attempt to split the difference between the belligerents, but instead would probe beneath nationalistic division to discover the real causes of conflict. It would reveal the frustrations of economic and moral needs, the resistance to change, the static and impractical character of international relations that had characterized the prewar period. The mediators might do something about these. For example, they might consider

---

[74] "Program for a Constructive Peace of the Woman's Peace Party," Jan. 10, 1915, in *The Overthrow of the War System*, ed. Lucia Ames Mead (Boston, Forum Publications, 1915), pp. 125–28; "Resolutions of the International Congress of Women at the Hague," May 1, 1915, *Women at the Hague*, pp. 150–59. Jane Addams later acknowledged the debt of the Woman's Peace Party to the Union of Democratic Control, and called attention to resemblances between the Hague program and the Fourteen Points, without, however, claiming any influence over Wilson. See "Public Address," May 12, 1919, *Bericht des Internationalen Frauenkongress* (Zurich, May 12–17, 1919), p. 196.

[75] Julia Grace Wales, "Continuous Mediation Without Armistice," Pamphlet (Chicago, 1915), pp. 1–13, Woman's Peace Party Pamphlet, Society Publications, Hoover Institution; Degen, *Woman's Peace Party*, pp. 46–47.

. . . the necessity of feeding those people in the southeast portion of Europe who are pitifully underfed when there is a shortage of crops, in relation to the possession of warm-water harbors which would enable Russia to send them her great stores of wheat. Such harbors would be considered . . . not from a point of view of the claims of Russia nor the counter claims of some other nation, but from the point of view of the needs of Europe.[76]

The mediators would act for the international community just as Royce's insurance board and Veblen's technical administrators were to act. There was no evidence, however, that the belligerents would accept such an interpretation of the mediator's role, or, for that matter, the idea of mediation at all. In April 1915, at the joint invitation of the British, German, and Dutch suffragettes, women representing over fifteen countries met at the Hague. After electing Jane Addams chairman of the Congress, they adopted the platform and instructed Jane Addams, Alice Hamilton, Dutch leader Aletta Jacobs, and others to present the Wisconsin plan to neutral and belligerent leaders. These representatives soon discovered the two sides of public opinion in the belligerent countries, calling them the "democratic" and "imperialist" forces. Historian Arno Mayer has called them the "parties of movement" and the "parties of order."[77] They learned that the neutrals at least would support the plan on condition that President Wilson endorsed it.

In 1915 Wilson did not yet appreciate, as he would two years later, the significance (one might say the revolutionary significance) of the "parties of movement." Colonel Edward House had quietly explored with the British, French, and German governments the possibilities for American mediation, and had concluded that Addams naively misinterpreted the views of Lord Grey and others.[78] Moreover, he had been at work during the winter of 1915, while Addams' tour took place the following spring and summer, right after the sinking of the *Lusitania*. The positions of both sides had hardened. With Secretary of State Lansing opposing neutral mediation, and House ridiculing the innocent lady pacifists, Wilson declined

[76] "Women and Internationalism," pp. 132–33. Jane Addams repeatedly expressed her faith in the internationalism of scientists, labor unionists, women, and social workers, believing that a basic concern for the advancement of knowledge or of human welfare was the essence of this kind internationalism. See *Long Road of Woman's Memory*, p. 121; *Newer Ideals of Peace*, pp. 113–15; "Public Address," *Bericht des Frauenkongress*, p. 197; "Women's Special Training for Peacemaking," *Proceedings of the Second National Peace Congress* (Chicago, May 2–5, 1909), pp. 252–54; "International Cooperation for Social Welfare," *National Conference of Social Work: Proceedings* (1924), pp. 107–13.

[77] *Wilson vs. Lenin: Political Origins of the New Diplomacy, 1917–1918* (Cleveland, Meridian Books, 1964), pp. vii, 4–8; Emily G. Balch, "The Time for Making Peace," *Women at the Hague*, pp. 113–14.

[78] Charles Seymour, *The Intimate Papers of Colonel House*, 4 vols. (Boston, Houghton Mifflin, 1926–28), II, 22.

to risk his future usefulness by supporting an official neutral conference.[79]
The International Woman's Committee turned to support of an unofficial
neutral conference.

Just at this juncture the irrepressible Madame Schwimmer decided that
the whole plan needed funds, color, and publicity. She appealed to Henry
Ford for help. Ford lost no time in stepping front and center, and promptly
informed the press that he not only would finance a neutral conference at
Stockholm, but that he would attend himself and would hire a ship to bring
the delegates to the meeting. He would have the "boys out of the trenches
by Christmas." Jane Addams realized that Ford's showmanship was dis-
couraging the most serious participants, but she decided to go to the
conference without committing either the Woman's Peace Party or the
International Committee. But just before the *Oscar II* sailed forth on a
wave of press ridicule, she experienced a serious recurrence of an old
kidney and bladder disturbance that sent her to the hospital. Emily Green
Balch took her place.[80]

PEACE AND BREAD

American entry into the war killed the last prospects for neutral mediation. Henry Ford had left the neutral conference expedition in Norway.
Madame Schwimmer also had resigned. But the Stockholm conference had
assembled. It addressed appeals to neutral and belligerent governments
alike, appeals embodying much of the Woman's Peace Party program. In
February 1917, after the United States broke diplomatic relations with
Germany, Ford withdrew his financial support and the conference ended a
short time later.[81]

More than the conference died in 1917. The Woman's Peace Party had
placed great faith in Woodrow Wilson. Disagreeing with his Caribbean
diplomacy, they nevertheless were convinced that he was a rational, peace-

[79] Degen, *Woman's Peace Party*, pp. 115–25; Ray Stannard Baker, *Woodrow
Wilson: Life and Letters*, 8 vols. (Garden City, N.Y., Doubleday, 1927–39), VI,
122–24.

[80] Degen, *Woman's Peace Party*, pp. 128–48; Louise Bowen to Lillian Wald, Dec. 1,
1915, Wald Papers; Chicago Woman's Peace Party to Aletta Jacobs, Dec. 13, 24, 1915,
Woman's Peace Party Correspondence, Addams' folder, Swarthmore College Peace
Collection; Addams to David Starr Jordan, Dec. 28, 1915, David Starr Jordan Peace
Collection, Hoover Institution.

[81] *Peace and Bread*, pp. 41–46; Neutral Conference for Continuous Mediation:
"Appeal to the Governments, Parliaments and Peoples of the Warring Nations,"
Easter 1916, *Towards an Enduring Peace*, pp. 243–46. The Stockholm program
resembled that of the International Congress of Women at the Hague with a much
greater emphasis, however, upon the particulars of self-determination. It called for the
restoration of Belgium and Alsace-Lorraine; for boundary adjustments between
Austria and Italy; and for autonomy for Armenia and other Turkish possessions.

loving man. Now Addams and the others felt a sense of betrayal. Was it too much for one man to formulate ideals and then live them, Addams asked. Had Wilson overvalued his own leadership in the future peace conference, as he once had at Princeton? The first note of real bitterness now crept into Addams' writings, measuring the depth of her disillusionment. It was as if Wilson's actions had awakened memories of George Pullman. "What was this curious break between speech and deed," she asked, "how could he expect to know the doctrine [of democracy] if he refused to do the will?"[82] But Wilson had no obligation to the pacifists, while many leaders of social reform did. Most of them abandoned the cause in 1917. The loss of friends, the public ridicule and misunderstanding, and the terrible treatment of conscientious objectors almost drove Jane Addams to complete despair. She never wrote more personally or perceptively than of the psychological effects of war upon the pacifists.

I experienced a bald sense of social opprobrium and wide-spread misunderstanding which brought me very near to self pity, perhaps the lowest pit into which human nature can sink. Indeed the pacifist in war time, with his precious cause in the keeping of those who control the sources of publicity and consider it a patriotic duty to make all types of peace propaganda obnoxious, constantly faces two dangers. Strangely enough he finds it possible to travel from the mire of self-pity straight to the barren hills of self-righteousness and to hate himself equally in both places.[83]

Fairly soon, Jane Addams found that her loyalty to her "vision of the truth" was not enough. If she hoped to make her stand practical, she would have to act. It is significant that the two most critical decisions in her life, the establishment of Hull House and her adherence to the cause of pacifism during the war, both stemmed from and answered "subjective" as well as "objective" needs. Both had religious overtones. Jane Addams returned to the religious symbol of bread for comfort, and found her new task in working for the Food Administration. She pleaded with American women to conserve food so that others might live. Although she recognized that Hoover's Food Administration was a wartime agency, she considered the implications of inter-Allied control of a common food supply enormous. For the first time an international agency had regulated commercial competition, not in response to an economic theory, but in response to primitive actual needs. If the League of Nations took up this work after the war, it

---

[82] *Peace and Bread*, p. 65. See also pp. 56–60 and 62 for Addams' mixed reactions to Wilson's foreign policies. Lillian Wald to Wilson, Jan. 24, 1917, Wald Papers, describes the pacifists' enthusiastic reaction to Wilson's "peace without victory" speech. The American Union Against Militarism was particularly active during the armed neutrality period, having several specific suggestions to prevent America from going to war. See Wald to Wilson, February 8, 1917, March 16, 1917, *Wald Papers*.

[83] *Peace and Bread*, p. 139.

would have all the positive incentive it needed to begin to create an international ethic and an international community.[84]

All her life Jane Addams had searched for union of the practical and the religious, for salvation and the new woman's role, for the humanitarian spirit and the action that should make the difference in the way men actually lived. This was the double meaning that "peace and bread" had for her. The wheat loaf symbolized man's primitive affections and mutual aid, the maternal impulse to nurture the young, the Russian peasant's longing to work the land in peace so that he and his family would not face starvation.[85] Bread now came to mean as well the small, practical beginnings of an international organization, not the grand creation as loudly heralded as Ford's peace ship, but quiet, effective work—the ending of the blockade as a beginning.

In 1919 the Second International Congress of Women, held in Zurich, telegraphed this appeal to the Versailles Conference, asking President Wilson to use his influence to keep the Inter-Allied Commissions in operation as relief agencies.[86] Then the League might extend credits for postwar reconstruction to all needy nations, whether former enemies or not. The international agencies should control strategic waterways, protecting the food trade against nationalistic interference. There should be a specific agency to guard the welfare of migratory laborers who had lost the protection both of their native land and of the nations where they worked. Finally, the mandates commission should act as a probate court protecting the interests of the mandated territories and not of the guardians.[87]

[84] "The World's Food and World Politics," *National Conference of Social Work* Pamphlet, no. 128 (1918), 2–5; "Statement of the Executive Board of the National Woman's Peace Party," Oct. 27, 1917, Pamphlet, p. 3, Woman's Peace Party, Society Publications, Hoover Institution. The Woman's Peace Party hoped that inter-Allied commissions, working on non-military problems, would become the "nucleus of a permanent international parliament." The contrast with J. B. Clark's idea of an Entente nucleus, united by the threat from outside, could not have been stronger.

[85] *Peace and Bread*, pp. 82, 93–94; "Tolstoy and the Russian Soldiers," *New Republic*, XII (Sept. 29, 1917), 240–42.

[86] This resolution of Mrs. Pethick-Lawrence was adopted unanimously. See *Bericht des Frauenkongress*, p. 195; *Peace and Bread*, pp. 160–61.

[87] *Peace and Bread*, pp. 95–96; "Labor as a Factor in International Relations," p. 5; "Women, War and Suffrage," *Survey*, XXXV (Nov. 6, 1915), 148–49; "The Potential Advantages of the Mandate System," *Annals of the American Academy of Political and Social Sciences*, XCVI (July 1921), 71–73; "Feed the World and Save the League," *New Republic*, XXIV (Nov. 24, 1920), 326. Addams and Alice Hamilton considered the food shortage so critical that they could not wait for governmental or League action, but personally distributed Quaker relief supplies in Germany, Austria, and Poland. Their report on the living conditions in postwar Europe and on the psychological aftermath of war stimulated other relief movements. See "Official Report of Jane Addams and Dr. Alice Hamilton to the American Society of Friends Service Committee, Philadelphia," *Nebraska Branch American Relief Fund for Central Europe* (1919), Pamphlet, 14 pp., Woman's Peace Party, Society Publications. Addams

This peculiar linking of the mystical and the practical had begun when Jane Addams explored the anthropological interpretations of the primitive adoration of such figures as the "corn mother." She believed that savage peoples had conceived of nurture and war as opposing forces. Their earliest training was not in fighting but in feeding the young. "Anthropologists insist that war has not been in the world for more than 20,000 years. It is in fact so recent that existing remnants of primitive people do not understand it." Whether or not the anthropology of her day actually confirmed such a generalization is questionable, but the uses that Jane Addams made of it are clear. "Could not the earlier instinct and training in connection with food be aroused and would it not quench the later tendency to war?"[88]

This, indeed, was a key question. Could such functionalism as Jane Addams advocated ever neutralize the conflicting interests of national states and dampen their ardor for plunging into war? In the 1940s most realists thought not. Jane Addams' latter-day critics have pointed out that her stress upon human solidarity neglected the ethnocentric character of human groupings. Critics of functionalism and communalism have maintained that getting the nations to work on programs such as health, food distribution, the fight against illiteracy, where they are likely to agree, does nothing to mitigate their actual struggles for power.[89] John Dewey, on the other hand, contrasted Jane Addams' realism with the mechanistic and force-ridden ideas of collective security and legal-political structures. He maintained that it was eminently more practical to seek to undercut nationalistic motives by appealing to actual needs than to rely upon force, whether national or international.[90] Paradoxically, some of the realists who criticized the world federalists in the 1940s used arguments for the slow growth of internation-

---

appealed to Congress for a thirty-three million dollar loan to supplement the work of the League and Hoover's American Relief Committee to ease the "hunger oedema" (see U.S. Congress, Senate, Committee on Banking and Currency, *Rehabilitation and Provisions for European Countries: The Need of Assistance in Exporting Our Goods and Rendering Financial Aid Generally in Rehabilitating European Countries: Addams' Statement*, Jan. 21, 1921, 66th Cong., third sess. (Washington, 1921), pp. 3–8.

[88] *Peace and Bread*, pp. 75–76, 78–80. For her ideas of the comparative lateness of war Addams was evidently relying upon Fraser's *The Golden Bough* and possibly upon Kropotkin's *Mutual Aid*. The "peacefulness" of primitive man was one of the communalists' unproven assumptions. Cf. Franz Boas, *Anthropology and Modern Life* (New York, Norton, 1928), pp. 67–68, 93–95, 97–98, for contrary anthropological conclusions.

[89] T. V. Smith, *et al.*, "Discussion of the Theory of International Relations based upon the Introduction by John Dewey to a Re-Issue of Jane Addams' *Peace and Bread in Time of War*," *Journal of Philosophy*, XLIII (Aug. 30, 1945), 478–79, 481; Frederick L. Schuman, *The Commonwealth of Man: An Inquiry into Power Politics and World Government* (New York, Knopf, 1952), pp. 335–43.

[90] John Dewey, "Democratic vs. Coercive International Organization," 1945, Introduction, *Peace and Bread*, p. xviii.

alism through small practical efforts[91] which resembled the basic tenet of Jane Addams' radicalism.

In the last analysis, Jane Addams' thought was indeed radical. So completely did she identify with all peoples that she refused to ally with any movement that was exclusively of one class or of one nationality. Her ideal remained the peaceful, classless community. And yet her radicalism, as active as it was, never became revolutionary. She neither planned nor advocated the violent destruction of one system of government in order to achieve something more humane. The processes of change were ever as important to her as the results. She unswervingly refused to sacrifice for a cause the precious lives of those for whom she fought. Her romantic discovery of the immigrants of Chicago sustained her and remained her raison d'etre throughout her life. A deep interest in human motives and the faith in human resiliency overcame even the disillusion of war. For in the closing years of her career she still hoped that people would work to create the international community because they would understand their mutual needs. For this most cosmopolitan of women the only eternal truths were those that might be called household truths.

[91] Carl Becker, *How New Will the Better World Be* (New York, Knopf, 1944), pp. 241–43; Edward Hallett Carr, *Nationalism and After* (London, Macmillan, 1945), pp. 64–70.

CHAPTER VI

Thorstein Veblen: The Community as a Theory of Revolution

The idols of his own tribe have crumbled in decay and no longer cumber the ground, but that release does not induce him to set up a new line of idols borrowed from an alien tribe to do the same disservice. By consequence he is in a peculiar degree exposed to the unmediated facts of the current situation; and in a peculiar degree, therefore, he takes his orientation from the run of facts as he finds them, rather than from the traditional interpretation of analogous facts in the past. In short, he is a skeptic by force of circumstances over which he has no control.

Thorstein Veblen, *The Intellectual Pre-eminence of Jews in Modern Europe*, 1919

The variations in communal internationalism are nowhere more evident than in the contrast between the humanitarians and the community's iconoclastic critic, Thorstein Bunde Veblen. For Royce, loyalty became the highest spiritual and moral reality. For Veblen, it represented an undue subservience to outworn institutions. For Addams, the settlement house was a viable means for creating a peaceful relationship between rich and poor. Veblen regarded it as an instrument of the leisure class culture transmitting "upper class proprieties" to those who hardly needed them.[1] Teaching and writing at the University of Chicago during the first decade of Hull House, Veblen looked with disdain upon the efforts of Chicago reformers. He regarded their activities as futile and compromising.

[1] Thorstein Veblen, *The Theory of the Leisure Class* (New York, Random House, 1934), p. 344.

Veblen refused to join any reform organization. He was the perpetual stranger, the "man from Mars," detached from the reformers' immediate concerns. He concentrated instead upon the long-term trend of events, but refrained from prophesying. Still less would he agitate. Yet there was hardly a work of his that failed to disturb the supporters of the established order. While Veblen's impersonality was sincere (he really did concern himself with seeing society as it was), it also masked a steadfast commitment to the commonweal. It was this combination of scientific detachment and implicitly humane commitment that attracted progressives to his works. As Morton White observed, an audience of progressives could hardly accept Veblen's amorality at face value. Veblen took the position that he was passing no judgment in calling the business culture wasteful and predatory; but waste and predation meant evil to his generation as unequivocally as pain and unhappiness had meant evil to the utilitarians.[2] Veblen's vocabulary barely concealed his subversive intentions. He used military terminology to describe the civilization the Spencerians believed peaceful. Since to most Americans business suggested creative energy, Veblen broke through that association with his destructive images—"business sabotage," "conspicuous waste," "kept classes." Sportsmanship no longer meant fair play; it became a "survival of prowess." The current wisdom was really an attachment to "imbecile" institutions. Whatever Americans regarded as signs of progress were "archaic" habits.[3]

Perhaps in interpreting Veblen strictly as a satirist, his readers were attempting to swallow him whole just as they tried to swallow Jane Addams in elevating her to sainthood. But Veblen acted as a catalyst for a radical discontent. The quiet scholar cloaked a humane hater, as fierce as his Viking ancestors in his portraits of the "force and fraud" of contemporary institutions.

Neither his vocabulary nor his philosophy, but rather his role as a probing skeptic, calls to mind the pre-revolutionary eighteenth-century *Philosophes,* especially those who inveighed against *l'Infame.* Like Voltaire and his contemporaries, Veblen mythologized a long-gone Golden Age, used an urbane wit to reveal fraud, and attacked the superstitious remnants of a feudal past clinging to the minds of his contemporaries. Whether he actually hoped to bring the "heavenly city" down to earth is another question, for he was not at all certain about progress, only about change and the resistance to change. Veblen's whole life and work abounded in

[2] *Social Thought in America: The Revolt Against Formalism,* 2nd ed. (Boston, Beacon Press, 1957), pp. 91–92.
[3] Daniel Aaron, *Men of Good Hope: A Story of American Progressives* (New York, Oxford Univ. Press, 1961), p. 239, compares Veblen's style, the linking of respectable and dishonorable words, with the conceits of the seventeenth-century metaphysical poets. Both were designed to "achieve a new and shocking perspective."

such ambiguities. He was at once detached and committed to the future, a hater yet not a misanthrope, a mocker of reformers and their inspiration. It is an appropriate irony that during the war—a war which he thought would enthrall men's minds—he became for the first time openly reformist. *An Inquiry into the Nature of Peace and the Terms of Its Perpetuation* (1917) was his most hopeful work.

BELLAMY, MARX, AND DARWIN

A rustic air clung to this cosmopolitan and erudite man. His Thoreauian isolation, his abiding hatred of constraint and authority suggested the classical yokel newly arrived in the great city. Nor was the rusticity merely pretense, for Veblen was, as Henry Steele Commager noted, a son of the Middle Border in the tradition of agrarian radicalism,[4] if not completely in that tradition. Certain elements of Veblen's thought are not clearly traceable to any specific influence, but a few parallels may be detected between Veblen and the agrarian Utopians (Edward Bellamy, for example) on the one hand and Karl Marx on the other.

Born to Norwegian immigrants in 1857, Veblen grew up in the isolated Scandinavian enclaves of Minnesota. He shared his father's contempt for the surrounding Yankee culture and his father's respect for learning and efficiency. The social world appeared in black and white contrasts to the immigrant farmers of the Midwest. The Yankee middlemen creamed the profits off the system, while the Norwegians broke their backs in toil. The city ladies sewed and attended church, while the immigrant women worked beside their husbands in the fields. The fundamental contrast of Veblenian economics between a goods-producing culture and a pecuniary one grew out of this youthful experience. His biting indictment of the American country-town ("the perfect flower of self-help and cupidity," an enterprise in collusion and salesmanship)[5] was as autobiographical a statement as he ever made.

Veblen's father shocked his Norwegian neighbors by sending his sons to a Yankee stronghold, Carleton College. When Thorstein went on to Johns Hopkins to study with Charles Spenser Pierce and Richard T. Ely, receiving his doctoral degree three years later in 1884 at still another university, Yale, the neighbors were quite sure that Thorstein was cut out for no useful occupation. He could obtain no appointment at any nearby institution of higher learning, for none had any use for a philosopher with

---

[4] *The American Mind: An Interpretation of American Thought and Character Since the 1880's* (New Haven, Yale Univ. Press, 1959), pp. 237–38.

[5] *Ibid.*, pp. 238–39; Veblen, *Absentee Ownership and Business Enterprise in Recent Times: The Case of America* (New York, Huebsch, 1923), pp. 142, 144.

atheistic tendencies. He appeared to do nothing but read endlessly in Mill, Kant, LaSalle, and the Marxists. His wife, Ellen Rolfe Veblen, reported that the work that left the deepest imprint on both their minds during the "critical period" before Veblen's lifework began was Bellamy's *Looking Backwards*. Bellamy, like Veblen, made much of the waste and class enmities of the capitalist system and of the useless inequality of women. Like both the Populist speakers who were inflaming the farm communities and Veblen himself, he regarded panics and depressions as part of the whole imbecilic economy.[6]

Although Veblen took no part in the farmers' revolts of the 1880's, he was deeply aware of them. The heavily debt-laden Veblens could not but listen with interest to Populist leaders. The Haymarket riot of 1886, the hundreds of strikes in Illinois alone that year, the frequent use of strike-breakers and state-militia, the economists who argued that unions destroyed the property basis of civilization—none of these passed unobserved.[7] Each was to play its part in molding Veblen's ideas about government and the vested interests.

Thorstein Veblen spent much time studying languages and translating the Icelandic sagas into English, but his familiarity with Scandinavian folklore did not really make him part of the highly ethnocentric little Norways. He went back to study economics at Cornell University and from there moved to the University of Chicago, then to Stanford, then to the University of Missouri, and in the 1920s at the New School for Social Research completed his academic career of ever-slow promotions, neglect, and apparent failure. Perhaps this most gifted of America's social scientists was too much for the university authorities. At Chicago, Stanford, and Missouri they found his domestic inconstancy almost as shocking as his ideas. Having shrugged off orthodox mores and theories with equal imperturbability, Veblen found that he belonged neither to the immigrant community nor to the academic one. He was rootless. The picture he drew in 1919 of the alienated Jew who regarded the ghetto culture and the surrounding gentile world with equal skepticism was thus very much a self-portrait. Veblen, too, was a marginal man taking his "orientation from the run of the facts" as he found them.[8]

His own marginality may have stimulated his interest in another alien-

[6] Joseph Dorfman, *Thorstein Veblen and His America* (New York, Viking Press, 1934), pp. 17, 40–41, 68–69.

[7] *Ibid.*, pp. 58–61, 63–64, 71, 88–89.

[8] Bernard Rosenberg, *The Values of Veblen: A Critical Appraisal* (Washington, D.C., Public Affairs Press, 1956), pp. 6–8; Max Lerner, "Editor's Introduction," *The Portable Veblen* (New York, Viking Press, 1960), pp. 9–10; Veblen, "The Intellectual Pre-Eminence of Jews in Modern Europe," 1919, *Essays in Our Changing Order*, ed. Leon Ardzrooni (New York, Viking Press, 1934), p. 229.

ated genius of political economy—Karl Marx. His intellectual debts to Marx were at least as great as his indebtedness to agrarian radicalism. Yet most of Veblen's writings on Marx are highly critical. He was no man's disciple. Veblen challenged Marx's conception of the class-struggle as a contest between the propertied and the propertyless and made occupational conflicts and technological determinism more important. He objected to Marx's labor theory of value and to the Hegelian framework of Marxian determinism. He could never accept the notion of inevitable progress which gave class-conflict its final and attainable goal.[9]

Yet these criticisms did not mean that Veblen totally rejected Marx. The central theme of Veblenian theory, the conflict between the business system (and its ideology) and the coming industrial order (and its mentality), was thoroughly Marxian. So was his contrast between a deterministic substructure, the state of the industrial arts, and the cultural superstructure. Both men insisted upon change as the prime reality of social life. By emphasizing the lack of final purpose in this change, Veblen made a Darwinian revision of Marxism. As Darwin observed in biological evolution—a pattern not predicated upon any previous concepts of natural law—so Veblen searched for a theory of economic evolution with similar reservations. Social change became for him a complex, cumulative sequence of cause and effect without natural harmonies or spiritual design.[10]

William Graham Sumner's naturalistic pessimism and his tendency to regard morals as mores enforced Veblen's own cultural interpretation of economic behavior. But Veblen appreciated that Sumner, using evolutionism to justify *laissez faire,* was promoting the same conservative absolutism that appealed to neo-classical economists like John Bates Clark. Sumnerism drove toward the eternal fitness of the capitalist economy as much as neo-classicism drove toward its naturalness. For Veblen, however, the capitalist culture did not answer man's needs. Its relation to the changing industrial order was one of conflict and hindrance. It lagged under burdens from the past. Thus Veblen's most lasting interests in how society changed as a whole, in the substructure of political and cultural institutions, and one of his most cherished values—serviceability to the community—linked him to the Marxian tradition.

[9] Veblen, "The Socialist Economics of Karl Marx and His Followers: I. The Theories of Karl Marx," 1906, *The Place of Science in Modern Civilization and Other Essays,* comps. Leon Ardzrooni, Wesley C. Mitchell, and Walter W. Stewart (New York, Huebsch, 1919), pp. 411, 415–16, 423–25, 430; Abram L. Harris, "Economic Evolution: Dialectical and Darwinian," *Journal of Political Economy,* XLII (1934), 51–52.

[10] "Socialist Economics of Marx," p. 416; Arthur K. Davis, "Thorstein Veblen and the Culture of Capitalism," *American Radicals: Some Problems and Personalities,* ed. Harvey Goldberg (New York, Monthly Review Press, 1957), pp. 281–83.

THE NEW PSYCHOLOGY AND ANTHROPOLOGY

Man's most fundamental preoccupations, according to Veblen, were economic. They concerned material survival and activities directed toward earning a living. Only when the economy reached a certain degree of efficiency was there time for indulging in wasteful emulation. Veblen became an economist not because he believed that one could separate economic from other types of behavior, but because he believed that studies of man's economic behavior would afford clues to the whole human culture. His interests were organic. He wished to make economics an evolutionary science by going beyond both neo-classical abstractions and the factual data of German historical economics to a "genetic account of unfolding process."[11]

The first step in devising a new economics was criticism of the old. Veblen found classical economics taxonomic. The classical conception assumed that man's economic traits were static and rational. The system provided no explanation for actual social change because it analyzed ideal abstractions rather than real economic behavior. For example, one of the major themes of John Bates Clark's *Essentials of Economic Theory* (1907) was the individual production of wealth. Clark took no account of the actual origins of property as anthropologists revealed them. Primitive men were not solitary hunters. They lived and worked in communities. Their real inheritance was the collective technological knowledge of the whole community. The neo-classical myth of the solitary hunter served only as an ideological defense of capitalism. In fact, primitive men neither understood nor practiced ownership. The loss of individual objects meant little to primitive peoples in contrast with the loss of large numbers of the tribe and the ensuing decline in community efficiency.[12] Thus Veblen indicated that economists could not in all truth consider capital an eternal economic factor. Man changed. His ideas of wealth changed with his environment. Moreover, man himself created the social environment that was the source of his economic preconceptions.

Objecting both to Marx's and to the conservative classicists' ideas of human nature, Veblen indicated that their hedonism was unrealistic. The utilitarian psychology used by all the rationalists pictured man as a passive receptor of pleasure and pain, reacting to his environment by making

[11] Veblen, *Place of Science:* "Why Is Economics Not an Evolutionary Science?" (1898), pp. 72, 77; "The Evolution of the Scientific Point of View" (1908), pp. 37–38; Wesley C. Mitchell, "Introduction," *What Veblen Taught* (New York, Viking Press, 1936), p. xxiii.

[12] "Why Is Economics Not an Evolutionary Science?" p. 68; "Professor Clark's Economics," *Place of Science,* pp. 184–86.

simple quantitative decisions. But man was neither passive nor rational. The new psychology, which destroyed this hedonism and modified Wundt's associational interpretation of mind, was supported both by biology and anthropology. Veblen's University of Chicago colleagues, Jacques Loeb and John Dewey, indicated that even man's sensations were self-activated. Dewey noted, "What we see, hear, taste, and smell, depends upon what we are doing and not the reverse."[13] The new psychology, in brief, conceived of man in terms of functioning, rather than as an inert being.

Upon this activist psychology, Veblen built his instinct theory of human nature. He was well aware of the treacherous vagueness of instinct psychology and of the lack of definition of the term "instinct" itself which justified the attacks upon it. But Veblen used "instinct" to reveal the sources of cultural change rather than unchanging human behavior. As Bernard Rosenberg observed, he "debiologizes and sociolizes it," making the modification of instincts by habits his central concern, and the conception of man plastic.[14] Veblen explained that instincts were more than complex groupings of what Jacques Loeb termed "tropisms." They were more pervasive inherited drives which combined with intelligence to direct human activity. They were malleable, as was man himself, and yet persistent.[15]

Veblen used instinct theory to direct attention to the conflict between human needs and the modern economic environment, to assert man's inheritance of peacefulness, and implicitly to provide standards of moral judgment. The instincts were always contaminated by habit, crushed by institutions. In opposing instincts and institutions, Veblen revealed that the former represented his own moral values.

The instinct of workmanship, the most pervasive human trait, for example, meant man's tendency to tailor his activity to a useful goal, to create objects necessary to the material well-being of the race. It entered into all man's more "complex and deliberate" activities, including the arts.[16] In elevating workmanship to such importance, Veblen was asserting the centrality of efficiency in his value system. Man survived not by waste and war but by laboring for the community. His advantage over other species was an advantage of creativity, not destructive powers (although, paradoxically,

---

[13] Dewey quoted by Dorfman, *Veblen*, p. 129; Harris, "Economic Evolution," pp. 53–59, contrasts Marxian rationalism with Veblenian instinct theory. Cf. Veblen, "Preconceptions of Economic Science II," 1899, *Place of Science*, pp. 134–35; "Preconceptions III," 1900, *Ibid.*, pp. 156–57; Edwin G. Boring, *A History of Experimental Psychology* (New York, Appleton, 1950), p. 475.

[14] *Values of Veblen*, p. 45; Veblen, *The Instinct of Workmanship and the State of the Industrial Arts* (New York, Macmillan, 1914), pp. 2, 12–13.

[15] *Instinct of Workmanship*, pp. 4–7, 10, 13, 32.

[16] *Ibid.*, pp. 25, 28, 31, 33.

workmanship increased those powers too). Veblen thus attacked the classical economic assumption that labor was naturally irksome.[17]

Of greater immediate concern in his internationalist thought was an
instinct he called the "parental bent." It meshed so completely with workmanship, defining the purposes of efficiency, that the two could hardly be
separated. The parental bent had a wider bearing than immediate concern
for one's own children. Like Addams' "family devotion" it became concern
for the race at large, particularly for the life of the next generation. It
made man a

. . . social animal; and . . . at the same time . . . substantially a peaceful
animal. The race may have wandered far from the ancient position of peacefulness, but even now the traces of a peaceful trend in man's everyday habits of thought and feeling are plain enough. The sight of blood and the presence of death, even of the blood or death of the lower animals, commonly
strike inexperienced persons with a sickening revulsion. In the common run
of cases, the habit of complacency with slaughter comes only as a result of
discipline. . . . In his unarmed frame and in the slight degree to which his
muscular force is specialized for fighting . . . man is to be classed with
those animals that owe their survival to an aptitude for avoiding direct conflict with their competitors.[18]

The question immediately arose then: How did men become habituated
to fighting? First, Veblen considered the self-contamination of the instincts
themselves. Under the barbarian culture, the parental bent itself induced
men to worship the chief, the king, the glory of the flag. It degenerated into
nationalism.[19] Second, there was some mutual contamination of the instincts. Although workmanship and the parental bent enforced each other,
workmanship alone made the community rich enough to afford emulation,
and strong enough to engage in preparations for war. Neither of these
instincts made war necessary, but their mutual corruption made it possible.

The third instinct, "idle curiosity," bore little relationship to the other
two except as a saving release from the pragmatic implications of workmanship. This playful bent, as strong in the modern scientist as in the
myth-making savage, defined man as an organism seeking knowledge for its
own sake. Possibly "idle curiosity" represented Veblen's own defense
against the business-oriented culture of the universities and the pragmatism
he considered its selfish rationalization. (Like Royce, Veblen objected to
pragmatism because it implied to him excessive individualism and the
"canons of expediency.")

Veblen asserted that the business-dominated universities produced "bar-

---

[17] "The Instinct of Workmanship and the Irksomeness of Labor," 1898, *Essays in Our Changing Order*, pp. 80–83.
[18] *Ibid.*, pp. 85–86.
[19] *Instinct of Workmanship*, p. 161.

barian knowledge." Once again his use of military images reveals his orientation. The university president became the bloated and futile "captain of erudition," a title suggesting more force than brains and a close association with "captains of industry." That Veblen even considered calling his work *The Higher Learning in America* (1918), "a study of total depravity," indicated the depth of his playful bitterness.

Idle curiosity also had an impact on Veblen's internationalist thought. It laid the foundation for his belief that the interests of true scientists and scholars were cosmopolitan and creative. Only the vested interests in universities, politics, and business divided them. During the war Veblen would propose that America save this higher learning by establishing a central office for the dissemination of bibliographical information and a house of refuge for "the wayfaring men of the republic of learning."[20]

Whether these three—workmanship, the parental bent, and idle curiosity—were the only instincts Veblen mentioned has been a matter of some debate, for he often designated emulation a "proclivity," and it stemmed from none of the other three.[21] At any rate, the good instincts formed only the core of human behavior. Their transformation by institutions (habitual lines of thought and action clinging stubbornly to man long after he had any use for them) was much more important. Believing that institutions were fundamentally corrupting, Veblen implied that progress would lie in a backward direction to the original instincts. This was not an unusual idea among the intellectual progressives of his day.[22] But Veblen used it in his own individual way. He thought of civilization as having developed in three main stages—the savage stage, the warring barbarian culture (the tendencies of both persisted later), and the modern business stage. He frequently hinted that there might be a fourth stage, more in accordance with human needs than the middle two—namely, an industrial republic, but he was not at all certain about progress in this direction.

The barbarian and business stages did not represent progress to him

[20] *Ibid.*, p. 87; "The Place of Science in Modern Civilization," 1906, *Place of Science,* pp. 8–9, 17, 19–23, contains some of Veblen's sharp criticism of pragmatism; "The War and the Higher Learning," 1918, *Essays in Our Changing Order,* pp. 340–46; Lerner, "Introduction," p. 11; Norman Kaplan, "Idle Curiosity," *Thorstein Veblen: A Critical Reappraisal,* ed. Douglas F. Dowd (Ithaca, Cornell Univ. Press, 1958), pp. 49–51.

[21] Myron W. Watkins, "Veblen's View of Cultural Evaluation," in *Veblen: A Critical Reappraisal,* pp. 253–54, emphasizes the contrast between "self-regarding proclivities" and "group regarding traits" considering emulation as instinctive as emulation. Stow Persons, *American Minds: A History of Ideas* (New York, Holt, 1958), p. 303, argues that fear, arrogance, race solidarity were instincts in Veblen's scheme, and emulation a proclivity. Max Lerner, "Introduction," pp. 41–42, contends that Veblen found man's primal endowment both good and peaceful. I agree with Lerner.

[22] David W. Nobel, "Veblen and Progress: The American Climate of Opinion," *Ethics,* LXV (July 1955), 285.

because the savage stage was closest of all to man's instinctual heritage. The savage stage, lasting longer than any other, gave human beings their "ineradicable sentimental dispositions" toward peacefulness and workmanship. The Christian ideal of human brotherhood, representing an ever-present challenge to the competitive system, persisted even into the twentieth century because it meshed so completely with man's original disposition.[23]

The downfall of the peaceful savage communities with their ethic of "live and let live" came when those communities emerged out of poverty. The superstitious savage respected the obvious outward signs of efficiency, such as the prizes of the hunt. A few braves exhibited greater force and strength than others and captured the tribe's wealth. Weaker men emulated them. This "proclivity for emulation" that had mysteriously entered Eden grew out of both technical proficiency and war. The chieftains went to war to acquire booty. Booty brought respect. The society changed to one of status and ownership when there were riches to be acquired. Soon there were vested interests in war.[24]

Veblen's disdain for war always bore the marks of his early association of its origins with the beginning of private ownership. He considered ownership itself the barbarian "habit of coercion and seizure reduced to a system." It began when the chieftains enslaved the members of other tribes, particularly women. Work thereafter had upon it the stamp of the woman-slave's inferiority and became irksome. The contrasting leisure and conspicuous wealth of the forceful class, the warriors, became honorific. Thus in *Theory of the Leisure Class,* Veblen indicated that waste, "conspicuous consumption," and the encumbrances of women's elaborate clothing represented an earlier predatory culture persisting into the present. Signs of wealth represented not work but prowess—superior force.[25]

Because war encouraged fraud and force in all human relationships, it even infected the drive for learning. Matter-of-fact knowledge without practical bearing (not conducive to an increase in wealth) was neglected. The animistic mentality flourished, encouraging organized religion, the morality of expediency in dealing with persons of higher rank, and technological stagnation.[26] War thus violated the three moral absolutes of the

[23] "Christian Morals and the Competitive System," 1910, *Essays in Our Changing Order,* pp. 203–204, 209, 218.

[24] "Instinct of Labor and Irksomeness of Work," pp. 90–91; *Theory of the Leisure Class,* pp. 16–17, 19. Veblen did not say that *no* fighting occurred during the savage stage, but that war as a way of life did not become fixed until later.

[25] *Theory of the Leisure Class,* pp. 17, 92–94, 170–71, 271–73; In *Essays in Our Changing Order,* see: "The Beginnings of Ownership" (1898), pp. 39, 43–44, 46, 48; "The Barbarian Status of Women" (1899), pp. 53–56; "The Economic Theory of Women's Dress" (1894), pp. 65–77; "Instinct of Labor and Irksomeness of Work," pp. 94–95.

[26] "Preconceptions I," p. 106; "Scientific Point of View," p. 45.

Veblenian ethos—the joy of producing useful objects efficiently, the concern for community welfare, the objective pursuit of truth. Although Veblen considered the traditional pacifism naive and futile, he too had a disposition in that direction.

He often associated technological advance with a temporary release from warfare. The entire feudal culture, for example, began to crack (but not disappear) with scientific humanism because the Renaissance represented a relatively more peaceful stage than the period that preceded it. Still later, in the eighteenth century, when Great Britain was increasingly free from continental embroilments, the handicraft system flourished and British nationalism began to evolve toward the ideal of the democratic commonwealth. For a brief span of time *laissez faire* was possible, and ideals of natural rights rooted themselves in the British mind. No sooner had the philosophy of this "quasi-predatory" culture been articulated than advancing technology made it obsolete. Industrial units grew too large for individual workmen to encompass with their own property or knowledge. "After the Industrial Revolution . . . it was no longer true even in [a] roughly approximate way that . . . equality before the law, barring property rights, would mean equal opportunity." By the twentieth century, industrial processes were so intricately interrelated that they were both world-wide and communal, but business remained individualistic and competitive.[27] The conflict between business and industry grew acute.

NATIONS, BUSINESS, AND WAR

Upon this conflict between business and industry, Veblen's analysis of modern life turned. In a sense the conflict began even in the late savage stage, in the first social distinctions between those who hunted and owned and those who worked. With the growth of barbarian culture, the distinctions grew stronger, as war, ownership, and honor coalesced. But in modern society they were strongest of all, industry producing goods and business (the "pecuniary" employments) producing nothing but money for the few owners. The dynamism of modern life was industrial. Businessmen merely established their natural right to get something for nothing. Thus Veblen, unlike Marx, viewed capitalism not as a real advance over feudalism but as a perpetuation of it. The modern stage represented progress over barbarism only in its technological achievements. Business retained the force and fraud of barbarism.

[27] "On the Nature of Capital I," 1908, *Place of Science*, pp. 340–41; cf. *Imperial Germany and the Industrial Revolution* (Ann Arbor, Univ. of Michigan Press, 1966), pp. 111–12, 119, 121; *Instinct of Workmanship*, pp. 217, 223, 234–38; *The Theory of Business Enterprise* (New York, Scribner, 1904), pp. 15–17, 76, 78–80.

In his most daring contribution to economic theory, Veblen explained the cycles of depression and prosperity in terms of the industrial-pecuniary conflict. The dynamic tendency of industry to produce goods and lower the costs of production undermined existing capitalization of business, thereby depressing prices. Chronic depression was "normal to business under the fully developed regime of modern industry," Veblen observed in *The Theory of Business Enterprise* (1904). Only completely extraneous forces such as wars kept the system prosperous. Business cures, such as increasingly unproductive consumption, or the end of cut-throat competition through monopoly, could never free the system from its inherent decay.[28] In place of either continual war (and threat of war) or constant threat of another descending business cycle, Veblen considered the possibilities of socialism. He recognized, of course, that this alternative had occurred to many other men of his time, but he persisted through the 1890s in calling the socialism of his day more an expression of the emulative mentality—of the desire of workers to keep up leisure-class appearances—than an evidence of the desire to free industry from business control. On the other hand, this was not true of all the protests of his time. The "Army of the Commonweal" (Coxey's army) created the potential for a revolutionary frame of mind, which might mean the difference "between the civil republic of the nineteenth century and the industrial republic of the socialists."[29]

Veblen never said precisely what he meant by the phrase "industrial republic." When contrasted with the democratic commonwealth (British and American political ideals), it seemed anarchistic. Veblen took it as too obvious to need demonstration that all national political establishments upheld the supremacy of the ruling classes and the existing economic order. Therefore, the industrial republic suggested an economic condition more than a political one—a condition in which industry served real human needs. During the war Veblen considered the possibility of an elaborate governmental apparatus to bring about socialism, so that by 1918 his industrial republic seemed much less anarchistic than it had before. However, he had such a specialized conception of the state that he would have regarded the phrase "a socialized state" as contradictory.

The only certainty in the decade before World War I was the end of business domination in its contemporary form. Machine technology pro-

---

[28] *Theory of Business Enterprise*, pp. 178, 180–183, 185–186, 190–191, 250–251, 255; Paul M. Sweezy, "Veblen on American Capitalism," *Veblen: A Critical Reappraisal*, pp. 183–85.

[29] It was typical of Veblen to appreciate this march of the dispossessed which ended in fiasco rather than the organized political socialism of Debs and others that followed in its train some years later. His preference for the International Workers of the World over the more powerful unions of skilled laborers was similar. See "The Army of the Commonweal," 1894, *Essays in Our Changing Order*, pp. 100, 101, 103.

duced a matter-of-fact frame of mind among the technicians upon whom
the whole system depended—a change suggesting the coming of socialism.
But something very deep in human nature resisted an objective scientific
outlook. Perhaps there would be a "recrudescence of magic, occult science,
telepathy, spiritualism, vitalism, pragmatism."[30] Superstition favored the
growth of nationalism, which in turn protected business. But nationalism
also pointed backward to the barbarian culture and a militant feudalism. In
the predatory states, businessmen could not be completely dominant. Nevertheless, they supported this resurgence of feudalism by allowing a drift
toward war.

The direct cultural value of a warlike business policy is unequivocal. It
makes for a conservative animus on the populace. . . . Military training is
a training in ceremonial precedence, arbitrary command, and unquestioning
obedience. . . . The more consistent and the more comprehensive this military training, the more effectually will the members of the community (and
not only the soldiers) be trained into habits of subordination and away from
the growing propensity to make light of personal authority which is the
chief infirmity of democracy. . . . Habituation to a warlike, predatory
scheme of life is the strongest disciplinary factor that can be brought to
counter the vulgarization of modern life wrought by peaceful industry and
the machine process. . . .
In this direction, lies the hope of a corrective for "social unrest" and
similar disorders of civilized life.[31]

Thus even before 1914 Veblen perceived the underlying conflict between
industrial democracy and the military state. In no sense did he predict
World War I. His eyes sought not the immediate crises, but the overall
drift of Western society. Nevertheless, his understanding of this drift, and
of the deep forces of violence, totalitarianism, and revolution was far
keener than that of any other internationalist. While conservatives looked
fearfully, and radicals hopefully, to the Second International, Veblen surveyed it with a cold accuracy. Jane Addams believed the leaders of the
International who predicted a strike against the capitalist overlords in the
event of an international war. The workers would not fight their brothers.
But Veblen read the results of the Franco-Prussian War quite differently.
Since the 1870s the German Socialists had been breathing the chauvinist air
of the Second Reich, until by the first decade of the twentieth century they
were quite used to it. The "infection of jingoism has gradually permeated
the body of Social Democrats, until they have . . . reached such a pitch of

---

[30] *Instinct of Workmanship*, p. 334.
[31] *Theory of Business Enterprise*, pp. 391–93.

enthusiastic loyalty as they would not patiently hear a truthful characterization of."[32]

The Second International demonstrated, rather than contradicted, the
enormous power of aggressive nationalism as it deflected the course of the
modern, matter-of-fact frame of mind.

So thoroughly did Veblen associate war, ownership, and nationalism that
there was no room in his *Weltanschauung* for any conception of peaceful
patriotism such as Royce considered at least possible in rational loyalty. For
Veblen the forms of the polity were of no great importance. The essence of
the state remained the same in the twentieth century as in the sixteenth—a
dynastic establishment in which sovereignty (legalized domination) re-
sided. Such sovereignty, whether monarchial or popular, was always distinct from community. Communities abided by the voluntary rule of "live
and let live," but states commanded blind loyalty and exercised the power
this loyalty gave them.[33]

Veblen also distinguished between a community as a small group "known
by personal contact and common gossip" and the nation which was a
mythologized group believed to have common descent but actually bound by
habit and custom, not by heredity. The nation in turn was distinct from
the race. Consequently theories of racial purity of any one particular nation
(Veblen was discussing the Germans) could not be proved. Most European
nations were composed of "hybrid races."[34]

This discussion of German racial theory and Veblen's flat refutation of
it in 1914 have often led commentators to marvel at Veblen's astounding
foresight. There are passages in his war work that seem more directly
related to World War II than to World War I. But once again it was his
feeling for the fundamental pattern of beliefs in a culture that called forth
his anticipations of the future, and often Veblen was very wrong. He did,
however, correctly perceive the same way of life in industrial Imperial Germany as in industrial Imperial Japan. For Americans who were flattered by
Japan's imitative ways, and who did not perceive the selection in imitation,
Veblen's views must have come as startling news. He observed that Japan,
one of the Allies, was as aggressive as the Germans. The "opera bouffe"
mythology that made up the state religion led Japan down the same path of
conquest. German and Japanese nationalism as contrasted with that of the
English-speaking peoples was relatively simple. The Germanic ideal of
statesmanship was frankly forceful, while the British ideal had pretensions

---

[32] "The Socialist Economics of Karl Marx and His Followers: II. The Later
Marxists," 1907, *Place of Science*, p. 454.

[33] *Imperial Germany*, pp. 67–69, 161–67; *An Inquiry into the Nature of Peace and
the Terms of Its Perpetuation* (New York, Huebsch, 1917), pp. 9–13.

[34] *Imperial Germany*, pp. 4–6, 8–9.

of peacefulness and Britons had to be driven to force. The British were less habituated to self-abnegation. The machine discipline had trained them over a longer period toward a skeptical frame of mind. Their tradition of civil liberties gave added weight to an anarchistic bias.[35]

These distinctions and the whole attack upon the dynastic state in *Imperial Germany and the Industrial Revolution* led some officials of the Wilson administration to mistake *Imperial Germany* for useful pro-Allied propaganda. George Creel of the Committee of Public Information even considered using it. But the New York City Postmaster banned the work from the mails on the grounds that it violated the Espionage Act.[36] Perhaps he was correct. Veblen flattered the Americans and the British no more than he did the Germans.

The Veblenian interpretation of nationalism may be summarized as follows: All nationalisms are invidious, but some are more invidious than others. While British and American nationalism was more democratic than German nationalism in principle, there was little difference between them in practice. Just as a military regime had disciplined the Germans, large-scale organizations (both corporations and labor unions) had disciplined the British, with the result that their "sense of national solidarity" was "in a visibly better state of repair the last two or three decades than formerly was the case." What the British lacked in military ardor they supplied abundantly in "flunkeyism."[37]

The crowning irony of Veblen's analysis was his assertion that patriotism, so detrimental to the common man's material interests, was largely the work of the common man himself. Veblen stressed, as Max Lerner observed, "the willingness of the capturable mind to be captured, even more than the strategic position the captor holds."[38] In *An Inquiry into the Nature of Peace and the Terms of Its Perpetuation* (1917), a work that continued the analysis of *Imperial Germany*, Veblen defined patriotism as "a sense of partisan solidarity in respect of prestige" resting upon some invidious comparison between one's own nation and others.[39]

The patriotic spirit is the spirit of emulation . . . shot through with the sense of solidarity. It belongs under the general caption of sportsmanship, rather than workmanship. Now any enterprise in sportsmanship is bent on an invidious success, which must involve as its major purpose the defeat and humiliation of some competitor. . . . Its aim is differential gain as against a rival; and the emulative spirit that comes under the head of pa-

[35] *Ibid.*, pp. 103, 112–13, 133; *Nature of Peace*, pp. 83–84, 99, 104–105; "The Opportunity of Japan," 1915, *Essays in Our Changing Order*, pp. 251–52, 261–62.
[36] Dorfman, *Veblen*, p. 382.
[37] *Imperial Germany*, pp. 135, 172.
[38] "Introduction," *Portable Veblen*, p. 27.
[39] *Nature of Peace*, p. 31.

triotism commonly, if not invariably, seeks this differential advantage by injury of the rival rather than by an increase of home-bred well-being.[40]

The *Nature of Peace* provided plentiful examples of the way men sacrificed self-interest to national prestige. Men boasted of the size of their national armies, of the extent of national territory, and of governmental protection of investments abroad, all of which held only psychic values for them. For such intangibles as the national honor, a well-trained patriot gladly sacrificed his family's welfare and even his life.[41]

The prevalence and persistence of nationalism in one form or the other in all ages led Veblen to consider the possibility that it was an inherited trait. But he reminded readers that certain communities, such as the Eskimos and the ancient Icelandic Republic, evidently saw no use in it. Even the Chinese, who had quietly outlived and civilized their earlier militant conquerors, so lacked a serviceable national spirit that they entered modern international politics only as a "bone of contention." Nationalism, then, was not an inherited characteristic but a frame of mind that served the state and other vested interests all too well.[42]

PEACE OR THE PRICE SYSTEM

Both *Imperial Germany* and the *Nature of Peace* probed far deeper into modern social institutions than could be expected from any *pièce d'occasion*. Contemporary criticism of them often reflected the mistaken belief that they were only propaganda pieces. Therefore Veblen was considered either staunchly pro-Allied or a subversive pacifist—an issue which neither the Postmaster who banned *Imperial Germany* nor the critics who praised it could settle.[43] Of course, Veblen's tendency to play with satire while making deadly serious points was partially to blame. More important was the ambivalence of the works themselves. World War I had both brightened Veblen's hopes for revolution and deepened his fears about retrogressive forces. The long sweep of probabilities, which usually commanded Veblen's attention, now met his immediate short-range hopes. Veblen did care what happened.

Much of the *Nature of Peace* implied that Veblen preferred an Allied victory to a German one (but he offered a counter argument also, as we shall see) largely because Prussian feudalism represented a more immedi-

---

[40] *Ibid.*, p. 33.

[41] *Ibid.*, pp. 27–29, 67–70.

[42] *Ibid.*, pp. 4–5, 11–12, 45, 130.

[43] Dorfman, *Veblen*, p. 370. The reviewers' reactions reflected their political positions. Sometimes, however, a liberal reviewer could be highly critical. See George Mead, "Review of the *Nature of Peace*," *Journal of Political Economy*, XXVI (1918), 752.

ate danger than Allied imperialism. He examined in some depth the reasons for the power of resurgent militarism by relating 1914 to fundamental economic changes. Britain suffered the "penalty of taking the lead" in the industrial revolution. She encumbered her technology with capitalist institutions and clung to the old ways of designing machinery. Germany, by industrializing late, avoided the traditional British wastefulness and used the most advanced technology to build strategic railroads and to adapt shipping to naval uses. She was acquiring colonies for efficient exploitation and creating the best armaments. The immediate danger to the common man's well-being was this Prussian combination of technological efficiency with militaristic purposes.[44] But Germany had to strike quickly before other nations caught up with her. She needed to move before her own people acquired the new discipline of machine technology and lost their aggressive loyalty to the Prussian dynasty. Already the cloudy German romantic culture was falling into decay.[45]

A similar analysis applied to Japan. The people's obedience to the Emperor and love of the state religion could not last indefinitely. In the short run, however, the predatory schemes of both Germany and Japan might succeed. It was for this reason that Veblen was eager to bring American power to bear against Germany and to assure a peace that would destroy all remnants of Prussianism. Without explaining how the United States might deal with Japan, he implied that if Germany were removed, the Japanese would not present a substantial threat. America's power was great, but her people were notably lax about military preparations in the midst of peace. Thus the American position between two powers whose only purpose was "insatiable quest of dominion" would become very precarious, particularly if she relied upon national self-help and last-minute defenses in her traditional fashion.[46] Collective security was not enough, since the "quasi-predatory" states usually worked at cross purposes. More important, advanced military technology gave the advantage to the aggressor.

The first job of the Allies and the "league of neutrals" (Veblen referred to a league which should be neutral by virtue of its neglect of nationalism) was to eliminate the German imperial regime, root and branch. Methods applied to the eradication of German militarism could then be extended to all military establishments. The league should destroy war equipment; confiscate the industrial plant needed to produce it; cancel the Imperial war debt (considering German creditors "accessory to the culpable enterprise of the Imperial government"); and establish a "neutral surveillance" over

---

[44] *Imperial Germany*, pp. 136, 138–41, 143, 147, 189–94, 214, 217.
[45] *Ibid.*, pp. 227, 236–37, 244–45, 247–48.
[46] *Nature of Peace*, pp. 229–30.

German affairs, reducing her government to an administrative status until a democratic regime could replace it. Finally, the league should confiscate the estates of the Junkerdom in all dynastic regimes and use the proceeds to indemnify civilians in invaded territory.[47] Not even the postwar reparations settlement could come up to Veblen's revolutionary standards. Thus, he did not consider Versailles too hard a peace.

The alternative to such a peace, established by a strong league with considerable economic powers, was surrender to the Imperial dynasty. This suggestion, seemingly a typical touch of Veblenian irony, implied something more. Veblen's consideration of "peace without honor" was subversive— directed more toward liberating men from their patriotic subservience than toward establishing the importance of Britain's triumph over Germany. In the final count, Veblen asked, why should the common man care? Would he suffer harder usage under Prussian tutelage than under the vested interests? If he surrendered his patriotism would that be any great loss? Veblen called attention not to the real possibility of this event but to something more important—the "discrepancy between business expediency" (upheld by Britain and the United States) and "serviceability to the common good."[48] For him the only basis for a true resolution of the war would have been the defeat of both the capitalist Entente and the imperial powers by social revolutions. In his revolutionary hopes and expectations lay Veblen's real interest in a hard peace. Whoever demands unconditional surrender contemplates a long war. While one part of Veblen feared the nationalist reaction that would be encouraged by war, another part of him viewed the war as a great opportunity. It would destroy the material and psychological basis of the old order. It was the seedbed of revolution. What the conservative internationalists feared, Veblen embraced. The longer the war lasted, the stronger the growth of popular skepticism regarding the necessity for rule by gentlemen. For a gentleman was necessarily "a wasteful affair." Even the British were losing faith in his fitness for survival. Their war government was vulgarized by large additions of cockney talents. Common soldiers rose rapidly into the officer class as their "betters" died nobly on the battlefields. If the war lasted long enough the

. . . common man . . . who gathers nothing but privation and anxiety from the owner's discretionary sabotage, may conceivably stand to lose his perception that the vested interests of ownership are the cornerstones of his life, liberty, and pursuit of happiness.[49]

Veblen hoped for even more specifically revolutionary means than the growth of the common man's skepticism. Like many progressives, he

[47] *Ibid.*, pp. 239–40, 257, 271–72.
[48] *Ibid.*, p. 160. Cf. pp. 151–56, 161.
[49] *Ibid.*, pp. 254–55. Cf. pp. 245–47, 253.

viewed the war as an opportunity for social engineering. After the House-Lippmann Committee for the formulation of American peace terms (The Inquiry) rejected Veblen's application for membership,[50] he found a minor position on the Food Administration. Some of his proposals—for example, those for the suspension of retail merchandising in the country town; for the voluntary nationalization of agricultural labor; and for a punitive taxation of employers of menial servants—appear deliberately outrageous challenges to the Wilson administration. Veblen was seriously hopeful about other measures, however. Price-fixing and the federal distribution of seed, the cessation of the War Department's persecution of the International Workers of the World and recruitment of these wobblies for harvesting of grain—all these proposals he defended on grounds of efficiency. The incorporation of small private banking into the postal savings system and the nationalization of mail-order retailing on the grounds of efficiency appeared immediately advantageous.[51] But Veblen hoped that such changes would not be, as he maintained they would, "for the duration only." Using such techniques, experts could create a socialist economy. This was the wartime implication of his discussion of the "industrial republic."

In brief, Veblen abandoned for the duration his erstwhile association between war and barbarism and established a new one between war and revolution. He did seem to think that the war might make the "world safe for democracy," but in his own terms, not in Wilson's.

Unlike Herbert Croly, who argued that a war government might change capitalism into a "humanitarian democracy" by using a "competent and responsible" vanguard of "anti-socialist" experts, Veblen looked for the "disestablishment" of capitalism altogether. Like John Dewey, he temporarily lost an appreciation for the more critical position of pacifist-progressives such as Jane Addams and Randolph S. Bourne. Addams and Bourne doubted that the pragmatic intelligence could survive an alliance with nationalism. Bourne's break with Dewey on this score is well known. He saw the failure of the "philosophy of intelligence" to create values which efficiency might serve.[52]

---

[50] Dorfman, *Veblen*, p. 380. Cf. Lawrence E. Gelfand, *The Inquiry: American Preparations for Peace, 1917–1919* (New Haven, Yale Univ. Press, 1963), pp. 71 ff., has an excellent discussion of the personnel practices of the Inquiry, including a description of their standards of "loyalty."

[51] In *Essays in Our Changing Order;* see "Menial Servants during the War" (1918), pp. 273–74; "Farm Labor for the Period of the War" (1919), pp. 290, 293–95, 298, 302–15; "Farm Labor and the IWW" (1918), p. 331; Dorfman, *Veblen*, pp. 383–86.

[52] Sidney Kaplan, "Social Engineers as Saviors: Effects of World War I on Some American Liberals," *Journal of the History of Ideas*, XVII (June 1956), 352–53, 360–61; Christopher Lasch, *The New Radicalism in America, 1889–1963: The Intellectual as a Social Type* (New York, Knopf, 1965), pp. 206–207; cf. Eric Goldman,

Not until Versailles did Veblen give up his faith in war as an instrument of revolution. By 1919 he realized the extent of the discrepancy between his conception of international peace and that of Wilson. For the climax of Veblen's revolutionary ardor came in his description of the "league of neutrals."

Veblen's league was nothing less than an instrument for destroying the *status quo*. In spite of his suggestion that the league at first should have a "British air," he actually had no preference for Anglo-American domination. Instead he contemplated an international administration run by scientific experts. The league was to reduce national states to administrative divisions, which in the last analysis might be climatic or topological or linguistic as the experts chose, ignoring both political boundaries and political demands.[53]

None of the communalists carried the opposition between the community and the national state system this far. Neither Royce nor Addams actually suggested the disestablishment of the state. But Veblen would have had "peace by neglect," meaning the neglect of everything encompassed in the phrase national interests, and more fundamentally the neglect of capitalism as well. For Veblen there were no justifiable national interests, only the interests of the common man as opposed to those of the absentee owners and their political lackeys.

He contended, for example, that the common man could relinquish his citizenship with all its personal and pecuniary rights without any actual loss. In English-speaking countries, aliens were not notably worse off than citizens, and the first thing they wished to drop was their allegiance to the mother-country.[54] The "neutralization of citizenship" would relieve men of perilous international complications brought about by the national protection of citizens residing abroad. "In the material respect no individual would be any worse off, with the doubtful and dubious exception of the expatriate fortune-hunter who aims to fish safely in troubled waters at his compatriots' expense."[55]

Equally important for the achievement of peace was the disallowance of all trade discriminations, tariffs, subsidies, consular establishments, and extraterritoriality. These remnants of the mercantilist period had no uses other than the competitive advantage of national states in war, or the profits of the traders. Certainly it made no difference to the common man where

---

Rendezvous With Destiny: A History of Modern American Reform (New York, Vintage Books, 1959), pp. 209 ff.

[53] *Nature of Peace*, pp. 231–32, 235–36, 245, 269; "Outline of a Policy for Control of the 'Economic Penetration' of Backward Countries and of Foreign Investments," 1917, *Essays in Our Changing Order*, pp. 368–69.

[54] *Nature of Peace*, pp. 209–10.

[55] *Ibid.*, p. 212.

his food was produced or what flags flew on the ships that carried his material necessities. Even the traders might find, by a careful calculation of costs, that the expenses of military and consular establishments far outweighed their supposed benefits.[56]

Whether Veblen actually expected the abandonment of trade discrimination and citizenship is a moot question. Probably he did not. And that distinguishes the *Nature of Peace* from the other internationalist works of the period. In Veblen's analysis of the conditions for perpetual peace there appears almost no evidence that he expected these conditions to be fulfilled. Certainly he did not look to their immediate fulfillment by the men then holding the reins of power. If one views the book as a challenge more than as a set of proposals, Veblen's revolutionary intention becomes apparent.

The efficacy of the work depends upon the validity of Veblen's analysis of the necessary conditions for peace. In his discussion of trade discriminations, it is evident that Veblen was carrying the economic interpretation of imperialism very far. The analysis owed a great deal to the rather specialized interpretation he had made of John Hobson's *Imperialism: A Study* (1902). Neglecting the psychological and moral factors by which Hobson modified economic determinism, Veblen viewed the whole colonial question as an outgrowth of trade privileges. He selected from Hobson one major point: the contrast between the economic pressures of surplus capital for investment (which drove governments into imperialist adventures) and the "exorbitant costs" of such adventures to the common man.[57] However valid this point, Veblen, who had made so much of the common man's bamboozlement by the interests, might have been expected to say more about the drives for national power and prestige that stirred the imperialist conscience of ordinary citizens. He did not do so in 1917 because he was discussing what the league might do, and he evidently thought it could do little to relieve men of the burden of their patriotism. A world without patriotic illusion represented to Veblen what the classless society represented to the Marxists—a kind of heaven on earth. But Veblen had much less faith in heaven than the Marxists.

Although the inquiry neither asked for, nor was favorable to, Veblen's suggestions for a league of neutrals, in his more hopeful moments he offered them. The mandates system, which was incidental in most American peace plans, lay at the heart of Veblen's league. It was certainly not the same system that finally emerged from the Versailles Conference. Veblen's plan had no national mandatory authorities at all. He insisted that the league have direct administrative control over all backward areas, not just

---

[56] *Ibid.*, pp. 24–27, 206–208.

[57] "Review of J. A. Hobson's *Imperialism: A Study*," *Journal of Political Economy*, VII (1903), 311–19; *Nature of Peace*, pp. 24–27, 259.

the former German colonies. To prevent monopolistic exploitation, the league guardians should enforce a strict free-trade regime preventing, wherever possible, national protection of traders and investors.

Most important of all, Veblen's attitude toward capital investment in underdeveloped areas was unique. He believed that "industrial penetration" of the outlying areas would "be too swift for the continued well-being of the native population." Many of their natural resources were not really needed by the industrial powers in any case. Therefore, the league should not encourage investment even if the investors did not have national protection. The guardians should protect the backward areas from those so eager to develop them.[58] Thus even Veblen's most specific suggestions reflected his respect for the primitive cultures that were threatened by the very technology he also admired. His mandates proposals indicated an attitude fundamentally at variance with that of liberal and socialist admirers of progress, who felt satisfied with equal rights for the colonies and with an equitable distribution of colonial resrouces.

Veblen's suggestions for colonial administration included no proposal for the emergence of the colonies into nationhood. The primary obligation of his league of neutrals would be to "discard or at least disregard, distinctions of nationality so far as the sentimental preconceptions of its constituent peoples would allow." Peace depended on the abolition of national frontiers, not upon the creation of new nations. Veblen looked for the "submergence of national divisions and national integrity" wherever possible.[59] No party of the left, in Western Europe at least, exhibited such bland disregard for the impulse to self-determination as did Veblen.

Since Veblen was deeply aware of the contrasts of nationalities and too realistic to expect these contrasts simply to disappear, one can account for his unequivocal opposition to the national states only by examining his interpretation of nationalism in relation to economic change. He believed that the ongoing forces for change in the world were technological knowledge and the material conditions of industrial life. The material substructure and the intellectual inheritance together created the whole modern apolitical culture.

Modern culture is drawn on too large a scale, is of too complex and multiform a character, requires the cooperation of too many and various lines of inquiry, experience, and insight, to admit of its being confined within national frontiers, except at the cost of insufferable crippling and retardation. The science and scholarship that is the peculiar pride of civilized Christendom is not only international, but rather is homogeneously cosmopolitan; so that in this bearing there are in effect no national frontiers.[60]

[58] "Economic Penetration," pp. 371–73, 377.
[59] *Ibid.*, p. 368.
[60] *Nature of Peace*, p. 39.

Because national states had emerged when industrial technology was small-scale, because by 1918 they hindered industrial efficiency and world-wide knowledge, sabotaging the world community in a fruitless quest for national self-sufficiency, the real interests of the common man demanded the abandonment of the useless polity. Veblen's conclusion was simple and bold. "As an industrial unit, the nation is out of date."[61] Here again he made an observation about the requirements for perpetual peace instead of presenting an immediate alternative. He realized that patriotism and the price-system were not easily laid aside. If the underlying factors in modern civilization were cosmopolitan, the institutional factors were not. There was a very large cultural lag between the two. Veblen expected it to persist.

The final meaning of disregarding frontiers, colonies, trade discrimina-tions, and citizenship was revolution. So long as the "keepers of the established rights" held power, such a revolution was impossible. If, for example, a general strike occurred in a major country or if any strike presaged revolution, the national establishments singly, or by collective security, would suppress it. Therefore, the "disestablishment of the rights of property and investment" was "not a simple matter of obsolescence through neglect."[62]

Veblen perceived that the statesmen would inevitably combine against revolution. If he had been a revolutionary planner, he might have indicated some ways and means for seizing power. He would have been called upon to answer such questions as: Who would lead the revolution? How could they seize control of strategic resources? What would be the relationship of revolutionary leaders to the masses? He might even have ended the *Nature of Peace* with a call for action. But the *Nature of Peace* was an inquiry, not a manifesto. Veblen recognized the virulence of the common man's patriot-ism, remarking wryly that it was "not a spirit of innovation."[63] His dark appreciation for the depth of nationalist attachments was the major intel-lectual (if not emotional) factor that prevented his revolutionary commit-ment. Once again he retreated into disengagement. The choice for mankind, he noted, lay between peace and the price-system. . . .

This current scheme of investment, business, and sabotage, should have an appreciably better chance of survival in the long run if the present con-ditions of warlike preparations and national insecurity were maintained, or if the projected peace were left in a somewhat problematical state, . . .

On the other hand . . . the cause of peace and its perpetuation might be materially advanced if precautions were taken beforehand to put out of the way . . . those discrepancies of interest and sentiment between nations and classes which make for dissension and eventual hostilities.[64]

[61] "The Passing of National Frontiers," 1918, *Essays in Our Changing Order*, p. 388.
[62] *Nature of Peace*, pp. 328–29, 363.
[63] *Ibid.*, p. 330.
[64] *Ibid.*, pp. 366–67.

The conclusion indicated the degree to which Veblen considered patriotic animosities, as much as capitalism itself, part of a determining substructure —the extent to which he departed from Marxist materialism. David Riesman has suggested that Veblen, in anticipating the persistence of patriotism, may have been naming the evil in order to ward it off.[65] If so, 1917 still offered that inverse evidence of Veblen's flickering hope. But the dark descended soon enough.

"DEMENTIA PRAECOX"

In the end it was Versailles and its aftermath more than the war itself that cast the shadow. Early in 1918, in an address before the National Institute of Social Science, Veblen said that if Americans really wanted peace they would have to do two things: (1) disallow "discretionary control" or management of any enterprise whose owner did not personally "direct the work in fellowship with his employees," and (2) administer as a public utility all businesses which had reached such a stage of "systematisation" that they could be handled from an office by accountancy methods. The government of experts should act for the public and displace the "absentee owners."[66] If Veblen actually expected this from the Wilson administration, then neither the "Mid-Victorian" Fourteen Points nor the Versailles Treaty could meet his expectations. Once again he was pointing out the necessity of revolution.

The whole significance of Veblen's reactions to Versailles turns upon the fact that a revolution had already taken place in Russia. Whether the peace was too hard (Veblen thought not) or too soft was not fundamentally the issue. The treaty expressed the panic of the vested interests in confronting the Russian revolution, as well as their determination to revive, with only minor modifications, the *status quo ante*. Veblen criticized John Maynard Keynes's *Economic Consequences of the Peace* (1920) for failing to consider seriously the common interests of Wilson and his European counterparts. "Of course this compact for the reduction of Soviet Russia was not written into the text of the treaty; it may be said to have been the parchment upon which the text was written."[67] The peace remained unstable largely because American intervention had not defeated Germany, but rather had prevented her conclusive defeat. Probably the Allies would have negotiated for this "peace without victory" even without American aid because their own interests depended upon preserving "the rule of the kept classes in Germany." What Keynes had ignored was the continual modifi-

---

[65] *Thorstein Veblen: A Critical Interpretation* (New York, Scribner, 1960), p. 124.
[66] "A Policy of Reconstruction," 1918, *Essays in Our Changing Order*, p. 396.
[67] "The Economic Consequences of the Peace," 1920, *Essays in Our Changing Order*, p. 464.

cation of the indemnity provisions, which in any case would not fall upon the absentee owners and which could be borne by the propertyless who would finally pay.[68]

Veblen was not resorting to conspiratorial history. He placed the blame for the peace terms on Wilson much less than did Keynes. He fully realized that neither did Wilson intend to revive European imperialism nor was he letting himself be fooled. On the contrary, Wilson fought hard for the liberal peace. But as the Allies confronted a Europe threatened by revolution, Wilson realized that America and Europe did have a common ground after all—the protection of their vested interests. With this realization Wilson's mid-Victorian liberalism and European imperialism united for the preservation of "commercialized nationalism"—Versailles.

The contrast, of course, was with a Veblenian peace that should answer the industrial needs of the future. The abatement of mid-Victorian liberalism required a revolutionary shift in power—from the statesmen to the production engineers—providing, of course, that the engineers were sufficiently enlightened to abandon the "awestruck political lieutenants of the vested interests."[69] Just how the engineers would achieve (or seize) power and when they might become enlightened enough to revolt, Veblen did not specify. These methodological details (which would have seemed more than details to an active revolutionist) did not trouble Veblen in 1919. Two years later he would reconsider the question of a Soviet of Engineers. In 1919 he was simply contrasting the possibility with Versailles. Apparently he could not decide whether some elitist engineers' society or the actual Soviet Union had a greater potentiality for the community. But in either case he was no man to dwell in Utopia. He began to measure the reality at hand.

After the November Revolution, Veblen considered the possibility that the Soviet Union might make democracy in his terms meaningful. His tendency to defend the underdog may have had something to do with his discovery of the Soviets. But so did his conception of democracy itself as "that frame of mind by virtue of which a people chooses to be collectively fortunate rather than nationally formidable."[70] Since 1904, at least, Veblen had considered representative institutions merely the political expression of business institutions. The Soviet's lack of a formal parliamentary structure troubled him little by 1919. He compared the Soviets to New England town meetings,[71] a sly reminder of America's own revolutionary traditions. The Soviets represented in Veblen's schema the same participatory democracies

---

[68] *Ibid.*, pp. 468–69.
[69] "Peace," 1919, *Essays in Our Changing Order*, p. 419.
[70] "Economic Penetration," p. 364.
[71] "Between Bolshevism and War," 1921, *Essays in Our Changing Order*, p. 441.

as had neighborhood organizations in Addams' and the provinces in Royce's.

Commentators have since speculated upon Veblen's possible response to Stalin's Russia—a power that borrowed technology and fiercely drove its own people in order to become both industrially and nationally formidable. The question, like so many other "ifs," becomes by its very nature unhistorical. Remembering the actual condition of Lenin's Russia and recalling Veblen's own distaste for constraint and dogma, one can hardly picture him the obedient Stalinist.[72] Yet the attempt to enlist his prestige for anti-Communism, posthumously, is even more ludicrous, since Veblen considered economic realities of prime importance. In spite of some earnest Bolshevik propaganda and the "red scare" in the West, the Soviet Union of 1920 was hardly ready to attack its neighbors—most of whom were engaged in attacking it. On the contrary, as Veblen recognized, the threat that the Soviets posed to the West was more a reflection of the condition of postwar Europe than of Soviet intentions. In brief, the threat was to the common man's faith in the vested interests.[73]

Not only had the Versailles Treaty made the world safe for the vested interests; it had also extended nationalism. To Veblen the principle of self-determination meant that the common man would have to bear the burdens of the national right to make war. Self-determination did not fulfill democracy. It sabotaged the democratic ideal of "live and let live." For the liberals of his day this was a paradoxical viewpoint indeed—denying as it did the relationship between freedom and national integrity. But Veblen never identified nationhood with freedom. Nationalities were communities of language and tradition which might be quite free without political separatism. The Welsh and Scots, for example, were nationalities, but not nations, and none the worse for British rule. The Irish were as hard-ridden by the vested interests and the "priestly pick-pockets" of their own island as by the British bureaucracy. The common man's need for a nation, which was only "an organization for collective offence and defence," was questionable to say the least.[74]

Whatever distinctions Veblen had drawn between the dynastic states and the democratic commonwealths had entirely disappeared by the 1920s. His appraisal of nationalism grew more polemical and bitter. The idea of

[72] Rosenberg, *Values of Veblen*, p. 105; Lerner, "Introduction," p. 39.
[73] "Bolshevism is a Menace to Whom?" 1919, *Essays in Our Changing Order*, pp. 412–13.
[74] *The Vested Interests and the Common Man* (New York, Huebsch, 1919), pp. 147–48.

sovereignty, he wrote, would doubtless appear to Freudians as "an inferiority complex with benefit of clergy."[75] He then attacked nationalism itself in the spirit of an evangelist discussing Adam's fall.

Born in iniquity and conceived in sin, the spirit of nationalism has never ceased to bend human institutions to the service of dissension and distress. In its material effects it is altogether the most sinister as well as the most imbecile of all those institutional encumbrances that have come down out of the old order. The national mob-mind of vanity, fear, hatred, contempt, and servility still continues to make the loyal citizen a convenient tool in the hands of the Adversary. . . .[76]

Clearly none of Veblen's playfulness and hardly any of his disinterested manner remained after 1919. He was not really disillusioned with the statesmen of Versailles, for he had expected little of them in the first place. Rather, it was the end of the common man's skepticism that drove him near despair. The matter-of-fact frame of mind died in postwar America as the potential skeptics turned red-baiters. This was hardly news, of course. For Veblen, however, it meant the conclusive abandonment of democratic hopes. Addams, who retained her faith in her neighbors, appeared quite gentle in her condemnation of those who learned their patriotic lessons too well—gentle, that is, by comparison with Veblen. Nothing could match Veblen's biting indictments in his *Dial* editorials of the American mass mind. The war had shocked Americans into a "dementia praecox." The power of organized religion, the "puerile credulities," the persecutions and deportations of advocates of "constructive sedition," the baiting of wobblies and conscientious objectors and pacifists for "excessive sanity," all signified mental derangement.[77]

Without any hope for a popular revolution Veblen turned to the engineers. The elitism of his earlier thought grew stronger. Only the action of a small group of technicians could build a rational and efficient economy. The engineers, being indispensable to the working of modern industry, had only to withdraw their support from business and prepare in an organized way to take it over. They would have to work out some arrangement with the mechanics and technicians of the major industries, but Veblen was not sure what this arrangement might be. In any case, the Soviet of Technicians was the only alternative to the continued rule by absentee owners.[78]

It is unlikely that Veblen actually contemplated such a revolution. Certainly he made no preparations for it in spite of his tenuous relationships

[75] *Absentee Ownership*, p. 26.
[76] *Ibid.*, pp. 38–39.
[77] "Dementia Praecox," 1922, *Essays in Our Changing Order*, pp. 427, 429–30.
[78] *The Engineers and the Price System* (New York, Viking Press, 1921), pp. 52, 69, 74–76, 80–82, 165–68.

during the latter half of 1919 with certain leaders of the American Society of Mechanical Engineers. One of the engineers working on the Giant Power Survey, Morris L. Cooke, after several discussions with Veblen on the social role of the engineer, concluded: "He was a bully good counselor but only as to theory. There was too little physique there to help on action." And Max Eastman remarked that Veblen's Soviet of Technicians proved to be a "soviet of abstractions."[79] Veblen lacked, among other things, any deeply rooted and creative faith in the coming revolution. He recognized that the engineers were as excessively loyal to the price system as was any other segment of the population.[80] They had not yet caught up with the social implications of their own work. And Veblen could not lead them into the necessary action. He turned his back upon organizations; he had none of the political leaders' hunger for power, and even refused to consider the means of achieving power. In short, he remained Thorstein Veblen, not Lenin.

Such apolitical thinking, carried to extremes as in Royce's and Veblen's plans, could never match the effectiveness of political activism. Even the theoretical clarity of these men was marred by excessive noninvolvement. For example, Veblen's "industrial republic" was supposed to fulfill the promise of the democratic commonwealth. It was to create "neighborly fellowships of ungraded masterless men given over to 'life, liberty, and the pursuit of happiness.' "[81] But Veblen's later works implied that the Soviet of Technicians should be the instrumentality of revolution. The instrument suggests far more concentrated authority than the anarchistic, egalitarian vision could hold. Veblen refused to examine closely either means or ends. That would have made him a Utopian instead of a critic. And so both the hazy goal and the contradictory method remained, along with Veblen's more pervasive commitment to unending (rather than teleological) change. A contrast to Marx, the theorist as leader, suggests once again that Veblen was not completely committed to revolution. If he had been, he would have had to face the obvious difficulty that no concentrated authority, however scientific and disinterested, could remain apolitical.

In addition, the question of the relationship of the engineer-leaders to the mass of the population demanded an answer even in theory. Veblen presumed that by allowing the free working out of industrial forces, the engineers would perform their tasks for the welfare of the whole population. But perhaps the people would have their own opinions as to what constituted their welfare. As John Dewey observed in 1926, the American people had no more reason to acknowledge the rule by the experts than they

---

[79] Quoted in Dorfman, *Veblen,* pp. 455, 460.
[80] *Engineers and the Price System,* pp. 137–38.
[81] *Absentee Ownership,* p. 28.

had to accept in such an unquestioning manner the rule by vested interests. Experts could supply facts, but no expertise could make the process of coming to decisions a conventionalized routine.[82] Decisions affecting the lives of large numbers of people were in their very nature political; and if a system were democratic, even in Veblen's sense, some institutions for popular control had to be provided.

Because Veblen's economic theory left little room for the close examination of political processes, he evidently was "not troubled" by this limitation. His was not in any sense a theory calling for action. In spite of the clear revolutionary tenor of his later thought, he never really planned a revolution. Dr. Louis Jaffe observed of Veblen's brief stay in Washington:

I suspect . . . [that] his secret desire was that the world should remain as it was. Such mastery as he had was based upon his knowledge of its idiosyncracies. He hated the thought that it might escape from the forms which he could despise to forms which he would have to accept.[83]

This is too dark a picture of Veblen's intentions, which were critical for the sake of a better creation. But it does point to the fact that Veblen did not visualize that better creation clearly. He kept his eyes on the powerful obstructions to change more than upon the revolutionary potential. It was the cultural lags and enslaving habits that commanded his attention, not the Utopia. Other men would try to use Veblenian criticism not only to understand business cycles, depressions, and national conflicts, but to some extent to cure them. The failure of the technocracy movement of the 1930s[84] only illustrated the difficulty of applying even Veblen's most sophisticated theories to complex, changing realities. This difficulty Veblen, the master-skeptic, would have appreciated.

[82] Kaplan, "Social Engineers as Saviors," p. 363.

[83] Quoted in Riesman, *Veblen: A Critical Interpretation*, pp. 124–25.

[84] Dorfman, *Veblen*, pp. 510–14. The technocrats, followers of Howard Scott, were reported to have surveyed the American economy and concluded that continued unemployment was inevitable unless the engineers managed the economy and the price system were abandoned. The newspaper accounts, and several of the "technocrats" themselves considered Veblen's *The Engineers and the Price System* the Bible of the movement. Others claimed that Veblen had learned from Scott. The movement, which was an overnight sensation in late 1932, had died before "much of 1933 had passed." Its chief effect seems to have been to attract more people to Veblen's theories.

CHAPTER VII

Woodrow Wilson: The Polity as an Instrument of National Policy

We are participants, whether we would or not, in the life of the world. The interests of all nations are our own also. We are partners with the rest. What affects mankind is inevitably our affair as well as the affair of the nations of Europe and of Asia.

Woodrow Wilson, Address before the League to
Enforce Peace, May 24, 1916

I can fancy those men of the first generation that so thoughtfully set this great Government up, the generation of Washington and Hamilton and Jefferson and the Adamses—I can fancy their looking on with a sort of enraptured amazement that the American spirit should have made conquest of the world.

Woodrow Wilson, Address, Kansas City, Mo.,
September 6, 1919

Veblen's savage indictment of the vested interests signaled the return of community distrust of politics. For a brief moment during the war years, doubts had been suspended and institutions had become acceptable as instruments for change. Royce had pictured the belligerents turning toward the insurance community. Veblen believed that the demands of wartime efficiency might revolutionize the state. Jane Addams, in spite of her pacifism, worked to transform the Food Administration into an agency of

179

international cooperation. This quickened tempo of hope concealed the deeper distrust of the instruments of power and of those who used them.

In large measure the hopes were a tribute, as resounding as the applause of Paris, to Woodrow Wilson and to what he represented. For although Wilson never sought a compromise with community ideals, although his internationalism was very limited in scope, the significance of his commitment impressed internationalists of all persuasions. The central position the League of Nations occupied in Wilson's later wartime foreign policy indicated, to most American internationalists, that an opportunity had arrived for the realization of a new international structure. Ideals would at last be supported by power. Neither the tardiness nor the limitations of Wilson's devotion to the cause could detract from his glittering promise of a new order. Wilson's devotion was significant because it portended achievement. Not only at critical moments in the history of American neutrality but during the war as well, Wilson had directed the attention of the masses of America and of Europe to the programs of the European Left and of American and British League groups. While in 1918 and 1919 he had deliberately brought internationalist ideals to bear against the German military and the Russian Bolsheviks, both his oratory and his methods held great promise. For by uniting internationalism with national purposes and wartime fervor, Wilson was experimenting with the union of ideals and interests. He seemed for a time to be preparing the ground for a truly popular internationalism.

President Wilson's internationalism did not and could not flow from a commitment to ideals alone. The office that gave him the opportunity to carry out a new policy severely limited his range of choices. He was responsible not to a set of universal ideals but to the American people and their national interests. Those interests might or might not accord with the highest social ethics. As the President understood American goals (even short-range goals), they did fuse with universal goals. Nevertheless his approach to international ideals was necessarily different from the path chosen by those who were not themselves responsible for the formulation of policy. Instead of simply formulating plans to fulfill ideals, Wilson selected ideals with which to carry out plans. Virtually every aspect of his internationalist thought bore a dual meaning. Self-determination accorded with his fundamentally atomistic view of international society. But Wilson's defense of self-determination proved very useful in shattering the resistance of the Central Powers. Of course, all the internationalists believed that they were answering the needs of their society. But they engaged in the dialogue by choice, whereas the President sought a road to a stable world of necessity.

Two additional forces influenced Wilson's attempts to pattern his foreign policy—the pressures of his domestic opponents and the need to respond to immediate crises in a revolutionary world. In spite of Wilson's 1912 victory and of Democratic control over both houses of Congress from 1913 to 1918, in spite of Wilson's strong control over his party and of his successful record of legislative achievement, he was at a double disadvantage in foreign affairs. His partisan and personal opponents, Theodore Roosevelt and Henry Cabot Lodge, having a different picture of the means of achieving American preeminence in world affairs, had long held leadership in this area. Public interest in, and understanding of, foreign affairs was very limited at best. Traditional views of Europe as old and corrupt militated against the kind of deeply involved Americanized world order that Wilson envisioned.

Moreover, throughout his years in the presidency Wilson had faced innumerable problems growing out of revolutionary changes taking place in Mexico, in China, and in Russia. He found himself weighing the impact of immediate decisions, which he could not avoid, upon long-range purposes. While in domestic affairs he could play the role of reformer, confident that both the public temper and his own increased awareness of the means to set in order the American economy supported him, in foreign affairs neither his knowledge nor his support was as certain. The world he confronted was already in a primary state of disintegration. As a reformer he had to take care to conserve the stability essential to American interests.

By 1918 every action or postponement of action had some effect upon his major decisions: How much reform should there be within the traditional state system in order to rid that system of its ancient imperial rivalries and alliances? How far did the changes have to go in order to lessen the attraction of Bolshevism? Would the resistance to revolution necessarily play into the hands of the keepers of the old order?[1]

In the formulation of his concept of the new order, however, Wilson was more certain. At no time did his ideals, which were both nationalist and internationalist, deny any demand that served the enlightened self-interest of the United States. Wilson viewed the expansion of American economic, political, and moral influence as essential to a peaceful world. While community thinkers often contrasted the goals of national ambition with those of world peace, Wilson envisioned them as virtually identical so long as the goals in each case could be considered American. It was the American mission to bring justice, democracy, and prosperity to the world. For these purposes the world needed an instrument to preserve stability, to prevent aggression, and to filter political change. That instrument was the

[1] N. Gordon Levin, Jr., *Woodrow Wilson and World Politics* (New York, Oxford Univ. Press, 1968), pp. 2–9, gives an excellent analysis of Wilson's anti-imperialism contesting Bolshevism.

League of Nations. Peace as well as prosperity followed upon the increasing influence of American capitalism. The President's frequent statements of American disinterestedness, and of the likemindedness of the world peoples implied that among the enlightened and those with a broad perspective there existed a common understanding of the requirements of peace.

A LEADER OF MEN

Wilson's predilection for the liberal polity grew out of his long-held tendency to view institutions as well as men as moral agents. Whether studying British and American government while still a young man, or reforming the structure and teaching system of Princeton University when he was its President, or proposing reforms in the relations of business and government after he had become President of the United States, Wilson displayed a similar political moralism. Certain political and economic arrangements, he believed, degraded men. Other structures ennobled them. Thus the institutions themselves in a sense either embodied or failed to embody moral standards.

A highly righteous, much beloved and admired father, the Reverend James Ruggles Wilson, a leading Southern Presbyterian minister, had shaped the foundations of this moralism in the days of Radical Reconstruction in Georgia. Young Wilson grew sensitively aware of, as well as very proud of, the fighting Covenanter tradition of his parents' past. And he used the strictest standards in judging not only himself but his fellows and the political life around him. Reading avidly the liberal journals, the *Edinburgh Review* and E. L. Godkin's *Nation,* he saw a contrast between high moral accomplishment of the Manchesterian liberals and the gross corruption of the Gilded Age.[2] Perhaps because Wilson learned to speak with precision and power, perhaps because his father was so respected as a preacher and because the South so clearly lacked high-minded leaders (at least, white Southerners who had supported the Confederacy so thought), Wilson studied with intense interest reports of liberal England. In the England of William Ewart Gladstone, his hero, men of true principles and generous literary and oratorical talents were respected. Real political leadership emerged.

Oratory and writing, the use of language to persuade others occupied much of Wilson's attention during his undergraduate years at Princeton. Still admiring Gladstone, he wrote of other powerful men. The success of

[2] Henry Wilkinson Bragdon, *Woodrow Wilson: The Academic Years* (Cambridge, Harvard Univ. Press, 1967), p. 10.

Otto von Bismarck was measured, John Bright admired, William Pitt worshipped.[3] And always his delight in these men served to sharpen the contrast with an impoverished South. He believed that the irresponsibility and cynicism of his own time grew out of the tyranny of congressional power and a corrupt rule that inverted the South's normal social order. The attempted social revolution of Reconstruction he associated with the destruction of liberty and progress, the stable traditions of liberal Britain with the assurance of both.[4] It seemed clear to Woodrow Wilson, even as he wrote his first book, *Congressional Government,* and turned his back upon the profession of law to enter Johns Hopkins in 1883, that the open exercise of power in Parliament by a prime minister and his cabinet developed the best leadership in a democracy and served to educate the people themselves in democratic processes.[5] Perhaps President Wilson's taste for open diplomacy and for direct appeals to the people, as well as his marked aversion to forcible occupation of another's land, both bore the mark of his Southern recollections of Congressional Reconstruction.

Certainly his anti-revolutionary concepts of democracy and his concern for the quality of leadership sprang from both personal and academic sources. He wanted to learn, he confided to his fiancee, Ellen Louise Axson, in 1883, "the arts of persuasion," the present forces and the "possibilities of the future" that he might develop skills in enlisting others for his purposes. He sought knowledge in order to exercise power.[6] There was, then, nothing cloistered about Wilson's conception of the historian and college teacher. Though the scholarly life appeared a less direct route to the world of power and action than did the law, yet Wilson found it a valuable and enlightening one; and it rarely diverted him from his main interest and goal—politics.

In Herbert Baxter Adams' famous seminar at Johns Hopkins, Wilson absorbed the Anglo-Saxonism of his teacher while cultivating an interest in what would later become the New History as offered by his friend, Frederick Jackson Turner. Like the New Historians, Wilson would become

[3] In *The Public Papers of Woodrow Wilson,* 6 vols. (cited hereafter as *Public Papers*), eds. Ray Stannard Baker and William E. Dodd (New York, Harper, 1925–27), see: "Prince Bismarck," Nov. 1877, I, 1–10; "William Earl Chatham," Oct. 1878, I, 11–18; "John Bright," March 1880, I, 43–59; and "Mr. Gladstone, A Character Sketch," April 1880, I, 63–88.

[4] Wilson's notes on Green's *History of the English People,* July 27, 1878 indicates some interesting historical parallels. See, Arthur S. Link (ed) *The Papers of Woodrow Wilson,* 3 vols. (cited hereafter as *Wilson Papers;* Princeton, Princeton Univ. Press, 1966–67), I, 391, and II, 27, 37.

[5] Link, *Wilson Papers,* II, 215, 218, 266, 267; Arthur S. Link, *Wilson: The Road to the White House* (Princeton, Princeton Univ. Press, 1947), pp. 13–15.

[6] Link, *Wilson Papers,* II, 499.

a reformer who realized the connection between domestic economic structure and foreign policy.[7] His conception of American foreign economic policy, especially trade expansion, appeared to bear the marks of Turner's understanding of the significance of the closing of the frontier. However, his conception of democracy was far more traditional and conservative. Like the two British political analysts he most admired, Edmund Burke and Walter Bagehot, Wilson contrasted the turbulent revolutionary discontents of France with the organic development of British democracy. He believed that the American "spirit" creating free institutions was fundamentally "Saxon." Slowly evolving self-government "elevated the masses" almost to the level of their leaders, while Jacobinism brought chaos, oppression, and reaction. Wilson's faith in popular judgment was qualified by his insistence upon enlightened leadership. The people knew best only when properly directed and inspired. He never believed, as did the truly conservative Butler, that the masses were fundamentally irrational; nor did he share Holt's cheerful faith in their goodness. Wilson's democratic faith was circumscribed by his insistence that the institutions must allow for the development of popular understanding and for the progress of popular self-control.[8]

Wilson's concepts of leaders and followers, institutions and morality, strongly contrasted with community ideals as both Addams and Veblen understood them. Addams had seen the American people of the 1890s as more knowledgeable than the traditional leaders—more understanding of the core of democratic ethics. In 1898 Wilson viewed the people "as clay in the hands of the consummate leader." For Addams the lowliest were an inspiration. But Wilson saw them as men to be supplied with a leader's power and methods. Veblen looked upon the major technological changes of the twentieth century as being in direct conflict with American leadership and institutions. But Wilson held that strong leaders perceived the direction of the underlying forces of their time and persuaded others to use them.[9] The spread of self-government and private enterprise were themselves forces.

In spite of Wilson's discussions of democratic society in organic terms, the heart of his system of thought was far from organic. In the very center

[7] Arno J. Mayer, "Historical Thought and American Foreign Policy in the Era of the First World War," *The Historian and the Diplomat,* ed. Francis L. Loewenheim, (New York, Harper, 1967), pp. 80–81.

[8] "The Significance of American History," Sept. 9, 1901, typescript in Speech file of the Woodrow Wilson Papers, Manuscript Division, Library of Congress (cited hereafter as Wilson MSS); Harley Notter, *The Origins of the Foreign Policy of Woodrow Wilson* (Baltimore, Johns Hopkins Press, 1937), pp. 19–22; Woodrow Wilson, *The State: Elements of Historical and Practical Politics* (Boston, Heath, 1889), pp. 173, 464–68, 575, 595–97.

[9] Woodrow Wilson, *Leaders of Men,* T. H. Vail Motter, ed. (Princeton, Princeton Univ. Press, 1952), pp. 25–26, 28, 50, 53.

stood the lonely individual, responsible for his own conduct and risking, as Wilson used to love to say, "the integrity of his own soul." Wilson never separated the political and economic aspects of his philosophy from this moral individualism. His Calvinist background established the belief that God tested the moral worth of each man in the life of action. If the Puritan was a moral athlete, then Wilson remained a Puritan all his days. But the darker aspects of Calvinism, the deep sense of man's unworthiness and inevitable sin were abandoned for the more popular nineteenth-century belief that man not only could remake himself, but was obliged to do so. This obligation entailed the restraint of every selfish passion and the cultivation of altruism and thoughtful reason.[10]

Above all he realized that no man could shift the responsibility for his own conduct. This assumption, together with his own economic cautiousness, led him to challenge progressive ideas of accepting and regulating monopoly. "One really responsible man in jail, one originator of the schemes . . . contrary to public interest legally lodged in the penitentiary would be worth more than a thousand corporations mulcted in fines. . . ."[11] And the fundamental moral atomism did not completely leave him. He remained respectful of the implications of "this lonely dying." It meant that each man separately had to remain faithful to his own ideals; had to answer to God's absolute standard of righteousness.

And yet in the days of the social gospel and during his Presidency Wilson could hardly avoid some concession to social duty. By 1914 he had come to believe that Christianity meant more than just saving one's own soul. It meant lifting one's brother, serving the nation, enlightening one's fellows. Wilson considered that groups of men, and nations as well as individuals, might have to answer to God's will and judgment.[12]

Neither Wilson's appreciation of the relationship between society and institutions nor his sternly moral psychology implied an integrated scholarly outlook. His contributions to American political theory and to the study of American history were far from original. At graduate school he had neglected his opportunities to study the advancing newer psychology. His psychological and social insights during this period appeared personal rather than academic. As Merle Curti has observed, Wilson's own habit of reining in his emotions led him to value self-restraint and to assume that others could exercise it. He especially commended the qualities of dispas-

[10] "The Ministry and the Individual," 1909, *Public Papers*, II, 178; Arthur S. Link, *Wilson the Diplomatist* (Chicago, Quadrangle Paperbacks, 1965), p. 14.
[11] "The Author and Signers of the Declaration of Independence," July 4, 1907, Speech File, Wilson MSS.
[12] "Militant Christianity," 1914, *Public Papers*, III, 200, 208; Henry R. May, *Protestant Churches and Industrial America* (New York, Harper, 1949), p. 230.

sionate judgment and dignified self-control as standards of national behavior during American neutrality.[13]

The characteristics he admired implied an almost aristocratic poise: easy genuineness, "robust moral sanity," enough courage to stand by convictions and state them openly, especially when principles were involved; enough practical good sense to slow the pace of change when popular understanding required.[14] In spite of his personal romanticism, of his belief that love and altruism were the saving graces of human nature, Wilson's psychology lay very much within the old pattern of the rational tradition.

THE NEW FREEDOM IN A REVOLUTIONARY WORLD

The Manchesterian Liberals, whose statesmanship Wilson so admired, reinforced his regional biases toward light government and free trade. In virtually his first public statement outside of university clubs, Wilson testified before the United States Tariff Commission in Atlanta in 1882 and condemned the protective tariff as a bounty for the inferior manufacturer. Implied in his arguments were the classically liberal assumptions of a harmony of interests among consumers and the enlightened manufacturers.[15] The actual condition of the American economy in the midst of an organizational revolution he ignored.

Yet Wilson was not rigidly committed to any abstract system. One year after his testimony, after exposure to Richard T. Ely's seminar in political economy at Johns Hopkins, he confessed that some governmental intervention for the purpose of integrating "enterprise and capital into these islands of competition which keep prices at a proper level of justice" would be a practical homage to the principles of Adam Smith. He was already approaching, although he was far from arriving at, his 1912 position calling for regulated competition—government intervention for the protection of the enterprising man entering the economy but acceptance of the bigness that followed naturally from efficiency.[16] The passivity of laissez faire accorded neither with American realities nor with Wilson's active intelligence.

[13] Merle Curti, "Woodrow Wilson's Conception of Human Nature," Midwest Journal of Political Science, I (May 1957), 1–3; Wilson, "American Neutrality," Aug. 19, 1914, Public Papers, III, 158.

[14] Woodrow Wilson, On Being Human (New York, Harper, 1916), pp. 23–24.

[15] Statement before the US Tariff Commission, Atlanta, Sept. 22, 1882, Wilson Papers, II, 141; William Diamond, The Economic Thought of Woodrow Wilson (Baltimore, Johns Hopkins Press, 1943), pp. 170–71, indicates the connection between Wilson's early Manchesterian beliefs and certain aspects of his foreign policy.

[16] Wilson's notes on Adam Smith, 1883, Wilson Papers, II, 541; Diamond, Economic Thought of Wilson, pp. 28–33.

It was policy-making rather than economic theory that attracted both the academic historian and the presidential candidate. His was preeminently a political rather than an economic interest. Thus, of the classical school he retained only the belief that the enlightened self-interest of competitors served both private profit and community need. The government should enforce the justice of natural competition, should assure business of stability and predictability, and should mediate between labor and capital in order to avoid "the Scylla of socialism and the Charybdis of plutocratic power."[17] The implications of Wilson's New Freedom were directly pertinent to his international thought. First, there was the idea that an enterprise (or nation) which grew by inherent power and efficiency served everyone's interest automatically. Secondly, Wilson's dark suspicions of special privilege and monopolistic practices, the strangling of the opportunities of others, translated into his abhorrence of the evils of the traditional imperial nations—militarism and suppression of the people. Thirdly, Wilson's early concern over the tariff had by 1912 developed into a full-fledged commitment for the expansion of the merchant marine and for the open door for American manufacturers all over the world. The U.S. market was not big enough for the American economy.

If prosperity is not to be checked in this country, we must broaden our borders and make conquest of the markets of the world. That is the reason that America is so deeply interested in . . . breaking down . . . that dam against which all the tides of our prosperity have banked up . . . the protective tariff. I would prefer to call it the restrictive tariff.[18]

Well before the 1912 campaign, when Wilson was completing the last volume of his *History of the American People* (1902) he indicated how he reconciled the expansion of American trade with the view that America had a humanitarian and ethico-political mission in the world. The Spanish-American War, he asserted, had come during a critical transformation in American life. The economy was so strong that the United States was emerging from her debtor position. Her industrial and agricultural surpluses required a world market. The spaces of the continent were "reduced to the uses of civilization," and young men looked for careers beyond the old frontiers. The closing of the frontier both directed American attention outward and thrust her economy into the interdependent world. She now competed with all the powers for the coveted markets of the awakening East, and therefore found the foothold in the Philippines essential.[19]

[17] Diamond, *Economic Thought of Wilson,* pp. 65–73.
[18] Address, Gloucester, N.J., Aug. 15, 1912, *A Crossroads of Freedom: The 1912 Campaign Speeches of Woodrow Wilson,* ed. John W. Davidson (New Haven, Yale Univ. Press, 1956), p. 47.
[19] *A History of the American People,* Vol. V: *Reunion and Nationalization* (New York, Harper, 1902), pp. 265, 296.

There was little doubt in Wilson's mind about American economic success in this world competition once the barriers of tariff and inadequate merchant marine had been removed.[20] Significantly, he viewed this economic expansion as an expansion of political influence too—an influence not only in America's possession, the Philippines, but throughout the Far East. Just one year after John Hay's Open Door Notes proclaiming American commitment to equal trading rights and to the political independence of China, Wilson observed:

The East is to be open and transformed, whether we will or no; the standards of the West are to be imposed upon it; nations and peoples who have stood still the centuries through are to be quickened, and . . . [to be made] part of the universal world of commerce and ideas. . . . It is our peculiar duty, as it is also England's, to moderate the process in the interests of liberty: to impart to the peoples thus driven upon the road of change, so far as we have the opportunity or can make it, our own principles of self-help; teach them order and self-control in the midst of change; . . .[21]

In brief, America's material power would become the vehicle of her moral influence and vice versa. Self-government, which Wilson, like all members of the polity, believed a peculiarly Anglo-American gift, was now to be developed among other peoples under American tutelage. Evidently in 1901 Wilson was still emphasizing the organic character of political liberty and its spiritual force, for he asserted that no people could give another the "gift of character." Yet the "common training" that bound the American generations was about to be shared.[22]

The meaning of the Wilsonian vision of America's mission was tested almost as soon as Wilson entered upon his first term as President. In China, in the wake of the shattered ancient order, a struggling revolutionary movement awaited the actions of an international consortium which some members of President Taft's administration had devised to dilute exclusive Japanese control over Manchurian railroads. The American bankers would not go in without Wilson's consent. But to Wilson the whole thing smacked again of government-protected privilege, of an infringement upon Chinese sovereignty, and was unnecessary in any case for the expansion of American influence in China. In breaking with the consortium, Wilson inadvertently allowed the temporary expansion of Japanese influence, but he also carved out a unique sphere of American moral-political influence with the Republic. The United States became, it appeared, China's friend. This friendship did American investment no harm when,

[20] In *Crossroads of Freedom,* see: Speech of Acceptance, Sea Girt, N.J., Aug. 7, 1912, pp. 33–34; and Address, Philadelphia, Oct. 28, 1912, pp. 487–89.
[21] "Democracy and Efficiency," March 1901, *Public Papers,* I, 412.
[22] "Significance of American History," p. 10.

somewhat later, Wilson agreed that it was not so immoral, after all, for American economic strength to block the Japanese.[23]

In Latin America, where the pattern of American intervention to protect the area near the Panama Canal Zone had become well established, Wilson and his near-pacifist Secretary of State, William Jennings Bryan, faced innumerable problems. It was easy enough to be anti-imperialist when some other power was intervening, or when the territorial integrity of the weak nation accorded with American interests. In the Caribbean, both American business and American security required stability, but Latin America was entering a period of increasing chaos. Mexico experienced the deep convulsions of a true twentieth-century revolution. Although Wilson believed in self-determination and in the peaceful settlement of disputes, he insisted that the South American Republics be taught to elect good men. Ironically, Wilson's very concern that the Mexican and Caribbean governments represent their people as well as protect American interests eventuated in a good deal more American intervention than either Roosevelt or Taft had found necessary. Nor were the Caribbean governments particularly democratic after the United States had taken a hand in their affairs.[24]

The upheaval in Mexico illustrated, as well as did any pattern of events, the contradictions of Wilson's political ethos operating in the midst of revolution. First, Wilson refused recognition of the Huerta government because Victoriano Huerta had come to power by betraying the revolution and by murdering his chief, Francisco Madero. The other conservative powers dealt with the *de facto* government, not only because it was there, but because Huerta seemed likely to restore the ancient rule of dictatorship and foreign investment. Having failed to persuade the man he would not acknowledge as ruler of Mexico that he ought to reform, Wilson succeeded in isolating Huerta diplomatically.

Thus far Wilson had protected the American position against the European interests. However, while condemning Huerta for his undemocratic practices, and while cautioning Americans to respect Mexico's right of self-determination, Wilson found an occasion for military intervention at Vera Cruz. Then as the Constitutionalists' first chief, Venustiano Carranza, assumed power, Wilson, whose liberal ideals should have been satisfied,

[23] Arthur S. Link, *Wilson: The New Freedom* (Princeton, Princeton Univ. Press, 1956), pp. 284–88; William Appleman Williams, *The Tragedy of American Diplomacy*, rev. ed. (New York, Delta, 1962), pp. 68–79. Williams denies Link's contention that Wilson's cancellation of the consortium was naive and self-sacrificing. Emphasizing the importance of economic advantages in Wilson's moralism, Williams sees the cancellation of the consortium as a first step toward greater expansion of American economic predominance in the Far East.

[24] Selig Adler, "Bryan and Wilsonian Caribbean Penetration," *Hispanic American Historical Review*, XX (May 1940), 205; Arthur S. Link, *Woodrow Wilson and the Progressive Era 1910–1917* (New York, Harper, 1954), pp. 93–94 ff.

took a different tack. Where before he had wanted liberty for the Mexicans, now he wanted order. Carranza was alternately too weak or too stubborn for *de jure* recognition. The State Department carefully estimated the pliability of "Pancho" Villa. It is ironical Wilson eventually felt compelled to send General Pershing in pursuit of this bandit Villa upon whom the President and Bryan, misinformed, had briefly pinned their hopes.[25] Many of Wilson's actions proved antithetical to his intentions. Hoping to contain the Mexican revolution at a stable and democratic level, he found American policy being shaped by its unexpected turnings. In order to have a responsible government in Mexico City—a government which would make American military intervention unnecessary—Wilson intervened. To give the Mexican people the right to choose their own form of government, he tried to dam up their revolution. To win their friendship, he insulted their dignity.

Yet, paradoxically, Wilson succeeded in the broadest sense. He protected and extended the American liberal view of the right government for Mexico. He controlled the claims of special American interest while backing the interests of the American political and economic system in general. The only failure was the failure of his highest, international ideal —the ideal of national freedom and self-determination. And this was most ironic of all. As he wrote Lindley M. Garrison, the Secretary of War, "There are . . . no conceivable circumstances which would make it right for us to direct by force or by threat of force the internal processes of what is a . . . revolution as profound as that which occurred in France." Wilson was resisting conservative pressures for an American assumption of power. The date was August 8, 1914. American marines were at that very moment in possession of Vera Cruz.[26]

It was the Mexican revolution, with all its implications for extended disorder in the Hemisphere, that first drove Wilson to consider an international organization as the vehicle for American responsibility. Since he later saw the League of Nations as an extension of this Pan-American idea—a Monroe Doctrine for the world—the context is significant. In the fall of 1914 Wilson's most confidential advisor, Colonel Edward M. House, proposed a pact for a mutual guarantee of political independence and territorial integrity. The number of functions this Pan-American Pact was to serve is in itself a revelation of Wilson's frame of mind, which House understood perhaps better than any of the President's other associates.

The first purpose of the Union was the allaying of Latin suspicions of

---

[25] Link, *Wilson and the Progressive Era*, Ch. 5; Lloyd C. Gardiner, "American Foreign Policy, 1900–1921: A Second Look at the Realist Critique of American Diplomacy," *Towards a New Past: Dissenting Essays in American History*, ed. Barton J. Bernstein (New York, Pantheon, 1968), pp. 215–19.
[26] Wilson MSS.

the United States. The interests of the Americas, House wanted it understood, were entirely mutual. All wanted to preserve their own independence. None wanted intervention in the others' affairs. All wanted peaceful settlements of disputes. Since the Wilson administration's own policies were weakening the American-created instrument for such settlements, the Central American Court of Justice, the hesitancy of the Hemisphere's ambassadors was understandable.[27] Nevertheless, a good deal more than a peace move was intended.

The 1914 proposal of the pact, as Wilson phrased it, revealed the second purpose. The pact would guarantee not only the territory of the states and their political independence, but also their "republican form of government." (The United States action in Mexico indicated that Wilson might not be easily satisfied on that score.) It contained also a pledge for complete governmental control of munitions manufacture and sale. It was, in short, a proposed pact for protecting the right kind of governments. In addition, House viewed the instrument in its broader implication as the fulfillment of an American mission. The policy would "weld the Western Hemisphere together [and] . . . serve as a model for the European nations when peace is at last brought about. I could see that this excited his enthusiasm."[28]

The following fall, the task of pushing the proposal among the ambassadors of Argentina, Brazil, and Chile fell to the new Secretary of State, Robert Lansing, while House and Wilson were still conditioning their recognition of Carranza by demands for political amnesty, land reforms, and protection of foreigners' just claims.[29] The incongruity of urging a pledge for nonintervention in this context seems to have occurred to no one except the Latin ambassadors themselves. But it was only when the private negotiations for the pact had failed, and when President Wilson had made a public declaration of general American purposes in the hemisphere at the Pan American Scientific Congress on January 6, 1916, that the full implications became apparent. The Monroe Doctrine, Wilson declared, had not stated how the United States would use her power in the Western Hemisphere. Now the United States would make this clear. She would join her neighbors in guaranteeing international peace and arbitration in the Americas, and, in order to do this, would ask for an agreement prohibiting revolutionary expeditions outfitted against neighboring countries, or arms supplied to revolutionists in other countries.

You see what our thought is, gentlemen, not only the international peace of America but the domestic peace of America. If American States are constantly in ferment, if any of them are constantly in ferment, there will

[27] Charles Seymour, *The Intimate Papers of Colonel House,* 4 vols. (Boston, Houghton Mifflin, 1926–28), I, 209–10.

[28] *Ibid.,* pp. 207–209.

[29] *Ibid.,* pp. 216, 221, 224–25.

be a standing threat to their relations with one another. It is just as much to our interest to assist each other to the orderly processes within our own borders as it is to orderly processes in our controversies with one another.[30]

Thus, at its very inception, the Wilsonian concept of an international organization, here a Pan-American organization, had its own distinctive emphasis. It was to be an organization for the protection of each single state as well as for the protection of all—a proposition somewhat different from the accepted British and American League to Enforce Peace ideas. And there was a suggestion in it, too, that only the stable and constitutional governments would be worthy of such membership and such protection. The Mexican revolution had perhaps nourished the seed, planted long before by Edmund Burke. The just polity should be a road away from revolution.

"THE RIGHT IS MORE PRECIOUS THAN THE PEACE"

During almost three years of European conflict, 1914 to 1917, the United States struggled to maintain her neutrality. This struggle critically shaped American ideas about preventing future wars. Yet during the same three years, Woodrow Wilson, who would shortly become the world spokesman for a liberal peace, for the most part avoided consideration of specific features of a league. His position and the maintenance of American neutrality necessitated caution. Wilson realized that the major effect of detailed commitments to a league would be to arouse counterproposals or domestic opposition to the league.[31] Public discussion might be interpreted either by his partisan enemies, or by overconfident or over-anxious Entente powers as a prelude to American entry.

Yet it was the President's own conviction as much as the exigencies of the situation that led him to delay discussion. For most internationalists the prospective league or prospective communal activities were virtually ends in themselves. Beyond them lay a progressively more peaceful world. For Wilson, however, the prospective league was an instrument of peace, largely because it was to be an instrument of America's foreign policy. American dedication to national rights and just settlements was the critical peacemaking factor. The league structure was to develop around that. The United States would sacrifice provincial selfishness, but not practical self-interest, by joining such a league, for she would have a major part in its decisions.[32]

[30] *Public Papers*, III, 444.

[31] Seymour, *Intimate Papers of Colonel House*, IV, 7, 49.

[32] Wilson, Memorial Day Address, May 30, 1916, *Public Papers*, IV, 194–95. For additional references to America's unique mission in the world, see also pp. 6–8, 233, 244, 323.

Wilson's interpretation of American neutrality and belligerency both point to this nationalistic interpretation of internationalism, this crucial reversal of means and ends. Even the timing of his relatively few statements about league structure (before 1918) point to it. When the demands of American neutrality dictated silence, Wilson was silent. When Wilson's goals for America as a mediator dictated a statement about a league, he made such a statement. In this regard, as in so many others, Wilson's idealism consisted, as Daniel M. Smith has observed, not in "ignoring of practical considerations but [in] the exalting of noble purposes and goals."[33]

As we have seen, the forms of international proposals emerged not only from *Weltanschauungen* and from interpretations of the causes of wars in general, but from particular understandings of the origins of the first world war. Wilson, who understood from personal experience the social disruption and fundamental corruption that followed in the wake of a great war, viewed the war in Europe as a crisis in the old order of secret diplomacy and imperial dominance.[34] To a far more pronounced degree than his second Secretary of State, Robert Lansing, or, for that matter, than most conservative men of the polity, he took a neutral position on the origins of the war. "It will be found before long," he remarked in confidence to a New York *Times* reporter in December 1914, "that Germany is not alone responsible for the war and that some other nations will have to bear a portion of the blame in our eyes." And this statement came even as he recognized that American interests would be served if, on the one hand, the Entente Powers won, but if, on the other, their victory over the Central Powers was not totally crushing.[35]

The President's public statements were, of course, more circumspect. His own example encouraged Americans to withhold judgment about the war. But this self-control did not indicate passivity. The war was an American concern "almost as if we were participants," because America's detachment from Europe enabled her to play a role of crucial importance in bringing about a peaceful world order.

> We are . . . a true friend to all the nations of the world, because we threaten none, covet the possessions of none, desire the overthrow of none. Our friendship can be accepted and is accepted without reservation because it is offered . . . for a purpose which no one need ever question. . . . Therein lies our greatness. We are the champions of peace and of concord. And we should be very jealous of this distinction . . . because it is our dearest pres-

[33] *The Great Departure: The United States and World War I* (New York, Wiley, 1965), p. 25.
[34] Address to League to Enforce Peace, May 27, 1916, *Public Papers*, IV, 185.
[35] Arthur S. Link, *Wilson: The Struggle for Neutrality, 1914–1915* (Princeton, Princeton Univ. Press, 1960), p. 53.

ent hope that this character and reputation may presently, in God's providence, bring us . . . the opportunity to . . . obtain peace in the world and reconciliation and a healing settlement . . .[36]

This was ever the critical argument that tipped the balance in favor of neutrality. So long as America herself was neutral, the chance of a peace of reconciliation and justice existed, because the belligerents might turn to America in a more rational moment and ask for mediation. A peace along America's "ancient principles" would necessarily be just. Wilson's frequent public statements about the matter only confirmed his priavte position. When Charles W. Eliot, former President of Harvard University, early in the war suggested intervention (a very exceptional position even for pro-Allied Americans in 1914), Wilson replied: "It would add to the burden already put upon mankind by this terrible war if the only neutral nation should withdraw from the position of influence afforded her by her neutrality."[37] Although Wilson took account of the public sentiment for neutrality, it was not the primary factor in determining his position. Always the question was how America could best maintain her extraordinary influence and use it for the "service of mankind." During the years of neutrality, the American mission meant primarily dedication to the task of bringing a healing peace which should be at once moderate and respectful of the rights of all nations—large and small.

As the war on the Western front reached a stalemate, the sea war intensified and American neutral rights were threatened. The interests of the United States dictated the freest possible trade with both sides, but the belligerents' interests required control and restriction. America's prewar business associations had been chiefly with the Allies, and her wartime shipping was going largely to them. Naturally Britain was trying to preserve this situation while Germany tried to reverse it. Soon matters grew deadly serious. While British sea practices cost Americans cargoes and cash, German practices cost noncombatant lives. While Britain's naval predominance was generally in America's national interest, Germany's attempt to reverse the balance was not.

Wilson realized the complexity of the legal issues, but significantly expanded the principles even while he attempted to confine the quarrel. America's neutral trading rights became the fundamental rights of humanity, to which she was dedicated as a member of the family of nations.[38] The submarine issue was dangerous not only because it threatened to pull the United States into war, but because if it were mishandled it would make the United States a belligerent accidentally on a petty or legalistic basis. Thus

---

[36] Second Annual Address to Congress, Dec. 8, 1914, *Public Papers*, III, 224–25.
[37] Wilson to Eliot, Aug. 14, 1914, Wilson MSS.
[38] In *Public Papers*, see: Wilson to Senator Stone, Feb. 24, 1916, III, 123; and Wilson, Address to Congress, April 19, 1916, III, 158.

self-interest, even narrowly conceived, and the protection of American lives and property, as well as the vision of America at the peace table shaping the future of a free Europe, necessitated attempts at mediation. The surest way of keeping America out of war was to end the hostilities before America was pulled in.

Of the complexities of American attempts at mediation, we shall mention only three, most directly related to Wilson's conception of the American mission for world peace: First, the famous House-Grey negotiations and the memorandum which emerged from them in 1916 illustrated the degree to which America's rather universalist neutralism clashed with the Allies' strategic plans. Although Colonel House's diplomacy was skillfully directed toward a cooperative policy, the belligerents fundamentally rejected the President's role as mediator. Secondly, these negotiations stimulated Wilson's ideas about a postwar league and indeed provided the context for the first exchanges between Britain and the United States on this subject. Thirdly, as the implementation of the House-Grey agreement failed, Wilson found himself going beyond the immediate need of mediation diplomacy and adapting and Americanizing the liberal peace programs of the European democratic Left.

The American role of peacemaker began, paradoxically enough, even before the war had broken out. The astute Colonel House, sensing an impending danger, visited Europe in 1913 and again in the summer of 1914 in order to persuade the ministries of Britain, France and Germany to accept the United States' good offices in composing naval rivalries. House also had a plan for the mutual consultation of the Great Powers about matters involving the "backward nations"—a plan which vaguely resembled Marburg's more elaborated ideas.[39]

By 1915 House's attempts at mediation had, of course, become more urgent. The United States had in large measure acquiesced in Britain's maritime system, which the British cautiously, and for the most part legitimately, applied. But Germany's submarine warfare constituted a major threat to America's peace. Britain's Foreign Secretary, Sir Edward Grey, knowing how essential it was to Britain to keep American friendship, hinted that the British would be willing to listen to House's ideas concerning the peace. It was in Britain's interest to shape American neutrality more toward acceptance of the British blockade, or hopefully to allow the Germans to drive the United States into the war. If, however, both of these courses failed, Grey hoped to involve the United States in a postwar international organization. He believed in calling in the new world to redress the balance of the old.[40]

[39] Seymour, *Intimate Papers of Colonel House*, I, 239–40, 256, 275.
[40] Quincy Wright, "Woodrow Wilson and the League of Nations," *Social Research*, XXIV (Spring 1957), 76–79; Link, *Wilson: Struggle for Neutrality*, pp. 218–19.

American interests reversed Grey's means and ends. House and especially Wilson hoped that the European nations would continue to balance one another off, thus keeping America free to pursue her own initiatives, and above all to end the war quickly. Thus, they acquiesced in an open pledge for American involvement in a postwar league, not to add to British strength in Europe, but to encourage peace talks. To Grey the goal was pro-British American involvement; to House, friendly but independent American command of the diplomatic situation. The belligerents' fundamental drive was for all-out victory, America's for a moderate peace.

In the course of negotiating with Grey in 1915, House proposed that some postwar conference rewrite the law of war at sea. There should be lanes of safety for all shipping, neutral and belligerent. Grey seized upon this suggestion to transform it into a proposal for collective security. The powers should guarantee all merchantmen, regardless of location, immunity from capture. If any nation violated this immunity, the signatories would unite to attack it. Later Grey enlarged the suggestion further to apply to aggression on land as well. At first House demurred at this bold suggestion for ending America's traditional policy of noninvolvement.[41] Yet each time the Americans engaged in negotiations for mediation, the British raised the question of America's postwar participation in a league.

In the fall of 1915, Grey once more hinted at Britain's conditional interest in American mediation. Wilson encouraged House to proceed. The President had some rather dire predictions about the postwar prospects should Germany win. Thus, House evolved an understanding with Grey which suggested that if the Allies' goals were reasonable, they had nothing to lose from American mediation. The House-Grey memorandum of February 1916 provided that when the Allies should tell Wilson they were ready, the President would call a peace conference. If Germany refused to attend or rejected reasonable offers, the United States would "probably" enter the war on the Allied side. As Arthur S. Link has observed, this memorandum did not promise American involvement but was an effort to avert it, at a time when German actions seemed to be giving Americans very few options.[42]

Shortly thereafter, however, relations with Germany improved markedly while those with Britain deteriorated. In March 1916 the Germans had torpedoed without warning the French Channel packet *Sussex*. After Wilson threatened a break in diplomatic relations with Germany, the Imperial Government agreed that its submarine commanders would here-

---

[41] Edward H. Buehrig, "Woodrow Wilson and Collective Security," in *Wilson's Foreign Policy in Perspective*, ed. Edward H. Buehrig (Bloomington, Indiana Univ. Press, 1957), pp. 43–47.

[42] *Wilson the Diplomatist*, pp. 46–50.

after use the traditional maritime rules of visit and search. Following this major concession the Germans even suggested that they would welcome American peace pressures. Wilson, knowing that the Germans' self-restrictions were conditioned upon American moderation of Britain's sea warfare, feared the resumption of unrestricted submarine methods. During the same period, moreover, the State Department was occupied almost daily with British interference with the mails, with British restrictions upon American trade, and with the bitter anti-British feelings aroused by the suppression of Ireland's Easter Rebellion.[43]

The need for mediation was clear. Anglophiles as well as neutralists were increasingly anxious for a settlement. Thus to induce Britain to invoke the House-Grey Memorandum, Wilson took one of his most important decisions. He would declare to Europe and to the American people that the United States was prepared for the sake of a just peace to end her historic isolation and to join a collective security organization—a league of peace. So directly was this related to Wilson's mediation attempts that the President originally intended to issue a direct call for a peace conference at the same time. But Grey led House to believe that the Allies would regard such a move as unfriendly.[44] Nevertheless, Wilson held out the bait. Britain wanted America to give a pledge of postwar internationalism. She now had such a pledge.

To the tremendous enthusiasm of Holt and Marburg and the dedicated internationalists of the polity, Wilson gave his declaration on May 27, 1916 at a large public meeting of the League to Enforce Peace. And yet, in contrast to the detailed plans of these league campaigners, Wilson's statements were very bare indeed. Their whole significance lay not in their content but in their context. The relation to the House-Grey negotiations was very clear as Wilson called for a

universal association of nations to maintain the inviolate security of the highway of the seas for the common and unhindered use of all nations of the world, and to prevent any war either contrary to treaty covenants or without warning and full submission of the guarantee of territorial integrity and political independence.[45]

This last phrase revealed the atomism that underlay Wilson's most basic conceptions of international organization, whether he spoke of a worldwide league or of a Pan American Union. The first public league promise also suggested the effects of the mediation process as they coincided with

---

[43] Robert Lansing Desk Diary, May 11, 15, 17, 20, 1916, Robert Lansing Papers, Manuscript Division, Library of Congress; Arthur S. Link, *Wilson: Campaigns for Progressivism and Peace* (Princeton, Princeton Univ. Press, 1965), pp. 13–16.

[44] Link, *Wilson: Campaigns for Progressivism and Peace,* p. 20.

[45] *Public Papers,* IV, 188.

Wilson's own ideals of America as a city on the hill. The war came, he noted, "out of secret counsels," while America was denied her longed for opportunity for contributing her good offices in order to avert the struggle. Wilson called for a "more wholesome diplomacy," meaning the end of "selfish aggression" and competitive armed alliances. Above all, the President asserted, America's convictions centered upon three fundamentals: the right of people to choose their own sovereignty, the right of small states to enjoy protection in their territorial integrity, and the right of the world to be free from "every disturbance of its peace that has its origin in aggression. . . ."[46]

Thus the President wanted not only mediation but a liberal and Americanized postwar world. His attempt to win this through mediation failed. The war had already cost too much. In the fall of 1916, when the military balance favored Germany, Allied resistance to mediation grew stiffer. But Germany once more tempted Wilson to move. The President, the Imperial Government implied, should increase pressure on Britain, since Germany was considering another change in submarine policy.

Wilson's reelection in 1916 furnished a renewed impetus toward peace, while the increased tempo of German sinkings made his task even more urgent. Late in November 1916 the President drafted a note calling for an open statement of the belligerents' war aims. For a variety of reasons, ranging from anticipated resentment by the belligerents to the possible damage to American prestige should they reject it, he delayed sending the note. The message was heavy with references to the effects of the war upon neutrals and to America's determination to chart her own course rather than find herself driven in. Yet most significant of all (from the viewpoint of Wilson's concept of the American role in world politics) were the President's pointed references to the possibilities of popular resentment against the European rulers. If the war continued for long, Wilson predicted, there would come a "reaction, political upheaval, a resentment that can never cool. . . ."[47]

This was the President's last appeal to the governments alone. After December 1916 Wilson addressed not only the warring powers, but a larger and more congenial audience, their peoples.

His famous "peace without victory" appeal of January 22, 1917 made certain assumptions about those peoples of Europe and about Americans too—assumptions he maintained in spite of the contrary evidence about the psychology of war. He believed that men preferred justice to revenge, "peace without victory" to a military triumph; he believed that the new

[46] *Ibid.*, p. 187.
[47] Ray Stannard Baker, *Woodrow Wilson: Life and Letters*, 8 vols. (Garden City, N.Y., Doubleday, 1927–39), VI, 385; see also pp. 381–82, 384, 386.

order need contain none of the fearful and hateful emotions of the old.[48] With this firm faith he tried to build a blaze of pacifist desire behind the backs of the military. Instead, the belligerents resolved all the more firmly for all-out victory.

Yet, in one important sense Wilson's assessment of the situation was correct. If the powers *could* have emerged from their national ambitions and their hatreds, if the German civilians could have held out longer, then a moderate peace, free access for all nations to the world's commerce, and limitations on armaments were at least part of the medicine the patient needed. The President realized, too, that by 1917 the "peace without victory" could not represent a return to the *status quo ante*. Europe was already transformed. His declaration of moderation was this time directed not only at keeping America out of war but at creating in Europe a *Pax Americana*. Thus he framed his proposals as a new Monroe Doctrine and added:

I am proposing government by the consent of the governed . . . freedom of the seas . . . moderation of armaments. . . .

These are American principles, American policies. . . . And they are also the principles and policies of forward looking men and women everywhere . . . of every enlightened community. They are the principles of mankind and must prevail.[49]

Ironically they became the principles that justified American entry into the war—an entry which made total Allied victory, rather than peace without victory, possible. At the very moment that Wilson appealed to Europe, and especially to Germany, to accept his mediation, the German high command used evidence of Allied intransigence and of Germany's readiness for an effective submarine blockade to tip the balance against his peace moves. Was American neutrality worth the restrictions of the *Sussex* pledge? The Kaiser and the military decided it was not.[50] In February the sinkings of neutral as well as belligerent vessels began.

Americans were deeply divided and largely anti-war, but that was not decisive. After the publication of the Zimmermann telegram, interventionist sentiment grew; but the President held out against intervention.[51] The

---

[48] *Public Papers,* IV, 409–10.
[49] *Ibid.,* p. 414.
[50] Ernest R. May, *The World War and American Isolation 1914–1917* (Chicago, Quadrangle Paperbacks, 1966), pp. 412–15; Link, *Wilson the Diplomatist,* pp. 77–81. Link believes Chancellor Bethmann-Hollweg largely responsible for not challenging the military. May shows him outmaneuvered.
[51] The Zimmermann telegram, in the opinion of Arthur S. Link, shocked the American people even more than had the German invasion of Belgium or the sinking of the *Lusitania*. In the text of the message Germany's foreign minister, Arthur Zimmermann, offered President Carranza of Mexico an alliance with the Imperial Government

Russian revolution, the March revolution, broke the Eastern front, strengthened the Central Powers, and also justified Lansing's characterization of the struggle as one between Autocracy and Democracy. How much effect this had upon the President's acceptance of belligerency it is difficult to say. We do know that in the days preceding Wilson's decision to go to war (he arrived at the decision on March 19, 1917), the fate of the Russian revolution was a major preoccupation. But perhaps the deepest-lying motive of all, and the one, as Arthur S. Link has observed, most difficult to prove, was Wilson's desire to shape the peace.[52] As a neutral there was little more that he could do unilaterally to bring mediation. He did not choose to work with the Conference of Neutrals; whether because of his desire to keep mediation in American hands or because he believed that such efforts would be ineffectual, we do not know. But as a belligerent, as the most powerful belligerent, America could use her strength not only to shorten the war, but to shape the peace; and it was this postwar settlement for which the President finally asked Americans to fight:

But the right is more precious that the peace, and we shall fight for the things which we have always carried nearest our hearts,—for democracy, for the right of those who submit to authority to have a voice in their own Governments, for the rights and liberties of small nations, for a universal dominion of right by such a concert of free peoples as shall bring peace and safety to all nations and make the world itself at last free. . . .[53]

"THE ROAD AWAY FROM REVOLUTION"

The United States entered the war as an Associated Power, not as an Ally. This designation implied more than independent (if coordinated) military command, more than national egotism. America had different goals from the Allies and presumably a more detached outlook. The Europeans, having suffered enormous losses and having gained nothing, were bitter and vengeful. But more important to the American liberals and their leader, Woodrow Wilson, was the belief that the Allies shared the old

---

in the event of war between Germany and the United States. Germany was to help Mexico to recover Texas, New Mexico, and Arizona. Mexico in turn was to persuade Japan to shift to the German side. The British intercepted the note and the State Department verified it. Wilson made it public on March 1. The effect upon anti-war sections of the country was palpable even though the note did nothing to prevent a pacifist filibuster of Wilson's bill for arming American ships. Recent evidence, as Link notes, connects this major diplomatic blunder with a Latin American specialist in the German Foreign Office, a man named von Kemnitz. It seems probable that Zimmermann discussed the idea of the proposal, if not the actual dispatch, with the Kaiser. The Supreme Command's support of the project "can be inferred" (Link, *Wilson: Campaigns for Progressivism and Peace*, pp. 342–46, 354–59, 433–36).

[52] *Ibid.*, pp. 394–96, 400–401, 405, 414–15; Lansing's Desk Diary, March 15, 19, 1917.

[53] Address to Joint Session of Congress, April 2, 1917, *Public Papers*, V, 16.

imperialism of the Central Powers. They too engaged in the traditional intrigues, in the cynical play of power; they too traded peoples from sovereignty to sovereignty. From all these the New World had abstained, or so Americans believed. By proclaiming the United States an Associate, Wilson conceived of America's purpose as higher: not only to break German militarism but to create a new order of national freedom and peace.

The President's understanding of the Allies' purposes was confirmed by the discovery of their secret treaties. These treaties justified the long-held demand of most liberal groups for open diplomacy. Yet Wilson cautioned House against open discussion of war aims with the British because he believed America's very purity would reveal conflict.

England and France *have not the same views with regard to peace that we have* by any means. When the war is over we can force them to our way of thinking, because by that time they will, among other things, be financially in our hands; but we cannot force them now, and any attempt to speak for them . . . would bring on disagreements, which would inevitably come to the surface in public. . . . If there is to be an interchange of views at all, it ought to be between us and the liberals in Germany, with no one else brought in.[54]

If Wilson overestimated the degree to which even American economic power could drive the Allies toward a moderate and just peace, once the threat of German victory was entirely removed, he accurately forecast the possibilities of the United States' moral leadership over the liberal peace movement—providing, of course, he was willing to use American power to effect real changes in Europe.

The difficulties were enormous. The war had severely weakened the middle-class base of European liberalism—a liberalism weak enough in Central and Eastern Europe even in peacetime. Moreover, Wilson himself was unsympathetic to the more profound changes favored by the European socialist Left.[55] In 1919, after an initial embrace, the socialists became more disillusioned with the President as he proved reluctant to push reform hard, fearing to split America off from the Allies. "Mr. Wilson is the world's greatest Liberal," H. N. Brailsford of Britain's Independent Labour Party observed. "Like all Liberals, he is destined to perpetual illusion, because he will not understand that a capitalist world will act after its own kind."[56]

Increasingly, however, Wilson found some harmony of interests not only with the enlightened and liberal Europeans but even with representa-

---

[54] Baker, *Life and Letters,* VII, 180. (Italics in Baker's text.)

[55] Levin, *Wilson and World Politics,* pp. 162–67.

[56] Arno J. Mayer, *Politics and Diplomacy of Peacemaking, 1918–1919* (New York, Knopf, 1967), p. 193.

tives of the old order. He was driven, if not to their defense, at least
to their side by the descent of Central and Eastern Europe into chaos and
revolution. In March 1917 Wilson had welcomed the Russian revolution
and had sentimentalized about the great Russian people, whom he frequently thereafter called great, generous, and lovable.[57] But the Russian
revolution, like the Mexican and the Chinese revolts, refused to stop
at that stable, democratic, and moderate level Wilson desired. In October, Lenin and the Bolsheviks seized power in Petrograd; and the complex, and to most Americans, obscure Russian civil war was under way.

The Soviets presented no immediate threat to US interests. The United
States' economic and social base was immeasurably more secure and prosperous than were those of Central or even of Western Europe. Rather, it
was President Wilson's vision of a peaceful world order, based upon
liberal nationalism and reformed capitalism, that Lenin challenged.

Both Lenin and Wilson sought the allegiance of the European Left. Both
could claim freedom from the old imperialism. Wilson believed that political democracy and economic justice demanded no more than the break-up
of the old monopolies of imperial power—the New Freedom and a just
peace. Lenin insisted that it was capitalism itself that bred war, that a
complete destruction of the economic base of the West was essential and
inevitable. Wilson had proclaimed that free enterprise and freedom for the
individual were one and the same. Justice demanded economic opportunity
for the masses within the private competitive system. Lenin saw Wilson's
impulse to shore up capitalism by reform as the major obstacle to his goal of
converting the war into a world revolution.[58]

At various times, Wilson, influenced by House, considered the possibilities of bringing the Bolsheviks into the Western polity, the conference, and the League—reforming them by accommodation. For the most
part, however, he could not bring himself to drive hard for accommodation
against the counterrevolutionary thrust of Marshall Foch, Winston
Churchill, Clemenceau, and other conservative spokesmen. He opposed
their plans for large-scale military intervention while hoping that a limited
American intervention in Archangel and Siberia would somehow encourage
the liberal and democratic anti-Bolshevik forces without restoring the
reactionaries.[59] In the final analysis, however, Wilson relied neither upon
accommodation nor upon counterrevolutionary intervention but upon economic aid, particularly in the form of relief, to halt both the spread of
communism in Central Europe and the growth of Russian loyalty to the
Bolsheviks. He believed that time and food and security would make the

[57] *Public Papers*, V, 13, 49–51, 71–72; VI, 101, 107–108.
[58] Levin, *Wilson and World Politics*, pp. 7–8.
[59] *Ibid.*, pp. 87 ff.

Russians wiser, and that in the interim the Allies should confine their "efforts to keeping Bolshevism out of the rest of Europe." Although at various times referring to the Bolsheviks as "consummate sneaks," tyrants, "monopolists" representing "nobody but themselves," Wilson viewed communism as threatening largely because it grew upon Europe's weaknesses.[60] He did not subscribe to the conspiratorial notions of his more fearful colleagues—a position which encouraged his resistance to massive military intervention. He told the Council of Four at Versailles in March 1919:

In my view, any attempt to check a revolutionary movement by means of deployed armies is merely trying to use a broom to sweep back a high tide. Besides, armies may become impregnated with the very Bolshevism they are sent to combat. . . . The only way to act against Bolshevism is to eliminate its causes. This is a formidable task: What its exact causes are, we do not know.

In any case, one cause is that the peoples are uncertain as to their future frontiers, the governments they must obey, and at the same time, are in desperate need of food transport, and opportunities for work. There is but one way to wipe out Bolshevism: determine the frontiers and open every door to commercial intercourse.[61]

Before Wilson could put to the test this concept of self-determination and the open door, the implied challenge of Bolshevism became a direct one. The Eastern front was in a state of collapse; and the Bolsheviks desperately needing peace, entered into negotiations with the German military. While temporarily willing to sacrifice large slices of Russian territory in order to gain the time necessary to consolidate his rule, Lenin counted upon postwar revolutionary upheavals in Europe to undermine the *dictat* by Germany. Appealing to the German and European Left, as well as his own people, with his programs of peace, land, and bread, Lenin published the Czarist secret treaties. Wilson now had to dissociate the United States from these much discredited, reactionary war aims. He wanted also to convince the Allies to moderate their demands, and to respond to Europe's cries for open diplomacy and scientific frontiers, in order to weaken at the same time both German resistance and the appeal of Bolshevism.

On January 8, 1918, the President delivered before Congress his Fourteen Points address, one of the most effective combinations of war propaganda and noble aspiration of the twentieth century. The Points themselves derived from Inquiry studies of the programs of the European Left. These all showed a remarkable coincidence of goals—open diplomacy

---

[60] *Public Papers*, VI, 70, 100, 106, 143, 441; John M. Thompson, *Russia, Bolshevism, and the Versailles Peace* (Princeton, Princeton Univ. Press, 1967), pp. 44–45, 383.

[61] Paul J. Mantoux, *Paris Peace Conference, 1919: Proceedings of the Council of Four, March 24—April 18*, Trans. John Boardman Whitton (Geneva, Droz, 1964), p. 35.

and parliamentary participation in the acceptance of treaties; arbitration and adjudication of disputes; nationalization of the arms industries, followed by disarmament; restoration of Alsace-Lorraine and Belgium and national self-determination for all peoples; "no annexations or indemnities"; and an international organization to keep the peace and represent all peoples.[62] The Wilsonian translation was more remarkable for its service to American interests—both in containing Lenin's appeal and in weakening German resistance—than for its originality. With regard to "equality of trade conditions," for example, Wilson explained that he did not contemplate the end of all tariffs, but only the end of discriminatory tariffs. All the members of the prospective League of Nations would give one another most-favored nation treatment, and there would be an open door all over the world even in colonial empires.[63] This proposition, modifying capitalism little more than Wilson had proposed to modify it while still a Georgia lawyer, involved no sacrifice of American interest. A country like the United States that was very short on territorial empire and yet swiftly emerging as the dominant commercial and industrial power of the world had little to fear from reciprocal tariffs. Wilson correctly insisted that this left each nation free to determine its own economic policies, and yet he could defend with equal validity US entry in the League by asserting:

If you don't want me to be too altruistic, let me be very practical. If we are partners, let me predict we will be the senior partner. The financial leadership will be ours. The industrial primacy will be ours. The commercial advantage will be ours. The other countries of the world are looking to us for leadership and direction. Very well, then, if I am to compete with the critics of this league as a selfish American, I say I want . . . to be inside . . . and help to run it.[64]

Appeals of this nature did not easily fit in with Wilson's own tendency to present the American role as a selfless mission for justice. But he was quite comfortable with the truth that the statement contained. The Allies' apprehensions with regard to American commercial domination of the continent were simply accepted by Wilson and his economic advisors as one of the unalterable conditions of 1919, as unalterable as the Allies' need for American support.[65] Many of the other points to which Wilson adhered closely, in contradistinction to the positions of the French and the British, accorded with this

[62] Arno J. Mayer, *Wilson vs Lenin: Political Origins of the New Diplomacy* (Cleveland, Meridian Books, 1964), pp. 339 ff.; Link, *Wilson the Diplomatist*, pp. 92–93.

[63] Wilson to Senator F. M. Simmons, Oct. 28, 1918, *Public Papers*, V, 289.

[64] Address, St. Louis, Mo. Sept. 5, 1919, *Public Papers*, V, 640.

[65] Edward N. Hurley to Wilson, Dec. 12, 1918; and Bernard Baruch to Wilson, Dec. 3, 1918, Wilson MSS.

sense of American economic strength and willingness to enter into free international commercial competition. The League mandate system originated in the plans of the British Labour Party and of Jan Christian Smuts of South Africa, but Wilson, more than the Allies, favored it. His plans had envisioned trusteeship by small neutral nations reporting to the League, but he accepted British and French and Japanese trusteeship over the former German colonies—provided no economic blockade could be instituted by the trustee; and provided also that economic exploitation of the resources of the area was open, and the mandated territories were demilitarized.[66]

Similarly the United States, having suffered no civilian casualties nor destruction of territory, and fearing no postwar German competition, could well press for moderate indemnities, while the French, justifiably suspicious and insecure, could not. The interests of the United States and Britain, reflecting different trade positions, conflicted over freedom of the seas.

Even the Point concerning the "autonomous" development of the peoples of the crumbling Hapsburg Empire coincided with American interests, for Wilson did not contemplate the destruction of the economic unity of Central Europe. But he did want to end "the system by which adventurous and imperialist groups in Berlin and Vienna and Budapest could use the resources of this area in the interests of a selfish foreign policy."[67] The contest with France over the size of these successor states (which states emerged even before Versailles and therefore could not be denied) was indeed a contest for scientific frontiers, but it was at the same time a contest between French security interests and America's moral and political influence. It was in America's interest to establish the kind of frontiers to which a League guarantee could be given—frontiers that would closely approximate the ethnic distribution of the Europeans.

Yet by the end of 1918 Central Europe had plunged so deeply into chaos and economic ruin that proclamations of self-government were quite meaningless without some strong economic presence to support the new régimes. The answer to Bolshevism had to be massive and imaginative. Herbert Hoover, the US Food Administrator, understood the coincidence of humane needs and American interests. Pleading with Wilson to lift the blockade and allow food to flow even into the former enemy territories, Hoover insisted, "Even a partial revival of the ordinary activities of life

---

[66] Official American Commentary on the Fourteen Points, Oct. 1918, in *Intimate Papers of Colonel House*, IV, 194–95.

[67] Report by Inquiry to President Wilson, Jan. 1918, in Ray Stannard Baker, *Woodrow Wilson and World Settlement*, 3 vols. (Garden City, New York, Doubleday, 1923), III, 24–25, 28.

within enemy territories will tend powerfully towards the end of Bolshevism and the stabilizing of governments." Wilson agreed whole-heartedly; and in January 1919 the battle began against chaos in Central Europe and against repeated French resistance to food relief to the Germans (at least until the reparations could be paid).[68] Thus the initial postwar support for the successor states was neither a French alliance nor the League of Nations. It was American economic power and American determination to fill empty stomachs in order to stop Bolshevism that built the first shelter for the atomistic new order in Central Europe.

The Fourteen Points, by their very atomism, contained many contradictions. The call for self-determination made the tariff and disarmaments reductions exceedingly difficult to fulfill, since the new nations might well consider heavy armaments and discriminatory tariffs their national prerogative.[69] The prospective League, theoretically their protector and unifying force, actually could exercise no major restriction upon their actions. It would be an instrument of their sovereignties. The mandate system was caught in a vise between the principle of training for self-government and the practice of rewarding the Allies. Wilson's idea that the League would be strengthened by this possession of "property" was contradicted by his own naval chiefs, who pleaded with him to oppose any Japanese trusteeships in the Pacific and to divert the Japanese to Siberia.[70] Evidently the military did not view mandates as truly international property any more than the traditionally imperialist powers did. Nevertheless, in view of the great national awakening in Africa and Asia at the time and the overall effect of the League mandate system, there is considerable justification in Arthur S. Link's observation that the whole arrangement presaged the end of colonial empires.[71]

Perhaps the most contradictory feature of the Versailles Peace was the crown of the Fourteen Points, the League of Nations. Was it to be an instrument for keeping permanent the Allied victory, or an instrument for reconciliation? Was it an organization of self-ruling free nations only, or a great and universal association? The first step toward a world government, or the dying gasp of nineteenth century nationalism?

These contradictions reflected a deeper conflict of purpose for the Fourteen Points. As war propaganda directed at weakening German resistance they were somewhat effective.[72] But they were soon to be used for an

[68] Hoover to Wilson, Jan. 1, 1919, in Herbert Hoover Archives, Hoover Institution.
[69] Karl Schmid, "Some Observations on Certain Principles of Woodrow Wilson," *Confluence*, V, Pt. 1 (Autumn 1956), 265.
[70] Naval Chiefs and Josephus Daniels to Wilson, Dec. 3, 1918, Wilson MSS.
[71] *Wilson the Diplomatist*, p. 113.
[72] John Snell, "Wilson's Peace Program and German Socialism, January—March, 1918," *Mississippi Valley Historical Review*, XXVIII (Sept. 1951), 213; Mayer, *Wilson vs. Lenin*, pp. 376–78.

entirely different purpose—as America's idealistic base for concluding peace. In this guise, they could merely arouse, but never fulfill the tired peoples' chiliastic expectations. Unless Wilson was willing to compromise with the Allies' very real security needs, the forces of revolution would flourish and the power base of international liberalism shake. Thus in order to influence the peace in the direction of liberal idealism at all, major compromises with the old order were necessary. And the French and British necessarily demanded considerable modification of the reparations stipulations and of the ideal of freedom of the seas enunciated by a rich and distant power. Moreover, as N. Gordon Levin, Jr. has shown, Wilson himself swung between the desire to establish a moderate peace reintegrating Germany into the national structure and the desire to mete out to the militarists righteous punishment. The latter position cost Wilson the support of the European social-democrats, but in any case the Left underestimated the degree to which the anti-revolutionary Wilson was willing to accommodate to the Allies.[73]

On the whole, Wilson appeared to view the League of Nations as a channel through which Europe could be stabilized and democratized in the image of liberal American institutions. Anything that departed from that ideal either in tolerance for the old Right or in bowing before Bolshevism quickened the President's resistance. This, rather than any particular structure of the League, held his interest.

In 1917 Wilson did not even consider the possibility that the League might have a permanent structure. He was most reluctant to commit himself to anything that would challenge the Senate's prerogatives or would place American forces at the disposal of an international body. Rather he insisted that the only promise that could be made was League protection for the integrity of small nations. Everything else had to wait upon experience.

My own conviction . . . is that the . . . constitution of the League must grow and not be made ; that me must *begin* with solemn covenants, covering mutual guarantees of political independence and territorial integrity (if the final territorial agreements of the peace conference are fair and satisfactory and *ought* to be perpetuated), but that the method of carrying out those mutual pledges should be left to develop of itself, case by case.[74]

The league theorists could begin with the questions of membership and sanctions; but since Wilson the President would be responsible for commanding those sanctions or advocating particular membership, he had to begin with the idea of a limited treaty—a covenant. The word carried with it all the poor American beginnings, the original weakness of colonial institutions combined with the great strength of their Puritan earnestness, and that was Wilson's intention—not legalistic intricacy but moral commit-

[73] Levin, *Wilson and World Politics*, pp. 125–32, 156–64.
[74] Seymour, *Intimate Papers of Colonel House*, IV, 16. (Italics in Seymour)

ment. When, at Versailles, the French asked for an international general staff and for guaranteed military sanctions—a structure that would have meant a strong military alliance supporting the Versailles decisions—Wilson replied;

> To propose to realize unity of command in time of peace, would be to put forward a proposal that no nation would accept. The Constitution of the United States forbids the President to send beyond its frontiers the national forces. . . . . The only method by which we can achieve this end lies in our having confidence in the good faith of the nations who belong to the League. . . . When danger comes, we too will come, and we will help you, but you must trust us. . . .[75]

The League of Nations, based as Wilson saw it upon a promise to protect the independence of its members, had many purposes both immediate and long-range. In the first place, in the context of French demands for security, it was an implied American promise of military aid, a promise which Wilson hoped would disarm Congressional critics by being indirect. Secondly, it was supposed to counter French demands for annexation of large slices of the German western industrial frontier. Actually, the French, and especially Clemenceau, had much less faith in a League of Nations than did Wilson. They demanded an American as well as an Anglo-French security treaty, a demilitarized Rhineland, and at least temporary occupation of the Saar. Yet the original interpretation of the territorial guarantee by Walter Lippmann of the Inquiry implied a moderate peace. Germany would remain very much a power in Europe, and therefore even the future security of Alsace-Lorraine depended upon a League supporting territorial adjustments.[76] Wilson was not willing to convert the League into a totally punitive instrument—a general staff subservient to France's desire for a perpetually second-class Germany.

Third, Article Ten of the Covenant constituted, for Wilson, a self-denying pledge, but not only that. It was in his mind, as it had been in Holt's, closely tied in with sanctions and with the promise of peace, because disturbance of the peace was equated with aggression against small nations. In interpreting the Article to American audiences Wilson tended to fall into the oversimplifications of some members of the League to Enforce Peace. He used the invasion of Belgium as the classic case of violation of territorial integrity, implying that a league with such a guarantee would have prevented the war.[77] Finally, Wilson liked to read the specific wording of the Article in order to point up some national advantages:

[75] Minutes of the League of Nations Commission, Paris Peace Conference, Feb. 11, 1919, Department of State, National Archives, Doc. No. 181.1101/8.

[76] American Inquiry Document No. 741, Archives of the Inquiry, Department of State, National Archives.

[77] In *Public Papers*, Vol. VI, see: Address at Des Moines, Sept. 6, 1919, p. 25; Address in Spokane, Sept. 12, 1919, p. 152; and Address in San Diego, Calif. Sept. 19, 1919, p. 293.

The Members of the League undertake to respect and preserve as against external aggression the territorial integrity and existing political independence of all Members of the League.

In case of any such aggression, or in case of any threat of aggression, the council shall advise upon the means by which this obligation shall be fulfilled.[78]

The United States would have a permanent vote on the Council (whose decisions had to be unanimous). Thus there could be no effective Council advice unless the Americans approved. Since the Council's vote was only advisory, the US Congress retained the final decision on the use of American forces.

To suggest the American origin of the Article, to place it within the correct tradition, Wilson cited the need for such a territorial guarantee backed by the League in the Far East. Territorial integrity was closely tied to open commercial opportunity as John Hay himself had perceived. Yet Japan's seizure of Shantung, a violation of the Open Door, was not preventable without guarantee. Wilson promised correction by use of Article Ten and Article Eleven of the Covenant.[79] Justice would come to China. It was as close a union of ideals and national self-interest as one could find.

The major problem raised by Article Ten was the one pointed out by conservative Elihu Root—the problem of accommodating change. Although Root himself was willing to accept the Article temporarily in order to use the League as a defense against Bolshevism, he foresaw the danger of enshrining the *status quo*.[80] Wilson realized the same danger and, in fact, was not willing to allow the Covenant to become simply the guarantor of Versailles and nothing more. He first acceded to the British request to omit the word "guarantee" from the Article and then had added a long clause to the Article indicating how the League might accommodate change. If ethnic or political changes influenced the reality or justice of national boundaries, then territorial readjustments, perhaps involving material compensation, could be made by vote of three-quarters of the delegates to the League Assembly. This provision meant, as Quincy Wright has observed, giving the League the right of international eminent domain. At French insistence, a weakened version of the article became Article Nineteen, thereby lending to the territorial article the rigidity the French originally desired.[81]

Wilson was not content a covenant that forced postponement of international action until territory was actually violated. He had in mind a

[78] David Hunter Miller, *The Drafting of the Covenant,* 2 vols. (New York, Putnam, 1928), II, p. 661.

[79] In *Public Papers,* Vol. VI, see: Address in Omaha, Sept. 8, 1919, pp. 41–43; and Address in Helena, Sept. 11, 1919, pp. 132–33.

[80] Elihu Root to Will Hays, March 29, 1919, in *Men and Policies,* eds. Robert Bacon and James Brown Scott (Cambridge, Harvard Univ. Press), pp. 262–63.

[81] Wright, "Wilson and the League of Nations," p. 73; Buehrig, "Wilson and Collective Security," pp. 57–58.

strong and alert international instrument for reintegrating world order. He revived his old desire to reform the polity in order to prevent revolution, to do justice to the weak in order to avoid the abyss of Jacobinism. He pictured the League as a positive opportunity for American liberal guidance of other nations. His favorite article, Wilson used to say, was Article Eleven, which encouraged the nations to bring to the attention of members of the League circumstances threatening the peace. To Wilson this meant a chance to focus international attention, and possibly pressure, on any small disorder which might have dangerous international repercussions. He rejoiced in this right to "butt in," for it might well obviate the need for military action.[82] Clearly the lessons of Mexico were painful to him, and he was casting about for some international means of exerting a stabilizing influence upon a revolutionary world. The League's good offices and the League's commitment to each nation's political independence internationalized America's mediatory ambitions.

In assessing the various means of preventing aggression, Wilson showed a preference for economic over military sanctions. Strengthening House's first draft he provided that even in case of *threat* of aggression, the guilty nation should confront a total blockade, complete financial isolation, and a vote of the League Council advising on the use of force to make the blockade effective.[83] The President liked to assure Americans that it was the very strength of this economic weapon that precluded military action:

> . . . [If] any member state violates that promise to submit either to arbitration or to discussion, it is thereby *ipso facto* deemed to have committed an act of war against all the rest. . . . We absolutely boycott them. It is provided in that instrument that there shall be no communication even between them and the rest of the world. They shall receive no goods; they shall ship no goods. They shall receive no telegraphic messages; they shall send none. . . . It is the most complete boycott ever conceived in a public document, and I want to say to you with confident prediction that there will be no more fighting after that. . . . [Peaceful] processes are more deadly than the processes of war. Let any merchant put it to himself, that if he enters into a convenant and then breaks it and the people all around him absolutely desert his establishment and will have nothing to do with him— ask him after that if it will be necessary to send the police.[84]

In brief, Wilson's version of the League Covenant with its permanent arbitral procedures, its sanctions and its atomism, its registering of approved (and therefore gradual) change, reflected an enlarged Monroe Doctrine as Wilson understood it. Like the Monroe Doctrine it depended

[82] Seymour, *Intimate Papers of Colonel House,* IV, 268; Baker, *World Settlement,* III, 106; Wilson, *Public Papers,* VI: Address at Helena, Sept. 11, 1919, p. 134; and Address at Tacoma, Sept. 13, 1919, p. 170.

[83] Wilson's First Draft of the Covenant, in Baker, *World Settlement,* III, 92.

[84] Address, Kansas City, Mo., Sept. 6, 1919, *Public Papers,* VI, 3.

upon Anglo-American cooperation and enforcement even though it was pre-eminently an American document. Like the twentieth-century interpretation of that Doctrine, it was to protect governments both from external aggression and from revolutionary upheavals that might invite interference. Like Wilson's missionary version of the Doctrine, the League was to protect free and representative governments, and to release pressures for change gradually and legally in order to prevent violent revolution. Through arbitration and "international eminent domain" the League of Nations would moderate and correct the Treaty rather than enforce it.

Even before the Council of Four met, Wilson anticipated the necessity for these provisions. The victory of the Republicans in November 1918 had weakened his bargaining position. The Allies' parliamentary victories only made an already chaotic situation still more difficult.[85] Wilson knew he would have to compromise; and when, in fact, he was compelled to trade his position, he asserted that the final resolution would be the League's. This may be what he meant when he remarked at the second plenary session of the Versailles conference:

Settlements may be temporary, but the action of the nations in the interest of peace and justice must be permanent. We can set up permanent processes. We may not be able to set up permanent decisions. . . .
[The United States] would feel that it could not take part in guaranteeing those European settlements unless that guarantee involved the continuous superintendence of the peace of the world by the associated nations of the world.
Therefore, it seems to me that we must concert our best judgment in order to make this League of Nations a vital thing . . . it should be the eye of the nations to keep watch upon the common interest. . . .[86]

In spite of this flexibility in Wilson's concept of the League of Nations, his was not an organic ideal. The real strength of the League lay in not the growth of supranational loyalty, but its coincidence with existing (if enlightened) national interests. Wilson never anticipated nor desired League functions to become supranational. They were to remain emphatically political. The whole League structure was a structure for stability. The President's frequently reiterated pleas for a just peace, a strong

---

[85] Seymour, *Intimate Papers of Colonel House,* IV, 362. House recorded the effects of the domestic pressures on the conference as follows: "The American delegation are not in a position to act freely. The elections of last November in the United States have been a deterrent to free action by our delegates. The British elections and the vote of confidence Clemenceau received in the French Chamber of Deputies, put the finishing touches to a situation already bad. If the President should exert his influence among the liberals and labouring classes, he might possibly overthrow the governments in Great Britain, France, and Italy; but if he did, he would still have to reckon with our own people and he might bring the whole world into chaos. The overthrow of governments might not end there, and it would be a grave responsibility."

[86] Jan. 25, 1919, *Public Papers,* V, 396–97.

League, and a reformed capitalism were, as he called them shortly before he died, the "road away from revolution." When Clemenceau had asked for annexations and had accused Wilson of believing that the world "is governed by abstract principles," the President had replied honestly and forcefully, "I greatly fear the transformation of [popular] enthusiasms into despair as violent as Bolshevism, which says: 'There is no justice in the world: our only course is to avenge by force the injustices formerly committed by force.'" Bolshevism, then, was the deep revulsion of the masses to the tyranny and arrogant inhumanity of the old regimes. Wilson was not confident of a simple solution, but he believed that a beginning must be made in meting out justice to each ethnic group, in securing homelands, and in freeing world commerce to work its beneficent influence.[87]

Fearing that a popular resentment of the devastation of the postwar world might turn against all the victors, Wilson limited to some degree the purely punitive response to Germany. But the same fear, as well as his own commitment to self-determination, made him hold back from an all-out Allied invasion of Soviet Russia. Containment rather than crusading—and for very practical reasons—was Wilson's response to Bolshevism. He believed that the military crusade urged by Winston Churchill and Marshall Foch would have several undesirable effects. American support for intervention would awaken strong progressive opposition in Congress (as indeed had America's role in the limited Siberian and Archangel expeditions).[88] It would lend US power and prestige to the most selfish French interests, while serving no specific American purpose. It might well result in the temporary restoration of the reactionary White Russians, rather than the rare liberals. But most significantly of all, it would make the Bolsheviks the national defenders of Russia against a foreign invasion, and thus augment the Russians' loyalty to Lenin.[89]

The disadvantages of negotiating with the Bolsheviks were less apparent, although the ideological and temperamental obstacles seemed formidable. At various times Wilson contemplated this option, all the while hoping that the Bolsheviks would fall of their own dead weight. For him any compromise with revolutionary socialism was out of the question, but Colonel House encouraged hopes that the communists might be liberalized within some acceptable coalition. In Paris the famous mission of William Bullitt, founded in part upon this hope, had the support only of the British and American liberals. The mission appeared to have House's approval. The liberals assumed incorrectly that Wilson was ready to recognize Lenin's

---

[87] Mantoux, *Paris Peace Conference*, p. 47.
[88] Mayer, *Politics and Diplomacy, 1919*, pp. 331–35.
[89] *Ibid.*, p. 329; Mantoux, *Paris Peace Conference*, pp. 33–35.

rule over most of European Russia. But most Americans in Paris opposed negotiations, and the President had left for Washington before the mission started.[90] By the time Bullitt returned, all prospects for recognizing Lenin's régime had been foreclosed.

A third option, fully and enthusiastically embraced by the President and supported by Lansing, House, and most of the American delegation, had opened up. This was the famous Hoover-Nansen plan, presented by Herbert Hoover on March 28, 1919. In a brilliant summary of "the key tenets of the Wilsonian view of the Bolshevik problem,"[91] Hoover proposed that "some Neutral of international reputation for probity and ability" gain financial and diplomatic support from the Northern neutrals and create an agency to distribute food and needed civilian supplies to the Russians. The only condition imposed upon the Bolsheviks would be the stipulation that they halt military action "across certain defined boundaries and cease their subsidizing of disturbances abroad." The relief agent, to be supplied by the United States and the neutrals, would need only agreements for the equitable distribution of supplies. Concurrently Wilson should make a strong public statement indicating just what were the goals of Bolshevism and how he accounted for its appeal. Of course its "utter foolishness as a basis of economic development," in comparison with American private enterprise should be pointed out. Hoover indicated the many advantages of this course. It required no recognition of Lenin's régime. It could test the possibilities of moderating the régime. It called for no military crusade in support of reaction (a course that went deeply against the American grain).[92] There were other implicit advantages which Hoover had no need to mention. His recommendation called for a cease-fire leaving large areas of Russia in the hands of the White Russians and with foreign troops still encamped. It demonstrated to the peoples of Russia and Central Europe alike both America's strength and her good will. It involved no submission to the interests or policies of the conservative Europeans. Above all, this humanitarian action was the most promising road away from revolution if, as both Hoover and Wilson believed, Bolshevism was not only an ideology but a protest against the way in which the world worked. In the closing months of his life, Wilson hoped that a "Christian concept of justice," a willingness to promote the welfare and happiness of others could but turn the Russian people toward liberal democracy.[93]

[90] Thompson, *Bolshevism and the Versailles Peace,* pp. 105–15, 135–52; Levin, *Wilson and World Politics,* pp. 210–15.
[91] Mayer, *Politics and Diplomacy, 1919,* p. 27.
[92] *Ibid.,* pp. 24–27.
[93] Wilson, "The Road away from Revolution," *Atlantic Monthly,* CXXXIII (Aug. 1923), 145–46.

In view of the partial coincidence of actions proposed by Jane Addams and by Herbert Hoover, we should examine the differences in intention and in construction between the communal aspirations and the Hoover proposal. The relief and reconstruction plan proposed by the British Labour Party, a plan Addams endorsed, required an immediate agreement to lift the blockade. Hoover, too, regarded this action as a necessity virtually at the time of the armistice. But six months later his aides found the blockade still strongly in effect throughout Eastern and Central Europe.[94] The Labour plan called for the granting of credits to enemy and liberated countries alike by a League of Nations that would become thereby a "world goverment actually in being." Hoover's plan meant American financing, in large measure by the Food Administration, and special appropriations from Congress. When the peace was signed, the American Relief Agency became a private organization with voluntary financing. Moreover, Hoover's intricate organization disbanded with his proposal for "some economic interarrangement" among the nations of Central Europe with regard to railroad management, coal distribution, and customs conventions. American cooperative participation in the Hoover plan was temporary and limited, a matter of the postwar emergency. Once the natural play of economic forces had resumed, Hoover expected a large reservoir of good will to remain as the American legacy in Central Europe.[95]

More fundamental than these operative contrasts—unilateral and private American financing as opposed to economic internationalism—were the fundamental attitudes toward community actions. For Addams the inter-Allied agencies were but preliminary to permanent League agencies. For Addams, as well as for Royce and Veblen, community functions such as insurance, relief, and mandate control were compelling engagements that would enable men to outgrow their national antagonisms. They bore the mark of no particular nation but were from the beginning either international or cosmopolitan. They were to become the agencies for transcending the state-system. They were to create a common interest which was, by definition, thwarted by the sovereign states with their competitive nationalism.

In Hoover's plan, the strength of humanitarian instinct was clear. The desire to perform the essential tasks of restoring a normal economy and

[94] Jane Addams, *Peace and Bread in Time of War*, reprinted with a 1945 introduction by John Dewey (Boston, G. K. Hall & Co., 1960), pp. 209–10; Alonzo E. Taylor, "Report on the Economic and Industrial Conditions in Central Europe, April 1919," *Organization of American Relief in Europe, 1918–1919*, ed. Suda Lorena Bane and Ralph Haswell Lutz (Stanford, Stanford University Press, 1942), pp. 381–82.

[95] Hoover to Wilson, June 24, 1919, Hoover Archives.

feeding and curing hungry and sick populations was plain for all to see. But the circumstances that called these humane actions into being and the goals that President Wilson pursued by means of the Hoover plan were pre-eminently political and national rather than communal. Food relief was America's way of stopping communism. Wilson appealed to Congress in January 1919 for an additional five million dollar appropriation for food relief to Roumania "in the interests of national defense." And Henry White, the only Republican on the American Commission for peace, wired to Henry Cabot Lodge in support of this move: Bolshevism "now completely controls Russia and Poland and is spreading through Germany." The "only effective barrier now apparently possible against it is food relief as Bolshevism thrives only on starvation and disorder."[96] The United States was just beginning, as Arno J. Mayer has observed, to use its enormous economic power as an instrument of political control.[97] Wilson's lack of interest in community ideals when the practice was divorced from the national interest underscored his general tendency to Americanize and politicize all aspects of internationalism. Raymond Fosdick recalled that as the President was boarding the *George Washington* to go to France, some sweatshop workers on their way to another fourteen-hour day pointed to the ship, and one said: "But do you see that boat? There's a man aboard her that's going to Europe to change all this." Upon being told the story, Wilson replied that it frightened him to think how much people expected of him, but he did not think it possible to consider industrial matters at the conference. The President mentioned the incident to House and added that he wished the conference could issue a statement limiting the maximum hours of labor to eight a day. He favored an international labor conference taking up such matters. In any case, these issues were not relevant to the peace.[98]

During his Western tour in defense of the League, Wilson occasionally referred to the embryonic International Labor Organization as an instrument for teaching the world the American method of labor peace. The American discovery that capital and labor shared a community of interests was a crucial one for avoiding revolution.[99] Perhaps it occurred to the President to appeal to a symbol of prospective security in the midst of strikes and a burgeoning red scare. Significantly, however, he failed to mention what the community thinkers inevitably saw in such organizations

[96] Wilson to Tumulty, Jan. 9, 1919 and White to Lodge, Jan. 8, 1919, Wilson MSS.
[97] *Politics and Diplomacy, 1919,* p. 17.
[98] Thompson, *Bolshevism and the Versailles Peace,* p. 44; Seymour, *Intimate Papers of Colonel House,* IV, 284–85.
[99] In *Public Papers,* Vol. VI, see: Address in Des Moines, Sept. 6, 1919, pp. 16–18; and Address in St. Paul, Sept. 9, 1919, pp. 60–61; also Levin, *Wilson and World Politics,* pp. 166–67.

—the shared identity of groups across national lines. It was precisely this mode of identification by class, or by profession, or according to interest, rather than by nation that the men of the polity avoided.

Thus in spite of the generosity of American relief and of his occasional interest in international labor settlement, Wilson's internationalism was highly political and not different in essentials from that of other anti-revolutionary members of the polity. The substance he offered to flesh out the bones of the polity was expanding American economic power and a moral influence that he regarded as but another side of that power. Rather than denigrate national interests by his appeals to idealism, he elevated them to universal significance. He sincerely believed that America was created to make the world "safe for democracy." His atomistic League in the last analysis was a vision of a multitude of cooperating liberal democracies, ethnically varied, different in power, but with the same political culture— American liberalism.

Little wonder, then, that Wilson staked so much on this Covenant and conceded so little. He asserted that by rejecting the League, Congress was rejecting not only international cooperation but America's world leadership. "Shall we keep the primacy of the world," he asked his fellow citizens, "or shall we abandon it?"[100]

[100] Address in St. Paul, Sept. 9, 1919, *Public Papers*, VI, 89.

CHAPTER VIII

An After Word

*O small dust of earth
that walks so arrogantly,
trust begets power and faith is
an affectionate thing.*

Marianne Moore, "In Distrust of Merits," 1944

*Most generations stone their prophets. This is not Wilson's
tragedy. It is America's tragedy. It is the tragedy of the next
generation.*

Raymond B. Fosdick to Mrs. Fosdick, March, 1920

American internationalism bore the hallmarks of the pre-atomic age.
Although not of a uniformly sunny temperament, it was characterized more
by hope than by despair. Josiah Royce, whose Christianity more than his
metaphysics made him a realist, still insisted that the future was not beyond
human control. Thorstein Veblen, while wryly observing that not only
capitalists but patriots, too, will run true to form, nevertheless clung to his
faith in revolution. Our present sense of events riding men and of life itself
becoming a mockery awaited another war and Hiroshima. For this
reason the internationalists are better understood as participants in a dialogue with one another than as prophets for the post-industrial age. It is not

217

that their dialogue is irrelevant, but rather that the chance of reviving internationalism necessarily depends upon the emergence of men and women who would impart another meaning to the term. Unless one accepts a grim biological determinism, the recurrence of wars has historical dimensions. The tragedy of one age penetrates the future, but it does not repeat itself exactly.

In 1914 the great tragedy seemed a great opportunity.[1] The war triggered a virtual explosion of peace plans. Popular attention once more focused upon foreign affairs; and the memory of the Spanish-American War might well have served as a warning that the American people might, once again, revive the theme of the old song, "I Don't Care."

In many respects, President Wilson himself represented a great opportunity. The American sense of mission had been essentially an isolationist concept. America was a non-Europe. Wilson skillfully made the theme activist and internationalist. Just because America was a non-Europe it was her duty to institute a new international age, to make her truth universal and to lead Europe into a repudiation of the old ways. Wilson, because he was leader of the polity as well as leader of the nation, insisted upon the unity of national and international goals, and colored the whole of institutionalism with this unity. And yet there is little evidence to support the contention that the American people, as opposed to the communalists and intellectuals, failed to support the League because it was too nationalistic. Jane Addams insisted that for the common man the League was "self convicted of the old diplomacy" and that it did not dare enough. Wilson argued for the Covenant in terms of its American coloration.[2] If one assumes the importance of small beginnings, then the President had the better of the argument. But, of course, the more fundamental question at issue was the League's role as defender of the Treaty and as projector of American power.

While nationalism and political internationalism constituted the core of the League debate, this does not imply that the American people rejected communalism. The whole issue of communalism was cut out of the public debate altogether. The possible choices of 1919 and 1920 presented themselves rather as follows: adherence to the League as contained within the Versailles Treaty and with Article Ten as Wilson insisted; acceptance of the League on Henry Cabot Lodge's terms, that is, with nationalistic modifications and without Article Ten; total rejection of the Covenant but with America's traditional isolation modified by the demands for trade expansion which were clearly evident during the Wilson period.

[1] Josiah Royce, *War and Insurance* (New York, Macmillan, 1914), p. 1.
[2] *Public Papers of Woodrow Wilson*, eds. Ray Stannard Baker and William E. Dodd, 6 vols. (New York, Harper, 1925–27), VI, 1–2 9, 16, 31, 89, 121, 146–47, 171, 199, 304–305.

In retrospect, what is truly remarkable about these three choices, in view of the sense of futility and disillusionment that accompanied American failure to join the League, is their fundamental similarity. If Wilson conceived of the League as a fulfillment of the American purpose, and if Lodge believed that Wilson's kind of membership meant too much European control, did either one really demand great sacrifices on the part of a nationalistic people? Did either of these men, or for that matter their earnest supporters, even consider the possibility that *Pax Americana* might become an inappropriate response to the twentieth-century world?

Only because Wilson was unable to come to an agreement with the nationalists did the United States accept, by default, the third choice. And yet the choice was not truly isolationist. In major respects, both Wilson and Lodge could have been satisfied. The United States was Europe's creditor, a two-ocean power, and the commercial master of the West. Far from losing the industrial primacy of the world, America had gained it. Far from retreating into isolation, America was committed to open-door engagement.[3]

There was indeed a loss, and it was precisely the loss, after all, that Jane Addams understood. The ordinary people, she observed, "distrusted the League because it was so indifferent to the widespread misery and starvation of the world." It hesitated to repair the damages of war and "refused to become the tentative instrument of the longed for new age."[4] In brief, by ignoring the community and arguing only on nationalistic terms within the framework of the polity, America's leaders succeeded in educating the public not at all. The League awakened no loyalty because America was made a substitute for the League. Collective security became national security and it remained that. The option of community allegiance, internationalized relief, open and eager participation in the specialized agencies never entered into the League debate at all.

Yet not the whole burden of responsibility fell upon Wilson. As President of the United States he did obey his primary obligation, which was to America's vital interests as he understood them. Rather, the responsibility for the decline of internationalism, in any terms but Wilson's, rests with the internationalists themselves, partly for neglecting the education of the public, but more fundamentally for cherishing their differences. The intellectual divergencies among the internationalists were so sharp that they

[3] William Appleman Williams, *The Tragedy of American Diplomacy,* rev. ed. (New York, Delta, 1962), pp. 123–41, 158–59.
[4] *Peace and Bread in Time of War,* reprinted with a 1945 introduction by John Dewey (Boston, G. K. Hall, 1960), p. 201.

failed to understand the degree to which their views supplemented one another in theory, or could be made to serve one another in practice. The institutionalists, for example, believed that the long-range interests of the national states were harmonious, and that an entity they called "world public opinion" not only existed, but agreed with America's fundamental purposes of national self-determination and League cooperation. These assumptions suggested nothing less than the existence of a world community. The men of the polity surely knew that the world of Adam Smith, however perfect as an ideal, had long since ceased to exist. As the Rockefellers and the Carnegies made perfect competition a myth, so the power of the United States and the birth of twentieth-century revolution made international harmony a dream. The question remained then: how attain the harmony upon which every political and legal scheme critically depended?

This was the fundamental issue which communalism was designed to resolve. For the community thinkers assumed that there was no actual harmony of interests and that the national state system created conditions injurious to such harmony. As Royce so succinctly stated, the nations were related to one another in "dangerous pairs." The activities the communalists proposed—international insurance, the protection of the weak and the poor, the disallowance of trade discrimination—were designed to promote just such a world public opinion, or better an international realization of common condition and common destiny.

But turning the matter entirely about, one is hard pressed to learn how these very activities could have been performed without the adherence and devotion of the national states to a formal, legal international organization. If these communal activities were to survive, they needed permanent institutions—at the very least, an international bureaucracy just for the bookkeeping! Thus the two approaches to internationalism were logically and practically complementary. The problem for the historian, however, is not an exercise in logic. Historically, polity and community diverged, and the polity dominated public consciousness. It is the predominance of the polity as well as the nature of the divergence that concerns us.

The contrasting world views of the internationalists may be briefly summarized:

Where the institutionalists concentrated upon political and legal reconstruction, the communalists fixed their attention upon the moral and practical implications of national exclusiveness. For the most part, some version of the old reason-will psychology, implying that man's duty was the restraint of his lower nature, satisfied the institutionalists. But the communalists viewed human nature in more dynamic terms, often, though not always, emphasizing the peacefulness of human instincts. The men of the polity, as has been observed, combined an acceptance of large organizations with traditional *laissez-faire* mentality. For this reason, among others, they were not dissatisfied with the American socio-economic order.

But the communalists frequently expressed more critical views of American society and could not accept any vision of the future which implied a *Pax Americana*. The strong tinge of moral imperialism and Anglo-Saxonism that colored the polity was by and large absent from communal thinking. Thus, the sense of America's mission in the world, so predominant in Wilson's thinking, was shared in some degree by the institutionalists; but it was thoroughly repugnant to Veblen and hardly less so to Addams and Royce. Finally, the major ideational contrast between the two groups concerned the character of world society. The men of the polity, even those who defined society as an organism, as Wilson did,[5] adhered to a formal atomistic view of international organization. The communalists viewed world society as a changing, organic whole.

Divergencies such as these went far deeper than any conflict about the expediency or morality of specific foreign policies. They were fundamentally arguments about the meaning of American life in the age when the nation first became a world power. In the early twentieth century, at a time when foreign policy had not yet become either a specialized study or a popular obsession, the reflections of the internationalists bore a close relationship to their broadest views of life and to their interests in domestic affairs. This, if anything, increased the likelihood of their views winning an audience. There was a barrier of expertise, and the internationalists strongly appealed to popular activism. Yet, shortly after the war, the programs of the communalists were all but forgotten and those of the polity, especially the President's, were remembered as a dramatic failure. It was almost as if during Wilson's tour and illness the old internationalism had burned itself out in the process of feeding the flame of Wilson's own cause and personal mission.

Yet long before the tour, internationalism had become identified with institutionalism; and not only the positions of the internationalists but the environment of wartime America itself contributed to the public predominance of the polity. In the first place, the men of the polity consciously tailored their programs for public acceptance. They were thoroughly familiar with the facts of political life and with the methods of building organizations and of publicizing views. Secondly, the content of institutionalism, particularly its emphasis upon America's mission, flattered the national ego. Thirdly, and perhaps most fundamentally, the communalists offered programs which may well have appeared too imaginative and

[5] *The Political Thought of Woodrow Wilson*, ed. E. David Cronon (Indianapolis, Bobbs Merrill, 1965), p. 23.

too experimental in view of the increasingly anti-revolutionary orientation of American foreign policy in a world shaken by revolution. It was difficult to satisfy the public longing for stability by proposals for fundamental changes in the *status quo*. Inevitably such proposals invited the most damning charge a twentieth-century American could make: they were impractical.

Perhaps a more searching investigation would shed more light on the reasons for this institutional predominance. The accommodation of the men of the polity to large organizations—an accommodation that exerted a profound influence upon their own thought—may well have influenced their standing with their American audience. As university presidents, publicists, and former Cabinet members, the men of the polity represented a certain wisdom about foreign policy. At least many Americans assumed so. During Wilson's presidency, Elihu Root and Nicholas Murray Butler, representatives of the Republican Old Guard, doubtless attracted relatively little popular following. Nevertheless they spoke for the Carnegie Endowment for International Peace and for the American Association for International Law, both of which symbolized considerable knowledge of foreign affairs. The leaders of the League to Enforce Peace, including former President Taft, were even more persuasive. By December 1916 they had built a national organization with branches in all but three states and were receiving considerable editorial and financial support.[6]

In comparing this situation with that of Addams, Royce, and Veblen, one is immediately struck by the fact that each was well known for talents in areas other than politics. Royce's *War and Insurance* caused a momentary flurry of interest among book reviewers, but no public figure ever regarded his suggestions or referred to them as practical. Even his admirers said comparatively little about the internationalist aspects of his thought. They remembered him chiefly as America's leading idealist metaphysician and the philosopher of loyalty, who offered a unique interpretation of the community.[7] The response to Veblen's *Nature of Peace* was similar—momentary strong interest, considerable controversy over his meaning, followed by comparative neglect.[8] His reputation as an iconoclast precluded his accept-

[6] Ruhl Bartlett, *The League to Enforce Peace* (Chapel Hill, Univ. of North Carolina Press, 1944), pp. 61–62, 65.

[7] See: *Papers in Honor of Josiah Royce on His Sixtieth Birthday* (New York, Longmans, 1916), *passim;* C. M. Blakewill, "Royce as an Interpreter of American Ideals," *International Journal of Ethics,* XXVII (April 1917) 306–16; Morris R. Cohen, "Josiah Royce," *Science,* N.S. XLIV (Dec. 1, 1916), 772–74.

[8] Joseph Dorfman, *Thorstein Veblen and His America* (New York, Viking Press, 1934), pp. 370–71, 381–82, indicates the strong interest aroused by Francis Hackett's review in the *New Republic.* Bernard Rosenberg, *The Values of Veblen: A Critical Reappraisal* (Washington, D.C., Public Affairs Press, 1956), p. 102, mentions the neglect of Veblen's plans after this initial controversy.

ance by the Inquiry. The Food Administration ignored his proposals. His followers, a relatively small group of academic economists and engineers, paid little attention to his internationalism.

One reason for this neglect, although perhaps not the most important one, was the non-organizational, apolitical bent of Royce's and Veblen's most famous writings. Jane Addams, on the other hand, possessed very strong organizational talents. She was the leader of a national pressure group, the Woman's Peace Party, even though the strength of her group never matched that of the League to Enforce Peace. Although at the height of its successes, early in 1916, the Woman's Peace Party had almost forty thousand members, after the United States entered the war, membership dwindled and the remaining pacifists became the objects of public opprobrium.[9]

Addams' strict pacifism during the war was only the most obvious explanation of her declining prestige. Of far greater significance was the uncompromising character of the communalists' ideas when measured against the prevalent wartime distrust of any innovation that did not contribute to the war effort itself. By comparison with the political internationalists, the communalists were uncompromising. They believed, as Addams later wrote of the wartime pacifists, that "man's primary allegiance is to his vision of the truth, and that he is under obligation to affirm it."[10]

The leaders of the League to Enforce Peace and of the world court movement, on the other hand, lived in a world of political compromises. Their very plans stemmed from a conscious tailoring of ideals to win public approval. Holt abandoned his federalism, first for the league of peace, later for collective security, because he thought his earlier ideas ran ahead of popular acceptance. Lowell's rejection of the international police proposal was based in part upon his estimate of what kind of international organization the major powers would subscribe to. Both Root and Butler had doubts about collective security, in large measure because they assessed American willingness to assume international responsibilities in terms quite different from those of Wilson.

This contrast between the communalist and institutionalist positions reflects, at least in part, a social contrast between men close to the center of political responsibility and influenced by its demands, and those comparatively distant from it. As Johan Galtung has noted, there is a consistent difference in the estimates of practicality in foreign policy alternatives between men familiar with the decision-making process and those on the periphery of political influence. Peripheral opinions are likely to be both

[9] Marie Louise Degan, *The History of the Woman's Peace Party* (Baltimore, Johns Hopkins Press, 1939), p. 156; Addams, *Peace and Bread,* pp. 10, 127, 139–40.

[10] *Peace and Bread,* p. 151.

more critical and more absolutist. They tend to emphasize either-or alternatives or to call for the establishment of a wholly new order. Thus we find such contrasts as these: peace or the price system, international insurance or exacerbated conflict. The men near the center, on the other hand, tend to concentrate on shorter-range alternatives and on more partial solutions.[11] Galtung's analysis is only partially applicable to the communalists and the institutionalists, both of which groups oversimplified solutions to a large degree. Nevertheless, his emphasis upon the contrast between the ideals of insiders and outsiders affords one explanation for the communalist-institutionalist difference.

The institutionalists were more familiar with the social realities of the policymaker's world. Root himself directly experienced these realities; he knew that the necessity for immediate and expedient short-range decisions could sometimes mold long-term ideals in unexpected ways. The leaders of the League to Enforce Peace, in frequent contact with men close to the governments of Great Britain and the United States, continually estimated the effects of their decisions upon public opinion and upon the policymakers. Marburg's correspondence with Lord Bryce affords a prime example of this type of adjustment for the sake of public acceptance. The questions frequently at issue were: Would the American government initiate such a policy? Would British and American opinion support it? To the institutionalists, the world of expedient compromise represented reality.

The reality of the communalists, on the other hand, was largely an apolitical one. It concerned the possibilities of fundamental alterations in the antagonistic nature of international relations. That it could be just as realistic is indicated by such judgments as Addams' prediction that the Russian soldiers would choose peace and bread rather than a continuation of the war. (Root, on the contrary, attributed the defections from the Russian army to the influence of German propaganda.)[12] Royce appreciated the contrast between the strength of national bonds and the weakness of international loyalty. The institutionalists failed to see the significance of this. Veblen perceived that the common man's patriotism contradicted his own interests. The men of the polity took a different view of patriotism.

This very critical awareness of nationalism limited the communalists' appeal, especially in a political climate of one hundred percent Americanism. While the institutionalists understood the strength of national loyal-

[11] "Foreign Policy as a Function of Social Position," *Journal of Peace Research*, I, no. 4 (1964), 211–14.

[12] Addams, "Tolstoy and the Russian Soldiers," *New Republic*, XII (Sept. 29, 1917), 240–42; Root to Robert Lansing, June 17, 1918, and Supplementary Report, Aug. 27, 1918, forwarded Lansing to Wilson, in U.S. Department of State. *Papers Relating to the Foreign Relations of the United States, 1918: Russia* (Washington, D.C., 1931), I, 121–22, 128, 147–53.

ties, at least to the extent of acknowledging how little international authority the sovereign nations would tolerate, they were apparently unconcerned
with the impediments national self-regard would create once international
institutions began to function. Moreover, their defense of national independence ran counter to their faith in what Wilson had called the "common
legal conscience in mankind."[13] Upon examination, this conscience proved
to be far from common. It included such Western and even predominantly
American ideas as federalism, respect for private property, judicial review,
and arbitration of international disputes. How flattering it was to think that
Americans had a unique perception of universal moral and legal principles
and therefore a unique obligation to foster them! The communalists were
not able to appeal to the public in this way. While both Royce and Addams
lauded the nobility of wartime patriotism and unity, Addams considered it
to have been bought at a fearful cost, and Royce suggested that it lacked the
spirit of loyalty to loyalty. Neither idea was particularly appealing to a
highly nationalistic people. Veblen's conception of patriotism as "honorific," magical, and self-deceptive appeared downright shocking to the wartime public. None of the community thinkers believed that the international
organization should mirror the existing American polity. None regarded
national honor as anything but destructive, and yet Americans presumed
that during the war their honor as well as their rights were at stake.

In brief, the community conception of patriotism as ethically and scien-
tifically backward challenged prevalent notions of the superiority of civilized peoples. This challenge made all the less acceptable such unprece-
dented ideas as the neutralization of trade and citizenship, the international
protection of migratory workers, and international insurance. What Addams called a needed "scepticism as to the values of established institutions," was quite unpopular in postwar America.[14] In a world of revolutionary disintegration, Americans were beginning to cast about for security
rather than challenge. If Wilson's appeals for the League satisfied any
popular longing, it was the longing for stability and permanence.

But the outward semblance of order did not seem trustworthy to the
communalists. During the Averbuch affair in Chicago, Addams learned that
appearances might be deceiving and might very well conceal social disintegration.[15] Royce's California history and Pauline Christianity had taught

[13] Woodrow Wilson, *The State: Elements of Historical and Practical Politics*
(Boston, Heath, 1889), p. 625.
[14] *Peace and Bread,* pp. 187–88.
[15] During the public excitement over the assassination of President McKinley, the
Chicago police shot and killed a Russian Jew named Averbuch whom they suspected of
anarchism. Averbuch had been on a quite innocent errand to the house of the chief of
police. They then arrested two of his friends and proceeded to question his sister at
great length. Not only did the incident reinforce the Russian Jews' traditional distrust

him the same lesson. In Veblen's system, financial depression only revealed the sickness of an outwardly efficient economy. Thus, communal internationalism divorced the ideal of order from the idea of permanency and substituted the goal of a changing order. Genuine stability grew out of the experience of cooperative relationships, the realization of common purpose such as that achieved in small and primitive societies.

The very conditions the communalists criticized diminished the chances of initiating communal plans. How could a sense of universal brotherhood arise in a world torn by national animosities? What people would persuade their governments to experiment with new means of international cooperation when those governments were so deeply committed to preserving order in a revolutionary era, and when the people themselves were contributing to the red scare? The crowning irony of the communalists' position was that the initiative for realizing even apolitical peace proposals rested with the governments. The statesmen were most reluctant to grant any authority to international agencies which, by providing security, education, and welfare, would ultimately undermine the foundations of national loyalty. As Veblen realized, the vested interests were not about to commit suicide.

As the League of Nations emerged in 1920, considerably weaker for the American defection, it was hardly the reversal of the old diplomacy which Wilson expected. This reversal actually had been expected to take place not through formal structure alone but through American participation and predominance. Instead, this complex political and legal instrument for the peaceful settlement of international disputes, now highly Europeanized, allowed the old diplomacy to work in some new ways.

And yet the traces of the league movements, American and British and continental, still remained. The regularly meeting Assembly, the Secretariat, and the Council combined the institutional idea of permanent structure with the practices of the European concert of powers. The Council's application of sanctions to enforce consideration of disputes, but not the award itself, reflected the essential idea of the League to Enforce Peace. The concept of sovereignty was protected by the requirement of unanimity in substantive Council decisions, by the explicit inclusion of regional understandings, and by the national states' exclusive prerogatives over domestic affairs. The agreement on the part of the powers to delay war while the Council inquired into the dispute, or while it was arbitrated, derived both from the recommendations of the Hague conferences and from Bryan's cooling-off treaties. Only the mandates provisions and the inclusion of

---

of police authority, but it revealed the deep division within the urban community especially between the poor immigrants and the law enforcement officials (see *Twenty Years at Hull House, with Autobiographical Notes,* New York, Macmillan, 1910, pp. 404–405, 414–16).

international unions bore any resemblance to the community ideal. Was the League, at its birth, fossilized by the old ways? Did the institutionalists' drive for stability make the League irrelevant in a revolutionary world? There was danger inherent in such a blanket condemnation—a point where worldliness could pass into cynicism—and the devoted Wilsonians and internationalists recognized this. The honest had to confess, as Walter Lippmann insisted, that the League at its birth was no more than the sum of the Great Powers. The hopeful had to work, as Raymond Fosdick insisted, for the day when it might become something more and outgrow its attachment to the Treaty.[16]

The League of Nations suffered unquestionably from its excessive politicizing and its wartime birth. Wilson and all the men of the polity assumed that Germany's "flagrant bad faith" and the Bolsheviks' repudiation of ancient obligations were exceptional. They rested their beliefs upon an assumed resemblance between nations and gentlemen. Nations honored their commitments and obeyed the law. Violations of law and treaty obligations stemmed either from misinterpretation or from evil intentions. The legalists and advocates of collective security quarreled over the kinds of sanctions necessary to enforce this gentlemen's code—over the distance one could go while preserving both sovereignty and national interests. But the basic commandment of the code itself was clear: Thou shalt honor contracts.

If any contract could have equated national interest and general interests, the League should have worked. The fact that it failed was not the result of mechanical imperfections. Rather the failure suggested that the nations, whether members or not, had discovered no common interests. The League lacked the power to enforce its decisions, or even to mediate quarrels, not because the Covenant needed revision, but because the national states gave it no power and the citizens of the states gave it no loyalty. America's failure to join was only the beginning. Even the members of the League failed to use the machinery available when the crisis did come in the 1930s. The question therefore remains: Was machinery enough?

As for the chimera of world public opinion, it remained just that. The moral force to compel the use of power never was brought to bear. One may attribute this failure to the amorality of national states, or to the necessity of self-interest in the state system. But in the last analysis there was nothing inevitable about short-sightedness. The failure of the League was a human failure. The decision for war or peace both in the short and the long range remained with national leaders and the populations who

---

[16] Raymond B. Fosdick, *Letters on the League of Nations* (Princeton, Princeton Univ. Press, 1966): Fosdick to Lippmann, July 14, 1919, pp. 9–10; Lippmann to Fosdick, Aug. 15, 1919, pp. 10–12.

supported them. In a world of conflict and self-interest, these elements of contingency remained: popular intelligence, individual wisdom, or lack of it, courage or irresolution. The atomism of the polity proved a more accurate reflection of international morality than contradictory expectations for a universal rule of law. It was not that men loved peace less, but their nations more. In short, the failure of the League reflected the absence of a true international community.

Thus, the quest for community, essentially a moral quest, appeared all the more compelling. Royce, Addams, and Veblen, for all their shortcomings, appreciated the emptiness and futility of a political structure without the sense of community. Yet, they too predicated their search upon unprovable hypotheses. How could one demonstrate that a true international community would emerge from the social and creative core of human nature once national antagonisms declined, if those antagonisms did not in fact decline? No one could prove that advancing technology, international insurance, or cooperative welfare activities held the keys to peace. These were articles of faith. Veblen, it is true, remained a skeptic in this regard. He believed somewhat more firmly than the others that the cultural lag would persist. Nevertheless he, too, had faith—in technology and in the coming revolution.

If such experiments as Royce, Addams, and Veblen proposed could have been adopted, the year 1919 appeared the time for them. But was there ever a propitious moment? One has only to contemplate the possibility of the Allies' shipping food to Germany, devoting their resources to the reconstruction of Europe, abandoning tariffs, neutralizing citizenship, or sacrificing reparations by creating an international insurance fund, and the question answers itself. These activities were to create a radical new morality. The morality had to exist already in order to initiate the activities.

Jane Addams recalled something that will seem obvious to critics of the community. The survival of communities of the past depended upon great and overriding motives—motives which touched people who never led nations and who rarely expressed themselves except through action. Religious motives had been the strongest of these. Like many internationalists, Addams seemed more than wistful as she wondered whether a renewed sense of brotherhood would come to men in the way it had once come to primitive peoples—through caring for fundamental human needs, with the resulting religious awareness.[17]

Of the importance of the growth of such international loyalty, the men of the polity seemed unaware. The institutionalists had succeeded as practical initiators, but lacked the critical sensitivity to perceive the inadequacy of

[17] *Peace and Bread,* pp. 205, 220.

what they planned. The communalists were perceptive critics of the *status quo* who understood the motives of revolution, but they consistently lacked the power to effect changes. Insight and practical effectiveness had no meeting-ground.

What is likely to strike the modern reader finally is Veblen's recognition of man's patriotism contradicting his common sense; Royce's understanding of the evil limitlessness of the quest for power; Addams' portrait of the pacifist in wartime, isolated because loyal to the truth, misunderstood because excessively rational. And if this dark side of communalism appears more realistic to us than the hopeful suggestions for reform, this in itself reveals as much about our own age as about the world of 1919.

Bibliography

PRIMARY SOURCES

Manuscript Collections

Jane Addams MSS and Correspondence, Swarthmore College Peace Collection.

Papers of Emily Green Balch, Swarthmore College Peace Collection.

Papers of Nicholas Murray Butler, Columbiana Collection, Columbia University.

Papers of Andrew Carnegie, Manuscript Division, Library of Congress.

Carnegie Endowment for International Peace Archives, Special Collections, Columbia University.

Papers of John Bates Clark, Special Collections, Columbia University.

Papers of Franklin Henry Giddings, Columbiana Collection, Columbia University.

Herbert Hoover Archives, Hoover Institution on War, Revolution and Peace, Stanford University.

Archives of the Inquiry, Department of State, National Archives.

David Starr Jordan Peace Correspondence, Hoover Institution on War, Revolution and Peace, Stanford University.

Robert Lansing Papers, Manuscript Division, Library of Congress.

Papers of Theodore Marburg, Manuscript Division, Library of Congress.

New York Peace Society Archives, Swarthmore College Peace Collection.

Oral History Collection, Columbia University.

Papers of Elihu Root, Manuscript Division, Library of Congress.

Department of State, 1919 Archives, National Archives.

Papers of Oscar S. Straus, Manuscript Division, Library of Congress.

Papers of William Howard Taft, Manuscript Division, Library of Congress.

Papers of Lillian Wald, New York Public Library.

Woodrow Wilson Papers, Manuscript Division, Library of Congress.

Wilson-Bryan Correspondence, National Archives.

Woman's Peace Party Correspondence, Swarthmore College Peace Collection.

Newspapers and United States Government Documents

New York *Times,* 1907–20.

New York *Tribune,* 1902–12.

San Francisco *Chronicle,* October 1915.

San Francisco *Examiner,* October 1915.

Congressional Record. Senate. 61st Cong., special session, July 1, 1909, *Debate on Income and Corporation Taxes,* pp. 3991–4016.

————. ————. June 23, 1909, *Debate on the Payne-Aldrich Tariff,* pp. 3670–3721.

U.S. Congress, House. Committee on Military Affairs. *Hearing on the Bill to Increase the Efficiency of the Military Establishment of the United States.* 64th Cong., 1st sess., Jan. 13, 1916. Jane Addams' Statement, reprinted as pamphlet by the Woman's Peace Party. Chicago, 1916, pp. 3–14.

————, Senate. Committee on Foreign Relations. *Report of the Committee on Foreign Relations Together with the Views of the Minority upon the General Arbitration Treaties with Great Britain and France.* Senate Document No. 98, 62nd Cong., 1st sess., Aug. 3, 1911.

————. ————. Committee on Banking and Currency. *Rehabilitation and Provisions for European Countries: Hearings Relative to the Need of Assistance in Exporting Our Goods and Rendering Financial Aid Generally in Rehabilitating European Countries.* 66th Cong., 3rd sess., Jan. 21, 1921.

U.S. Department of State. *Papers Relating to the Foreign Relations of the United States, 1918: Russia,* I. Washington, D.C., 1931.

Society Publications and Published Collections of Documents and Papers

Baker, Ray Stannard. *Woodrow Wilson: Life and Letters.* 8 vols. Garden City, N.Y., Doubleday, 1927–39.

————. *Woodrow Wilson and the World Settlement.* 3 vols. Garden City, N.Y., Doubleday, 1923.

————, and William E. Dodd (eds.). *The Public Papers of Woodrow Wilson.* 6 vols. New York, Harper, 1925–27.

Bane, Suda Lorena, and Ralph Haswell Lutz (eds.). *The Blockade of Germany after the Armistice.* Stanford, Stanford University Press, 1942.

————. *Organization of American Relief in Europe, 1918–1919.* Stanford, Stanford University Press, 1943.

Bourne, R. S. (ed.). *Towards an Enduring Peace: A Symposium of Peace Proposals and Programs 1914–1916.* New York, American Association for International Conciliation, 1916.

Brown, Stuart Gerry (ed.). *The Social Philosophy of Josiah Royce.* Syracuse, Syracuse Univ. Press, 1950.

Central Organization for a Durable Peace. *Recueil de Rapports sur les Différents Points du Programme Minimum.* 2 vols. The Hague, 1916.

Cronon, E. David (ed.). *The Political Thought of Woodrow Wilson.* Indianapolis, Bobbs-Merrill, 1965.

Davidson, John Wells (ed.) *A Crossroads of Freedom: The 1912 Campaign Speeches of Woodrow Wilson.* New Haven, Yale Univ. Press, 1956.

Fosdick, Raymond B. *Letters on the League of Nations.* Princeton, Princeton Univ. Press, 1966.

Hull House Maps and Papers, a presentation of nationalities and wages in a congested district of Chicago. . . . New York, Crowell [1895].

Lasch, Christopher (ed.). *The Social Thought of Jane Addams.* Indianapolis, Bobbs-Merrill, 1965.

League to Enforce Peace. *Pamphlets 1915–1919,* Society Publications Collection, Hoover Institution.

———. *Enforced Peace: Proceedings of the First Annual National Assemblage of the League to Enforce Peace, Washington, May 26, 27, 1916.* New York, League to Enforce Peace, 1916.

League to Enforce Peace. *Independence Hall Conference, held in the City of Philadelphia, June 17, 1915.* New York, League to Enforce Peace, 1915.

———. *Win the War for Permanent Peace: Addresses Made at the National Convention of the League to Enforce Peace in Philadelphia, May 16, 17, 1918.* New York, League to Enforce Peace, 1918.

Latané, John H. (ed.). *Development of the League of Nations Idea: Documents and Correspondence of Theodore Marburg.* 2 vols. New York, Macmillan, 1932.

Lerner, Max (ed.). *The Portable Veblen.* New York, Viking Press, 1960.

Link, Arthur S. (ed.). *The Papers of Woodrow Wilson.* 3 vols. Princeton, Princeton Univ. Press, 1966–67.

Mantoux, Paul J. *Paris Peace Conference, 1919: Proceedings of the Council of Four, March 24-April 18,* trans. John Boardman Whitton. Geneva, Droz, 1964.

Mead, Lucia Ames (ed.). *The Overthrow of the War System.* Boston, Forum Publications, 1915.

Miller, David Hunter. *The Drafting of the Covenant.* 2 vols. New York, Putnam, 1928.

Mitchell, Wesley C. (ed.). *What Veblen Taught.* New York, Viking Press, 1936.

Papers in Honor of Josiah Royce on His Sixtieth Birthday. New York, Longmans, 1916.

Scott, James Brown (ed.). *American Addresses at the Second Hague Peace Conference.* Boston, Ginn, 1910.

Woman's Peace Party. *Bericht des Internationalen Frauenkongress.* Zurich, May 12–17, 1919.

————. *Pamphlets 1915–1919* (continues as Woman's International League for Peace and Freedom). Society Publications, Hoover Institution.

World Federation League. *The American Peace Commission: A Step Toward Definitely Organizing the World.* New York, World Federation League, 1910.

————. *The Peace Movement: The Federation of the World.* New York, World Federation League, 1910.

Individual Works

Addams, Jane. "Americanization," *American Sociological Society: Papers and Proceedings,* XIV (Dec. 29–31, 1919), 206–14.

————. "Arts and Crafts and the Settlement," *Chautauqua Assembly Herald,* XXVII (July 9, 1902), 2–3, 7–8.

————. "Bread Givers," Address at Rockford Seminary, April 21, 1880, Jane Addams MSS, Swarthmore College Peace Collection.

————. "Charity and Social Justice," Address, National Conference of Charities and Corrections, St. Louis, May 19, 1910. *Survey,* XXIV (June 11, 1910), 441–49.

————. "Child Labor Legislation—A Requisite for Industrial Efficiency," *Annals of the American Academy of Political and Social Science,* XXV (May 1905), 542–50.

————. "Class Conflict in America," *American Sociological Society: Papers and Proceedings,* XI (Dec. 28–31, 1907), 152–55.

————. *Democracy and Social Ethics,* ed. Anne Firor Scott. Cambridge, Harvard Univ. Press, 1964.

————. "Exercises in Commemoration of the Birthday of Washington," Address, Union League Club, Chicago, Feb. 23, 1903. Chicago, *Memorial Bulletin* (1903), pp. 6–9.

————. "Feed the World and Save the League," *New Republic,* XXIV (Nov. 24, 1920), 325–27.

————. "The Food of War," *Independent* LXXXIV (Dec. 13, 1915), 430–31.

————. "Impressions of Mexico," Address, Chicago, April 1925. Pamphlet, Woman's International League for Peace and Freedom: U.S. Section, Society Publications, Hoover Institution, pp. 1–2.

————. "In Memoriam, Henry Demerest Lloyd," Address, Chicago, Nov. 29, 1903. Jane Addams MSS, Swarthmore College Peace Collection.

————. "The Interests of Labor in International Peace," *Universal Peace*

Congress: Official Report of the Thirteenth Congress. Boston: Oct. 3–8, 1904, pp. 145–47.

Addams, Jane. "International Cooperation for Social Welfare," *National Conference of Social Work: Proceedings* (1924), pp. 107–13.

————. *Jane Addams: A Centennial Reader,* ed. Emily Cooper Johnson. New York, Macmillan, 1960.

————. "John Dewey and Social Welfare," *John Dewey The Man and His Philosophy: Addresses Delivered in New York in Celebration of His Seventieth Birthday.* Cambridge, Harvard Univ. Press, 1930, pp. 140–52.

————. "Labor as a Factor in the Newer Conception of International Relations," Address, National Conference on Foreign Relations of the United States, Academy of Political Science at Long Beach, New York, May 31, 1917. Pamphlet, Jane Addams MSS, Swarthmore College Peace Collection, pp. 1–7.

————. "Larger Aspects of the Woman's Movement," *Annals of the American Academy of Political and Social Science,* LVI (Nov. 1914), 1–8.

————. "Larger Social Groupings," *Charities,* XII (1904), 675.

————. *The Long Road of Woman's Memory.* New York, Macmillan, 1916.

————. "A Modern Lear: Strike at Pullman," *Survey,* XXIX (Nov. 2, 1912), 131–37.

————. *Newer Ideals of Peace.* New York, Macmillan, 1907.

————. "The Objective Value of a Social Settlement," *Philanthropy and Social Progress: Seven Essays . . . Delivered before the School of Applied Ethics at Plymouth, Mass., during the Session of 1892.* New York, Crowell 1893, pp. 27–56.

————. "The Operation of the Illinois Child Labor Law," *Annals of the American Academy of Political and Social Science,* XXVII (March 1906), 327–30.

————. "Patriotism and Pacifists in Wartime," Address, Chicago, May 15, 1917. Pamphlet, Jane Addams MSS, Swarthmore College Peace Collection, pp. 1–2.

————. *Peace and Bread in Time of War,* repr. with a 1945 introduction by John Dewey. Boston, G. K. Hall, 1960.

————. "Peace and the Press," *Independent,* LXXXIV (Oct. 11, 1915), 55–56.

————. "The Potential Advantages of the Mandate System," *Annals of the American Academy of Political and Social Science,* XCVI (July 1921), 70–74.

————. "The Present Crisis in Trade Union Morals," *North American Review,* CLXXIX (Aug. 1904), 178–93.

———. "Recent Immigration, A Field Neglected by the Scholar," Address, University of Chicago, Dec. 20, 1904, *University Record,* IX (Jan. 1905), 274–84.

———. "The Responsibilities and Duties of Women toward the Peace Movement," *Universal Peace Congress: Official Report of the Thirteenth Congress.* Boston, Oct. 3–8, 1904, pp. 120–22.

———. *The Second Twenty Years at Hull House, September 1909 to September 1929: With a Record of a Growing World Consciousness.* New York, Macmillan, 1930.

———. "The Significance of Organized Labor," *Machinists' Monthly Journal,* X (Sept. 1898), 551–52.

———. *The Social Thought of Jane Addams,* ed. Christopher Lasch. Indianapolis, Bobbs-Merrill, 1965.

———. *The Spirit of Youth and the City Streets.* New York, Macmillan, 1912.

———. "The Subjective Necessity for Social Settlements," *Philanthropy and Social Progress: Seven Essays . . . Delivered before the School of Applied Ethics at Plymouth, Mass., During the Session of 1892.* New York, Crowell 1893, pp. 1–26.

———. "Tolstoy and the Russian Soldiers," *New Republic,* XII (Sept. 29, 1917), 240–42.

———. "Tolstoy's Theory of Life," *Chautauqua Assembly Herald,* XXVII (July 14, 1902), 2–3.

———. "Toward Internationalism," *Women's Auxiliary Conference of the Second Pan-American Scientific Congress.* Washington, D.C., Dec. 28, 1915–Jan. 7, 1916, pp. 59–60.

———. "Trade Unions and Public Duty," *American Journal of Sociology,* IV (Jan. 1899), 448–62.

———. *Twenty Years at Hull House, with Autobiographical Notes.* New York, Macmillan, 1910.

———. "Votes for Women and Other Votes," *Survey Graphic,* XXVIII (June 1, 1912), 367–68.

———. "Women, War, and Suffrage," *Survey,* XXXV (Nov. 6, 1915), 148–50.

———. "Women's Special Training for Peacemaking," *Proceedings of the Second National Peace Congress.* Chicago, May 2–5, 1909, pp. 252–54.

———. "Work and Play as Factors in Education," *Chautauquan,* XLII (Nov. 1905), 251–55.

———. "The World's Food and World Politics," *National Conference of Social Work,* Pamphlet no. 128 (1918) 6 pp.

———, Emily G. Balch, and Alice Hamilton. *Women at the Hague: The International Congress of Women and Its Results.* New York, Macmillan, 1915.

Addams, Jane, and Alice Hamilton. "Official Report of Jane Addams and
    Dr. Alice Hamilton to the American Society of Friends Service Com-
    mittee, Philadelphia." Pamphlet of the Nebraska Branch American Re-
    lief Fund for Central Europe. n.p., 1919. Society Publications, Hoover
    Institution, pp. 1–14.
Angell, Norman. *The Great Illusion: A Study of the Relation of Military
    Power in Nations to Their Economic and Social Advantage.* New York,
    Putnam, 1910.
Baldwin, Simeon E. "The International Congresses and Conferences of the
    Last Century as Forces Working Toward the Solidarity of the World,"
    American Journal of International Law, I (1907), 564–78.
Bridgman, Raymond L. *World Organization.* Boston, Ginn, 1905.
Butler, Nicholas Murray. *Across the Busy Years.* 2 vols. New York,
    Scribner, 1939–40.
———. *The American As He Is.* New York, Macmillan, 1908.
———. "Andrew Carnegie—Benefactor,"*International Conciliation,* no.
    315 (Dec. 1935), 533–38.
———. (pseud. "Cosmos"). *The Basis of an Enduring Peace.* New York,
    Scribner, 1917.
———. "The Carnegie Endowment for International Peace," *International
    Conciliation* no. 75 (Feb. 1914), 3–14.
———. "The Education of the Neglected Rich," *Educational Review,*
    XXIV (Nov. 1907), 398–402.
———. "Ely's *Labor Movement in America,*" *Science,* VIII (Oct. 15,
    1886), 353–55.
———. *The Faith of a Liberal.* New York, Scribner, 1924.
———. "Greetings to the New Russia," *Greetings to the New Russia,*
    Carnegie Endowment for International Peace: Division of Intercourse
    and Education, no. 13. Washington, D.C., 1917, pp. 10–14.
———. *The International Mind: An Argument for the Judicial Settlement
    of International Disputes.* New York, Scribner, 1912.
———. "A League of Nations," *International Conciliation,* no. 131 (Oct.
    1918), 52–56.
———. *The Meaning of Education: Contributions to a Philosophy of
    Education.* New York, Scribner, 1915.
———. "Nationality and Beyond" (Aug. 8, 1916), *International Concilia-
    tion,* no. 107 (Oct. 1916), 3–10.
———. *Philosophy.* New York, Columbia Univ. Press, 1911.
———. "Review of Benjamin Kidd's *Social Evolution,*" *Educational Re-
    view,* VII (April 1894), 385–88.
———. *Scholarship and Service: The Policies and Ideals of a National
    University in a Modern Democracy.* New York, Scribner, 1921.

————. *True and False Democracy.* New York, Macmillan, 1907.

————. *Why Should We Change Our Form of Government?* New York, Scribner, 1912.

————. *A World in Ferment: Interpretations of the War for a New World.* New York, Scribner, 1917.

Butler, Nicholas Murray, and Elihu Root. *Problems Confronting the Carnegie Endowment for International Peace.* Pamphlet reprint of minutes of semiannual meeting of the Board of Trustees, Dec. 7, 1920. Washington, D.C., 1920.

Clark, John Bates. "Address," *Lake Mohonk Peace and Arbitration Conference,* II (1896), 36–39.

————. "Address," *Lake Mohonk Peace and Arbitration Conference,* III (1897), 73–77.

————. "Address," *Lake Mohonk Peace and Arbitration Conference,* VII (1901), 45–49.

————. "The After Effects of Free Coinage of Silver," *Political Science Quarterly,* XI (Sept. 1896), 493–501.

————. *The Control of Trusts: An Argument in Favor of Curbing the Power of Monopoly by a Natural Method.* New York, Macmillan, 1901.

————. "Do We Want Compulsory Arbitration?" *Independent,* LIV (Nov. 13, 1902), 2681–82.

————. "An Economic View of War and Arbitration," *International Conciliation,* no. 32 (July 1910), 1–10.

————. "Education and the Socialistic Movement," *Atlantic Monthly,* CII (Oct. 1908), 433–41.

————. *Essentials of Economic Theory as Applied to Modern Problems of Industry and Public Policy.* New York, Macmillan, 1907.

————. "If This League Fails," *New York Times,* June 1, 1919, p. 2.

————. "A Modified Individualism the Outcome of Wealth," *Independent,* LIV (May 1, 1902), 1066–68.

————. "Natural Forces That Make for Peace," *Lake Mohonk Peace and Arbitration Conference,* IV (1898), 91–94.

————. "On What Principles Should a Court of Arbitration Proceed in Determining the Rate of Wages?" *Publications of the American Economic Association,* 3rd ser., VIII (1907), 23–28.

————. "The Part of Organized Labor in the Peace Movement," *Lake Mohonk Peace and Arbitration Conference,* XIV (1908), 59–62.

————. "Peace as Assured by Economics," *Lake Mohonk Peace and Arbitration Conference,* V (1899), 72–78.

————. *The Philosophy of Wealth: Economic Principles Newly Formulated.* Boston, Ginn, 1886.

Clark, John Bates. "Powerful Agencies Working for Peace in the World," *Lake Mohonk Peace and Arbitration Conference,* XI (1905), 54–56.

——. "Recollections of the Twentieth Century," *Atlantic Monthly,* LXXXIX (Jan. 1902), 4–16.

——. "The Referendum in the United States," *Independent,* LIV (Feb. 20, 1902), 429–31.

——. *Social Justice Without Socialism.* Boston, Houghton Mifflin, 1914.

——. "Trusts," *Political Science Quarterly,* XV (June 1900), 181–85.

——. "Trusts, Present and Future," *Independent,* LI (April 20, 1899), 1076–80.

——. "A Workable League," New York *Times,* Nov. 11, 1918, p. 14.

——, and Sir George Paish. "A Proposed Standing Committee of the Powers," *Lake Mohonk Peace and Arbitration Conference,* XX (1914), 118–24.

Constant, Baron d'Estournelles de. "Program of the Association for International Conciliation," *International Conciliation,* no. 1 (1907), 1–4.

Davis, Hayne. *Among the World's Peacemakers: An Epitome of the Interparliamentary Union.* New York, Progressive Publishing Co., 1907.

Dewey, John. "The School and Social Progress" (1899), *American Social Thought.* Ray Ginger, ed. New York, Hill and Wang, 1961, pp. 17–32.

Fiske, John. *A Century of Science and Other Essays.* Boston, Houghton Mifflin, 1899.

Giddings, Franklin Henry. "Absolutist Communism," *Independent,* CIII (July 3, 1920), 13–15.

——. "Americanism in War and Peace," *Publications of the Clark University Library,* V, no. 5 (1917), 16 pp.

——. "Are Contradictions of Ideas and Beliefs Likely to Play an Important Group-Making Role in the Future?" *American Journal of Sociology* (May 1909), 784–98.

——. "The Bolsheviki Must Go," *Independent,* XCVII (Jan. 18, 1919), 88.

——. "The Concepts and Methods of Sociology," *Congress of Arts and Science: Universal Exposition, St. Louis, 1904,* ed. Howard J. Rogers. Boston, 1906, V, 787–99.

——. *Democracy and Empire.* New York, Macmillan, 1900.

——. "The Democracy of Universal Military," *Annals of the American Academy of Political and Social Science,* LXVI (July 1916), 173–80.

——. "The Economic Ages," *Political Science Quarterly,* XVI (June 1901), 193–221.

———. "The Ethics of Socialism," *International Journal of Ethics,* I (Jan. 1891), 239–43.

———. "The Greatness of Herbert Spencer," *Independent,* LV (Dec. 1903), 2959–62.

———. "The Immigration Tangle," *Independent,* CVI (Sept. 24, 1921), 144–45.

———. "Imperialism?" *Political Science Quarterly,* XIII (Dec. 1898), 585–605.

———. "The Intellectual Consequence of the War," May 1919, typescript in Giddings Papers, 22 pp.

———. "A Political Program," *Independent,* LIII (Sept. 27, 1900), 2305–2306.

———. *Principles of Sociology: An Analysis of the Phenomena of Association and Social Organization.* New York, Macmillan, 1896.

———. "The Quality of Civilization," *American Journal of Sociology,* XVII (March 1912), 581–89.

——— (ed.). *Readings in Descriptive and Historical Sociology.* New York, Macmillan, 1906.

———. "The Relation of Social Theory to Public Policy," *International Conciliation,* no. 58 (Sept. 1912), 3–13.

———. *The Responsible State: A Re-examination of Fundamental Political Doctrines in the Light of the War and the Menace of Anarchism.* Boston, Houghton Mifflin, 1918.

———. *Studies in the Theory of Human Society.* New York, Macmillan, 1922.

———. "A Theory of History," *Political Science Quarterly,* XXXV (Dec. 1920), 493–521.

———. "The United States Among Nations," *Independent,* XCVIII (June 14, 1919), 399–400.

———. "What Did It?" *Independent,* CIV (Nov. 20, 1920), 262.

———. "What Is Fair," *Independent,* XCVIII (June 21, 1919), 437.

———. "What the War Was Worth," *Independent,* XCIX (July 5, 1919), 16–17.

———. "Whom the Gods Would Destroy," *Independent,* LXXIX (Aug. 10, 1914), 195–96.

Holt, Hamilton. "An American Peace Commission," *Independent,* LXVIII (June 20, 1910), 1455–56.

———. "The Armament Octopus," *Independent,* LXXVIII (April 13, 1914), 80.

———. "Armament Scandals," *Independent,* LXXIV (May 1, 1913), 946.

———. "Article X—The Soul of the Covenant," *Independent,* C (July 5, 1919), 15–16.

Holt, Hamilton. "A Backward Glance and a Look Ahead," *Independent,*
LXXIV (Oct. 2, 1913), 5–6.
———. "A Basis for a League of Peace," *Independent,* LXXIX (July 20,
1914), 83–84.
———. "The Best Use for a Big Navy," *Independent,* LXXXVII (Sept.
4, 1916), 325–26.
———. "The Birth of the League of Nations," *Independent,* XCVII (Feb.
15, 1919), 217.
———. "The Bugaboo of Individualism," *Independent,* LVI (March 31,
1904), 743.
———. "Call the Third Hague Conference Without Delay," *Independent,*
LXXXVI (Dec. 4, 1913), 429–31.
———. "Can We Let Them Go?" *Independent,* L (July 21, 1898), 266.
———. "Concerted Peace," Central Organization for a Durable Peace.
Recueil de Rapports sur les Différents Points du Programme Minimum.
The Hague, 1916, II, 14–26.
———. "A Conference of the Neutral Nations," *Independent,* LXXXI
(March 29, 1915), 443–44.
———. "Cooperation or Intervention," *Independent,* LXXXVII (Nov.
27, 1916), 339–40.
———. "A Declaration of Interdependence," *Independent,* LXXXII
(June 14, 1915), 447–48.
———. "Democracy in America," *Independent,* LIV (Sept. 18, 1902),
2260–62.
———. "England's Proposal to Germany for a Naval Holiday," *Independent,* LXXVI (Oct. 30, 1913), 190–91.
———. "The Federation of the World," *Independent,* LXVIII (Feb. 24,
1910), 429–30.
———. "For a Conference of Neutral Nations," *Independent,* LXXXVII
(July 31, 1916), 143–44.
———. "For a Holy War," *Independent,* XCII (Dec. 15, 1917), 497–98.
———. "For the Greater Security of France," *Independent,* IC (July 19,
1919), 83–84.
———. "The Futility of Reservations," *Independent,* IC (Aug. 30, 1919),
237.
———. "Hawaii American Territory," *Independent,* L (July 7, 1898),
127.
———. "The High Duty of the United States," *Independent,* LXXIX
(Aug. 10, 1914), 195.
———. "How Shall We Keep Peace With Japan?" *Free Synagogue
Pulpit,* III (June 1915), 97–104.
———. "International Amity," *Independent,* LIV (Nov. 12, 1908), 1137.

————. "The Interparliamentary Union," *Independent,* LVIII (May 4, 1905), 1025–26.

————. "Labor Disputes," *Independent,* LII (Feb. 28, 1901), 517.

————. "The League or Bolshevism?" *Independent,* XCVIII (April 5, 1919), 3–4

————. "A League to Enforce Peace," *Independent,* LXXXII (June 28, 1915), 423–24.

————. "The Mediation Deadlock and the Way Out," *Independent,* LXXVIII (June 29, 1914), 543–44.

————. "The Monroe and Ishii Doctrine," *Independent,* XCII (Nov. 17, 1917), 309.

————. "Monroe and Wilson," *Independent,* LXXXV (Jan. 17, 1916), 73.

————. "No Divided Counsels at Washington," *Independent,* XCV (Aug. 17, 1918), 210–11.

————. "No Reservation," *Independent,* IC (Aug. 9, 1919), 183–84.

————. "An Open Letter to the President," *Independent,* CV (Jan. 25, 1921), 663.

————. "An Open Letter to 'The Thirty-One,' " *Independent,* CVI (Aug. 6, 1921), 47.

————. "Our Conditions to Spain," *Independent,* L (Aug. 15, 1898), 196–97.

————. "Peace Without Vengeance," *Independent,* LXXIX (Sept. 21, 1914), 396.

————. "A Practical Referendum," *Independent,* LVII (Dec. 1, 1904), 1277–78.

————. "Preparedness," *Independent,* LXXXIII (Sept. 6, 1915), 379–80.

————. "The President's Program of Preparedness," *Independent,* LXXXV (Feb. 14, 1916), 216–17.

————. "Pure Democracy," *Independent,* XCII (Oct. 27, 1917), 169–70.

————. "The Referendum," *Independent,* LIV (Nov. 20, 1902), 2789–90.

————. "A Remedy for Corruption," *Cosmopolitan Magazine,* XLIX (Sept. 1910), 301–16.

————. "The Republican Contribution to the Covenant," *Independent,* XCVIII (May 24, 1919), 275.

————. "The Representative with a Million Constituents," *Independent,* LXXX (Nov. 23, 1914), 281.

————. "Results," *Independent,* XCI (July 14, 1917), 45.

————. "Mr. Roosevelt at Christiania," *Independent,* LXVIII (Feb. 17, 1910), 376–77.

————. "The Senate Outlook for Ratification," *Independent,* IC (Aug. 2, 1919), 151–52.

Holt, Hamilton. "Socialism and Socialism," *Independent*, LVIII (Dec. 8, 1904), 1337–38.

———. "The Socialists," *Independent*, LVII (Nov. 17, 1904), 1165–66.

———. "The Solution of Industrial Peace," *Independent*, LXXIV (Feb. 6, 1913), 273–75.

———. "The Taft and Lodge Reservations," *Independent*, CI (Feb. 14, 1920), 244.

———. "A Task for the Thirty-five Neutrals," *Independent*, LXXXII (May 24, 1915), 308–309.

———. "Three Roads and One," *Independent*, LXXXIV (Nov. 22, 1915), 292–93.

———. "The Time Has Come," *Independent*, LXXXVI (May 22, 1916), 264–65.

———. "The United States Peace Commission," *North Atlantic Review*, CXCII (Sept. 1910), 201–16.

———. "Mr. Van Dyke and the Philippines," *Independent*, L (Aug. 15, 1898), 920.

———. "Wanted: A Final Solution of the Japanese Problem," *Independent*, LXXVI (Nov. 6, 1913), 236–37.

———. "The Way to Disarm: A Practical Proposal," *Independent*, LXXIX (Sept. 28, 1914), 427–29.

———. "Well Done, St. Louis!" *Independent*, LXXXV (March 27, 1916), 437–38.

———. "What Is This Treaty of Peace?" *Independent*, IC (July 12, 1919), 49–50.

———. "Which Is the Party of Progress?" *Independent*, LXXVIII (Oct. 9, 1916), 52.

———. "The Woman's Peace Congress," *Independent*, LXXXII (May 10, 1915), 228.

———. "Woodrow Wilson," *Independent*, XCVIII (Jan. 19, 1918), 89.

———. "Work for a Nobel Prize Winner," *Independent*, LXVIII (Feb. 24, 1910), 429–30.

———, and Hayne Davis. "A Constitution of the World," *Independent*, LXII (April 11, 1907), 826.

Hoover, Herbert. *The Ordeal of Woodrow Wilson*. New York, McGraw-Hill, 1958.

James, William. "The Moral Equivalent of War," 1910, in *Essays on Faith and Morals*, ed. Ralph Barton Perry. Cleveland, Meridian Books, 1962, pp. 311–28.

Kant, Immanuel. *Perpetual Peace*, trans. and ed. Lewis White Beck. Indianapolis, Bobbs-Merrill, 1957.

Lowell, Abbott Lawrence. "America's War and America's Opportunity," *A*

League of Nations. World Peace Foundation Bound Pamphlets. Boston, 1918, I, 5–8.

————. "An Appeal to Public Opinion," League to Enforce Peace Pamphlet No. 25, n.p., n.d., Society Publications, Hoover Institution.

————. *Conflicts of Principle.* Cambridge, Harvard Univ. Press, 1932.

————. "The Colonial Expansion of the United States," *Atlantic Monthly,* LXXXIII (Feb. 1899), 145–54.

————. *Essays on Government.* Boston, Houghton Mifflin, 1889.

————. *Governments and Parties in Continental Europe.* 2 vols. Boston, Houghton Mifflin, 1896.

————. "The International Policeman," *Independent,* LXXXII (June 14, 1915), 460–61.

————. "A League to Enforce Peace," League to Enforce Peace Pamphlet, Boston, 1915. Society Publications, Hoover Institution.

————. "Oscillations in Politics," *Annals of the American Academy of Political and Social Science,* XII (July 1898), 69–97.

————. *Public Opinion and Popular Government.* New York, Longmans, 1913.

————. *Public Opinion in War and Peace.* Cambridge, Harvard Univ. Press, 1923.

————. "The Status of Our New Possessions," *Harvard Law Review,* XIII (Nov. 1899), 153–59.

————, *et al.* "The Covenanter: Letters on the Covenant of the League of Nations," *A League of Nations.* World Peace Foundation Bound Pamphlets. Boston, 1919, II, 99–166.

————, and Henry Cabot Lodge. "Joint Debate on the Covenant of Paris," March 19, 1919, *A League of Nations.* World Peace Foundation Bound Pamphlets. Boston, 1919, II, 49–97.

Marburg, Theodore. "Admissions and Restriction upon Admissions of Aliens," *American Society of International Law: Proceedings of Fifth Annual Meeting.* Washington, D.C., 1911, pp. 88–95.

————. "Amendment of the Sheman Anti-Trust Law," *Annals of the American Academy of Political and Social Science,* XXXII (July 1908), 34–42.

————. "Apostles of World Unity, VI—Hamilton Holt," *World Unity,* I (March 1928), 411–15.

————. "The Backward Nation," *Independent* (June 20, 1912), 1365–70.

————. *Development of the League of Nations Idea: Documents and Correspondence of Theodore Marburg.* ed. John H. Latané. 2 vols. New York, Macmillan, 1932.

————. *Expansionism.* Baltimore, J. Murphy, 1900.

————. "Follow the Flag," *Independent,* XC (April 21, 1917), 162.

Marburg, Theodore. "Labor and Capital for Democracy," *Independent,* XC (July 9, 1917), 464.

———. *The League of Nations.* 2 vols. New York, Macmillan, 1917–19.

———. "The League to Enforce Peace—A Reply to Critics," *Annals of the American Academy of Political and Social Science,* LXVI (July 1916), 50–59.

———. "A Modified Monroe Doctrine," *South Atlantic Quarterly,* X (July 1, 1911), 227–31.

———. "The Obligation to Keep the Peace," *Independent,* LXXXIII (June 14, 1915), 461–62.

———. *Political Papers.* 2 vols. Baltimore, J. Murphy, 1898.

———. "Remarks," *Proceedings of the American Society for the Judicial Settlement of International Disputes.* Washington, D.C., Dec. 1910, pp. 73–76.

———. "Remarks of the Presiding Officer," *Proceedings of the American Society for the Judicial Settlement of International Disputes.* Cincinnati, Nov. 1911, pp. 81–88.

———. "Sovereignty and Race as Affected by a League of Nations," *Annals of the American Academy of Political and Social Science,* LXII (July 1917), 142–46.

———. "The World Court and the League of Peace," *Annals of the American Academy of Political and Social Science,* LXI (Sept. 1915), 276–83.

Mead, George. "The Psychological Bases of Internationalism," *Survey,* XXXIII (March 6, 1915), 604–13.

Moore, Marianne. *Nevertheless.* New York, Macmillan, 1944.

Reinsch, Paul S. *Public International Unions: Their Work and Organization. A Study in International Administrative Law.* Boston, Ginn, 1911.

Root, Elihu. *Addresses on International Subjects,* eds. Robert Bacon and James Brown Scott. Cambridge, Harvard Univ. Press, 1916.

———. "American Ideals During the Past Half-Century," *International Conciliation,* no. 210 (May 1925), 3–10.

———. *The Citizen's Part in Government.* New York, Scribner, 1907.

———. "The Codification of International Law," *American Journal of International Law,* XIX (Oct. 1925), 675–84.

———. *Experiments in Government and Essentials of the Constitution.* Princeton, Princeton Univ. Press, 1913.

———. "International Law at the Arms Conference," *American Society of International Law: Proceedings of the Sixteenth Annual Meeting.* Washington, D.C., April 27, 1922, pp. 1–10.

———. "International Law and the Peace Settlement," Minutes of the

Meeting of the Executive Council, American Society of International Law, April 17, 1919, *Proceedings* (1919), 45–64.

――――. "Japan and the United States," *International Conciliation,* no. 124 (March 1918), 13–19.

――――. *Latin America and the United States.* eds. Robert Bacon and James Brown Scott. Cambridge, Harvard Univ. Press, 1917.

――――. *Men and Policies,* eds. Robert Bacon and James Brown Scott. Cambridge, Harvard Univ. Press, 1924.

――――. *Miscellaneous Addresses,* eds. Robert Bacon and James Brown Scott. Cambridge, Harvard Univ. Press, 1917.

――――. *The Military and Colonial Policy of the United States,* eds. Robert Bacon and James Brown Scott. Cambridge, Harvard Univ. Press, 1916.

――――. *North Atlantic Fisheries Arbitration at the Hague: Argument on Behalf of the United States by Elihu Root,* eds. Robert Bacon and James Brown Scott. Cambridge, Harvard Univ. Press, 1917.

――――. "Opening Address," American Society of International Law; *Proceedings of Fifteenth Annual Meeting.* Washington, D.C., April 27, 1921, pp. 1–13.

――――. "The Permanent Court of International Justice," Minutes of the Meeting of the Executive Council, American Society of International Law, Nov. 13, 1920, *Proceedings* (1920), pp. 26–35.

――――. "The Permanent Court of International Justice," American Society of International Law; *Proceedings of the Seventeenth Annual Meeting.* Washington, D.C., April 26, 1923, pp. 1–14.

――――. "Remarks to the Executive Council of the American Society of International Law," April 27, 1918, American Society of International Law; *Proceedings* (1919), pp. 12–21.

――――. "The Spirit of Self-Government," *International Conciliation,* no. 62 (Jan. 1913), 3–14.

Royce, Josiah. *California from the Conquest in 1846 to the Second Vigilance Committee in San Francisco: A Study of American Character.* Boston, Houghton Mifflin, 1886.

――――. "Comment on Mary Whiton Calkins' article 'Royce's Philosophy and Christian Theism,'" *Philosophical Review,* XXV (1916), 295–96.

――――. "The Eternal and the Practical," *Philosophical Review,* XIII (1904), 113–42.

――――. *Fugitive Essays,* ed. Jacob Loewenberg. Cambridge, Harvard Univ. Press, 1920.

――――. *The Hope of the Great Community.* New York, Macmillan, 1916.

Royce, Josiah. "The Mechanical, the Historical, and the Statistical," *Science,* N.S. XXXIX (1914), 551–66.

———. *Outlines of Psychology.* New York, Macmillan, 1903.

———. *The Philosophy of Loyalty.* New York, Macmillan, 1908.

———. *The Problem of Christianity.* 2 vols. New York, Macmillan, 1913.

———. "Professor Royce on His Reviewer," *New Republic,* I (Dec. 26, 1914), 23.

———. "Provincialism Based upon a Study of Early Conditions in California," *Putnam's Magazine,* VII (1909), 232–40.

———. *Race Questions, Provincialism, and Other American Problems.* New York, Macmillan, 1908.

———. "Relations between Philosophy and Science in the First Half of the Nineteenth Century," *Science,* N.S. XXXVIII (1913), 242–54.

———. *The Religious Aspect of Philosophy.* Boston, Houghton Mifflin, 1913.

———. *The Social Philosophy of Josiah Royce,* ed. Stuart Gerry Brown. Syracuse, Syracuse Univ. Press. 1950.

———. *The Spirit of Modern Philosophy.* Boston, Houghton Mifflin, 1899.

———. *Studies of Good and Evil.* New York, Appleton, 1898.

———. *War and Insurance.* New York, Macmillan, 1914.

———. *William James and Other Essays in the Philosophy of Life.* New York, Macmillan, 1911.

———. "Words of Professor Royce at the Walton Hotel," *Papers in Honor of Josiah Royce on his Sixtieth Birthday.* New York, Longmans, 1916, pp. 279–83.

———. *The World and the Individual.* 2 vols. New York, Macmillan, 1900–1902.

Royce, Sarah. *A Frontier Lady: Recollections of the Gold Rush and Early California,* ed. Ralph Henry Gabriel. New Haven, Yale Univ. Press, 1933.

Straus, Oscar S. *Under Four Administrations from Cleveland to Taft.* Boston, Houghton Mifflin, 1922.

Sumner, William Graham. *The Conquest of the United States by Spain and Other Essays,* ed. Murray Polner. Chicago, Regnery, 1965.

Tocqueville, Alexis de. *Democracy in America.* Henry Reeve Text, ed. Phillips Bradley. 2 vols. New York, Vintage Books, 1954.

Tönnies, Ferdinand. *Community and Society (Gemeinschaft und Gesellschaft)* trans. and ed. Charles P. Loomis. New York, Harper Torchbooks, 1965.

Trueblood, Benjamin. *The Federation of the World.* 3rd ed., Boston, Houghton Mifflin, 1899.

Veblen, Thorstein. *Absentee Ownership and Business Enterprise in Recent Times: The Case of America.* New York, B. W. Huebsch, 1923.

————. *The Engineers and the Price System.* New York, Viking Press, 1921.

————. *Essays in Our Changing Order,* ed. Leon Ardzrooni. New York, Viking Press, 1934.

————. *Imperial Germany and the Industrial Revolution.* Ann Arbor, Univ. of Michigan Press, 1966.

————. *An Inquiry into the Nature of Peace and the Terms of Its Perpetuation.* New York, B. W. Huebsch, 1917.

————. *The Instinct of Workmanship and the State of the Industrial Arts.* New York, Macmillan, 1914.

————. *The Place of Science and Other Essays,* comps. Leon Ardzrooni, Wesley C. Mitchell and Walter W. Stewart. New York, B. W. Huebsch, 1919.

————. "Review of J. A. Hobson's *Imperialism: A Study,*" *Journal of Political Economy,* VII (1903), 311–19.

————. *The Theory of Business Enterprise.* New York, Scribner, 1904.

————. *The Theory of the Leisure Class.* New York, Random House, 1934.

————. *The Vested Interests and the Common Man.* New York, B. W. Huebsch, 1920.

————. *What Veblen Taught,* ed. Wesley C. Mitchell. New York, Viking Press, 1936.

Wales, Julia Grace. *Continuous Mediation Without Armistice.* Chicago, Woman's Peace Party, 1915, Society Publications, Hoover Institution.

Wells, David A. *Recent Economic Changes and Their Effect on the Production and Distribution of Wealth and the Well-Being of Society.* New York, Appleton, 1893.

Wilson, Woodrow. *A Crossroads of Freedom: The 1912 Campaign Speeches of Woodrow Wilson,* ed. John Wells Davidson. New Haven, Yale Univ. Press, 1956.

————. *A History of the American People.* Vol. V: *Reunion and Nationalization.* New York, Harper, 1902.

————. *Leaders of Men,* ed. T. H. Vail Motter. Princeton, Princeton Univ. Press, 1952.

————. *An Old Master and Other Political Essays.* New York, Scribner, 1893.

————. *On Being Human.* New York, Harper, 1916.

————. *The Papers of Woodrow Wilson,* ed. Arthur S. Link. 3 vols. Princeton, Princeton Univ. Press, 1966–67.

Wilson, Woodrow. *The Political Thought of Woodrow Wilson,* ed. E. David Cronon. Indianapolis, Bobbs-Merrill, 1965.

———. *The Public Papers of Woodrow Wilson,* eds. Ray Stannard Baker and William E. Dodd. 6 vols. New York, Harper, 1925–27.

———. "The Road away from Revolution," *Atlantic Monthly,* CXXXIII (Aug. 1923), 145–46.

———. *The State: Elements of Historical and Practical Politics.* Boston, Heath, 1889.

SECONDARY MATERIALS

Aaron, Daniel. *Men of Good Hope: A Story of American Progressives.* New York, Oxford Univ. Press, 1961.

Abrams, Irwin. "The Emergence of the International Law Societies," *Review of Politics,* XIX (July 1957), 361–80.

Adler, Selig. "Bryan and Wilsonian Caribbean Penetration," *Hispanic American Historical Review,* XX (May 1940), 198–226.

Ashworth, William. *A Short History of the International Economy.* 2nd ed., London, Longmans, 1960.

Atkinson, Henry A. *Theodore Marburg: The Man and His Work.* New York, Morton Littman Printing Co., 1951.

Bailey, Thomas A. *Theodore Roosevelt and the Japanese American Crisis.* Stanford, Stanford Univ. Press, 1934.

———. *Woodrow Wilson and the Lost Peace.* Chicago, Quadrangle Paperbacks, 1963.

Baker, Ray Stannard. *Woodrow Wilson: Life and Letters.* 8 vols. Garden City, N.Y., Doubleday, 1927–39.

———. *Woodrow Wilson and the World Settlement.* 3 vols. Garden City, N.Y., Doubleday, 1923.

Baldwin, Roger Nash. "The Reminiscences of Roger Nash Baldwin II," Oral History Collection, Columbia University. New York, 1954.

Barrett, Clifford (ed.). *Contemporary Idealism in America.* New York, Macmillan, 1932.

Bartlett, Ruhl. *The League to Enforce Peace.* Chapel Hill, Univ. of North Carolina Press, 1944.

Beale, Howard K. *Theodore Roosevelt and the Rise of America to World Power.* Baltimore, Johns Hopkins Press, 1956.

Becker, Carl. *How New Will the Better World Be?* New York, Knopf, 1944.

Beloff, Max. "Self-Determination Reconsidered," *Confluence,* V, Pt. 1 (Autumn 1956), 195–203.

Benson, Lee. *Turner and Beard: American Historical Writing Reconsidered.* Glencoe, Ill., Free Press, 1960.

Berthoff, Rowland. "The American Social Order: A Conservative Hypothesis," *American Historical Review,* LXV (April 1960), 495–514.

Birdsall, Paul. *Versailles Twenty Years After.* New York, Reynal & Hitchcock, 1941.

Blakewell, C. M. "Royce as an Interpreter of American Ideals," *International Journal of Ethics,* XXVII (April 1917), 306–16.

Blau, Joseph L. "Royce's Theory of Community," *Journal of Philosophy,* LIII (1956), 92–98.

Bogardus, Emory S. *A History of Social Thought.* 2nd ed. Los Angeles, Miller, 1928.

Boas, Franz. *Anthropology and Modern Life.* New York, Norton, 1928.

Boring, Edwin G. *A History of Experimental Psychology.* New York, Appleton, 1950.

Bragdon, Henry Wilkinson. *Woodrow Wilson: The Academic Years.* Cambridge, Harvard Univ. Press, 1967.

––––––. "Woodrow Wilson and Lawrence Lowell—An Original Study of Two Different Men," *Harvard Alumni Bulletin,* XLV (May 22, 1943), 595–97.

Brierly, J. L. *The Law of Nations: An Introduction to the International Law of Peace.* 6th ed., New York, Oxford Univ. Press, 1963.

Brownell, Baker. *The Human Community: Its Philosophy and Practice for a Time of Crisis.* New York, Harper, 1950.

Buehrig, Edward H. *Woodrow Wilson and the Balance of Power.* Bloomington, Indiana Univ. Press, 1955.

–––––– (ed.). *Wilson's Foreign Policy in Perspective.* Bloomington, Indiana Univ. Press, 1957.

Buranelli, Vincent. *Josiah Royce.* New York, Twayne, 1964.

Bury, J. B. *The Idea of Progress: An Inquiry into its Origin and Growth,* with an introduction by Charles A. Beard, New York, Macmillan, 1932.

Campbell, Charles S., Jr. *Anglo-American Understanding 1898–1903.* Baltimore, Johns Hopkins Press, 1957.

Carr, Edward Hallett. *Nationalism and After.* London, Macmillan, 1945.

Chambers, Clarke A. "The Belief in Progress in the Twentieth Century," *Journal of the History of Ideas,* XIX (April 1958), 197–224.

Clough, Shepard Bancroft, and Charles Woolsey Cole. *Economic History of Europe.* Boston, Heath, 1941.

Cohen, Felix S. *The Legal Conscience: Selected Papers of Felix S. Cohen.* New Haven, Yale Univ. Press, 1960.

Cohen, Morris R. "Josiah Royce," *New Republic,* VIII (Oct. 14, 1916), 264–66.

Commager, Henry Steele. *The American Mind: An Interpretation of American Thought and Character Since the 1880's.* New Haven, Yale Univ. Press, 1959.

Cotton, J. Harry. "Royce's Case for Idealism," *Journal of Philosophy,* LII (1956), 112–23.

Curry, George. "Woodrow Wilson, Jan Smuts and the Versailles Settlement," *American Historical Review,* LXVI (July 1961), 968–86.

Curti, Merle. *Peace or War: The American Struggle 1636–1936.* Boston, Norton, 1936.

———. *The Roots of American Loyalty.* New York, Columbia Univ. Press, 1946.

———. "Human Nature in American Thought—The Retreat from Reason in an Age of Science," *Political Science Quarterly,* LXVIII (Dec. 1953), 492–510.

———. "Woodrow Wilson's Concept of Human Nature," *Midwest Journal of Political Science,* I (May 1957), 1–19.

———. "Jane Addams on Human Nature," *Journal of the History of Ideas,* XXII (Oct. 1961), 240–53.

Davis, Allen F. "The Social Workers and the Progressive Party, 1912–1916," *American Historical Review,* LXIX (April 1964), 671–88.

Davis, Arthur K. "Veblen's Study of Modern Germany," *American Sociological Review,* IX (1944), 603–09.

Davis, Calvin de Armond. *The United States and the First Hague Peace Conference.* Ithaca, Cornell Univ. Press, 1962.

De Conde, Alexander (ed.). *Isolation and Security.* Durham, Duke Univ. Press, 1957.

Degen, Marie Louise. *The History of the Woman's Peace Party.* Baltimore, Johns Hopkins Press, 1939.

Diamond, William. *The Economic Thought of Woodrow Wilson.* Baltimore, Johns Hopkins Press, 1943.

Dorfman, Joseph. *The Economic Mind in American Civilization.* Vol. III, *1865–1918.* New York, Viking Press, 1949.

———. "The 'Satire' of Thorstein Veblen's *Theory of the Leisure Class,*" *Political Science Quarterly,* XLVII (1932), 363–409.

———. *Thorstein Veblen and His America.* New York, Viking Press, 1934.

Dowd, Douglas F. (ed.). *Thorstein Veblen: A Critical Reappraisal.* Ithaca, Cornell Univ. Press, 1958.

Duffus, Robert L. *The Innocents at Credo: A Memoir of Thorstein Veblen and Some Others.* New York, Macmillan, 1944.

Dudden, Arthur P. (ed.). *Woodrow Wilson and the World of Today.* Philadelphia, Univ. of Pennsylvania Press, 1957.

"Editorial Comment," *American Journal of International Law,* I (Jan. 1907), 129–30.

Elson, A. "First Principles of Jane Addams," *Social Service Review,* XXVIII (March 1954), 3–11.

Everett, John Rutherford. *Religion in Economics: A Study of John Bates Clark, Richard T. Ely, Simon N. Patten.* New York, King's Crown Press, 1946.

Farrell, John C. *Beloved Lady: A History of Jane Addams' Ideas on Reform and Peace.* Baltimore, Johns Hopkins Press, 1967.

Fenwick, Charles G. *International Law.* 3rd ed., New York, Appleton, 1948.

Finch, George A. "The American Society of International Law, 1906–1956," *American Journal of International Law,* L (April 1956), 293–312.

Fine, Sidney. *Laissez-faire and the General Welfare State: A Study of Conflict in American Thought 1865–1901.* Ann Arbor, Univ. of Michigan Press, 1956–7.

Fleming, Denna Frank. *The United States and the World Court.* Garden City, N.Y., Doubleday, 1945.

Fleming, Donald. "Social Darwinism," *Paths of American Thought,* eds. Arthur M. Schlesinger, Jr., and Morton G. White. Boston, Houghton Mifflin, 1963. pp. 123–46.

Fried, Alfred H. *Annuaire de la Vie Internationale,* Monaco, Institut International de la Paix, 1907, Vol. III.

Gabriel, Ralph Henry. *The Course of American Democratic Thought.* New York, Ronald Press, 1956.

Galtung, Johan. "Foreign Policy as a Function of Social Position," *Journal of Peace Research,* I, no. 4 (1964), 206–13.

Gardiner, Lloyd C. "American Foreign Policy 1900–1921: A Second Look at the Realist Critique of American Diplomacy," *Towards A New Past: Dissenting Essays in American History.* ed. Barton J. Bernstein. New York, Pantheon, 1968.

Gelfand, Lawrence E. *The Inquiry: American Preparations for Peace, 1917–1919.* New Haven, Yale Univ. Press, 1963.

Gillin, John L. "Franklin Henry Giddings," *American Masters of Social Science.* ed. Howard W. Odum. New York, Holt, 1927, pp. 191–228.

Ginger, Ray. *Altgeld's America: The Lincoln Ideal versus Changing Realities.* Chicago, Quadrangle Paperbacks, 1965.

Goldberg, Harvey (ed.). *American Radicals: Some Problems and Personalities.* New York, Monthly Review Press, 1957.

Goldman, Eric. *Rendezvous with Destiny: A History of Modern American Reform.* New York, Vintage Books, 1959.

Good, R. C. "National Interest and Political Realism: Niebuhr's 'Debate' with Morgenthau and Kennan," *Journal of Politics,* XXII (Nov. 1960), 597–619.

Handlin, Oscar. *The Uprooted: The Epic Story of the Great Migrations That Made the American People.* New York, University Library, n.d.

Hankins, F. H. "Franklin Henry Giddings, 1855–1931: Some Aspects of His Sociological Theory," *American Journal of Sociology,* XXVII (Nov. 1931), 349–67.

Harris, Abram L. "Economic Evolution: Dialectical and Darwinian," *Journal of Political Economy,* XLII (1934), 34–79.

Hayes, Carleton J. H. "Impressions of Nicholas Murray Butler," Oral History Collection, Columbia University. New York, 1960.

Hemleben, Sylvester John. *Plans for World Peace Through Six Centuries.* Chicago, Univ. of Chicago Press, 1943.

Higham, John. "The Reorientation of American Culture in the 1890's," *Origins of Modern Consciousness,* ed. John Weiss. Detroit, Wayne State Univ. Press, 1965, pp. 25–48.

Hinsley, F. H. *Power and the Pursuit of Peace: Theory and Practice in the History of Relations Between States.* Cambridge [Eng.], Univ. Press, 1963.

Hocking, Richard. "The Influence of Mathematics on Royce's Metaphysics," *Journal of Philosophy,* LIII (1956), 77–91.

Hofstadter, Richard. *The American Political Tradition and the Men Who Made It.* New York, Vintage Books, 1954.

———. *Social Darwinism in American Thought.* Boston, Beacon Press, 1955.

Holcolme, Arthur N. "Edwin Ginn's Vision of World Peace," *International Organization,* XIX (1965), 1–19.

Hollander, Jacob H. (ed.). *Economic Essays Contributed in Honor of John Bates Clark.* New York, Macmillan, 1927.

Homan, Paul T. *Contemporary Economic Thought.* New York, Harper, 1928.

Jessup, Philip. *Elihu Root.* 2 vols. New York, Dodd Mead, 1938.

"Josiah Royce," *Science* N. S., XLIV (Dec. 1, 1916), 772–74.

Kallen, Horace M. "Remarks on Royce's Philosophy," *Journal of Philosophy,* LIII (1956), 131–39.

Kaplan, Sidney. "Social Engineers as Saviors: Effects of World War I on Some American Liberals," *Journal of the History of Ideas,* XVII (June 1956), 347–69.

Kelley, Nicholas. "Early Days at Hull House," *Social Service Review,* XXVIII (Dec. 1954), 424–29.

Kennan, George F. *American Diplomacy 1900–1950.* New York, Mentor, 1964.

———. *Russia Leaves the War: Soviet-American Relations.* Princeton, Princeton Univ. Press, 1956.

Kohn, Hans. *The Idea of Nationalism: A Study in Its Origin and Background.* New York, Macmillan, 1944.

Kuehl, Warren. *Hamilton Holt, Journalist, Internationalist, Educator.* Gainesville, Univ. of Florida Press, 1960.

Lange, Christian L., and August Schou. *Histoire de l'Internationalisme.* 3 vols. Oslo, Publications of the Nobel Institute, H. Aschehoug, 1919–63.

Lasch, Christopher. *The New Radicalism in America, 1889–1963: The Intellectual as a Social Type.* New York, Knopf, 1965.

Leopold, Richard W. *Elihu Root and the Conservative Tradition.* Boston, Little Brown, 1954.

Leuchtenberg, William E. "Progressivism and Imperialism: The Progressive Movement and American Foreign Policy, 1896–1916," *Mississippi Valley Historical Review* (Dec. 1952), 483–504.

Levin, N. Gordon, Jr. *Woodrow Wilson and World Politics.* New York, Oxford Univ. Press, 1968.

Levine, Daniel. "Jane Addams: Romantic Radical, 1889–1912," *Mid-America,* XLIV (Oct. 1962), 195–210.

———. *Varieties of Reform Thought.* Madison, State Historical Society of Wisconsin, 1964.

Lewis, Cleona. *America's Stake in International Investments.* Washington, D.C., Brookings Institution, 1938.

Lindeman, E. C. "Community," *Encyclopedia of Social Science.* New York, Macmillan, 1937, III, 102–105.

Link, Arthur S. "A Portrait of Wilson," *Virginia Quarterly Review,* XXXII (Fall 1956), 524–40.

———. *Wilson: Campaigns for Progressivism and Peace, 1916–1917.* Princeton, Princeton Univ. Press, 1965.

———. *Wilson: Confusions and Crises, 1915–1916.* Princeton, Princeton Univ. Press, 1964.

Link, Arthur S. *Wilson the Diplomatist.* Chicago, Quadrangle Paperbacks, 1965.

———. *Wilson: The New Freedom.* Princeton, Princeton Univ. Press, 1956.

———. *Woodrow Wilson and the Progressive Era 1910–1917.* New York, Harper, 1954.

———. *Wilson: The Road to the White House.* Princeton, Princeton Univ. Press, 1947.

———. *Wilson: The Struggle for Neutrality, 1914–1915.* Princeton, Princeton Univ. Press, 1960.

Linn, James Weber. *Jane Addams: A Biography.* New York, Appleton, 1935.

Loewenberg, Jacob. *Royce's Synoptic Vision.* Baltimore, Johns Hopkins Press, 1955.

Lovett, Robert Morss. "Jane Addams and the Woman's International

League for Peace and Freedom," Address at Hull House, Oct. 26, 1946; reprinted as a pamphlet by the Woman's International League for Peace and Freedom. Chicago, 1946.

———. *All Our Years: Autobiography of Robert Morss Lovett.* New York, Viking Press, 1948.

Mann, Arthur. "British Social Thought and American Reformers of the Progressive Era," *Mississippi Valley Historical Review,* XLII (March 1956), 672–92.

Marriot, Sir John A. R. *Commonwealth or Anarchy: A Survey of Projects of Peace from the Sixteenth to the Twentieth Century.* London, Allan, 1937.

May, Ernest R. *The World War and American Isolation 1914–1917.* Chicago, Quadrangle Paperbacks, 1966.

May, Henry F. *Protestant Churches and Industrial America.* New York, Harper, 1949.

Mayer, Arno J. "Historical Thought and American Foreign Policy in the Era of the First World War," *The Historian and the Diplomat,* ed. Francis L. Loewenheim, New York, Harper, 1967, pp. 73–90.

———. *Politics and Diplomacy of Peacemaking, 1918–1919.* New York, Knopf, 1967.

———. *Wilson vs Lenin: Political Origins of the New Diplomacy.* Cleveland, Meridian Books, 1964.

McCloskey, Robert Green. *American Conservatism in the Age of Enterprise 1865–1910.* New York, Harper, 1964.

McCreary, J. K. "Religious Philosophy of Josiah Royce," *Journal of Religion,* XXX (1950), 117–31.

Mead, George. "Review of the *Nature of Peace,*" *Journal of Political Economy,* XXVI (1918), 752.

———. "The Philosophies of Royce, James, and Dewey in Their American Setting," *John Dewey: The Man and His Philosophy. Addresses Delivered in New York in Celebration of His Seventieth Birthday.* Cambridge, Mass., 1930, pp. 75–105.

Miller, David Hunter. *The Drafting of the Covenant.* 2 vols. New York, Putnam, 1928.

Morgenthau, Hans J. *Politics among Nations: The Struggle for Power and Peace.* 3rd ed. New York, Knopf, 1962.

———. *Scientific Man v. Power Politics.* Chicago, Univ. of Chicago Press, 1946.

Mowry, George. *The Era of Theodore Roosevelt 1900–1912.* New York, Harper, 1958.

Niebuhr, Reinhold. *Moral Man and Immoral Society: A Study in Ethics and Politics.* New York, Scribner, 1932.

————. *The Structure of Nations and Empires.* New York, Scribner, 1959.

Nobel, David W. "Religion of Progress in America, 1880–1914," *Social Research,* XXII (Winter 1955), 417–40.

————. "Veblen and Progress: The American Climate of Opinion," *Ethics,* LXV (July 1955), 271–86.

Northcott, Clarence H. "The Sociological Theories of Franklin Henry Giddings," *American Journal of Sociology,* XXIV (July 1918), 1–23.

Notter, Harley. *The Origins of the Foreign Policy of Woodrow Wilson.* Baltimore, Johns Hopkins Press, 1937.

Ogburn, William Fielding (ed.). *Technology and International Relations.* Chicago, Univ. of Chicago Press, 1949.

Olson, William Clinton. "Theodore Roosevelt's Conception of an International League," *World Affairs Quarterly,* XXIX (1958–59), 329–53.

Osgood, Robert E. *Ideals and Self-Interest in America's Foreign Relations: The Great Transformation of the Twentieth Century.* Chicago, Univ. of Chicago Press, 1964.

————. "Woodrow Wilson, Collective Security, and the Lessons of History," *Confluence,* V, Pt. 2 (Winter 1957), 341–54.

Pargellis, Stanley (ed.). *The Quest for Political Unity in World History.* Washington, U.S. Gov't. Printing Office, 1944.

Paul, Arnold M. *Conservative Crisis and the Rule of Law: Attitudes of the Bench and Bar 1887–1895.* Ithaca, N.Y., Cornell Univ. Press, 1960.

"Peace Through Insurance," *New Republic,* I (Nov. 14, 1914), 26.

Perry, Ralph Barton. *In the Spirit of William James.* New Haven, Yale Univ. Press, 1938.

————. *The Thought and Character of William James.* 2 vols. Boston, Little, Brown, 1935.

Persons, Stow. *American Minds: A History of Ideas.* New York, Holt, 1958.

Potter, David M. "The Historian's Use of Nationalism and Vice Versa," *American Historical Review,* LXVII (1962), 924–50.

Preston, Sydney and Alexander Ernest Sich, "Fire Insurance During the War," *War and Insurance: The Economic and Social History of the World War. British Series.* London, Oxford Univ. Press for the Carnegie Endowment for International Peace, 1927, pp. 57–97.

Pringle, Henry F. *The Life and Times of William Howard Taft.* 2 vols. New York, Farrar and Rinehart, 1939.

Randall, John Herman, Jr. "Josiah Royce and American Idealism," *Journal of Philosophy,* LXIII (Feb. 3, 1966), 57–83.

Reuter, Paul. *International Institutions,* trans. J. M. Chapman. London, Allen & Unwin, 1958.

Riesman, David. "Some Observations on Community Plans and Utopia," *Yale Law Journal,* LVII (1947), 173–200.

Riesman, David. *Thorstein Veblen: A Critical Interpretation.* New York, Scribner, 1960.

Rogers, Lindsay. "The Reminiscences of Lindsay Rogers," Oral History Collection, Columbia University, New York, 1958.

Rosenberg, Bernard. *The Values of Veblen: A Critical Appraisal.* Washington, D.C., Public Affairs Press, 1956.

Santayana, George. *Character and Opinion in the United States.* New York, Scribner, 1920.

Schmid, Karl. "Some Observations on Certain Principles of Woodrow Wilson," *Confluence,* V, Pt. 1 (Autumn 1956), 264–76.

Schneider, Herbert. *A History of American Philosophy.* New York, Columbia Univ. Press, 1947.

Schuman, Frederick L. *The Commonwealth of Man: An Inquiry into Power Politics and World Government.* New York, Knopf, 1952.

Schwarzenberger, Georg. *The Frontiers of International Law.* London, Stevens & Sons, 1962.

Scott, James Brown. *The Project of a Permanent Court of International Justice and Resolutions of the Advisory Committee of Jurists.* Carnegie Endowment for International Peace, Division of International Law, no. 35. Washington, The Endowment, 1920.

———. "Elihu Root's Services to International Law," *International Conciliation,* no. 207 (Feb. 1925), 3–54.

Scott, James Brown. "Elihu Root, Secretary of State, July 7, 1905–January 27, 1909," *American Secretaries of State and Their Diplomacy,* ed. Samuel Flagg Bemis, Vol. IX. New York, Knopf, 1929, pp. 193–282.

———. *The Hague Peace Conferences of 1899 and 1907.* 2 vols. Baltimore, Johns Hopkins Press, 1909.

Seymour, Charles. *The Intimate Papers of Colonel House.* 4 vols. Boston, Houghton Mifflin, 1926–28.

———. "The Paris Education of Woodrow Wilson," *Virginia Quarterly Review,* XXXII (Fall 1956), 578–93.

Shotwell, James T. "John Bates Clark, 1847–1938, A Tribute," *Carnegie Endowment for International Peace Year Book.* Washington, D.C., 1938, pp. 150–63.

———. "The Reminiscences of James T. Shotwell," Oral History Collection, Columbia University, New York, 1949.

Smith, Daniel M. *The Great Departure: The United States and World War I 1914–1920.* New York, Wiley, 1965.

———. "National Interest and American Intervention, 1917, An Historiographical Appraisal," *Journal of American History,* LII (June 1965), 5–24.

Smith, John E. "Royce on Religion," *Journal of Religion,* XXX (1950), 261–65.

———. *Royce's Social Infinite: The Community of Interpretation.* New York, Liberal Arts Press, 1950.

Smith, T. V., *et al.* "Discussion of the Theory of International Relations; Based upon the Introduction by J. Dewey to a Re-issue of Jane Addams' Peace and Bread in Time of War," *Journal of Philosophy,* XLIII (Aug. 30, 1945), 477–97.

Snell, John L. "Wilson's Peace Program and German Socialism, January–March, 1918," *Mississippi Valley Historical Review,* XXXVIII (Sept. 1951), 187–214.

Stapleton, Lawrence. *Justice and World Society.* Chapel Hill, Univ. of North Carolina Press, 1944.

Stimson, Henry L., and McGeorge Bundy. *On Active Service in Peace and War.* New York, Harper, 1948.

Stromberg, Roland N. *Collective Security and American Foreign Policy from the League of Nations to NATO.* New York, Praeger, 1962.

———. "The Idea of Collective Security," *Journal of the History of Ideas,* XVII (1956), 250–63.

Strout, Cushing. *The American Image of the Old World.* New York, Harper, 1963.

Thompson, John M. *Russia, Bolshevism, and the Versailles Peace.* Princeton, Princeton Univ. Press, 1967.

Tims, Margaret. *Jane Addams of Hull House 1860–1935: A Centenary Study.* New York, Macmillan, 1961.

Toth, Charles W. "Elihu Root 1905–1909," *An Uncertain Tradition: American Secretaries of State in the Twentieth Century.* ed. Norman A. Graebner, New York, McGraw-Hill Paperbacks, 1961, pp. 40–58.

Walters, F. P. *A History of the League of Nations.* London, Oxford Univ. Press, 1960.

Webster, C. K. *The League of Nations in Theory and Practice.* Boston and New York, Houghton Mifflin, 1933.

Weinberg, Albert K. *Manifest Destiny: A Study of Nationalist Expansionism in American History.* Baltimore, Johns Hopkins Press, 1935.

Whitaker, Arthur P. *The Western Hemisphere Idea: Its Rise and Decline.* Ithaca, Cornell Univ. Press, 1954.

White, Howard B. "Royce's Philosophy of Loyalty," *Journal of Philosophy,* LIII (1956), 99–103.

White, Morton G. *Social Thought in America: The Revolt Against Formalism.* 2nd ed. Boston, Beacon Press, 1959.

White, Morton G., and Lucia White. *The Intellectual versus the City: From Thomas Jefferson to Frank Lloyd Wright.* New York, Mentor Books, 1964.

Williams, William Appleman. *The Tragedy of American Diplomacy.* Rev. ed. New York, Delta, 1962.

Winkler, Henry R. *The League of Nations Movement in Great Britain 1914–1919.* New Brunswick, Rutgers Univ. Press, 1952.

Woodworth, Robert Sessions. "Josiah Royce," *National Academy of Sciences of the United States of America: Biographical Memoirs,* XXXIII (1959), 381–91.

Wright, Quincy. "Woodrow Wilson and the League of Nations," *Social Research,* XXIV (Spring 1957), 65–86.

Yoemans, Henry Aaron. *Abbott Lawrence Lowell 1865–1943.* Cambridge, Harvard Univ. Press, 1953.

Zimmern, Alfred. *The League of Nations and the Rule of Law 1918–1935.* London, Macmillan, 1936.

Index

Abbott, Edith, 124
Abbott, Grace, 124
Adams, Herbert Baxter, 182
Addams, Jane, 7–10, 14, 15, 18, 52–58, 87, 98, 100, 102, 109, 114–49, 150, 168, 169, 176, 179–80, 184, 214, 218–21, 224–25, 228–29; on factory system, 130–31; with Food Administration, 146, 179–80; and Tolstoy, 116–17, 125; background of, 118–21; on labor, 126, 132; on welfare state, 134–35; Progressive Party of, 19–20, 136–37; at Hull House, 20, 117, 120, 121–26; on socialism, 125; social milieu of, 16; on class isolation, 125; in Woman's Peace Party, 16, 139–46, 223; on women's suffrage, 135
Addams, John, 118–19, 120
Aguinaldo, Emilio, 33
Alabama claims arbitration, 17
Alaska boundary settlement, 13
Alienation, 97–98
Altgeld, John Peter, 124
American Association for International Law, 222
American Federation of Labor, 18
American Peace Society, 16, 69
American Relief Agency, 214
American Society for International Law, 23, 28, 46
American Society for the Judicial Settlement of International Disputes, 28, 56
American Society of Mechanical Engineers, 177
Anderson, Chandler P., 23
Angell, Norman, 11–12
Anglo-American arbitration treaty (1897), 69
"Army of the Commonweal" (Coxey's army), 161
Army War College, 37
Association for International Conciliation, 27
Austin, John, 40
Axson, Ellen Louise, 182

Bagehot, Walter, 184
Balch, Emily Green, 145
Baldwin, James Mark, 95
Baltimore Peace Society, 58

Barbarian culture, 158–59, 160
Barnard, Frederick, 26
Barnett, Canon, 120–21
Bartholdt, Richard, 27, 58, 69, 70
Bear Flag War, 92
Belgium, 46, 47
Bellamy, Edward, 152, 153
Bismark, Otto von, 183
Bluntschli, Johann, 17
Bolshevism, 49–50, 202–3, 205–6, 212–13, 215, 227; League of Nations and, 83–84, 209
Bourgeois, Leon, 27
Bourne, Randolph S., 168
Bradley, F. H., 94
Brailsford, H. N., 201
Brandeis, Louis D., 31
Brazil, 36, 44
Breckinridge, Sophonisba, 124
Bright, John, 183
Bryan, William Jennings, 56, 57, 128, 189, 190
Bryce, James Lord, 57, 58, 76, 224
Bullitt, William, 212
Burke, Edmund, 184
Burritt, Elihu, 17
Business stage, 158–59, 160–62
Butler, Nicholas Murray, 7, 12, 18, 26–53, 57–58, 60, 70, 77, 128, 184, 222, 223; on Latin America, 33–36; on law, 29–33; on *stare decisis,* 32; on arms race, 38; on Latin America, 34–35; on social reform, 28–32; at Columbia University, 26; on international mind, 22, 23–24; social milieu of, 16; during World War I, 44–47

Carnegie, Andrew, 3, 13, 18, 25, 27, 70
Carnegie Endowment for International Peace, 3, 19, 27–28, 53, 60, 222
Carranza, Venustiano, 189–90, 191, 199*n*
Catt, Carrie Chapman, 139
Cecil, Robert, 62
Central America. *See* Latin America
Central American Court of Justice, 35, 191
Chicago Emergency Peace Committee, 139
Child labor, 122, 129